how to
REHABILITATE
ABANDONED BUILDINGS

BY DONALD R. BRANN

Library of Congress Card No. 73-87513

Published by
DIRECTIONS SIMPLIFIED, INC.

Division of
**EASI-BILD PATTERN CO., INC.
Briarcliff Manor, N.Y. 10510**

Copyright 1974, DIRECTIONS SIMPLIFIED, INC. Entire contents are protected by copyright in the United States and in countries signatory to the Bern Convention and to the Pan American Convention. All Rights Reserved. No part of this publication may be reproduced, stored in a retrieval system, or transmitted, in any form or by any means, electronic, mechanical, photocopying, recording or otherwise, without written permission of the publisher. Printed in the U.S.A.

ACKNOWLEDGMENTS

The author expresses his appreciation to the Brooklyn Union Gas Company for the many before and after photos; to Owens Corning manufacturers of the fiberglass tub-shower; and to The Hydronics Institute for information concerning baseboard heating.

NOTE

Due to the variance in quality and availability of many materials and products, always follow directions a manufacturer and/or retailer offers. Unless products are used exactly as the manufacturer specifies, its warranty can be voided. While the author mentions certain products by trade name, no endorsement or end use guarantee is implied. In every case the author suggests end uses as specified by the manufacturer prior to publication.

Since manufacturers frequently change ingredients or formula and/or introduce new and improved products, or fail to distribute in certain areas, trade names are mentioned to help the reader zero in on products of comparable quality and end use. The Publisher.

All metric dimensions shown are approximate. Note page 253.

TO BE A WINNER

From childhood through much of our adult lives, we fight a continual war for survival with somebody or some situation over which we have little or no immediate control. As young adults, we soon discover the kind of job we want is hard to find and even harder to hold. A desire for success, a willingness to put in a full day's work, invariably creates animosity among those goofing off. Good will and good intentions are subject to group pressures. Loners invariably become targets for joiners. At every stage we face problems that flow from an ocean of sources. To settle a war that rages within requires a referee who dictates rules we must be willing to accept. Consider these terms for an armistice.

    Accept the fact that the moment you awake, conscious problems will fill that part of your day you owe to others.

    Recognize that every problem offers instant opportunity. Each solved provides more time to live with one less problem

    Continue to be a participant and a producer but still an individual. Learn to coexist with rancor, jealousy and especially with lame brain group leadership.

    Divide your mind, energy and each waking moment into spheres of activity. Spend as much as your job requires but make a daily investment in a **project** that pays extra dividends.

    Always remember, making an honest effort is one of life's greatest rewards.

    Your home is a physical presentation of you, the individual. Allow it to fall apart and you are the loser. Improve it and you create an important investment. Doing this work helps you establish a Shangri La time zone of activity—one which offers escape, satisfaction, and complete peace of mind.

Don R. Brann

TABLE OF CONTENTS

7 — Give Fate A Helping Hand
17 — Houses $1.00 each
19 — Financing
31 — The Instant John
33 — Important Plus Factors
39 — Tools Needed
42 — Roofing and Foundation Repairs
54 — Wet Basement
58 — Floor Repairs
63 — Window Repair, Replacement, Glazing
75 — To Build a Partition
78 — Removing a Wall
94 — Roughing in Service Lines
122 — Plumbing Wall Installation
127 — Insulation
128 — Installing Fiberglas Tub and Shower
146 — Toilet Installation
152 — Lavatory Installation
160 — Kitchen Modernization
220 — Panel Walls
229 — Install Suspended Ceiling
236 — Heating Tips
241 — Prefabricated Chimney
243 — Baseboard Radiation
246 — Iron Railing Repairs
247 — Front Step Repairs
248 — Important Do's and Don'ts
249 — The Magic of Good Direction

GIVE FATE A HELPING HAND

Once upon a time, the task of transforming an abandoned building into livable apartments was a truly discouraging uphill fight. Every step from obtaining a permit and financing, to being allowed to do the work, required more than brains and guts. Those who recognized the potential were usually given a royal run-around when they attempted to get a modernization permit. Accustomed to granting permits only to recognized professionals and those who had influence or payola, many building departments were staffed by little Caesars who dictated what must be done, how and who would be permitted to do it. In most cases the permit was contingent on the work being done by "approved contractors." Today the building inspector and his staff are as vitally concerned with rehabilitating buildings as the mayor is in seeking new industry.

Everyone concerned with the life of a city knows an exodus of taxpayers and an influx of welfarites spells disaster. Unless a community can attract people who care, who pay taxes, and/or rehabilitate property that can produce taxes, the life blood of the city begins to drain dry in its abandoned buildings. Cities from New York, Philadelphia, Wilmington, Baltimore, Washington to New Orleans and Seattle are waking up. One after another have reenacted parts of the Homestead Act of 1862 that offered free land to anyone who agreed to farm it. Today's version provides abandoned houses for $1.00, if the purchaser agrees to rehabilitate it within a specified period. Others offer tax incentives that almost guarantee sizeable Capital Gains.

Transforming an abandoned derelict into a desirable dwelling is no small feat of magic. But like most magic, it's a trick everyone can learn and perform when they join the act. Building a new house or rehabilitating an existing one starts with a shovel, a strong back and will to win. All of this nation's housing was manmade by people no smarter or dumber than yourself. Despite the great successes and enormous failures of the prefabbers, most home construction still requires doing one thing at a time.

Rehabilitation requires the same physical effort. While it takes one person longer than two, and some steps require two people, each hour invested pays a big, big bonus. Not only can anyone who qualifies get money to do the work, but also free advice concerning financing, planning, etc.

Buying and remodeling an abandoned building is an adventure in living. To some, it's a frightening voyage into the unknown. If you fear doing it, that's a good sign. Fear is one of life's most important stimulants. Harness its power and it can help you conceive and successfully accomplish some of life's richest dreams. The author assumes you have never done any of this work and explains HOW in non-technical, step-by-step directions.

Learning any profession, skill or trade requires reading, then practicing what you read. If you understand what you read, then match parts with pictures and follow a step-by-step sequence, you learn something new fast. Just as others learn to prune a bush, so can you install new framing, flooring, build or remove partition walls, etc. Everything is done one step at a time. Focus your mind on one step and before you know it, you'll be working on the twenty-second.

Every city has hundreds, many have thousands of abandoned buildings. Even the smallest community has abandoned stores, warehouses or factory buildings that contain four good walls on a solid foundation, plus a roof. While many need roofing repairs or a new roof, repointing loose brickwork, etc., what's left represents valuable potential. Those who take an abandoned building and turn it into living space quickly discover the results have magical repercussions. Doing the work provides a free education in one of today's highest paid and hardest to get into industries. Doing the work for your home permits your doing the same for others, over and over again. You become a contractor with one employee—You—until you decide to expand. Since you get dry behind the ears fast doing your first job, you can't easily be conned into paying someone who doesn't provide a full day's work for a day's pay.

It all begins with you. If you are basically yellow, lazy or just stupid, you will quickly find many easy ways to chicken out. If you have guts to do today what millions did yesterday, build their own shelter, you begin to live a new life. If you are at all interested, but still lack the courage to jump in, try out as a helper. When you make inquiry concerning a rehabilitation loan, (see page 21), get the address of others who are currently doing the work. Visit them to find out how they are doing. If you need experience, offer to help. Weekends of work in someone else's gold mine will convince you quickly.

Years ago a popular song contained the following refrain "You can be richer or poorer, it all depends on you." This book adds one additional area. You can now be a landlord or tenant with the decision still yours to make. Never in the history of this country have so many been offered so much in exchange for personal effort.

Renovating a brownstone or transforming an abandoned store into income producing apartments, provides a method of mining gold without leaving town. Those willing to work can make a fortune turning spare time into rental income. Like so many times in the past, opportunity continues to bang hard on the door of those willing to hear and act. Transforming a hole in the ground, four walls and a roof into living space is not an impossible dream and the rewards are terrific. You not only get more house at the lowest possible cost, rent-free living when you have other units to rent, but also earn a huge bonus in the form of a Capital Gains the day you decide to sell. Not having to pay inflated prices or even a real estate broker's fee, you only need concern yourself with getting a long term improvement loan at a government fixed rate, and in doing something you have never done before.

Everyone who owns a home knows the interest on a mortgage costs big dough. He also knows that financing charges on a car or household appliances can cost an arm and a leg. Those willing to accept an abandoned building for free, or at $1.00*, or at a cost far less than you normally pay for a building site, also

*At time of publication.

discover they can borrow practically all the money needed to buy materials, equipment and appliances, at a piddling 3%* interest rate. Three percent when mortgage money runs from 8% to 14% and higher*.

This book provides a guide that illustrates many of the problems you will meet and explains how to successfully solve each. Every hour you invest learning what goes where and when, will change your concept of living. You become a homeowner dependent on no one but yourself.

Most people who consider this job raise the following questions: "Can I do it. . . . I've never done any of this work before . . . I don't know the difference between a door jamb and a stud." These same thoughts passed through the minds of almost everyone of the thousands who have already done what you propose doing. All said the same thing, "I never thought I could do it," but each figured if others could, so could they.

*At time of publication.

To develop instant confidence see what others have done, then select a similar building and do the same thing. When you see what magic can be done, Illus. 1, 2, you realize your back as well as your brain will get plenty of exercise once you make a decision to do.

While you won't see many abandoned buildings available at bargain prices next door to one that has been rehabilitated, you can frequently find one around a corner, or a block away, or in another part of town. What you do to rehabilitate the house establishes a precedent. It encourages others to do the same thing. Like grass seed planted in the fall, by spring your efforts help seed a better neighborhood.

Since many abandoned buildings are in high crime areas, occupants of renovated brownstones invariably tell you it was their occupancy that helped make the streets safer. In a very real sense they helped carve out a homestead in a wilderness in much the same way colonists did a hundred years ago. While no one person stops crime instantly, it's surprising what bright street lighting, police whistles carried by all residents, block party get-togethers, plus a neighborly mutual assistance association can accomplish in creating a safer neighborhood.

Selecting an abandoned brownstone or store in what may still be a slum area, has many advantages few suburbanites obtain when they buy a house in an established neighborhood. The suburban home buyer finds many of his neighbors status seekers who withhold friendship until they ascertain his credit or social rating.

In most cities, the renovators have formed block and/or neighborhood associations for both social and muscle building. When two or more families band together and make friends with others who want to live the way of life they have discovered, their voices get action. The police and sanitation departments take notice of their needs. Garbage is hauled regularly, street lighting is improved and another street is reborn.

Talk to these "pioneers." Learn at first hand how they remodeled a brownstone. Also seek advice from the redevelopment authority. Many have a trained staff that advise you on architectural, financial and construction problems.

ANTICIPATE AND YOU WILL BE PREPARED

Rats infest most abandoned buildings so plan a systematic extermination. Human rodents also infest most slum areas so be prepared. While you can poison a rat, the law still protects the human species. If you expect a break-in and prepare for it in an offensive manner, you could get instant respect and the privacy you seek. Like rats, the word gets around. Knowing that the criminal seeks to steal anything he can sell, and anything he can steal is worth a try, you have to batten down every available point of entry. After removing the garbage, old plaster, rotted timbers, and certainly before you leave any tools, material or equipment overnight, plan on occupying the premises. If street level windows have been gutted, cover openings with ⅝ or ¾" plywood, Illus. 3. Measure X and Y. Cut panels to fit. Drill holes ¼" from edge. Place panel in position. Insert 1½ or 2" No. 10 flathead wood screws through panels and fasten each in place. Space screws every 12 to 18". When you finish rehabilitation, remove panels, install glass, putty up screw holes, paint frames. The plywood can be used for many different interior projects.

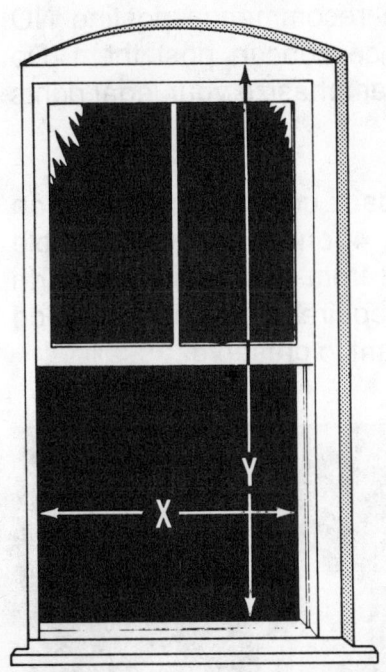
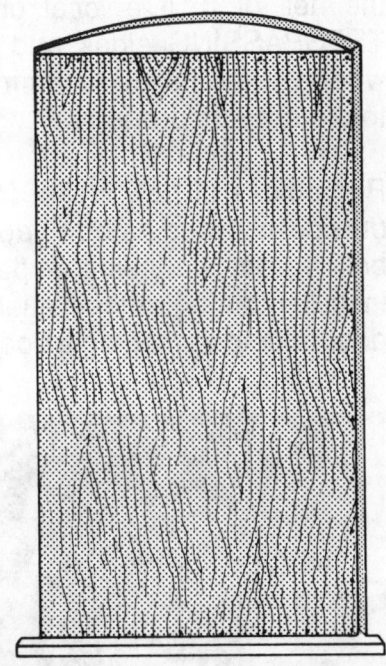

ALTERNATE METHOD OF PROTECTING WINDOWS

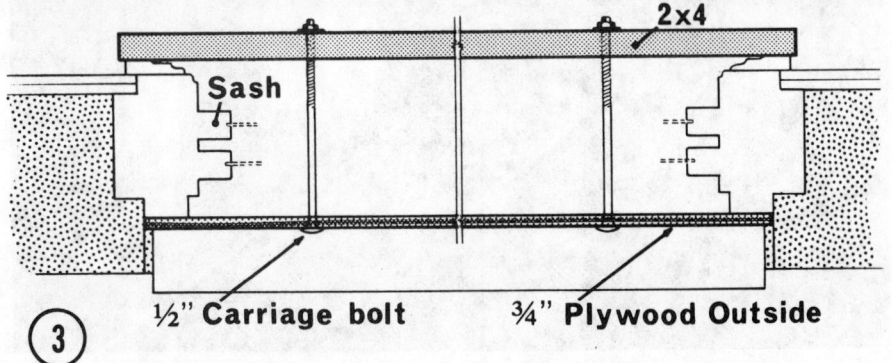

Many first time home modernizers paint signs on panels reading, "Have A Good Day," or "May The Lord Be Good To You," or "Good Health and Happiness." A friendly message generates friendlier feelings while it sometimes discourages graffiti by others. Painting or posting keep out signs on entry doors during reconstruction is currently considered of questionable value. Many slum dwellers enjoy breaking any law just for the hell of it. If a local ordinance recommends posting NO TRESPASSING signs and the police concur, post them. Do whatever the police recommend to emphasize your legal rights to protect your property.

Regardless of how well a front or back door fits the frame, an outside plywood "storm" door, Illus. 4, one that can be double bolted from the inside or padlocked from the outside, is worth installing during rehabilitation. This requires jimmying a plywood door prior to damaging a door you want to preserve.

A simple, battery powered trap switch, Illus. 5, connected to an 8 or 10" alarm bell provides psychological protection. Most petty thieves don't like to be detected. A blast from an alarm bell, a sudden flood of light, or the sound of a loud tape recorded voice phoning police headquarters, can deter an intruder. Complete details for installing all kinds of burglar alarms are described in Book #695 How To Install Protective Alarm Devices. A thief who trips an alarm bell or floodlights, a siren or telephone dialer that automatically notifies the police, will invariably leave the premises.

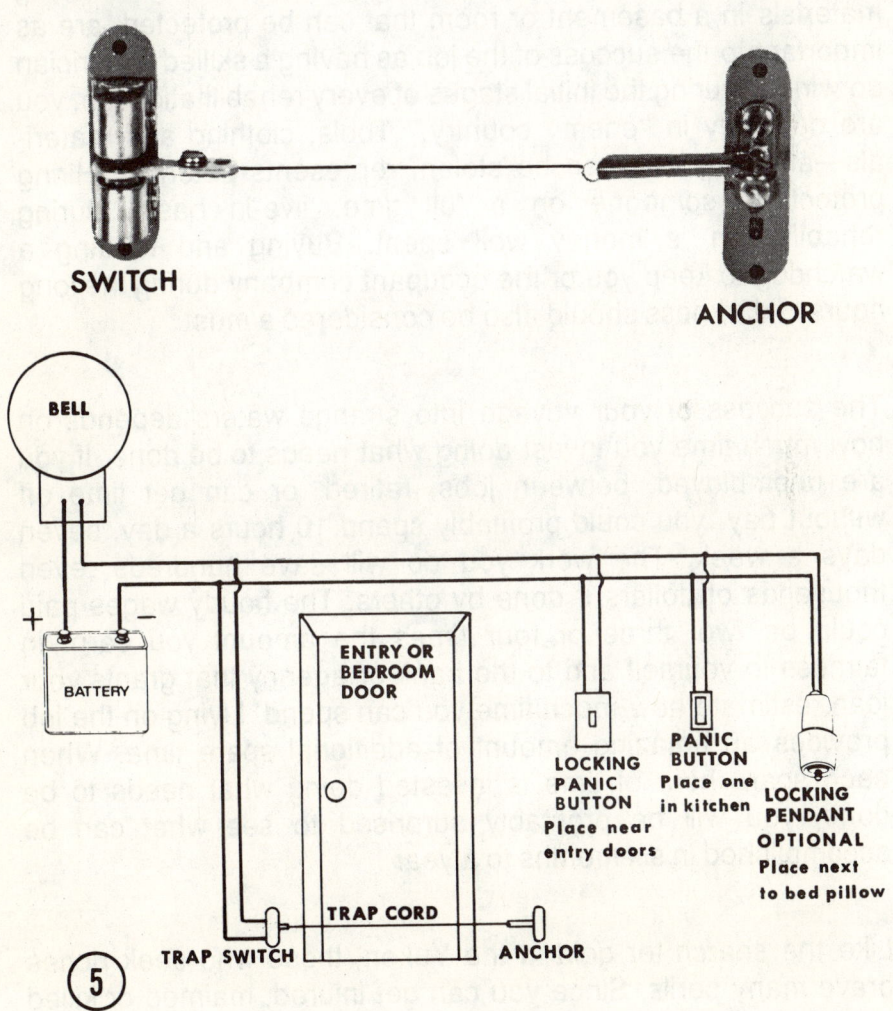

15

How you protect your property provides a clue as to how fast your house will be considered off limits. Since taking occupancy in an abandoned building is comparable to a first wave assault on an enemy stronghold, advice from a police captain or legal aide society lawyer can be helpful.

If you can afford to hire a helper, ask a local store owner for the names of those families who need and are willing to work. An unskilled, unemployed inner city resident, currently on welfare, can provide the manpower required to do much of the preliminary work. Removing refuse and storing building materials in a basement or room that can be protected, are as important to the success of the job as having a skilled electrician do wiring. During the initial stages of every rehabilitation job, you are definitely in "enemy country." Tools, clothing and materials—anything that can be stolen, represents potential. Hiring protection, someone on a full time, live-in basis, during rehabilitation is money well spent. Buying and feeding a watchdog to keep you or the occupant company during the long hours of darkness should also be considered a must.

The success of your voyage into strange waters depends on how much time you invest doing what needs to be done. If you are unemployed, between jobs, retired, or can get time off without pay, you could profitably spend 10 hours a day, seven days a week. The work you do will save hundreds, even thousands of dollars if done by others. The hourly wages paid could be two, three or four times the amount you earn. In fairness to yourself and to the bank or agency that grants your loan, estimate how much time you can spend. Living on the job provides an amazing amount of additional spare time. When each spare hour of time is invested doing what needs to be done, you will be profitably surprised to see what can be accomplished in six months to a year.

Like the search for gold in the Yukon, those who seek riches brave many perils. Since you can get injured, maimed or killed by a car on a trip to a suburban supermarket, as readily as you can get mugged and robbed in a slum, only the strong survive while the meek continue to pay rent.

HOUSES $1.00 EACH*

Like a plague, urban decay takes one victim then another and another. It spreads rapidly from house to house, block to block, until whole neighborhoods are devastated. Unchecked through years of lame brain inner city politics, vast areas, Illus. 6, containing some of the cities most valuable homesites, become uninhabitable eyesores no longer capable of paying taxes.

Like the hands of a clock that repeat a cycle, after decades of decay, slums are today being rehabilitated. Each rehabilitation attracts another, then another. Block after block is reborn with taxpaying homeowners who care about their property, street, neighborhood and their city.

In July, 1973, the wire services released stories that told how New York City officials were offering houses at $1.00 each. Their purpose was to revitalize slum areas. With 259 vacant houses in a racially mixed slum, the Philadelphia City Council also adopted what they call an urban homesteading bill. A survey indicates Philadelphia had a total of 30,000 abandoned buildings off its tax rolls, with hundreds more to be so certified.

Wilmington, Delaware, with over 1500 abandoned buildings, also adopted the Homestead Act and offered houses at $1.00. Officials in other cities were swamped with applicants. HUD estimates it had close to a quarter million abandoned buildings and apartments it would like to liquidate.

But don't be snowed. Houses at $1.00 each and abandoned buildings eligible for special tax benefits, as well as housing you can buy at a price you can afford, are valueless unless you can obtain a CO—Certificate of Occupancy—when a specified list of improvements are completed.

*At time of publication.

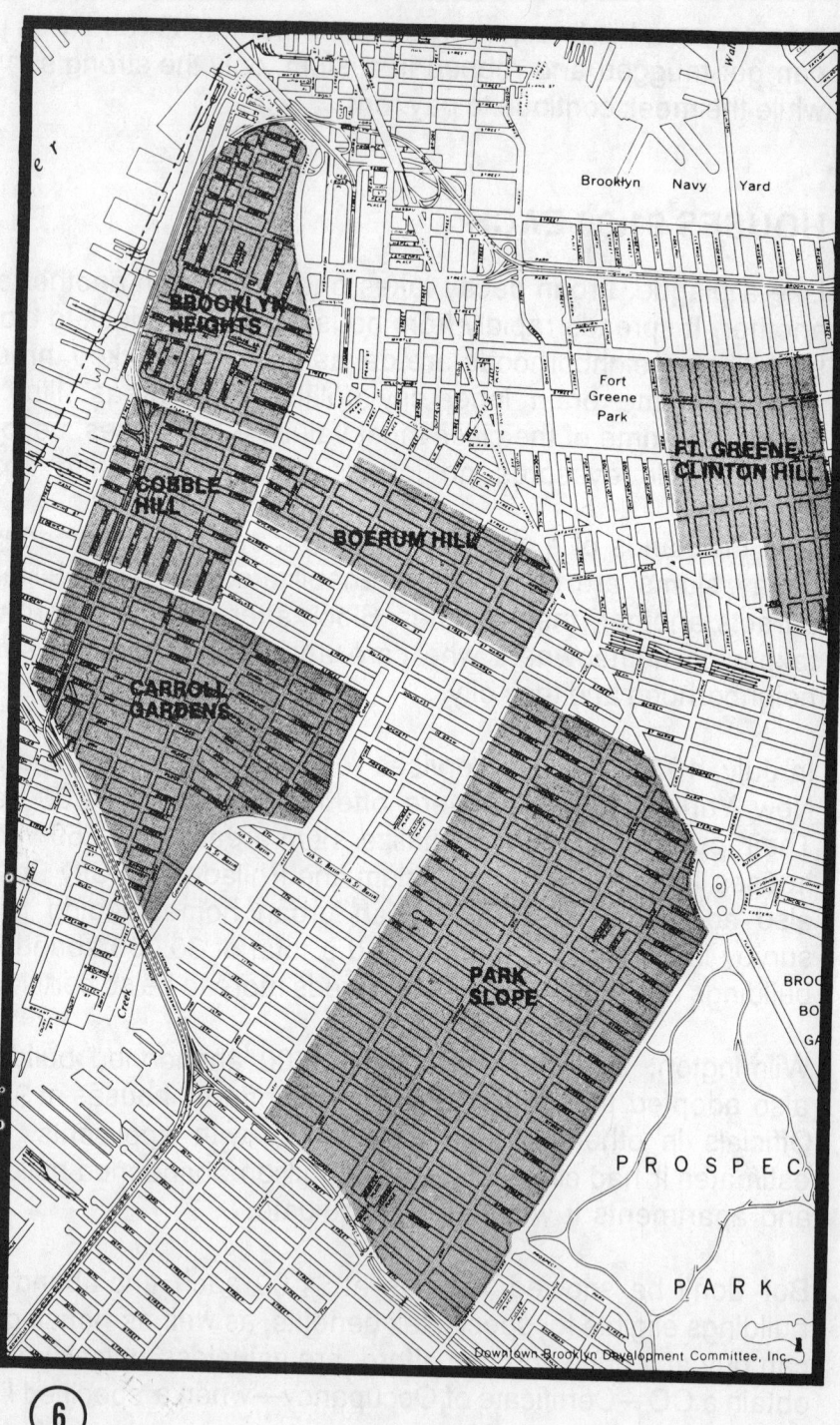

Before signing your name to a purchase agreement, get an opinion from the building department and/or Board of Health. Find out what they want done, what they will allow you to do, or who they want to do what. If possible, record the conversation so you don't miss any suggestions, or get their recommendations in writing. All your work could go for naught unless you are allowed to move in, accomplish what needs to be done, then become a landlord instead of a tenant.

Many years ago an elderly neighbor offered a bit of advice I have never forgotten and often followed. Never buy real estate until you learn how to appraise its value; never buy a business until you have worked for the owner. Rehabilitating an abandoned building is very much like going into business for yourself. If after reading through this book you still question your ability or desire to do the job, moonlight in your spare time helping someone who is going through what you plan on doing. Explain what you have in mind. They will be glad to have help.

Those seeking a house should check the urban renewal office to find out what areas are being razed, what buildings are to be left standing. A neighborhood police precinct can be of help in pinpointing both new and long time residents. A branch bank or savings and loan association, gas or electric company are all interested in what you plan on doing. Every store owner who's still in business will also give advice freely. Remember, you are a colonist in a new land. One where every family helps increase the safety of others. Regardless of color, nationality or religion, you are welcome and your efforts will be noted and appreciated.

TO OBTAIN FINANCING

Prior to purchase, evaluate what you get and what it will cost to make it habitable according to local codes. As this book goes to press, there are a number of government agencies ready, willing and wanting to loan money towards rehabilitation of housing units. The rate of interest will be exceptionally low when compared to other types of loans. New York City, like other cities hard hit by slum problems, has established tax free incentives* that give a rehabilitator tax benefits from 10 to 30 years.

Most urban renewal and redevelopment authorities have been established to help recognized builders improve large projects. New government agencies have been created to make individual rehabilitation loans. Since you represent an unknown quantity, one who may be here today and gone tomorrow, don't bring a satchel and expect a bundle of money during your first meeting. One good move is to go to the bank that holds, or had a mortgage on the property. Discuss how you plan to rehabilitate the basement and first floor to a point where you can move in, and you could find a very receptive audience. Don't underestimate what you can do or the value of the time and labor you invest. If there is any doubt concerning the cost of what you can do, talk to a local contractor, one who is doing, or has done work in the area. Ask him to give you a ball park estimate on the cost of putting a basement and first floor into a livable condition.

Certain government agencies are making quick loans of up to $1500.00 to qualified owner/occupants of one to two family dwellings located in specified urban renewal areas. "To be eligible, owner's income should be under $3000.00 per year. If it's over $3000.00, a direct grant may cover that portion of rehabilitation costs for which an available loan, the principal and interest payments on which, when added to the present housing expense, exceeds 25% of the owner's total monthly income."

If this sounds confusing, it is. It's a direct quote from the agency making the loan. But don't let it stop you. Rehabilitation loans are not hard to get. "Monthly housing expenses include payments for mortgage principal and interest, mortgage insurance premiums, service charges, hazard insurance, real estate taxes and special assessments, maintenance and repairs, heating and utilities and ground rent if same exists." Withal, if you think the government bends over to lend money,

*At time of publication.

you better believe it. They do, but to keep up a facade of progress, they keep changing the Section or Department giving money away, and they do a superb job of wording the offer to make it sound legal. One day they advertise loans under Section 312, the next week Section 312 has been replaced with another program. Those on the receiving end of a government rehabilitation loan really don't care what the Section number is, all they want is the dough when needed.

As this book went to press, One Direct Federal Loan for Rehabilitation contained these features:

A–This low interest Federal loan program is designed for urban renewal areas and the code enforcement areas to assist in upgrading the complete neighborhood. Under most circumstances, it will cover the rehabilitation on any conceivable (residential or commercial) property.

B–The applicant must be an owner or a tenant of property in a Title 1 urban renewal project or code enforcement project area. He must have the desire and ability to repay the loan and must not be able to obtain the necessary funds from other sources on comparable terms and conditions, i.e., a *three percent loan* from other sources.

(underlined by the author)

There are any number of interpretations under which a rehabilitation loan will be granted. It's up to the applicant to work out details with the local office. Some loans are made for up to 20 years at an interest rate of 3%. If you have any difficulty in getting a loan, write your Congressmen. Their office frequently gets action.

An applicant, who owns and occupies a one to four family building, may be eligible to incorporate existing debt secured by the property and the cost of rehabilitation into one loan. The terms of one type of loan goes on to say: "This will be considered whenever the principal and interest payments for rehabilitation costs, when added to payments on existing debts secured by the property would result in total monthly payments for principal and interest that exceed twenty percent of the applicant's monthly income. Such refinancing will ordinarily be considered only when rehabilitation costs represent one fifth or more of the principal amount of the loan."

If loan language seems confusing, don't be discouraged. What the Federal loan for rehabilitation tries to do is get you to borrow money at 3% to rehabilitate housing. And this provides OPPORTUNITY UNLIMITED for an able-bodied person, man or woman, who wants to make a career remodeling housing. With a 3% interest rate, it's real hard to miss.

For additional information concerning the generosity of the Federal Housing Administration lending program, note details concerning Section 220 (1), Section 203 and Section 221 (d) (2).

Let's assume you have found a house and a legal aide lawyer assures you a clear title is available. You have contacted the local urban housing or rehabilitation center and they have told you the many ways you can borrow sufficient funds to get the work started.

A modernization loan that's convertible into a long term first mortgage on the completion of work is the only sound way to borrow. Since the renovation of a brownstone or any building is an important piece of business, don't sign any agreement or borrow any money until a lawyer reads the agreement. As soon as you take title, or hours before, ask an insurance agent to provide the necessary coverage. As a property owner who may, or may not do all the work, you become an employer the moment you hire someone to do any work. Make certain liability insurance covers every need, not only from personal injury, but also from what the work might do to others.

CONSIDER THESE FACTS

Inspect houses that have been abandoned. Learn if they are city owned. Getting possession is comparatively easy. While those still to be classified as being abandoned may not be had for a buck, many can be bought at low cost if you assume outstanding liens. Make certain the purchase price includes the land. This gives you a complete foundation, four usable walls and a roof for much less than you can possibly duplicate, even if you built it yourself.

Purchasing an abandoned building puts you way ahead providing what's left is usable. Another big plus is whether you can live in the house while the work is being done. Even if it means camping out with a cookstove, a chemical toilet and one or two good watch dogs, it's important to occupy the premises as soon as you start work. Among the primary problems to solve before purchase are how long and how much will it cost to remove all trash, and how much spare time you can allocate to the work that needs to be done.

Like marriage, there are many preliminary areas of exploration that must be carefully inspected and intelligently assessed. The basic utilities, plumbing, electrical and heating normally require replacement. In many three and four story brownstones the gas line, while still usable, should be inspected by the gas company before new equipment is installed. If the line at the meter is intact, and there are no gas leaks evident, install a gas heater to keep your "temporary living quarters" comfortable during a winter of work.

Taking possession and occupying a building are two important first steps. In many parts of a city, vandalism of an empty building seldom sparks police action while a break-in of an occupied building warrants attention. Occupancy helps discourage new graffiti. Cleaning up existing graffiti can usually be accomplished by brushing on a paint thinner then rubbing clean with rags. While several applications are frequently necessary to remove thick paint, what isn't removed can be covered with paint. Carbon tet can also be used effectively. Always keep windows and doors open when using carbon tet or paint thinner.

When you find a likely prospect make a thorough inspection. Start with the outside. Rake debris away from the foundation. See if there are any cracks, broken blocks, or holes in the ground alongside the foundation. Note whether any wood framing is in contact with the soil. If you see any exposed wood framing, jab it with a screw driver or knife to see how much and how deep it's rotted. Note whether any existing leader pipes have channeled water into a basement, or have helped crack the foundation. A neglected leader pipe can create instant damage, particularly when water freezes. Inspect the basement and each floor for water stains and damage.

Don't allow piles of garbage, Illus. 7, abandoned furniture, cracked plaster or obsolete plumbing discourage you. In most houses all lead and copper piping has been ripped out. What you see is what you get. Sound floor joists and framing, Illus. 8, resting on a solid foundation wall is what you want.

25

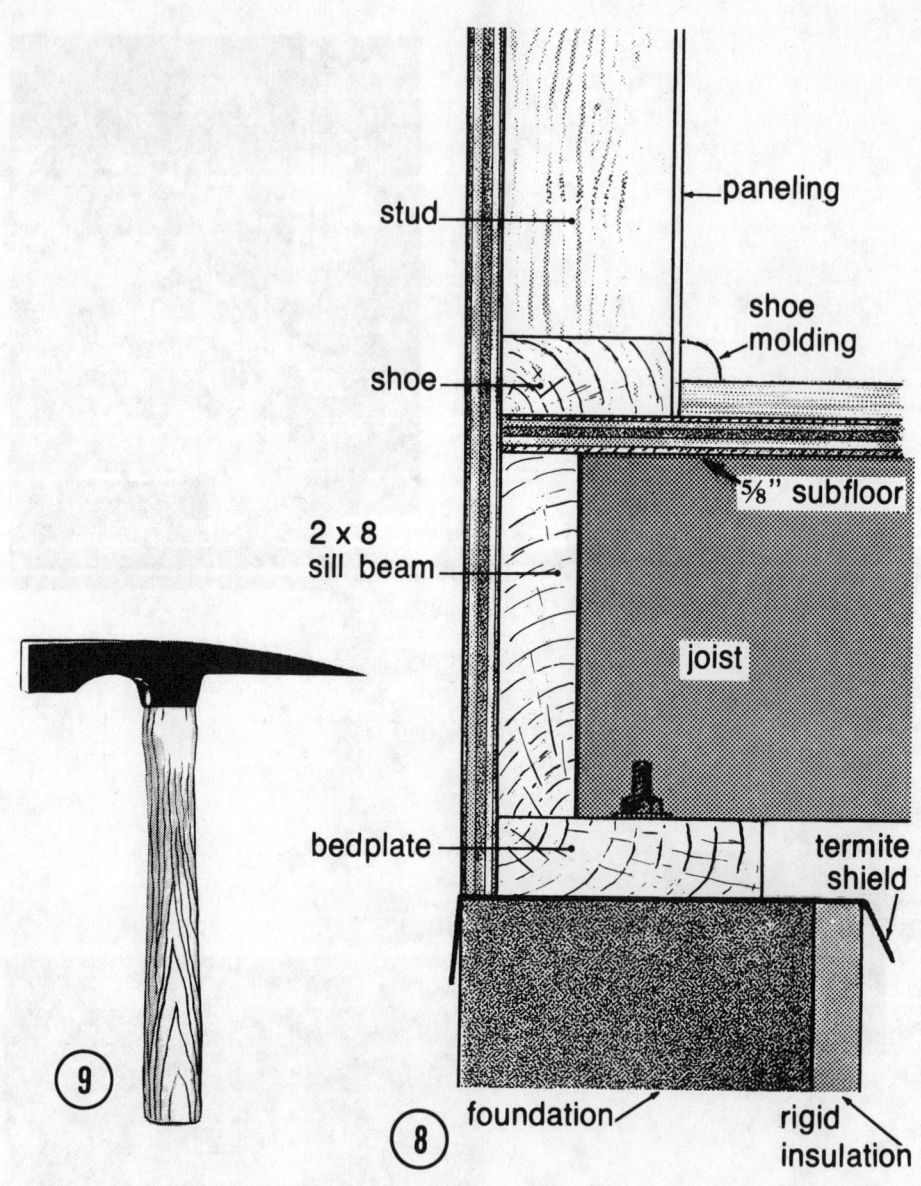

Use a mason's hammer, Illus. 9. Drive it into the ends of each joist, shoe and stud, especially under a kitchen or bathroom. If most of the timbers in the basement look O.K., work your way up each floor. Inspect the wall framing and ceiling joists even if it means pulling off some cracked plaster and lathe. Most damage is usually found under a kitchen or bathroom.

If the foundation is serviceably sound and the building inspector agrees to issue an occupancy permit when specific work is completed, the total cost of rehabilitation might be much less than you expect. Even those who don't do all the work effect considerable savings when they learn what needs to be done. By acting as your own contractor you effect substantial savings when buying materials. Always remember one historical fact, long before building departments established codes and issued permits, colonists built their own homes with hand tools and thousands of these homes still stand.

Choice of a building should be dictated by its initial cost and the number of solid floor and/or ceiling joists, studs and rafters you get. It's essential each floor be tested all over. If a floor can't support a heavy adult without movement, it should be stiffened. Unless floor boards and joists are solid, you will always have trouble with floor coverings.

Replace all rotted floor boards. You generally find rotted flooring under most bathrooms and kitchens. By nailing solid bridging, Illus. 10, in position needed, it's easy to nail replacement flooring. If floor is solid but rough, a rented sanding machine does a superb job restoring a floor.

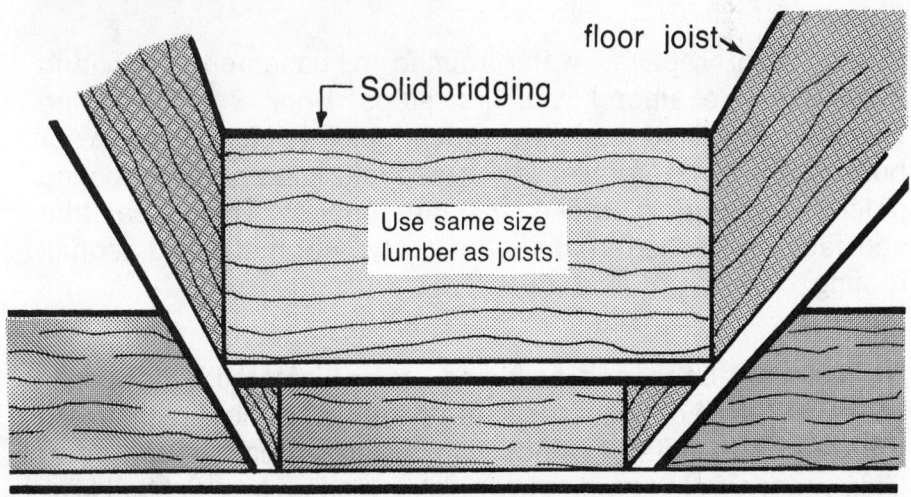

27

If a floor slopes while joists test O.K., don't worry. Floors, even in new houses frequently settle when framing dries out. Plastic underlayment as described on page 62, simplifies leveling.

As an owner and soon-to-be master craftsman, you will be patching or waterproofing a foundation one day, doing carpentry, roofing or dry wall paneling on other days. A careful survey and a long, long check list of what must be done helps convince most lending institutions you know and are willing to do a thorough job. This creates confidence. It also convinces a seller he had better move quickly before even more work needs to be done.

If you are one of the lucky few who get an abandoned building for a buck, remember the city needs you just as you need the building. Make inquiry from those who sit in on the transaction to find out if they can influence the sanitation department to pick up what you have to discard. Your first major job will be to remove all garbage, rotted timbers, cracked plaster, plus years of accumulated trash. Unless the sanitation department agrees to remove what you clean up, paying to have it hauled could be costly.

Making roof repairs, waterproofing a basement floor and foundation are among your first steps. Book # 696 Roofing Repairs Simplified contains much helpful information. Your building material retailer sells asphalt impregnated roofing patches that help make instant repairs. These can be satisfactorily applied to almost every type of metal and asphalt roofing.

Since most abandoned buildings are rat infested, as soon as you remove all debris, place rat poison following directions on package. Test different kinds with different foods as bait. A rat likes variety. Being smart they quickly wise up to a diet that kills, so a change of diet is important. Blank off each room that's baited so a watchdog or cat can't get in. Check results daily.

Since some brands kill more rats than others, use those that produce the best results. Keep renewing poison in each area until it's left undisturbed and you no longer see telltale droppings. Long after you have cleaned out an area, rats will reappear until the rooms are being lived in. It takes a lot of poison to discourage rats and mice from leaving familiar areas. Then by some code only a rat understands, the survivors say "to hell with it" and move out. Patch rat holes with a piece of galvanized tin or aluminum before covering with flooring, but give a rat ample time to leave before covering. Wait until there are no more droppings and no evidence of bait being eaten.

CAUTION:
> Many well-fed cats will eat a poisoned rat. Always drop dead rats in a polyethylene* bag. Tie the bag tight before dropping it into a covered garbage container. Many people love cats so don't alienate your new neighbors by destroying their loved ones.

As soon as you have removed all debris and have placed rat poison wherever you see a hole, start sealing up all windows and doors. Fumigate each room individually, do a floor at a time. Doing an entire house in one operation normally requires a commercial service.

One of the fastest ways to seal windows and doors is to tape polyethelyne over each opening. Polyethelyne comes in rolls in widths up to 20 ft. Cut pieces and tape in position, Illus. 11. This usually keeps fumigant in the area selected for the length of time needed.

Fumigants are deadly killers. Under no circumstances allow anyone or any animal into the area. Put all rooms off limits until directions on can suggest reoccupancy. Then cover your mouth and nostrils and quickly open windows and doors to air the area out thoroughly before using the room.

*Use a polyethylene bag from a dry cleaner.

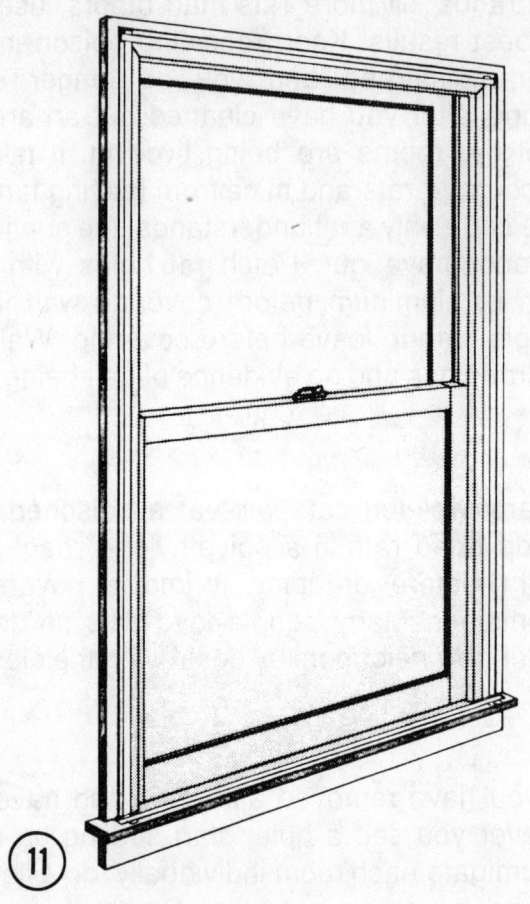

⑪

With care, one set of polyethelyne "curtains" can be used over and over again. As commercial fumigators tell you, doing a room at a time only drives mice, insects, vermin, etc., from room to room. One way to partially offset this traffic problem is to light fumigating candles in as many different areas, on as many floors as possible before leaving the premises. Allow each to burn down without opening a door or window. Place each candle in a coffee can containing an inch or two of sand or dirt. When all windows are sealed, start lighting candles on the top floor, then others on down to the basement. Get out fast. Keep your mouth and nose covered. In every case follow directions manufacturer of fumigant recommends. Post a "Danger Don't Enter" sign over entry doors.

INSTANT RELIEF

Assuming the house you buy is stripped of its facilities and you recognize the logic of moving in as soon as possible, the question of a workable toilet requires immediate attention. Your choice can range from an old-fashioned bedpan and plastic bags; a chemical toilet, Illus. 12, available from lumber, farm supply and mail order houses; a propane gas fired unit, Illus. 13, that can be used permanently; or a jet-powered john, Illus. 14, that can be installed below the waste line in a basement. Since a basement floor is usually below frost level, even before you heat the basement chances of a freeze-up are nil.

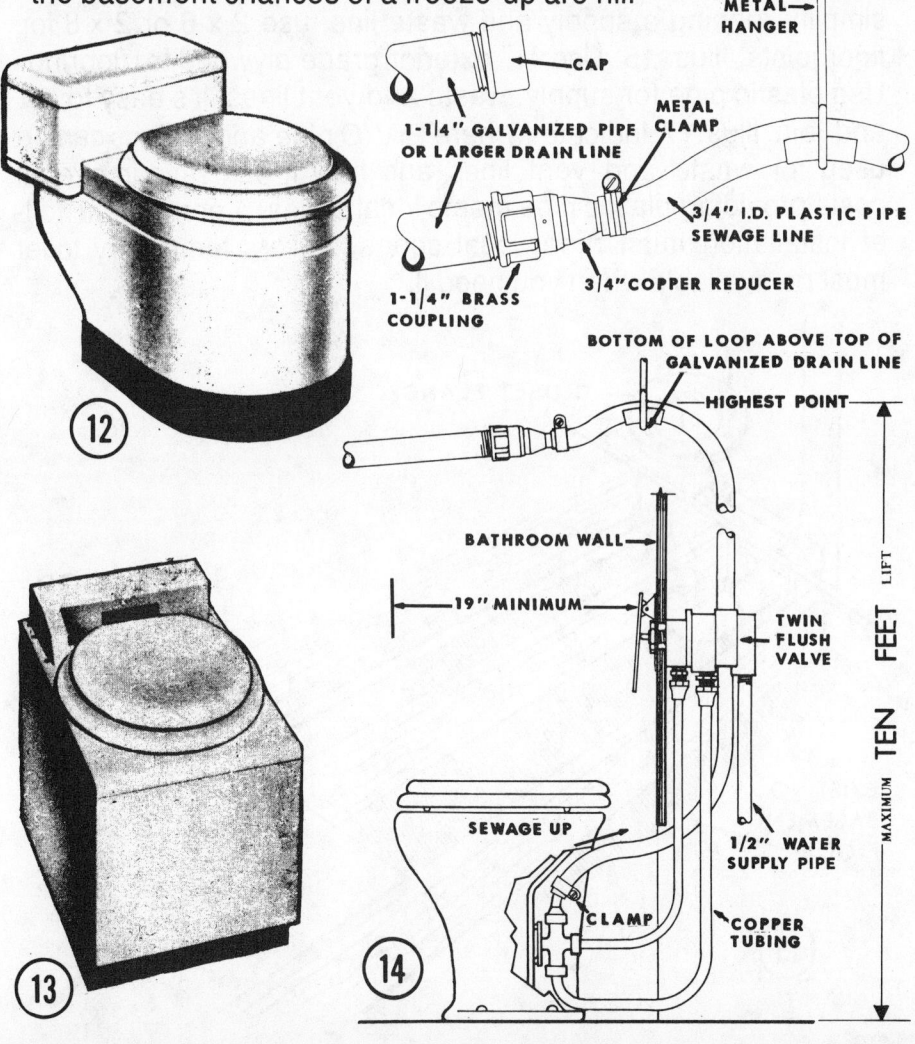

Where to locate a relief station during your first days on the job will help determine choice of equipment. Many families discover a clean basement provides one of the safest places to camp out in the earliest stage. It's the coolest place in summer, the warmest in winter, even with a temporary space heater. It also requires a minimum of material to lock up.

Those who want to install a permanent toilet in a basement, one that's below the waste line, should consider the jet stream pump powered toilet, Illus. 14. This toilet, designed for use below the waste line, flushes waste up to 10' height. Position a jet-powered toilet as close to waste line as convenient. To simplify running a supply and waste line, use 2 x 6 or 2 x 8 for floor joists, Illus. 15. Use ¾" exterior grade plywood for flooring. Use plastic pipe for supply, waste and vent lines. It's easy to cut and join. Illus. 17, indicates where P.V.C pipe and fittings can be used for waste and vent lines and how it can save in overall costs providing plastic pipe meets local codes. A permanent toilet installation must meet local codes, while a temporary toilet must be available when you need it.

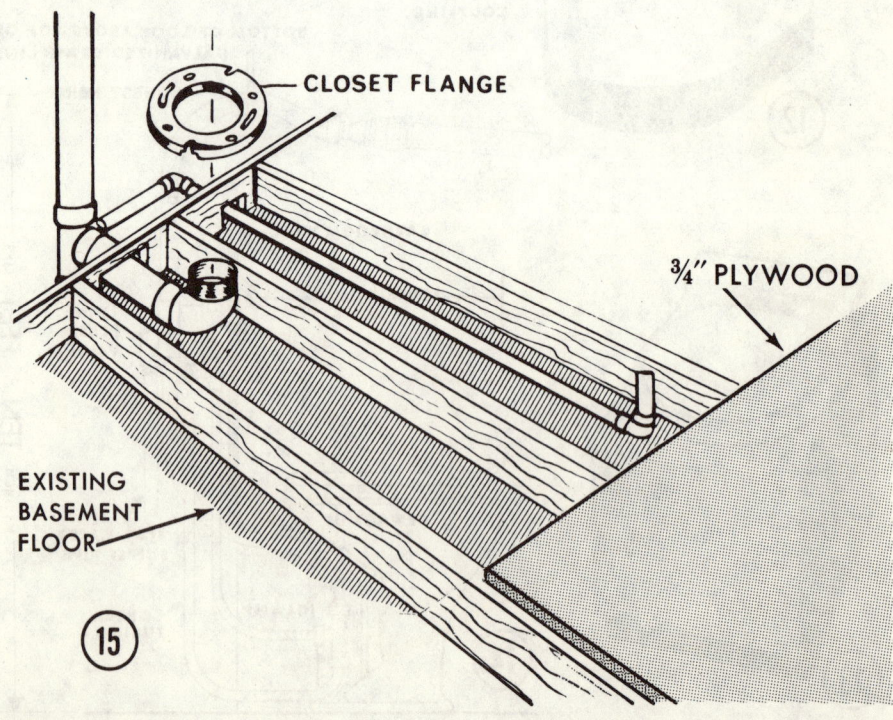

IMPORTANT PLUS FACTORS

To create a workable floor plan, you will want to make changes that complement your way of living while increasing the resale value of the property. Since few owners of an abandoned building can afford the services of an architect, do what others frequently do. Go through the magazines, real estate pages of your newspaper, and advertising folders offered by townhouse, leisure living and condominium builders. Note those floor plans that are approximately the overall shape of your house. If it's wider or narrower, longer or shorter, it really doesn't matter if the plan can be adapted to fit the space you have available. Important features to look for are the location of a usable waste line for kitchen and bathroom. Illus. 16 is a case in point.

This two story, two family plan places the waste, drainage and supply lines in a practical, workable arrangement. You could use this plan in a two story store, garage or warehouse rehabilitation job as readily as in a four story walkup. Illus. 17 shows a P.V.C. drainage system.

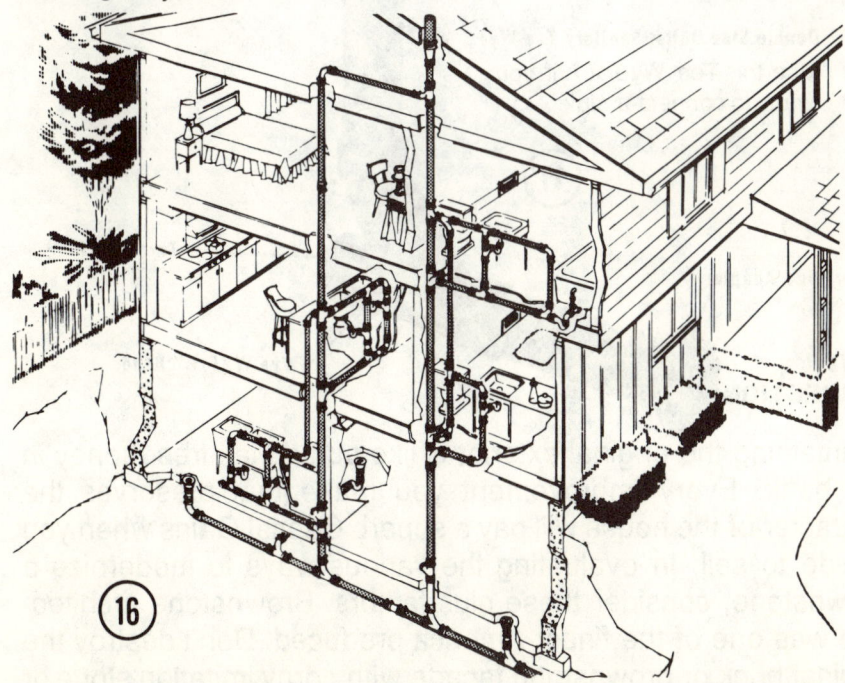

33

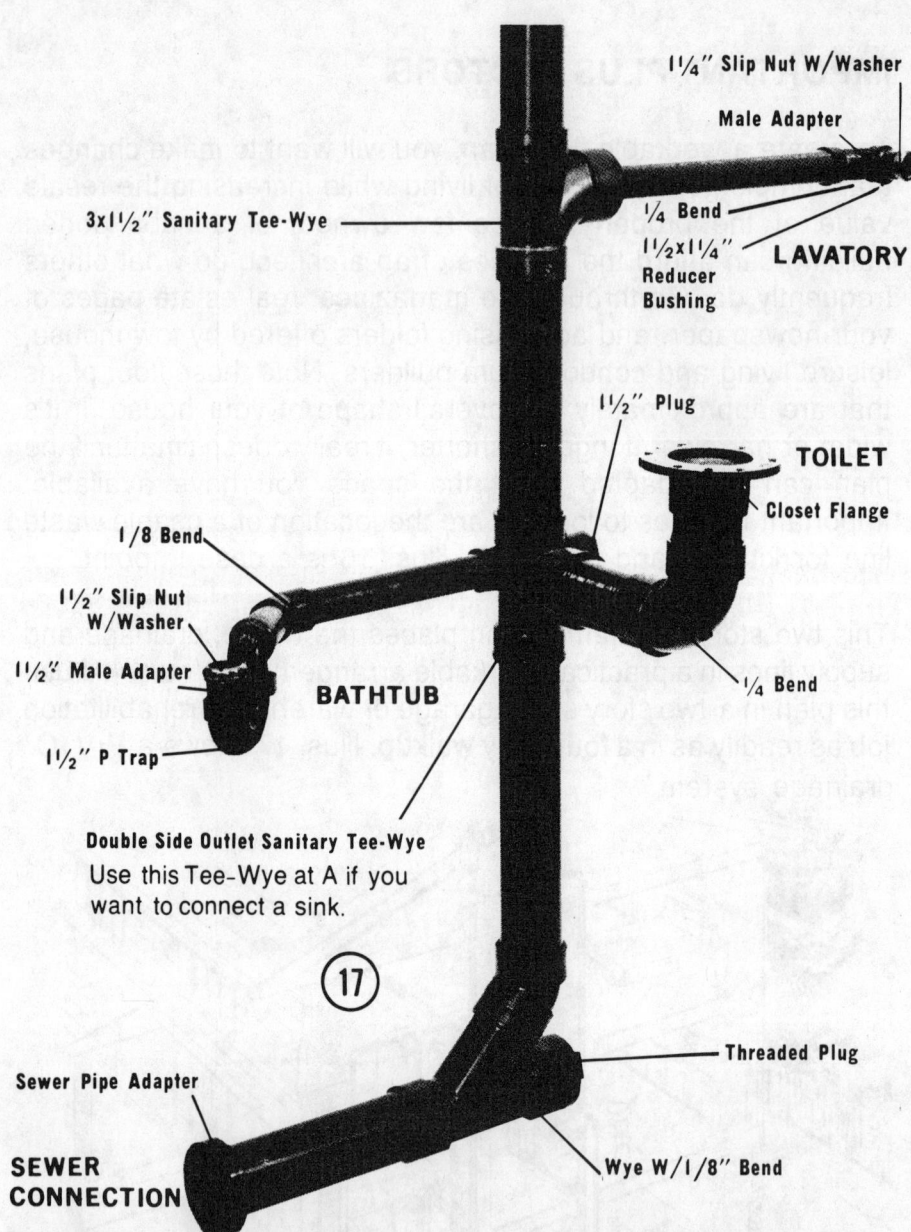

Maintaining the original exterior is like putting tax free money in the bank. Every improvement you make that preserves the character of the house will pay a superb Capital Gains when you decide to sell. In evaluating the various ways to modernize a brownstone, consider these plus factors. Brownstone architecture was one of the finest America produced. Don't destroy the original brick or brownstone facade with corny imitation stone or plywood. Whenever possible, keep the original size and style window, even if it means obtaining used ones from some other abandoned building. Only install replacement windows when you can't obtain matching wood windows. Aluminum or steel sash will change the character of the exterior and is only recommended when used replacements can't be had. Visit wreckers and lumber yards. If the building had tall or wide windows, you lose its charm with smaller ones.

Paint stores in brownstone neighborhoods normally carry acrylic and latex based paints in shades that complement the exterior of a brownstone. Where you see a renovated building that still maintains its original architectural beauty, phone the owner and make inquiry as to what they used and where they bought the product. They will be happy to help because everything you do to complement your building helps upgrade the neighborhood. Don't improvise. Don't guess as to the color, kind or method of application. Note those houses that have the same stone facade as yours, then get expert advice free directly from those who know how it was done.

Since many people are almost color blind when it comes to matching colors on a plastered wall, exterior finishes are even more difficult. The stone used to finish brownstones came from many different quarries. Some stone soaks up paints while others take very little.

Never buy exterior paint in any quantity until you have tested a patch in the least conspicuous place. Allow it to dry, even weather a bit, before buying sufficient quantities to do the entire house.

Painting trim and the exterior requires working off ladders or a scaffold. Since a scaffold provides greater freedom and is less tiring, rent what you need. The pipe scaffold, Illus. 18, or the build-it-yourself scaffold, Illus. 19, can be erected to height required.

Anchor the scaffold to the wood trim around a door or window.

Drive 8 or 10 penny nails temporarily into the trim and wire the scaffold to the nails. When you get ready to remove the scaffold, pull the nails, plug the holes with putty before painting the trim.

Another way to anchor a scaffold is shown in Illus. 18. A 2 x 4 is placed across a window opening. Wire is fastened to the 2 x 4 and to the scaffold. Old double hung windows will frequently close and lock over the wire.

A−2x4 or 2x6
B−2x4 or 2x6
C−2x6, 2x8 or 2x10
D−1x6

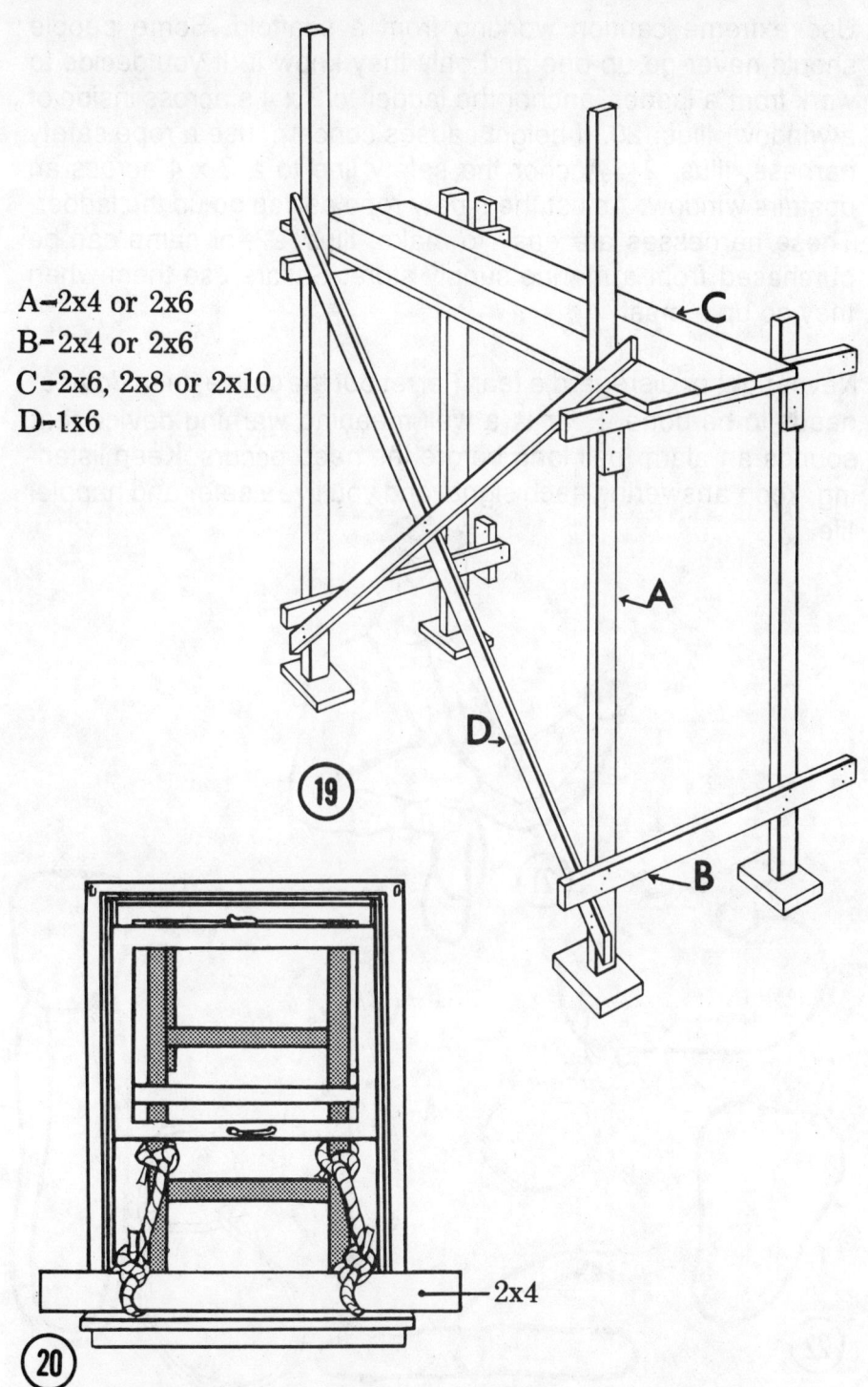

2x4

Use extreme caution working from a scaffold. Some people should never go up one and only they know it. If you decide to work from a ladder, anchor the ladder to 2 x 4's across inside of a window, Illus. 20. If height causes concern, use a rope safety harness, Illus. 21. Anchor the safety line to a 2 x 4 across an upstairs window. Adjust the safety rope as you go up the ladder. These harnesses are easy to make, Illus. 22, or same can be purchased from a marine supply store. Sailors use them when they go up a mast.

Never fight or disregard a fear. Ferret out the cause, then do what needs to be done. Fear is a well meaning warning device that sounds an alarm bell long before the need occurs. Keep listening, keep answering each signal and you live a safer and happier life.

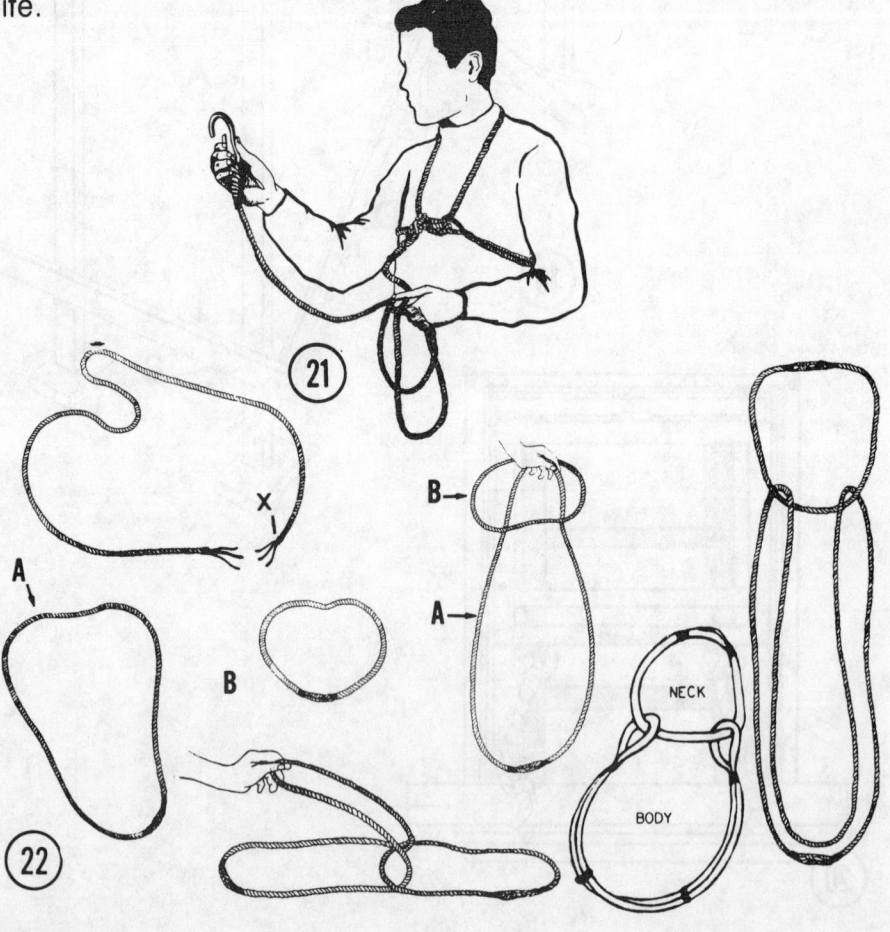

(22)

SAFETY LINE

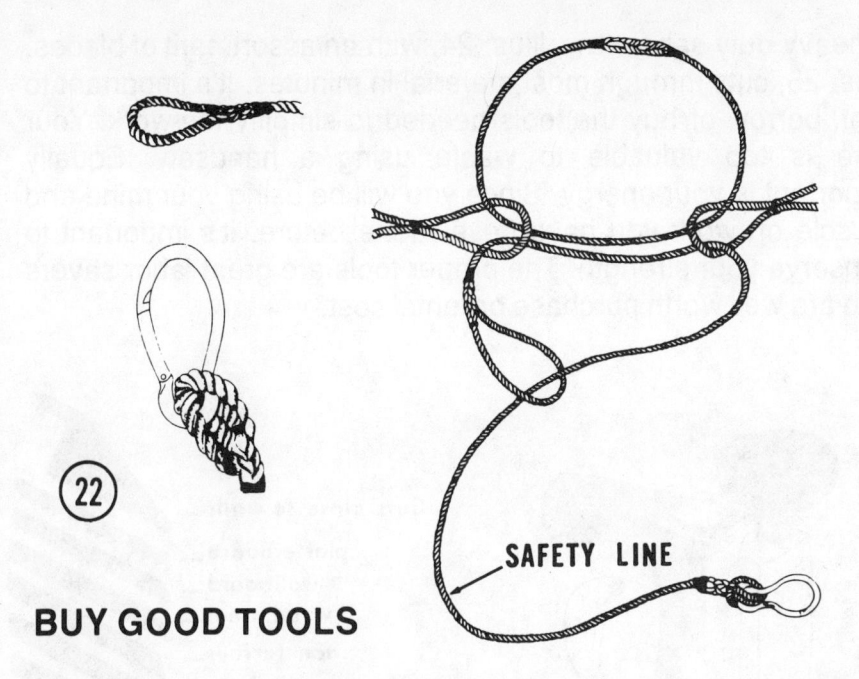

BUY GOOD TOOLS

Rehabilitating and maintaining a house requires a lot of tools so buy what you need and buy good quality. Most "first time" home improvers discover they are far more adept than they first imagined. Not only can they do masonry and carpentry with almost professional skill, but they enjoy doing it. If you see any future in this work, buy a radial arm and an electric hand saw. The radial arm saw is like having an experienced carpenter make all saw cuts. It's hard to make a wrong straight or angle cut with this saw, Illus. 23.

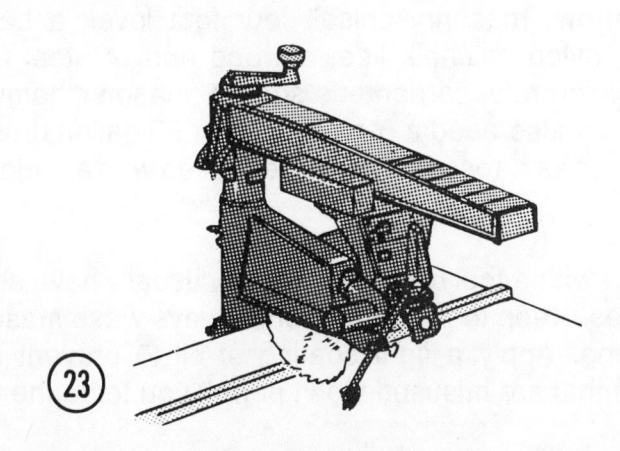

(23)

39

A heavy duty saber saw, Illus. 24, with an assortment of blades, Illus. 25, cuts through most material in minutes. It's important to rent, borrow or buy the tools needed to simplify the work. Your time is too valuable to waste using a handsaw. Equally important is your energy. Since you will be using your mind and muscle on work you have never done before, it's important to conserve your strength. The proper tools are great labor savers and are well worth purchase or rental cost.

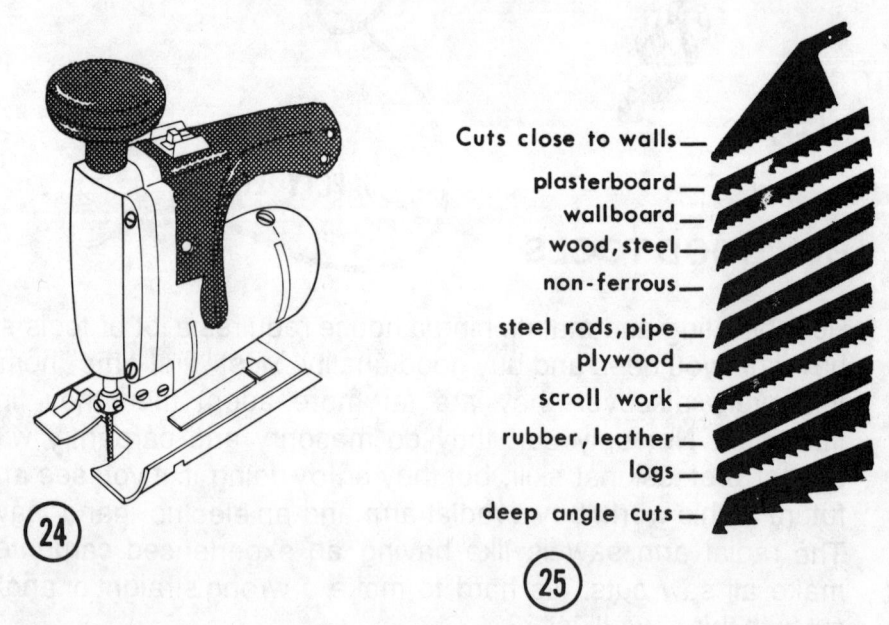

Cuts close to walls
plasterboard
wallboard
wood, steel
non-ferrous
steel rods, pipe
plywood
scroll work
rubber, leather
logs
deep angle cuts

(24) (25)

Concrete repairs require a shovel, mason's hoe, mixing tub or steel wheelbarrow, masonry chisel, four foot level, a ball of non-stretching nylon or chalk line, a wood and/or steel float, trowel, 6 ft. folding rule, carpenter's square, mason's hammer, Illus. 26. You will also need a 5 gallon can or 50 gallon drum to wash off tools, or as a reservoir for water mixed with an additive or anti-freeze.

Get acquainted with a tool rental store. They usually have all the tools a pro uses. Keep tools store fresh. Always wash masonry tools after using. Apply a light coating of oil to prevent rust. Concrete tools that are misused won't permit you to do the best kind of work.

LEVEL

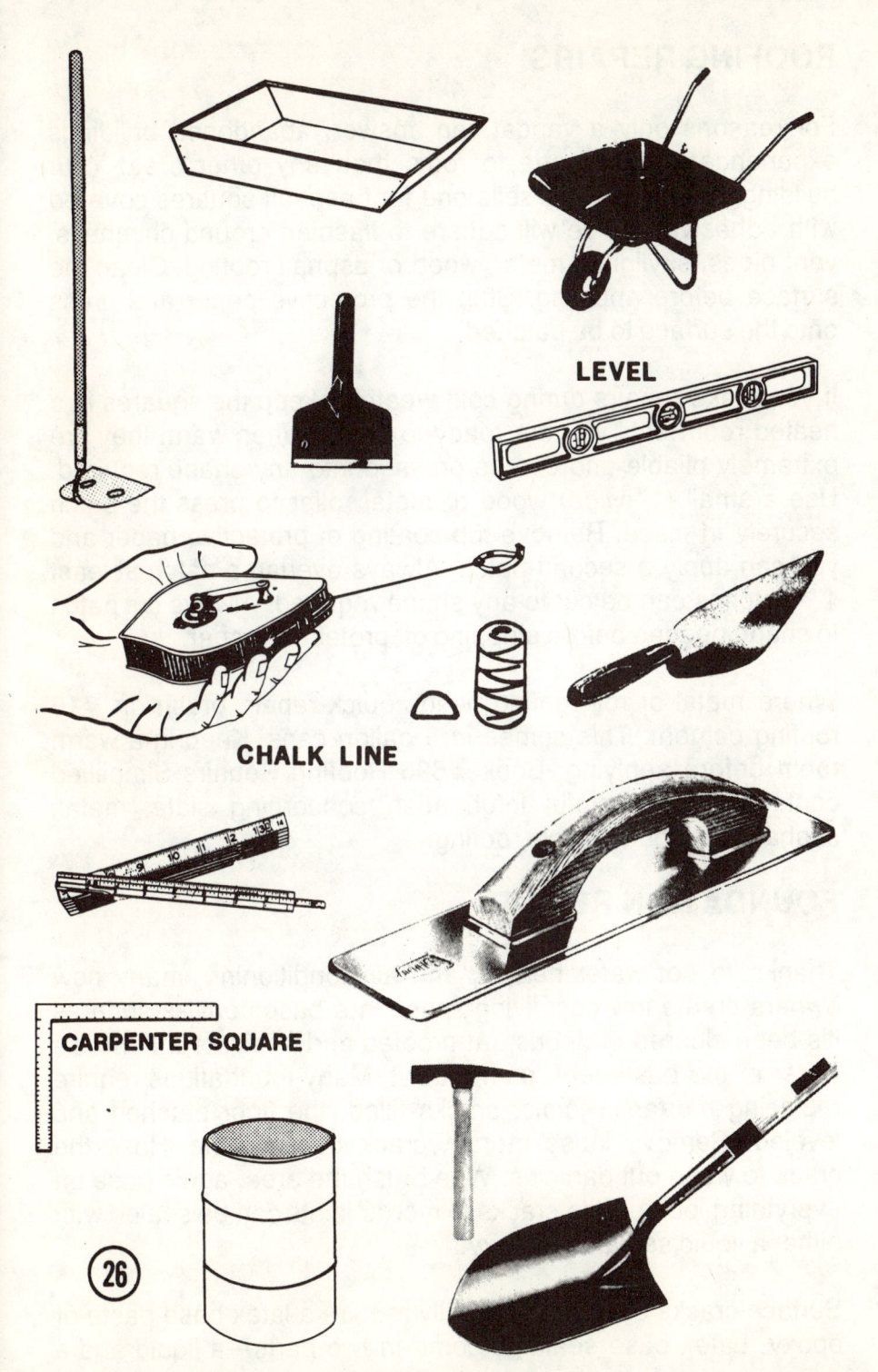

CHALK LINE

CARPENTER SQUARE

26

ROOFING REPAIRS

For reasons only a vandal can answer, abandoned buildings experience less damage to roofs than any other area. Your building material dealer sells one foot asphalt squares covered with adhesive. These will adhere to flashing around chimneys, vent pipes, skylights, metal, wood or asphalt roofing. Clean the surface before applying. Strip the protective paper and press onto the surface to be patched.

If you make repairs during cold weather, keep the squares in a heated room until you are ready to apply. When warm they are extremely pliable and can be pressed into any shape required. Use a small (1" wide) wood or metal roller to press the patch securely in place. Remove top coating of protective paper and you can apply a second patch. Always overlap a patch at least 1". Patches can be cut to any shape required. Always cut patch to shape needed before stripping off protective paper.

Where metal or roll roofing needs quick repair, brush on #15 roofing cement. This comes in 5 gallon cans. Keep in a warm room before applying. Book #696 Roofing Repairs Simplified contains much helpful information concerning slate, metal, asphalt and wood shingle roofing.

FOUNDATION REPAIR

Thanks to hot water heating and air conditioning, many new owners create low cost living space in a basement as soon as it's been cleared of debris, rat-proofed and fumigated. If there's water in the basement, pump it out. Many foundations require replacing mortar in joints, cracks filled, the floor patched and leveled. Remove loose mortar, cracked block, etc. Hose the crack to wash out particles. Wire brush the area, again hose off everything loose. Fine cracks in mortar joints can be sealed with either a liquid sealant or epoxy.

Surface cracks of any size usually require a latex base paste or epoxy. Latex base sealants come in two parts—a liquid and a powder. Epoxy also comes in two parts. Mix only as much as you can use immediately. Always note setting time directions on can specify. A third sealant, available at most lumber yards, is called a plug sealant. This can be used to plug sizable cracks even with water coming in.

After filling all cracks and holes in foundation, you can further waterproof a foundation wall with a slush coat consisting of one part portland cement, one part Anti Hydro, or equal waterproofing additive, to three parts water. Brush this over the dampened surface. While still wet apply a 3/8" thick coat of cement mortar, mixed as follows:

> One part Anti-Hydro to 10 parts of water. This is called gauging water. Mix one part portland cement to two parts of clear sand. Add gauging water. Apply a 3/8" thick coating to walls, Illus. 27, to a foot above grade level. Use a wood or metal float, Illus. 28, to spread the mortar.

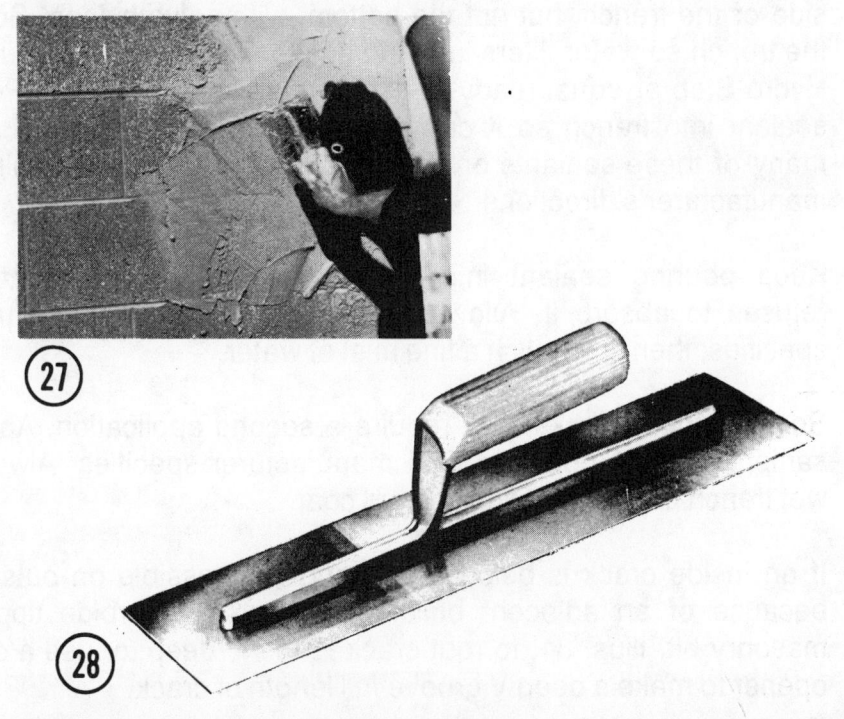

27

28

43

After the first coat begins to set, scratch the surface using a screwdriver or trowel, Illus. 29. Allow this coat to set thoroughly. Spray it daily with a fine mist. Allow to cure for a week.

Using the same mix, apply a second ⅜" coating using a float. Smooth this coat, Illus. 30. Allow to cure slowly by spraying daily with a fine mist. Allow to dry thoroughly. A week after you stop spraying, the wall can be painted with any masonry paint.

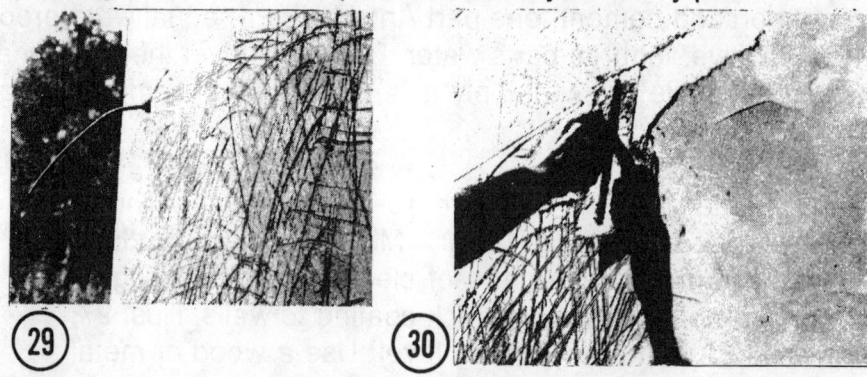

If you see an exposed, readily accessible crack on the outside, dig a trench so bottom of trench is level with crack. Cover the side of the trench, but not the bottom, with polyethylene. Soak the trench so water filters into and soaks the crack. Next pour in Hydro-Stop or equal ready-to-use masonry crack sealant. Pour sealant into trench so it can seep into crack. Since there are many of these sealants on the market, always read and follow manufacturer's directions.

Keep pouring sealant into trench until crack in foundation refuses to absorb it. Allow sealant to set time manufacturer specifies, then spray with a fine mist of water.

Some hairline cracks may require a second application. Apply same within 24 hours or time manufacturer specifies. Always wet trench before applying second coat.

If an inside crack is below grade and inaccessible on outside because of an adjacent building, etc., use a carbide tipped masonry bit, Illus. 31, to rout crack ½ to ¾" deep; or use a can opener to make a deep V groove full length of crack.

(31) Masonry Drill with Tungsten Carbide Tip

Apply a paste sealant, either latex or epoxy, Illus. 32. Since patching paste sets up fast, some within minutes, it's important to prepare the crack with water and follow manufacturer's directions. Smooth the surface as quickly as you pack the paste into the crack.

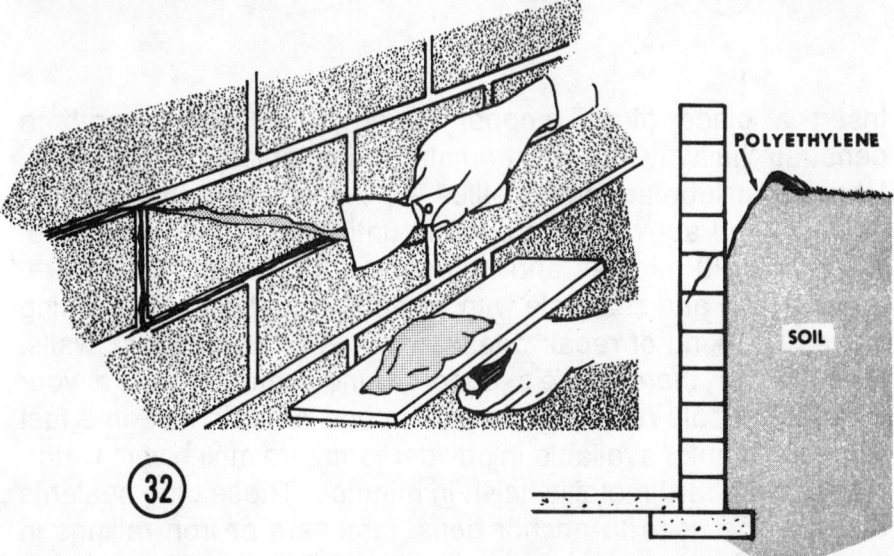

(32)

If you have a long crack or if a portion of the foundation wall is allowing water to enter at several different levels, draw a chart to accurately locate area. Where conditions permit, drive a crowbar or iron rod to depth required to service each crack.

Cracks that take in a lot of water should be sealed inside with paste sealant, and on outside with liquid sealer.

Another way of filling a crack below grade in a poured concrete wall, one that shows up on inside of basement, Illus. 33, is by drilling a ½" or larger hole at top of crack. Drill hole at a slight downward angle to a distance halfway through wall. Use a ½" or larger masonry bit.

(33)

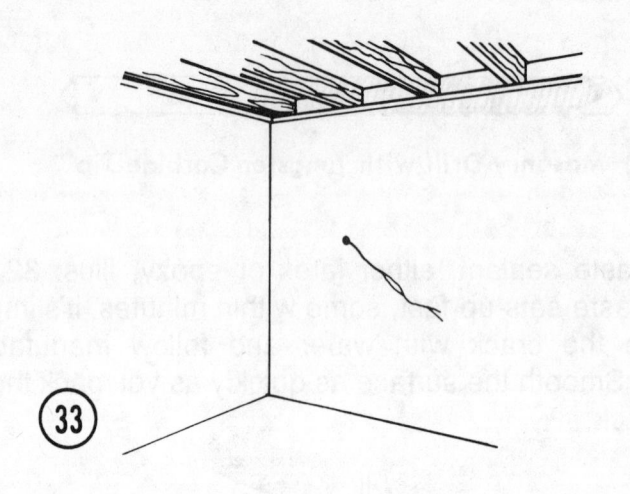

Insert a piece of ½" copper tubing of sufficient length to penetrate halfway into wall and still project at least 2" from wall. Use rubber tube and funnel, Illus. 34. Apply water, then sealant as described above. Keep pouring until it won't take any more. Wait 15 to 20 minutes and try again. If it still won't take more, remove pipe and seal hole with an epoxy or latex base patching paste. This kind of repair doesn't work in concrete block walls. Even where there there's underground water pressure your masonry supply retailer can recommend a sealant. Some fast setting sealants, available in powder form, are mixed with water. It dries to a hard metallic finish in minutes. These plug sealants can also be used to anchor bolts, fasteners or iron railings in concrete. Only mix as much as you need. Don't mix a new batch with any part of a previous batch. Most patching plug sealants are applied to a thoroughly soaked surface. Use a short bladed putty knife. Work the sealant in fast, deep and smooth, as quickly as possible.

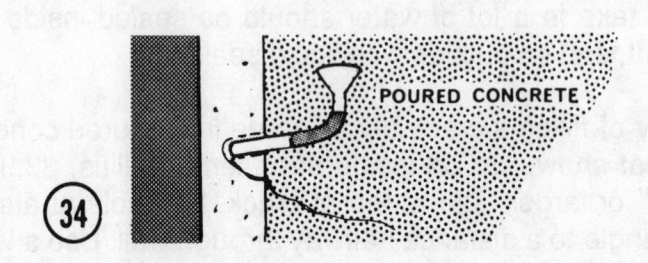

POURED CONCRETE

(34)

If you happen to buy a house next to an empty lot, or next to a house that's being wrecked, and your foundation is exposed, waterproofing the outside is good insurance. After applying a two coat mortar application and after mortar has been allowed to cure thoroughly, paint foundation with asphalt cement. While still wet embed #15 felt horizontally, Illus. 35. Start at bottom and overlap each course 6". Paint with hot tar or asphalt cement to thoroughly seal all lapped joints. Allow asphalt to dry thoroughly then use care when back filling with earth.

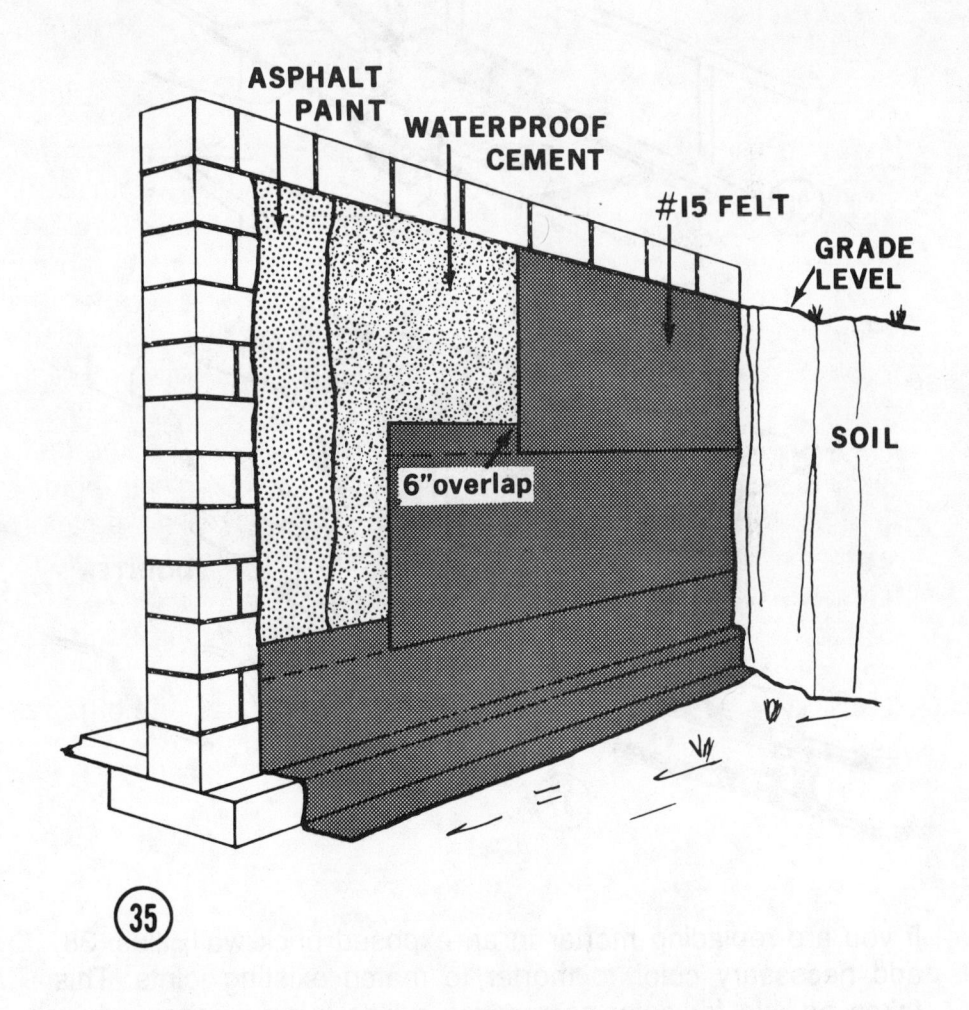

If you are replacing mortar in joints between bricks or blocks, use a float and trowel to pack mortar into joint, Illus. 36. Use a prepared mortar mix. This only requires adding water. Work the mortar into the joint. Use either a concave or convex jointer, Illus. 37, to finish the joint to match others.

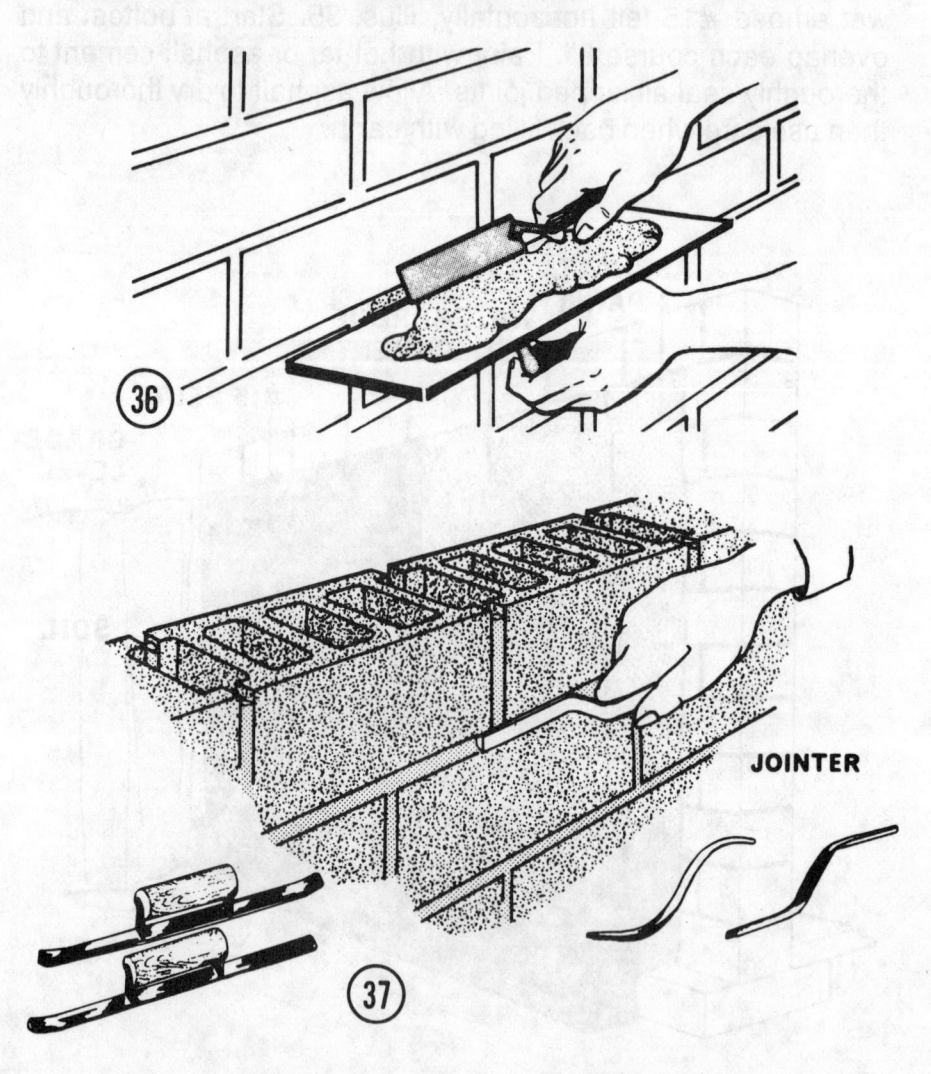

JOINTER

If you are replacing mortar in an exposed brick wall, Illus. 38, add necessary color to mortar to match existing joints. This takes an eye for color so practice a little in an inconspicuous place.

38

(38)

Cracks in a concrete floor or concrete foundation can be sealed and waterproofed with liquid or paste sealants following procedure outlined for walls. If the basement floor slopes badly or is cracked, consider covering the entire floor with 1" to 1½" of concrete.

Mixing concrete requires drinking-quality water, clean sand, gravel or crushed stone. Use sand and gravel free of silt, clay and loam. For small jobs, use the premixes. These are exactly what the name implies, an exact mixture. Add water as specified and they are ready to use. A gravel mix contains cement, sand and gravel. This is used to patch large holes. The gravel mix is used for concrete 2" or more thick.

A mortar mix contains cement, lime and fine sand. Use this to fill mortar joints.

A sand mix, cement and sand, is used for patching cracks, plastering, parging or stuccoing. 80 lbs. of premix will cover about 16 sq. ft., ¼" thick when used for plastering. The mortar mix is perfect for laying brick or blocks, and for repairing mortar joints in chimneys, etc.

Small amounts of concrete can be mixed in a steel wheelbarrow. Use a straight sided can or pail as a measure. One part cement, 2¼ parts sand, 3 parts gravel provide what is known as a 1-2-3 mix. Use this mix to level up a floor or build a platform for a washing machine, dryer, furnace, etc.

To estimate amount of concrete needed for various size areas, multiply the width by length to obtain square footage, then note chart, Illus. 39. If you want to estimate covering a floor with 1" of concrete, use ¼ amount noted under 4".

EXAMPLE:
If you wanted to raise up one end of a low basement floor with a 20' x 20' - 1½" thick slab.
Area = 20 x 20 = 400 sq. ft. x 1½" = 1.85 cu. yds.

CUBIC YARDS OF CONCRETE IN SLABS

Area in square feet (length × width)	Thickness in inches				
	4	5	6	8	12
50	0.62	0.77	0.93	1.2	1.9
100	1.2	1.5	1.9	2.5	3.7
200	2.5	3.1	3.7	4.9	7.4
300	3.7	4.7	5.6	7.4	11.1
400	4.9	6.2	7.4	9.8	14.8
500	6.2	7.2	9.3	12.4	18.6

(39)

When making small repairs with a prepared mortar mix, dump the contents in a wheelbarrow, spread it out, make a hole in the middle and add as much water as directions specify. Use a hoe to pull the dry mix into the water. If you have a sizable foundation repair job, use code specified mortar mixes. These specify using a Type M or N mortar mix. This is what each contains:

Type M— 1 part portland cement, ¼ part hydrated lime and not less than 2¼ or more than 3 parts sand by volume. This is a high strength mortar and is suitable for masonry below grade that is in contact with the earth, such as foundations, retaining walls, walks, sewers, manholes, catch basins.

Type N— 1 part portland cement, 1 part hydrated lime and not less than 4½ or more than 6 parts sand by volume. This mortar is considered a medium strength mortar and is recommended for exposed masonry above grade, walls, chimneys, and exterior brick and block work subject to severe exposure.

Always use a batch of mortar within 2½ hours after it has been mixed. Always add water when needed. Always keep it alive by turning it over with a trowel.

A bag of portland cement weighs 94 lbs*. It is equal to one cubic foot. One bag of cement, 2¼ cubic feet of sand, plus 3 cubic feet of gravel and between 4 to 5½ gallons of water makes approximately 4½ cubic feet of concrete.

Always store portland cement in a dry place. Only buy as many bags as you can use during the period you are working. Never lay bags on the ground or on a concrete floor, always on boards placed across blocks. Always cover with polyethelyne when not being used. Dampness, morning dew, even humidity, can harden cement.

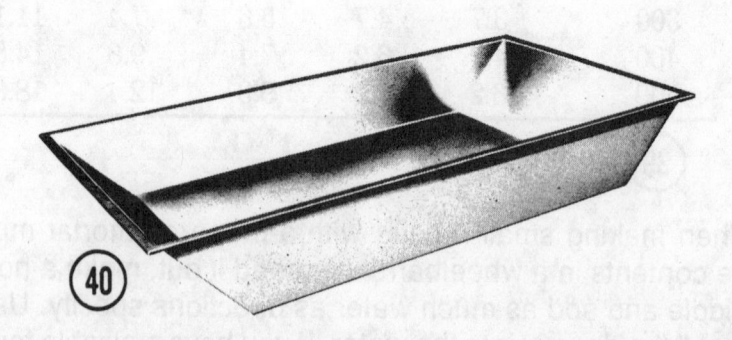

If you have a lot of concrete work to do, rent a mixing tub, Illus. 40. This provides the best way to mix a full bag of cement. A

*87.5 lbs. in Canada.

steel wheelbarrow can be used for smaller batches. Always use up a batch of concrete as quickly as possible, preferably within 30 to 40 minutes. In hot weather, in less time.

The secret to good concrete lies in accurately measuring all materials and in mixing the sand and cement thoroughly to one consistent color before adding gravel. Mix gravel, sand and cement thoroughly before adding water. Use only as much water as is needed to make a consistency that holds its shape when a handful is compressed. The exact amount of water is difficult to specify since the moisture content of sand varies.

A concrete floor can be hardened, made comparatively non-dusting, and waterproofed with the addition of Anti-Hydro Set or equal additive. This is especially important when pouring a basement or floor area where there's any question of dampness. Follow manufacturer's directions and add the exact amount of additive they specify to the water when mixing. In the case of readymix, always pour in the exact gallons of additive required according to the size of the load. Besides waterproofing concrete, it also acts as a hardener and dust inhibitor. Measure and mix additive in exact amount of water manufacturer specifies. Then use only as much of this water to a bag of cement as specified. Cut the top off a 50 gallon drum and use this as a reservoir for premixed water. If you buy readymix, ask the driver to pour the additive into the tank. Make certain it's thoroughly mixed before driver starts to pour.

Concrete requires time to cure. During this time spray with a fine mist. This should be done once or twice every 24 hours for at least three days. Always spray a basement wall with a fine mist. If the work is exposed to direct sunshine, cover with burlap, roofing felt or building paper. Remove same before wetting concrete.

Where building codes permit, owners of many brownstones convert the basement into an apartment. To obtain the largest amount of usable floor space install the heating system where the supply and return lines can be run along a partition or outside wall, or between ceiling joists. If you need to run a pipe below an existing concrete floor, an electric jack hammer, Illus. 41, simplifies cutting an 8 or 10" wide trench. Jack hammers are available on a rental basis. Always make the trench wide and deep enough to embed a copper line in sand. Screen the sand to make certain there are no nails or other metals. Draw a chart so you know where the pipe is buried. Test the pipe thoroughly before recovering with sand, then with 1" or 1½" of concrete. Use caution when drilling holes through a concrete floor. You never know where a water main or gas line may be buried. If you use a jack hammer don't drive the bit through the slab. Break the last ¼ or ½" with a hammer and chisel.

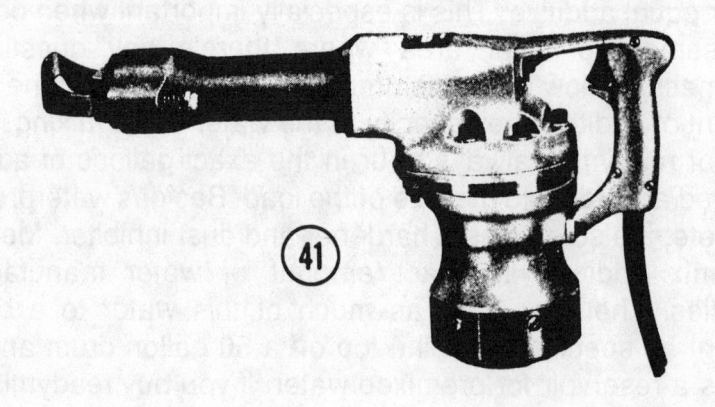

WET BASEMENT

There are many ways to resolve this problem. Where a flow of water can't be stopped, don't buy. An occasional "wet basement" can usually be controlled with a sump pump, Illus. 42. If you consider buying a house that has sump pump in the basement, you know the previous owner had a water problem. If the sump pump was connected to a dry well, the problem may not be solved. The well may have filled up. If the discharge line from a sump pump was connected to the cast iron waste line, make a long test. Run a hose from a water line. Let the pump run at some length to see if it takes the flow of water.

TO DRY WELL → ← ELECTRIC
CONCRETE
GRAVEL
SOIL
12"
14"

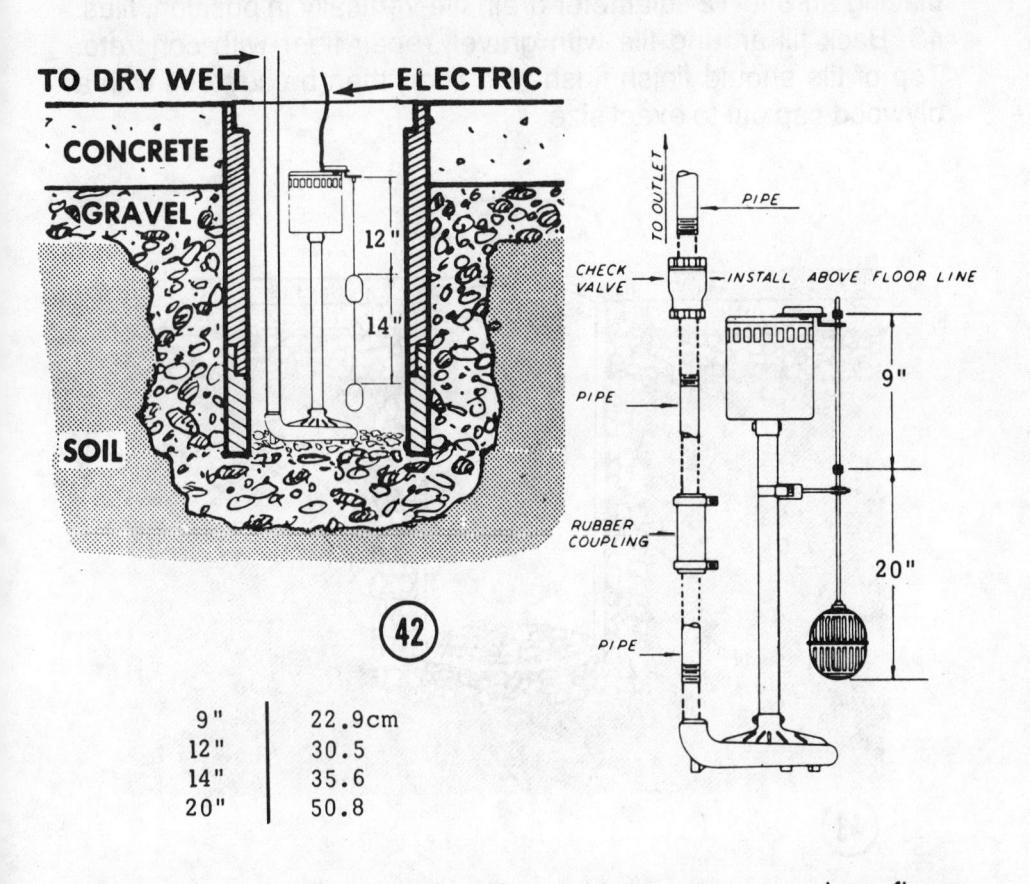

TO OUTLET
PIPE
CHECK VALVE — INSTALL ABOVE FLOOR LINE
PIPE
9"
RUBBER COUPLING
20"
PIPE

(42)

9"	22.9cm
12"	30.5
14"	35.6
20"	50.8

A sump pump will normally relieve water pressure under a floor and around footings. If there's no sump pump and you have water in one corner, it can usually be corrected by digging a 12" diameter hole, 12, 18 to 24" deep. Use a chisel and hammer to break through concrete or rent a jack hammer. Since a jack hammer does a lot of work fast, rent by the hour. Use with caution. The water in your basement may come from a damaged water main running under your basement floor. For this reason break open a small patch using a hammer and chisel and carefully inspect what's below even before using a jack hammer. If the water comes from a cracked main, call the water department and tell them it's an emergency. If you don't strike a gusher, open up the concrete to width and depth sump pump manufacturer recommends. Most manufacturers recommend filling bottom of sump pump hole with 3 to 4" of gravel, then placing an 8 to 12" diameter drain tile vertically in position, Illus. 43. Back fill around tile with gravel, repair floor with concrete. Top of tile should finish flush with floor, then be covered with a plywood cap cut to exact size.

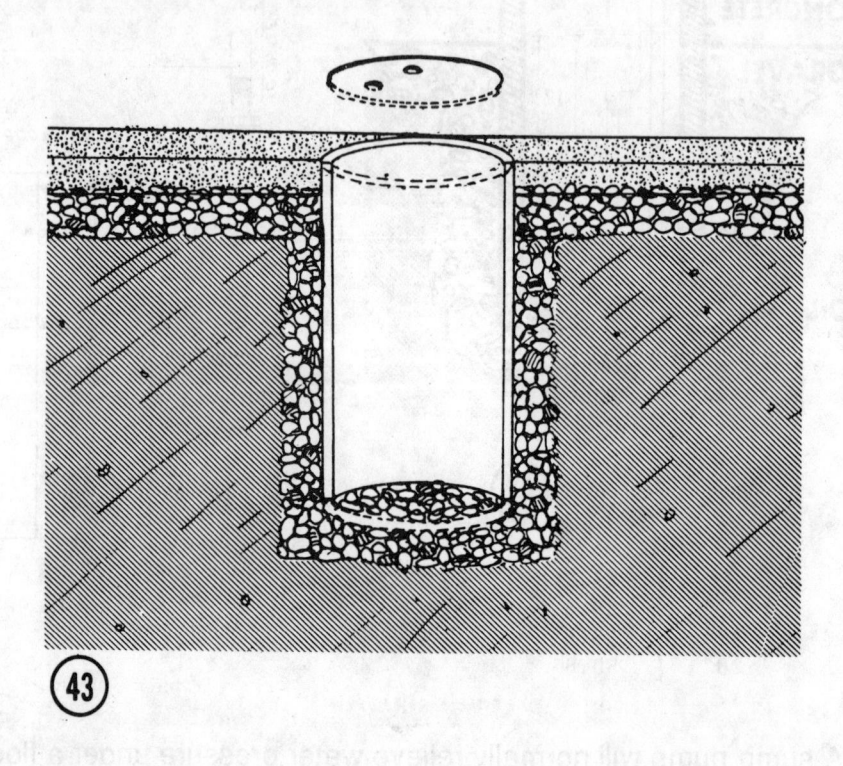

Drill holes in cap for pipe and electric line, several more to allow well to breathe.

CAUTION: Never plug in any electrical tool or piece of equipment when working in water, or when your hands or feet are wet.

INSULATE BASEMENT

If part of your basement foundation wall is above grade and a drop in temperature creates moisture, as well as a loss of heat, do this. After filling cracks and sealing foundation, cement rigid foam insulation to the inside wall with asphalt cement. Use 1" or 2" thick foam. This insulation should extend to floor, Illus. 44.

44

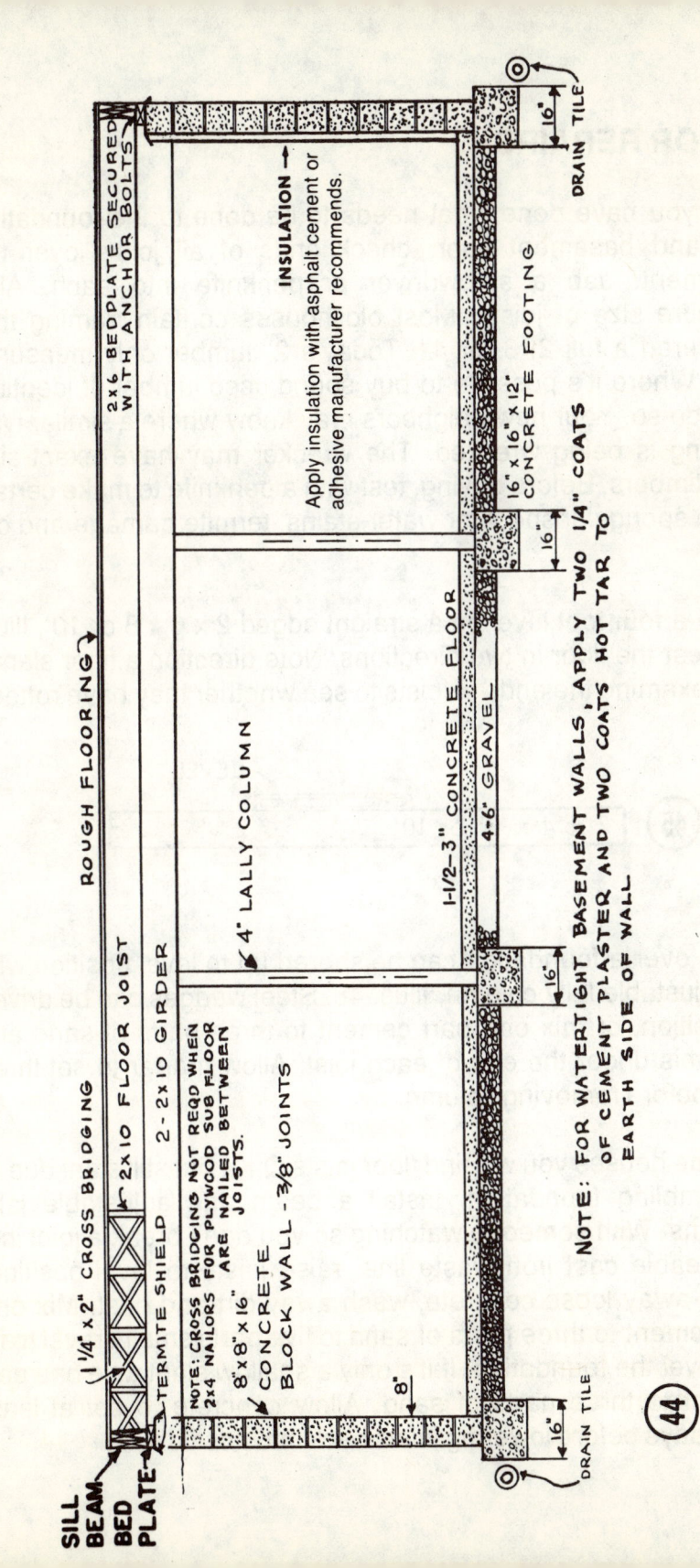

FLOOR REPAIRS

After you have done what needs to be done to the foundation wall and basement floor, check ends of all joists over the basement. Jab a screwdriver or penknife into each. Also measure size of joists. Most old houses contain framing that measured a full 2, 3, or 4". Today's 2" lumber only measures 1½". Where it's possible to buy sound used lumber of identical size, do so. Your new neighbors may know where a similar type building is being wrecked. The wrecker may have exact size solid timbers. Before buying, test with a penknife to make certain it isn't spongy. Inspect for water stains, termite damage and dry rot.

Place a four foot level on a straight edged 2 x 6 x 8 or 10', Illus. 45. Test the floor in two directions. Note direction a floor slants, then examine the ends of joists to see whether they have rotted.

(45) 2 x 4 x 8' or 10' — LEVEL

Joists over a foundation can be shored up to level position with an adjustable lally column, Illus. 46. Steel wedges can be driven in position, or mix one part cement to three parts of sand and flush this under the end of each joist. Allow mortar to set three days before removing column.

In some houses you will find floor joists O.K., but still slant due to a crumbling foundation. Install a beam and adjustable lally columns. With someone watching so you don't break a joint in a serviceable cast iron waste line, raise joists to level position. Clean away loose concrete, wash away dirt and dust. Mix one part cement to three parts of sand to five parts small gravel to fill and level the foundation. If it's only a shallow slant, use one part cement to three parts of sand. Allow concrete to set at least three days before lowering joists back into position.

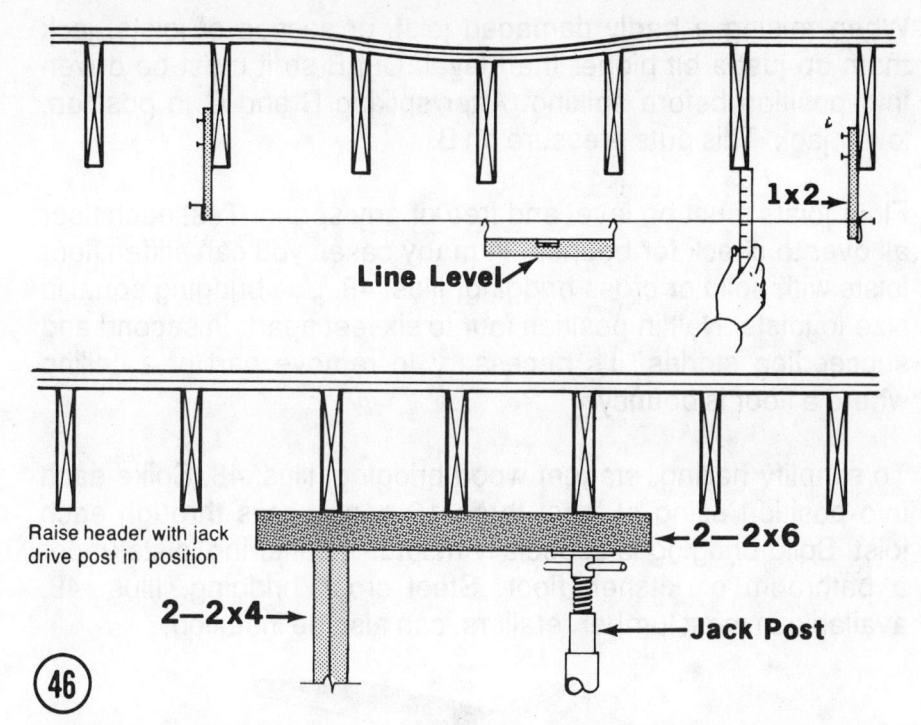

Figure 46 labels: Line Level; 1x2; Raise header with jack drive post in position; 2—2x4; 2—2x6; Jack Post

Another way to stiffen joists is to jack up joist to eliminate movement, then nail a 2 x 4A, Illus. 47, some distance from end of joist, preferably over a pier or girder. Use 16 penny nails. Cut 2 x 4 B to angle and length needed so you have to drive B into position tight against foundation and A. Spike it securely to joist. Spike 2 x 4C in position. C can butt against solid bridging or another A. Release jack. If you still get movement, replace jack in position and apply the same 2 x 4 stiffening to the opposite side. You can stiffen joists anywhere you find them using this method. B and C can be cut to any length required.

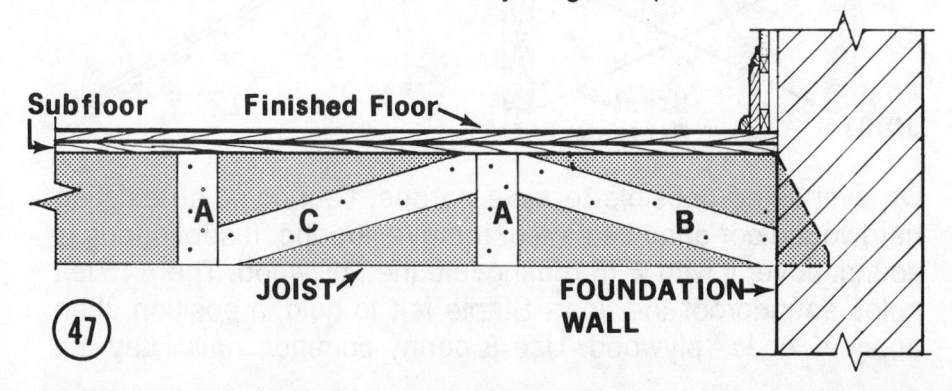

Figure 47 labels: Subfloor; Finished Floor; A; C; A; B; JOIST; FOUNDATION WALL

59

When raising a badly damaged joist, or section of joists, jack them up just a bit higher than level. Cut B so it must be driven into position before spiking. After spiking B and C in position, lower jack. This puts pressure on B.

Floor joists must be level and free of any spring. Test each floor all over to check for bounce. In many cases you can stiffen floor joists with solid or cross bridging, Illus. 48. Use bridging equal in size to joists. Nail in position four to six feet apart. In second and succeeding stories, it's necessary to remove part of a ceiling where a floor is bouncy.

To simplify nailing, stagger wood bridging, Illus. 48. Spike each into position using at least three 16 penny nails through each joist. Solid bridging is especially helpful in stiffening joists under a bathroom or kitchen floor. Steel cross bridging, Illus. 49, available in most lumber retailers, can also be installed.

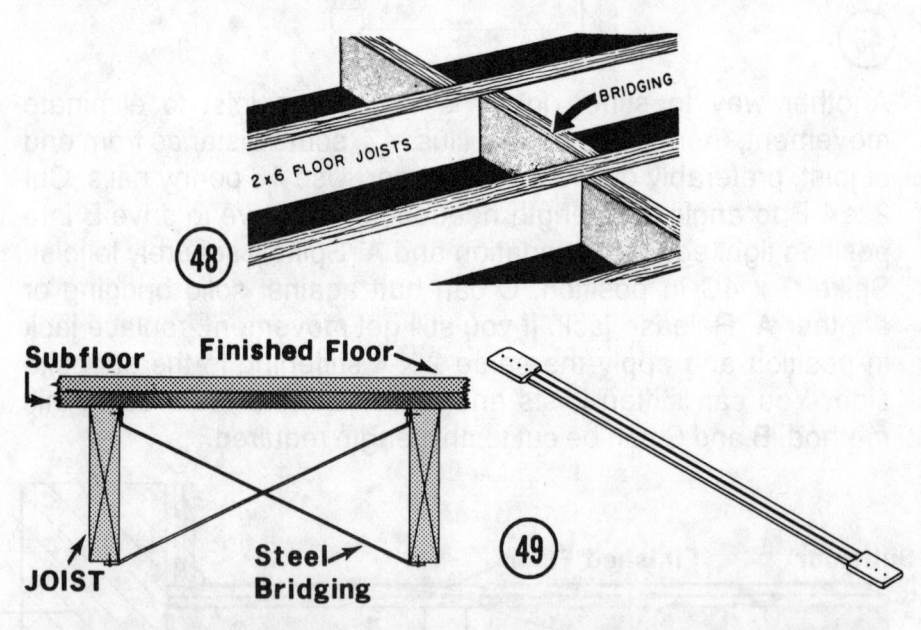

Do everything possible to save parquet flooring. If an existing hardwood floor can't be saved, remove flooring. If subflooring is sound, cover it with #15 roofing felt, then plywood. The #15 felt helps soundproof the floor. Staple felt to hold in position, then apply ⅜ or ½" plywood. Use 8 penny common nails. Lay out panels so ends don't line up over same joist, Illus. 50. For a top quality job, snap chalk lines to indicate joists and run a ribbon of adhesive along each line. Nail ⅜ or ½" plywood every 16" along perimeter and intermediate joists. Don't butt panels tight. Allow 1/16 to 1/32" between panels at sides and ends.

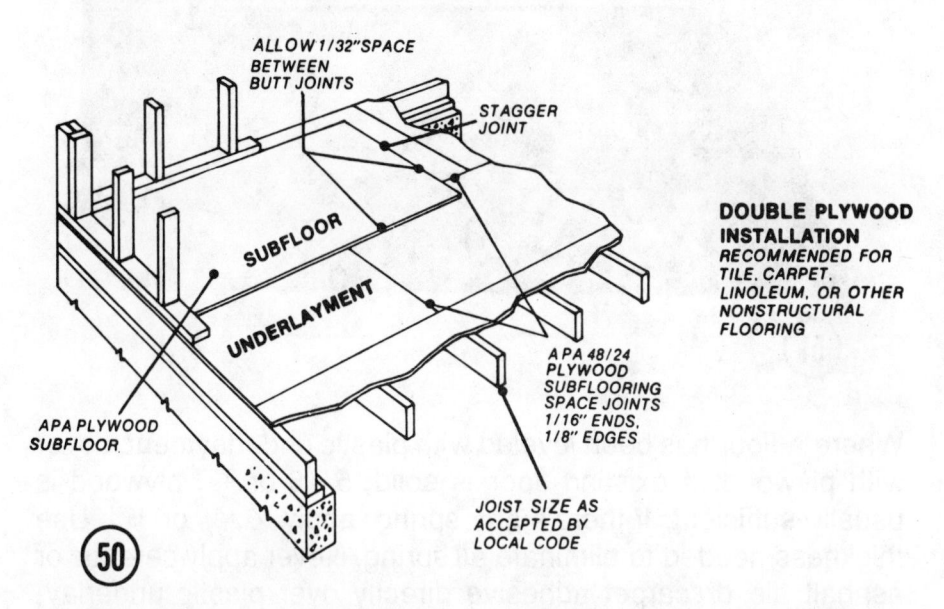

ALLOW 1/32" SPACE BETWEEN BUTT JOINTS

STAGGER JOINT

SUBFLOOR
UNDERLAYMENT

DOUBLE PLYWOOD INSTALLATION
RECOMMENDED FOR TILE, CARPET, LINOLEUM, OR OTHER NONSTRUCTURAL FLOORING

APA 48/24 PLYWOOD SUBFLOORING SPACE JOINTS 1/16" ENDS, 1/8" EDGES

APA PLYWOOD SUBFLOOR

JOIST SIZE AS ACCEPTED BY LOCAL CODE

(50)

Always use exterior grade plywood for subflooring in a bathroom or kitchen. Exterior grade provides an ideal base for ceramic or asphalt tile, linoleum or carpeting. The plywood eliminates movement while it provides a smooth and solid base for floor covering. The addition of plywood subflooring frequently necessitates removing all doors and sawing these ½ to ¾" less across the bottom.

Before installing plywood, inspect flooring to make certain there are no loose boards. If you find any, locate position of joists and drive 8 or 10 penny nails into joists. Check the subfloor with a level in two directions. Use a straight 2 x 4 x 8 or 10' and a level, Illus. 45. If you find a slight dip, level up the area with plastic underlayment, Illus. 51. This can be spread feather thin to almost a 5/16" thick in one coat. Allow each coat to dry length of time manufacturer specifies, then apply as many coats you need to level area.

(51)

Where a floor has been leveled with plastic underlayment, cover with plywood. If existing floor is solid, 5/16 or ⅜" plywood is usually sufficient. If there's any spring, apply ½, ⅝ or ¾". Use thickness needed to eliminate all spring. Never apply ceramic or asphalt tile or carpet adhesive directly over plastic underlayment. Few adhesives are compatible to plastic underlayment. Tile and carpet cements should be applied with a notched trowel, Illus. 52, to a clean, dust free plywood floor. Plastic underlayment is only a leveler. It does nothing to strengthen a floor.

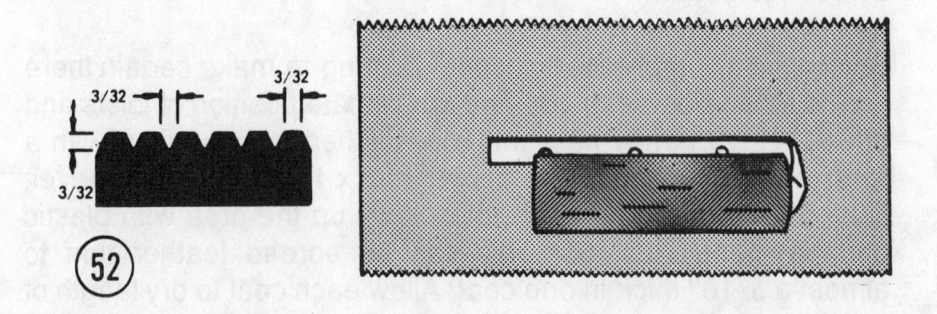

(52)

62

TO REPLACE WINDOWS

Since an architect selected the original windows to complement the character of the facade, keeping the originals or replacing them with their exact size and style is important, Illus. 53.

(54)

If you decide to replace wood windows with an easy to install wood, steel or aluminum replacement unit, it's not difficult. Illus. 54 shows the different style windows currently found in many buildings. Before deciding to replace, ascertain availability of the existing style in size you need. To determine size, measure each window at A, B, C, D and E, Illus. 55. If a replacement window is required, remove side and top stops, Illus. 56. Remove lower sash and cut sash cords. Allow weights to drop down. Remove parting stop, Illus. 57, and top sash. Again, cut cords. Remove pulleys. These are usually screwed to frame.

(55)

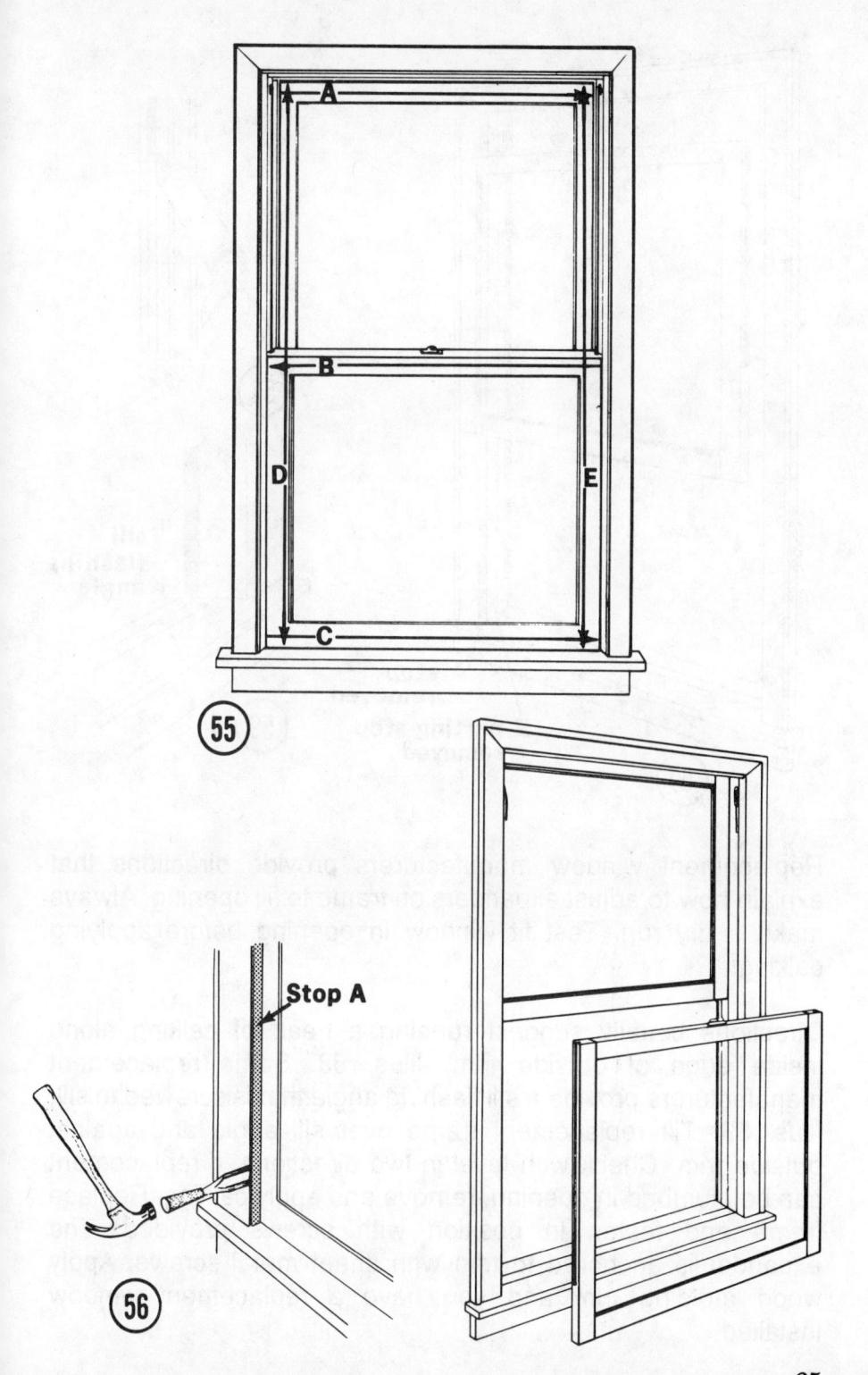

Stop A

(56)

65

A-stop removed
B-parting stop removed

sill flashing angle

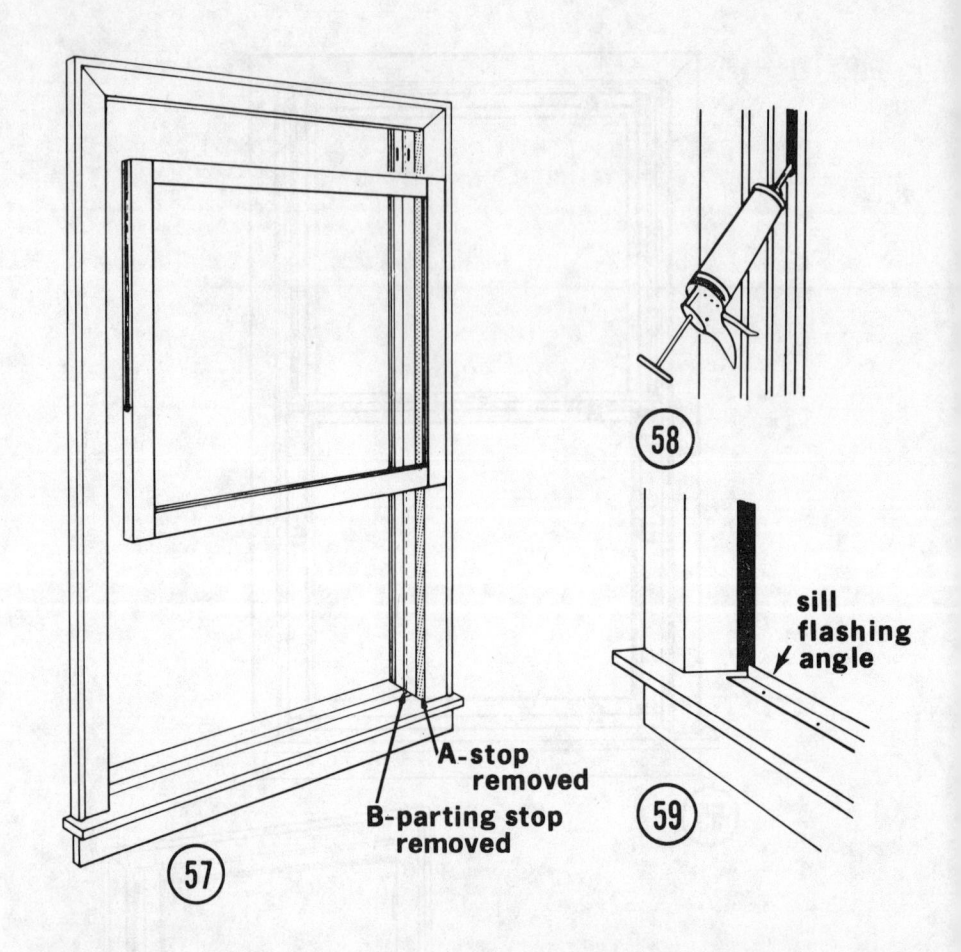

Replacement window manufacturers provide directions that explain how to adjust expanders on frame to fill opening. Always make a dry run. Test fit window in opening before applying calking.

Directions usually suggest running a bead of calking along inside edge of outside trim, Illus. 58. Some replacement manufacturers provide a sill flashing angle that is screwed to sill, Illus. 59. Tilt replacement frame over sill angle and against outside trim. Check with level in two directions. If replacement can be plumbed in opening, remove and apply calking. Replace frame and fasten in position with screws provided. The expander is anchored to trim with sheet metal screws. Apply wood molding trim and you have a replacement window installed.

REPAIRING DAMAGED SASH

In many cases you can salvage even damaged sash by removing and regluing. The sash in a double hung window is held in place with stops A, Illus. 56, and with a parting stop B, Illus. 57. The stops A are usually nailed in place with 3 penny finishing nails. Start at bottom of stop, or alongside any nail you see. Insert a 1" or 1¼" putty knife between stop and trim and pry up stop. Only pry a little at a time. If the stop doesn't budge, use a nailset. Drive nails through stop. If a putty knife is too flexible, use a flat chisel. Remove side stop, then top and parting stop. Plan on replacing stops if you have trouble removing them.

Carefully disconnect sash cord or chain. Tack end of cord temporarily to the trim. Replace sash cord where needed. Your hardware and lumber dealer sells replacement chain, Illus. 60. Cut to length needed.

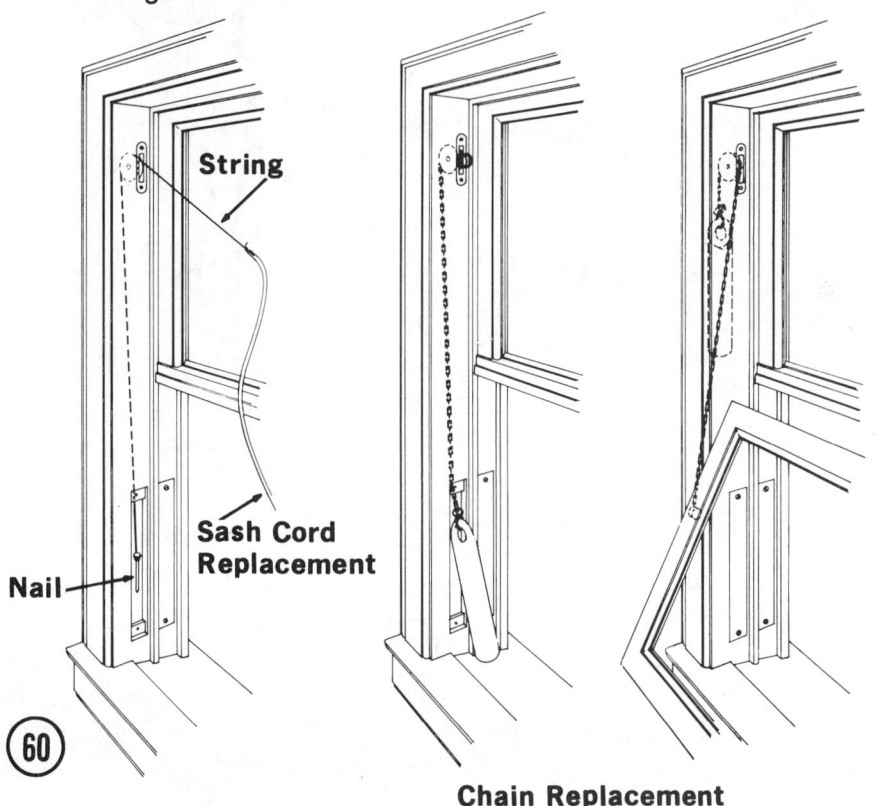

Chain Replacement

67

If existing sash only needs regluing, remove stops. Place sash in position noted with a broom handle or 1 x 2 across frame, Illus. 61. Thin down waterproof glue and soak the corners. Apply clamp to hold frame square while glue sets, Illus. 61. Fill holes, nicks or breaks with a wood filler. Sandpaper smooth. When painted you'll have difficulty finding the repair.

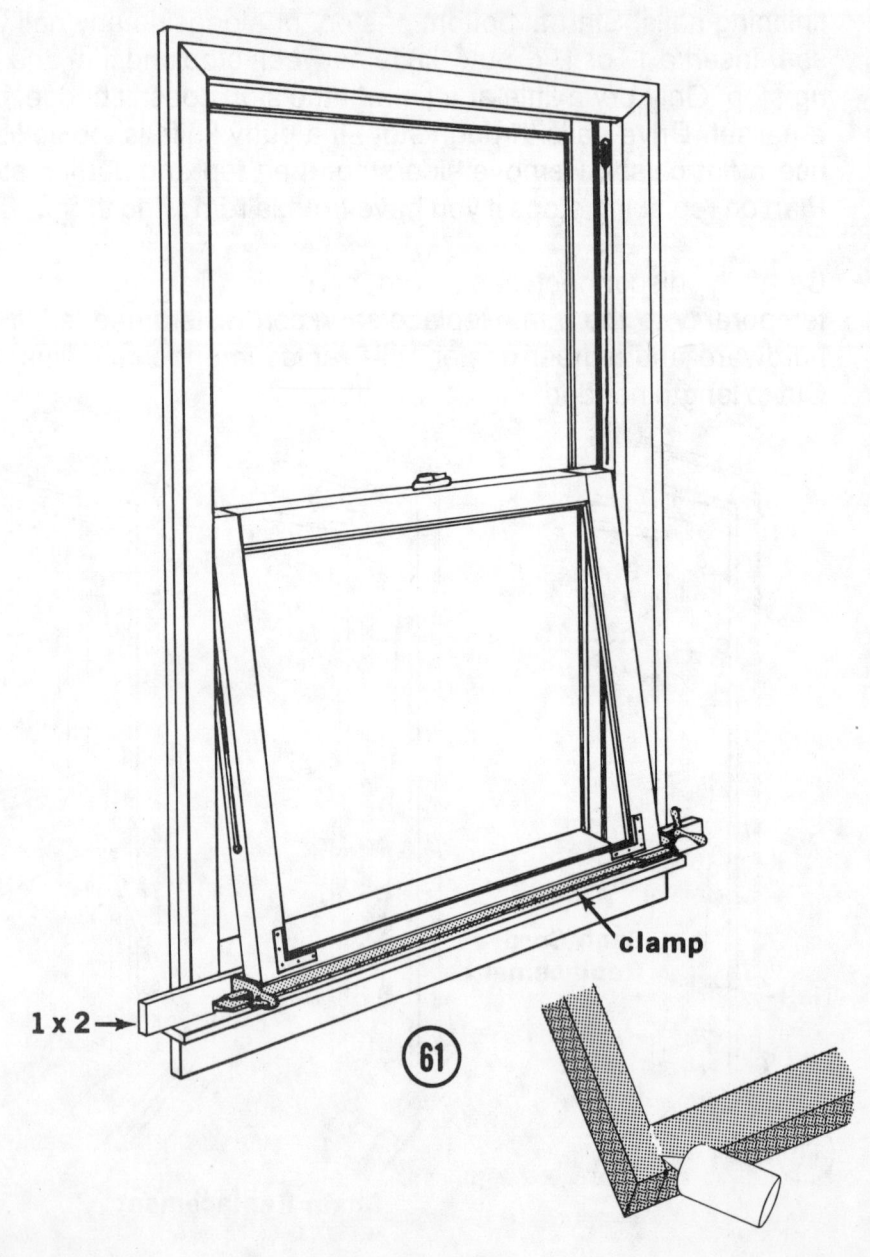

Another way to repair a sash without removing same is with a wood wedge, Illus. 62, and metal corner plates, Illus. 61, 63. Remove stops. Apply glue to crack. Drive wedge to tighten sash. Use care not to crack glass. While the wedge holds sash, fasten 2 or 2½" flat corner brackets in position shown.

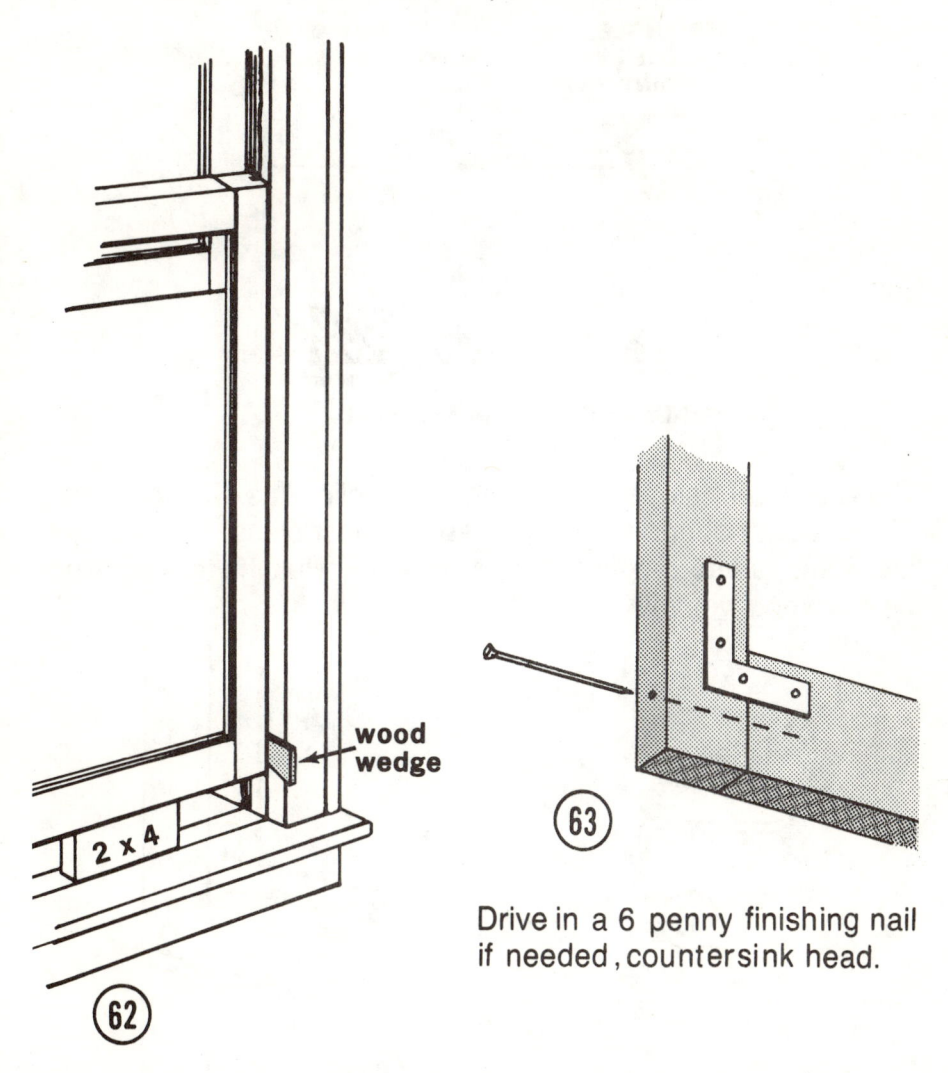

Drive in a 6 penny finishing nail if needed, countersink head.

Heat from a propane torch can be used to remove old putty prior to installing new glass. A street level window that's vulnerable to breakage should be glazed with Lexan or equal non-breakable acrylic. While more expensive than glass, its lifespan and safety factor more than warrant the cost.

FACTS ABOUT GLAZING

Glass in a wood frame is usually held in place with triangular glazier points and putty, Illus. 64; or a wood molding called a glass bead or putty bead.

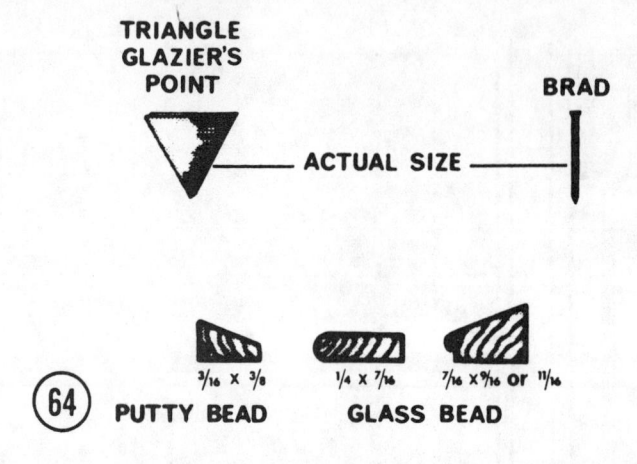

TRIANGLE GLAZIER'S POINT

BRAD

— ACTUAL SIZE —

(64) PUTTY BEAD   3/16 x 3/8   GLASS BEAD   1/4 x 7/8   7/16 x 9/16 or 11/16

Glass in steel frames is held with a wire clip, Illus. 65, and putty. The irregular shaped leg A presses against glass. The straight leg B snaps into a hole in frame, Illus. 66. Putty is then applied as in a wood window.

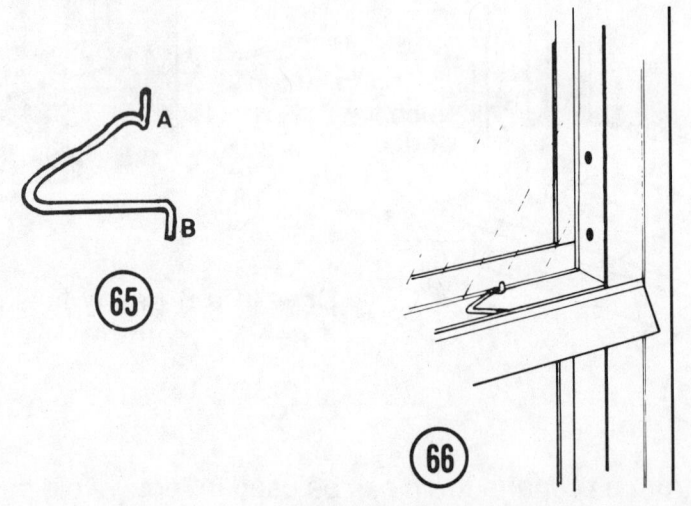

(65)

(66)

Some steel sashes were manufactured with a steel molding. This is screwed in the same position as a glass bead.

Aluminum window manufacturers use the kind of spring clip shown in Illus. 67. The shaped head fits under edge of glass, Illus. 68, 69, the legs are spread to butt against frame. Most glaziers use one close to the ends, one every 16 to 18". The putty is then applied and beveled.

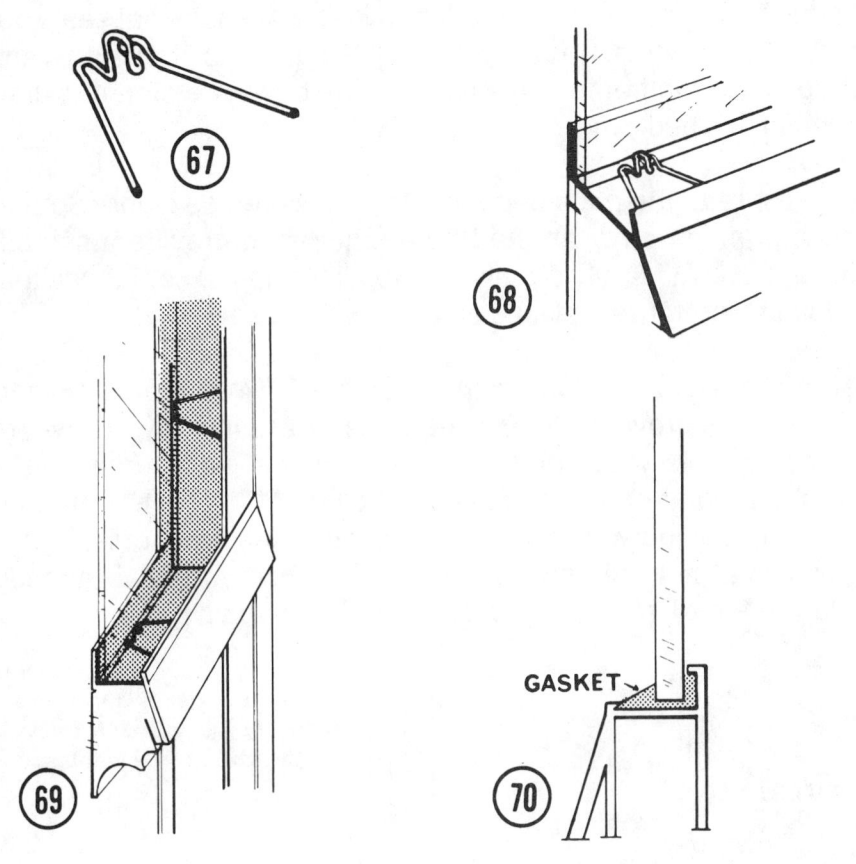

Some aluminum window manufacturers now set glass in a plastic or neoprene gasket, Illus. 70. This can be pryed out and reused. Since this may be difficult to replace, use care not to damage it. Always use the same thickness glass as originally installed. Do not use putty, or a putty bed, with this gasket. When replacing, apply vaseline on frame to help slide gasket in place.

Always remove broken glass and inspect old putty for clips. Always note how many and where these clips were installed.

After removing broken glass, scrape frame carefully to remove bits of old putty. If putty is hard, apply heat using a torch or soldering iron. When area is clean, paint rabbet with linseed oil or paint primer. When dry, roll out a ribbon of putty and spread it thin over area receiving glass. Use a putty knife. This is called a "putty bed" and is important. It provides a cushion that seals out cold air, prevents windows from rattling, while it absorbs any irregularities in frame or glass. Many windows are manufactured without this bed.

Don't spread the putty bed too thick. This creates globs. Spread only as much putty as the frame requires to provide a smooth base, Illus. 71. Apply a putty bed to all frames except those that contain a preformed plastic or neoprene gasket.

Always cut glass to size of opening, less 1/8" in overall width and height. This provides 1/16" clearance all around. If you have no confidence in your ability to measure the glass area, cut a cardboard pattern full size of opening less 1/8". Note how pattern fits into opening with just 1/16" clearance all around. Ask your glass retailer to match the pattern. Tell him you have already allowed for 1/8" clearance and he'll consider you a pro.

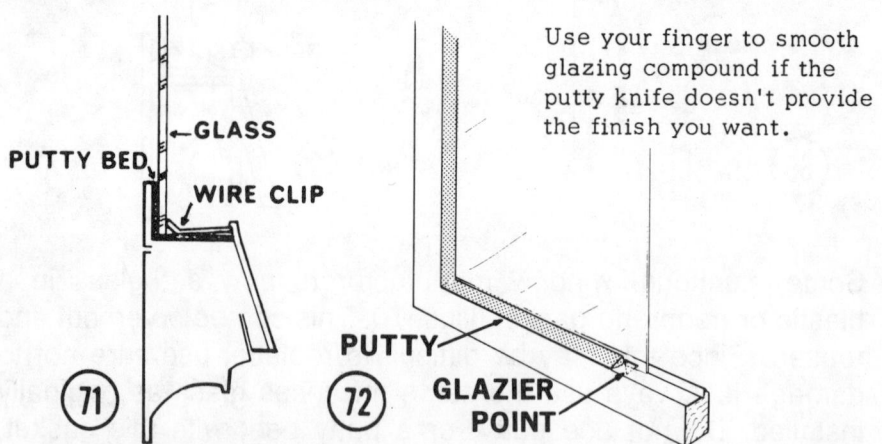

Use your finger to smooth glazing compound if the putty knife doesn't provide the finish you want.

WOOD WINDOW—PUTTY

Press glass into putty bed. Use edge of a chisel or screwdriver to press or tap glazier points in frame about 2" from corners of a small window; and every 10" from corner in a larger window. Glazier points need only be driven in about ½ their overall height, Illus. 72. Use care not to scratch glass. Never replace glazier points, Illus. 64, in the same holes.

Knead putty to make it pliable, then roll it into long strips about pencil thickness. Place it in rabbet, press and bevel with a putty knife, Illus. 72. The linseed oil or paint primer permits putty to bond to frame.

Allow putty to dry about a week before applying paint. When painting, seal putty to glass with a hairline of paint on glass.

WOOD WINDOW—GLASS BEAD

Remove all broken glass. Glass bead is usually nailed in place with small brads. Note where bead was nailed and insert a wood chisel, wide screwdriver or narrow putty knife in center, Illus. 73, preferably alongside a brad. Carefully raise bead, pull brads using pliers wherever nailed.

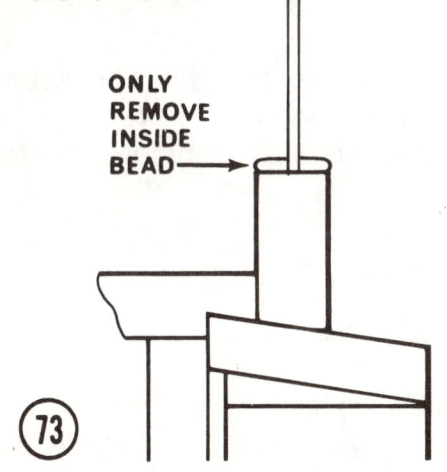

Carefully lift out inside bead at mitered corners. Never remove outside bead. Scrape away old paint and putty. Paint area with linseed oil. Spread a putty bed as outlined previously. Replace glass and renail bead along short sides first. Bow to insert longer lengths in position. Make new holes when renailing. Countersink heads of brads. Fill old and new nail holes with putty, then paint.

Because of warpage or paint build-up, the bead in many old frames is sometimes difficult to remove without damage. If damage occurs, repair with putty after replacing bead. When repainted, it's hard to find where the chisel scarred molding, or a new glass bead can be installed. If the original glass was installed without a bed of putty, you will find it necessary to file ends of miter to shorten overall length. Always maintain angle of miter.

STEEL SASH

Replacing a window in a steel sash requires special clips, Illus. 65, 66. The broken glass and old putty is removed. It's frequently necessary to use a propane torch to loosen old putty on a metal sash. Again apply a thin bed of putty before setting glass in place. Press one leg of spring slip against glass, the other leg snaps into predrilled holes in sash, Illus. 66. Putty is then applied as previously described.

If steel sash has metal glass beads, these are screwed to frame. Spray screws with Liquid Wrench, insert screwdriver in screw slot, hit screwdriver lightly with hammer. This frequently jars screws loose.

ALUMINUM WINDOWS

Glass in these windows is held in place with clips, Illus. 67, and putty. Again remove glass and putty. Apply putty bed and replace glass. Press clips into place. Place head under edge while legs press against frame. Bevel putty to width frame requires.

Always purchase double strength glass for larger windows, single strength for smaller windows.

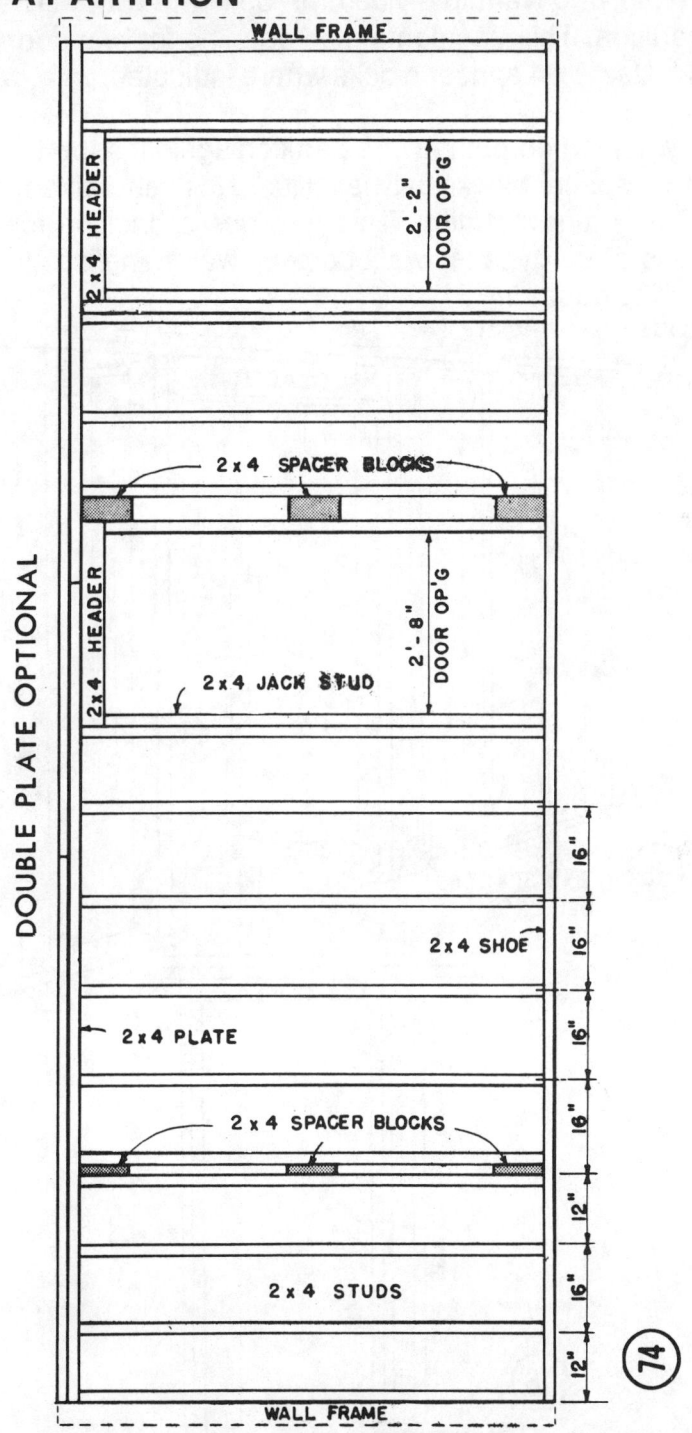

TO BUILD A PARTITION

Those who want to divide one room into two, will need to build a partition. This can contain an opening for one door or two, Illus. 74. Use 2 x 4 spacer blocks where indicated.

If you plan on butting one partition against another, Illus. 75, nail 2 x 4 spacer blocks flatwise, Illus. 76, flush with edge of studs on side butting partition. This provides a backing for wall B, plus nailors for gypsum wallboard or wall paneling. It also permits nailing door trim.

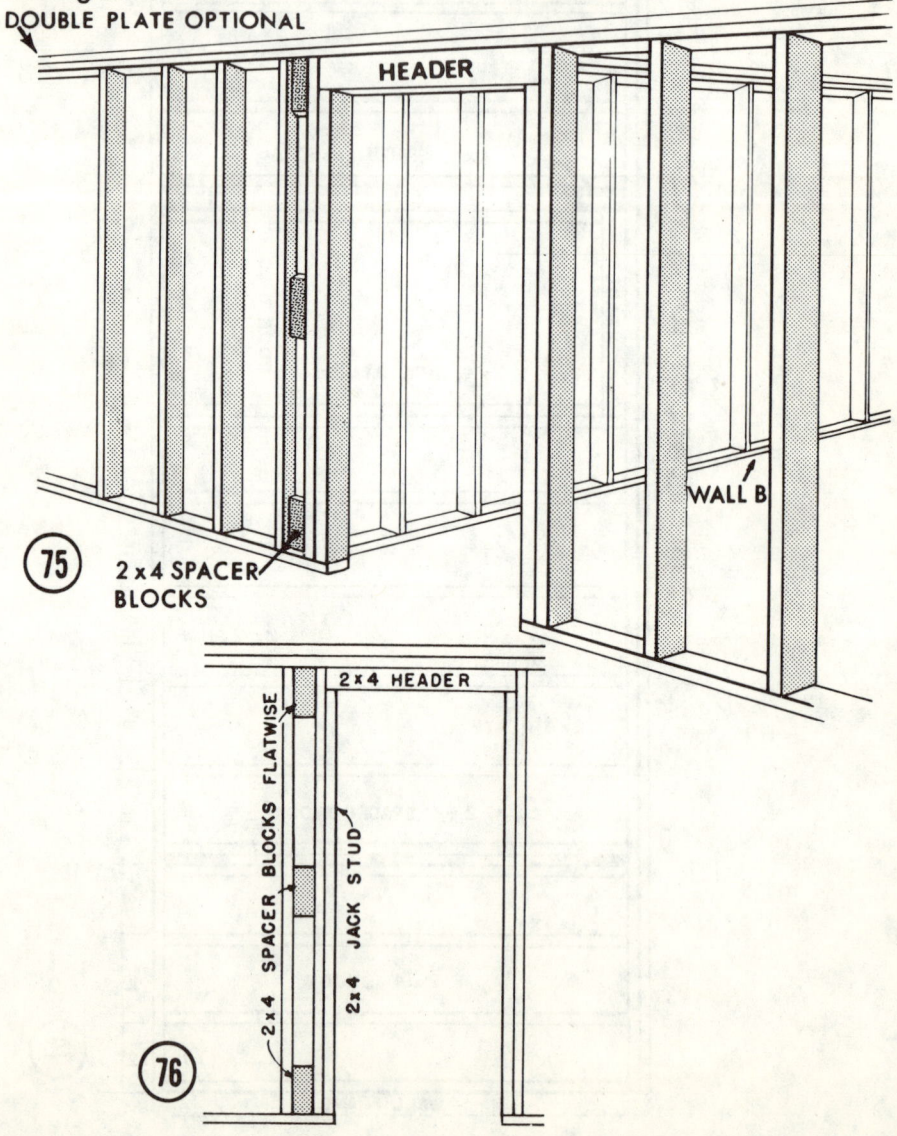

Cut shoe and plate to length required. Only a single plate is required since these partitions are not considered load bearing. Place shoe and plate side by side, Illus. 77. Measure 16" and draw center line to indicate position of each stud.

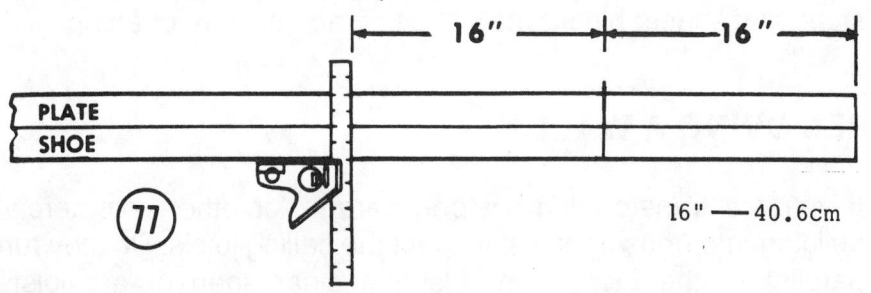

16" — 40.6cm

When nailing a plate across ceiling joists, nail into each joist with two 16 penny nails. When nailing a plate parallel to ceiling joists, position plate so it can be spiked to a joist or to solid bridging, Illus. 10.

After spiking plate in position, drop a plumb bob down from plate to locate exact position for shoe, Illus. 78. Snap a chalk line. Spike shoe in position to joists or to solid bridging. Cut each stud to length required so you can tap it into position. Check each stud with a level in two directions. Toenail studs to shoe and plate with 8 penny nails.

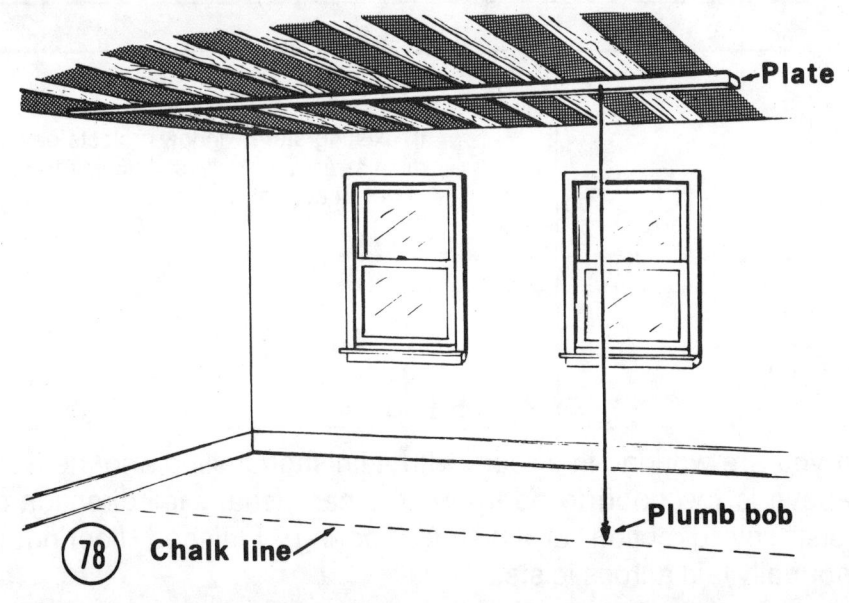

Nail studs in position required for a door opening, Illus. 74. Nail studs to header. Nail jack studs in position. Always frame opening to rough opening size door frame requires. Your lumber retailer will advise size of opening. After framing opening with studs and spacer blocks, saw shoe off across door opening.

REMOVING A WALL

If you are transforming a store, garage, or other commercial building into housing units, inspect the ceiling joists. Do they run parallel to the store front? Is it a clear span or are joists supported by a girder? Since a store display window or opening for a garage door will normally be framed with a header or beam of sufficient size to support the rafters and roof load, you only need to frame in opening with a single plate, shoe and studs, after removing existing window or door.

If joists run parallel to the header over a window, drop a plumb bob down from header to locate position for a shoe. Nail shoe in place. Nail studs 16 to 24" on centers. Frame opening for a door and or window, Illus. 79.

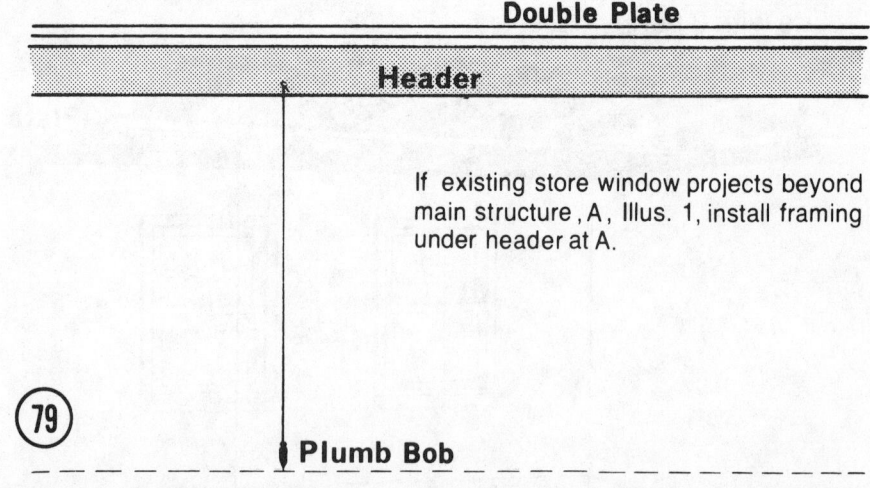

Double Plate

Header

If existing store window projects beyond main structure, A, Illus. 1, install framing under header at A.

(79)

Plumb Bob

If you are working in a room with a finished ceiling and the floor above is too good to open up, you can usually tell direction of joists by direction of finished flooring. Finished flooring is normally laid across joists.

TO FRAME IN A LARGE OPENING

One problem renovators frequently encounter during the planning stage of most rehabilitation work is the need to make two rooms into one or vice versa. The wall they want to remove or open up, is usually load bearing. This refers to a wall, one over one, Illus. 80, that supports the floor joists on the floor above. Building codes and sound construction require replacing a load bearing wall with a girder or header and studs, steel columns or wood posts, of sufficient size to support the load.

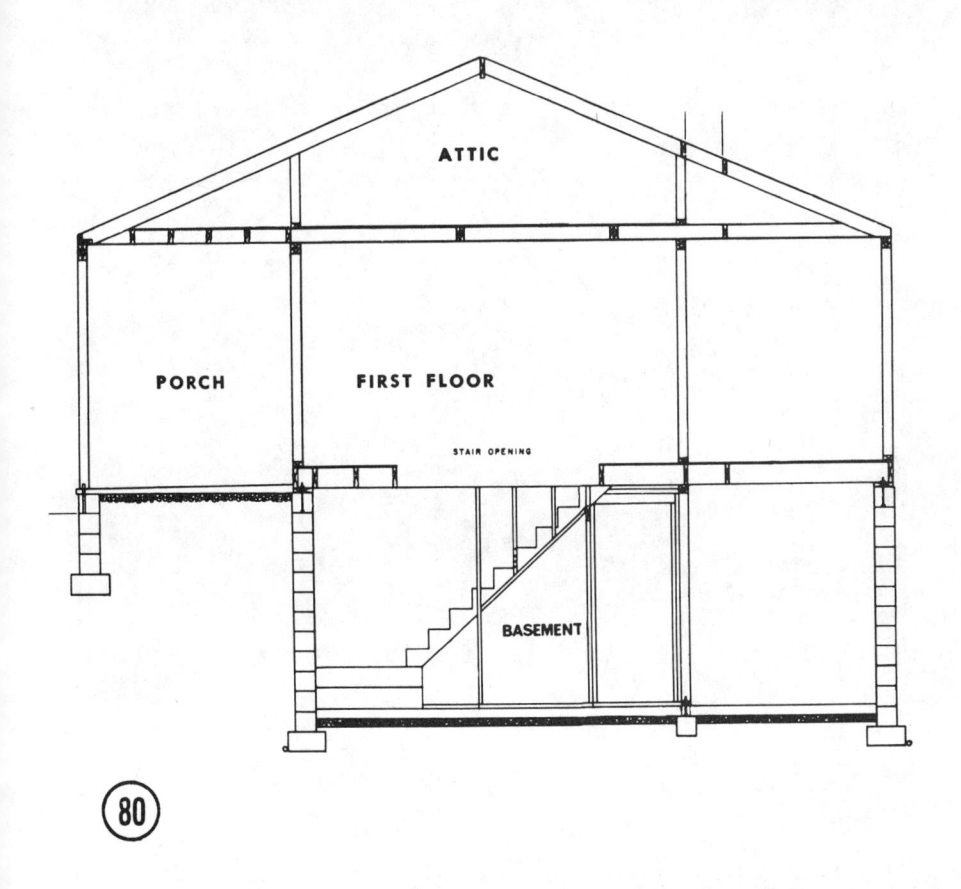

(80)

One way two rooms can be turned into one is by opening up part of a wall. This can be 6, 8, 10', or any size opening required, providing you install a header and studs or posts of sufficient size.

Locate position of stud A, Illus. 81. Using a saber saw, saw down edge of A. Remove crown molding on ceiling, shoe molding and baseboard on floor along wall to be opened. Remove lathe and plaster from both sides of wall within area to be opened.

(81) Left side of proposed opening.

Nail extra studs B in position, Illus. 82 alongside A.

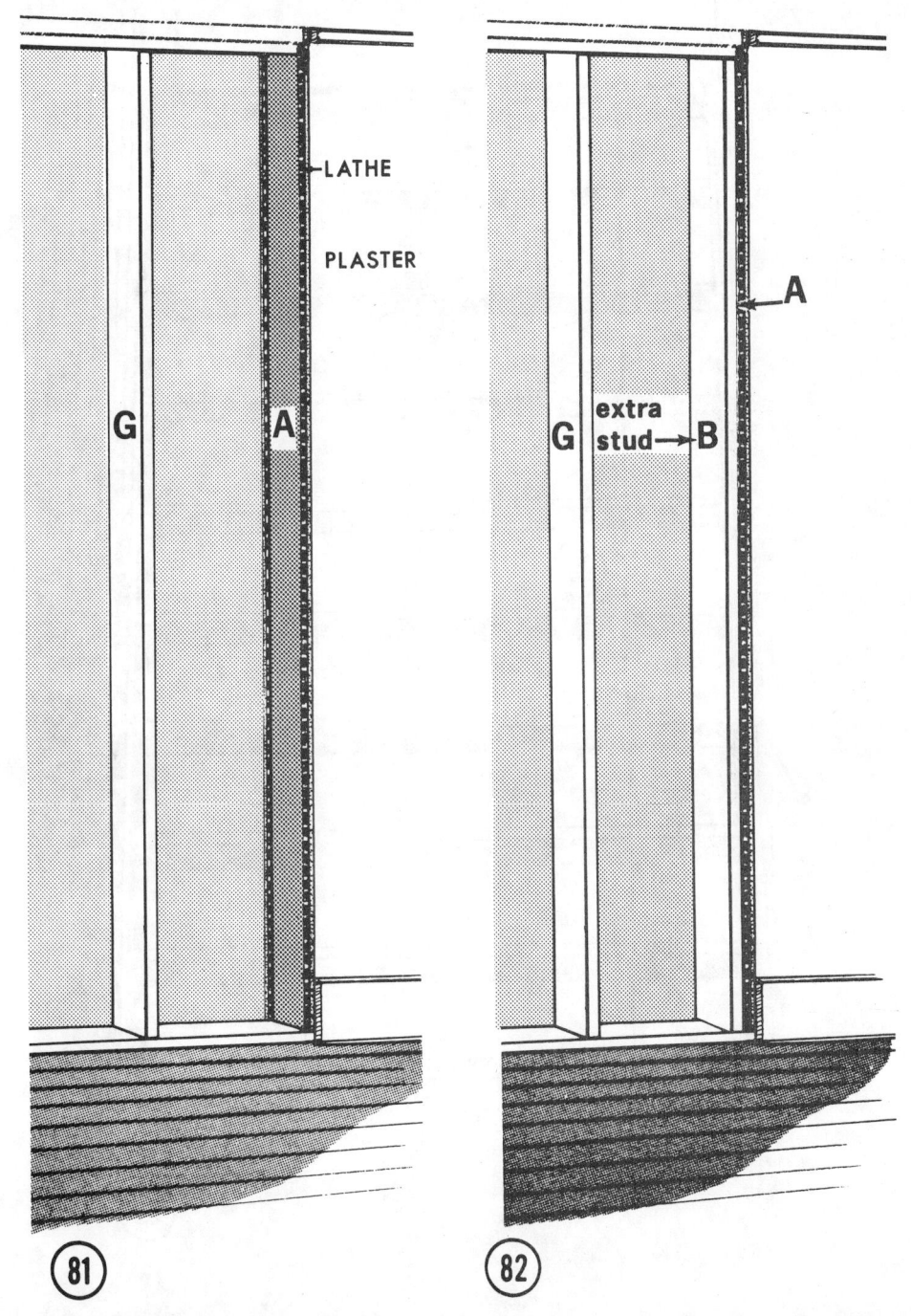

(81)

(82)

81

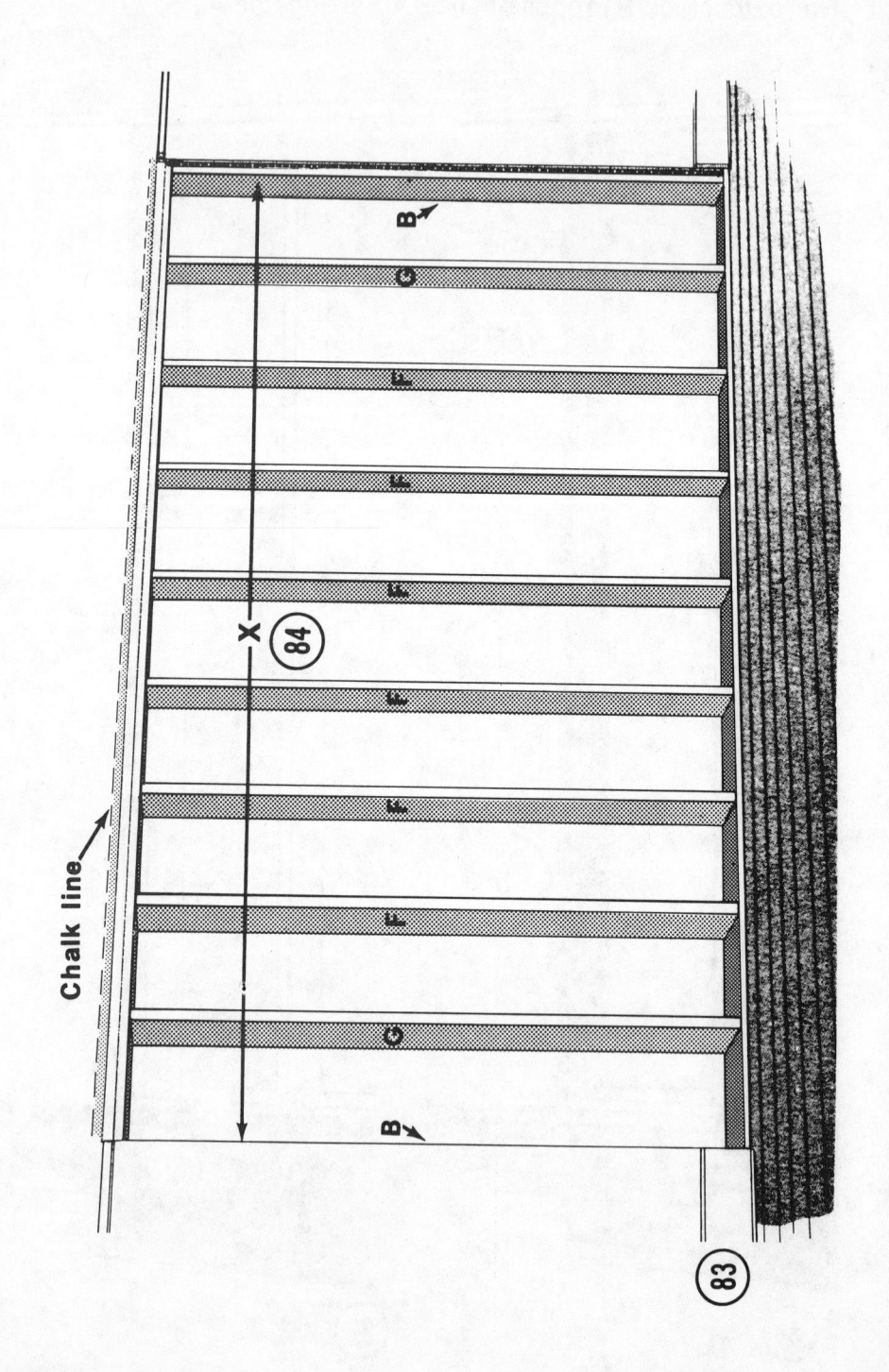

Chalk line

B
G
F
F
F
F
F
F
G
B

X
⑧④

⑧③

Snap a chalk line on ceiling 1½" from edge of plate, Illus. 83. Using a saber saw, remove lathe and plaster along this line. This permits new header to butt against joists.

Cut 2—2 x 6, 2 x 8, 2 x 10, 2 x 12 for headers D, (use size building inspector recommends), to full length of opening, plus studs G and B on each side. The size lumber will be determined by length of span X, Illus. 83, 84.

Cut 2 x 4 shoe C, Illus. 85, to length required. Nail in position edgewide to existing shoe and studs.

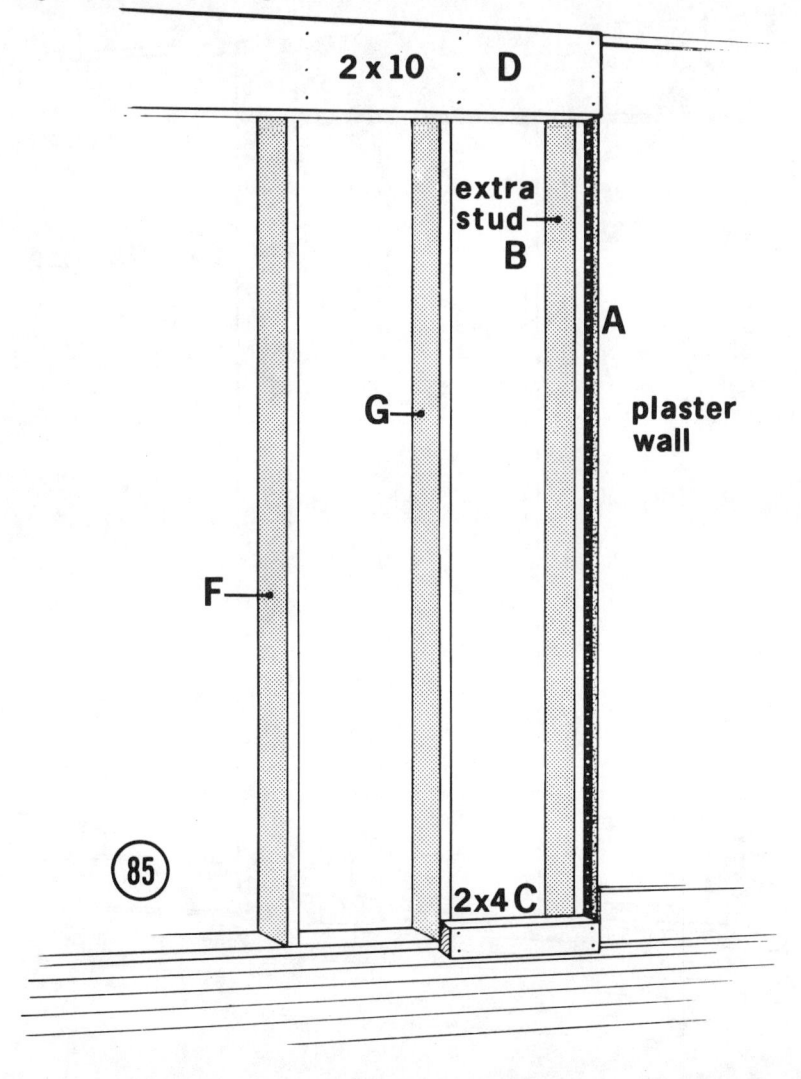

Raise and only temporarily nail header D in position to plate. Two 2 x 8's, one on each side of opening, are usually acceptable on spans up to 10', while 2 x 10 or 2 x 12's provide sufficient support for spans up to 12'.

To butt header D tight against joists, cut studs E, Illus. 86, slightly oversize so you have to drive them in position. Check E with level. When plumb, spike to stud with 16 penny nails. When header has been forced into position without raising joists above, spike it in place to each stud with 16 penny nails. Studs E and shoe C are nailed flatwise so they butt flush against D.

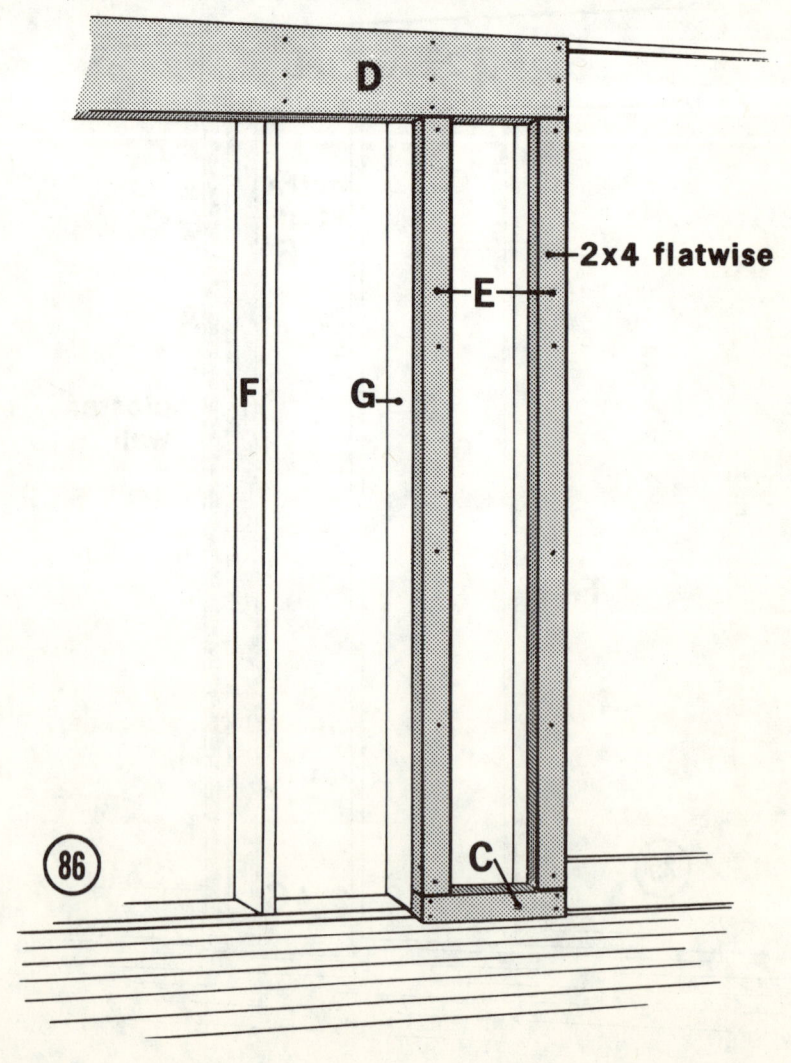

87

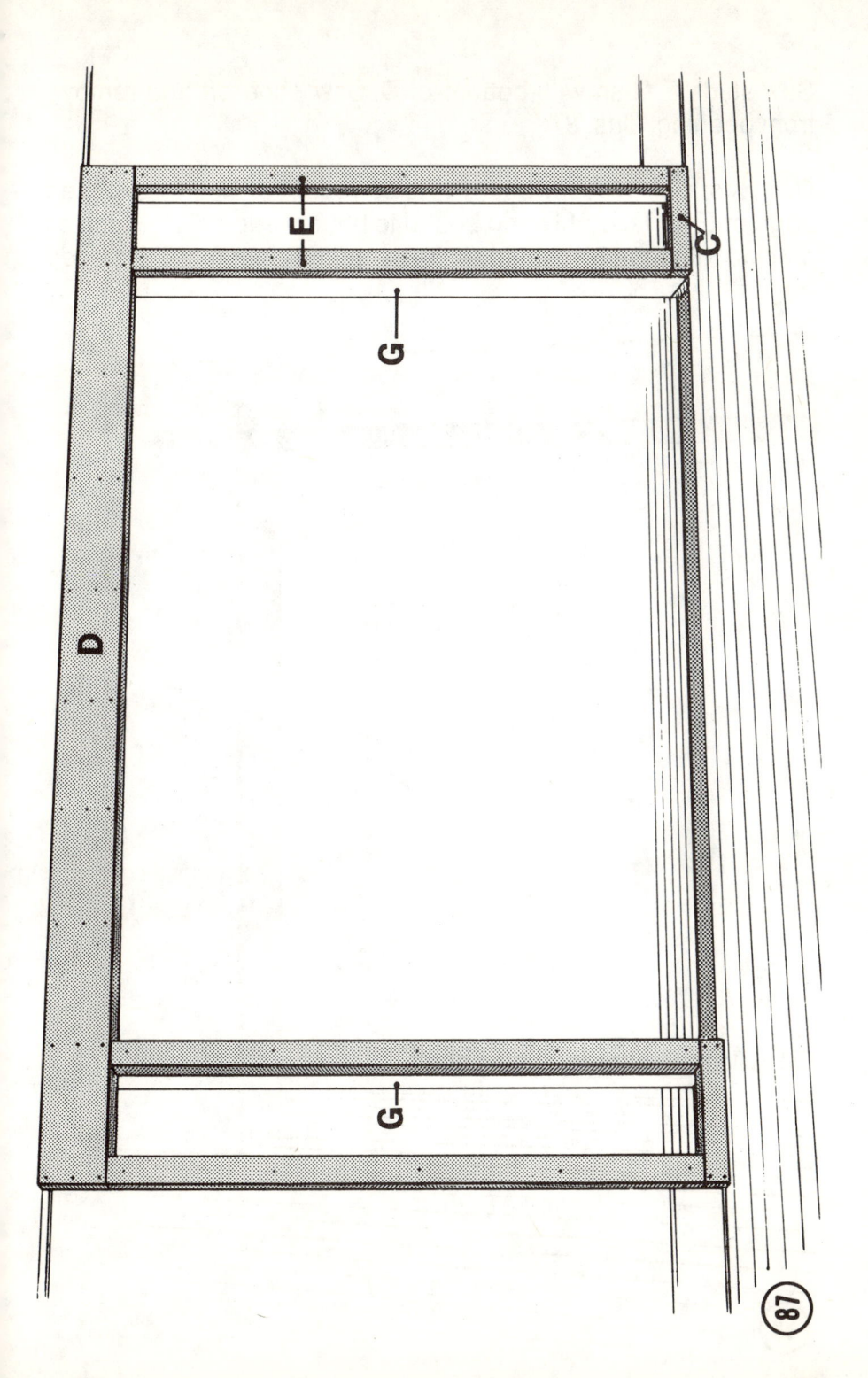

Saw studs F flush with bottom of D. Saw shoe off and remove from opening, Illus. 87.

Cut ½ or ⅝" gypsum board to size required. Nail to exposed edge of E, to face of D and E, and to bottom edge of D. Patch all cracks with patching plaster, then apply tape to all exposed edges, Illus. 88.

Fill in flooring after removing shoe.

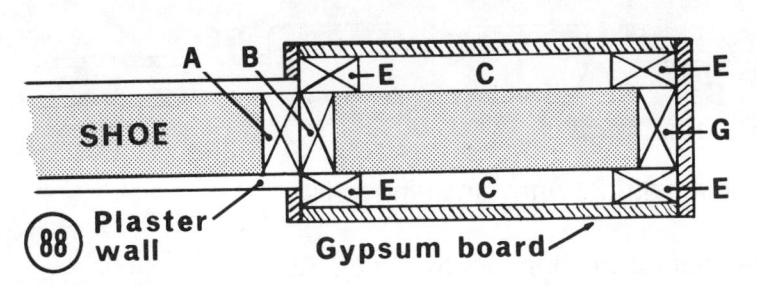

Miter cut crown molding as shown, Illus. 89. Miter cut ends of G and H to angle shown. When all pieces are cut to angle and length required they fit together as shown with bottom edge down.

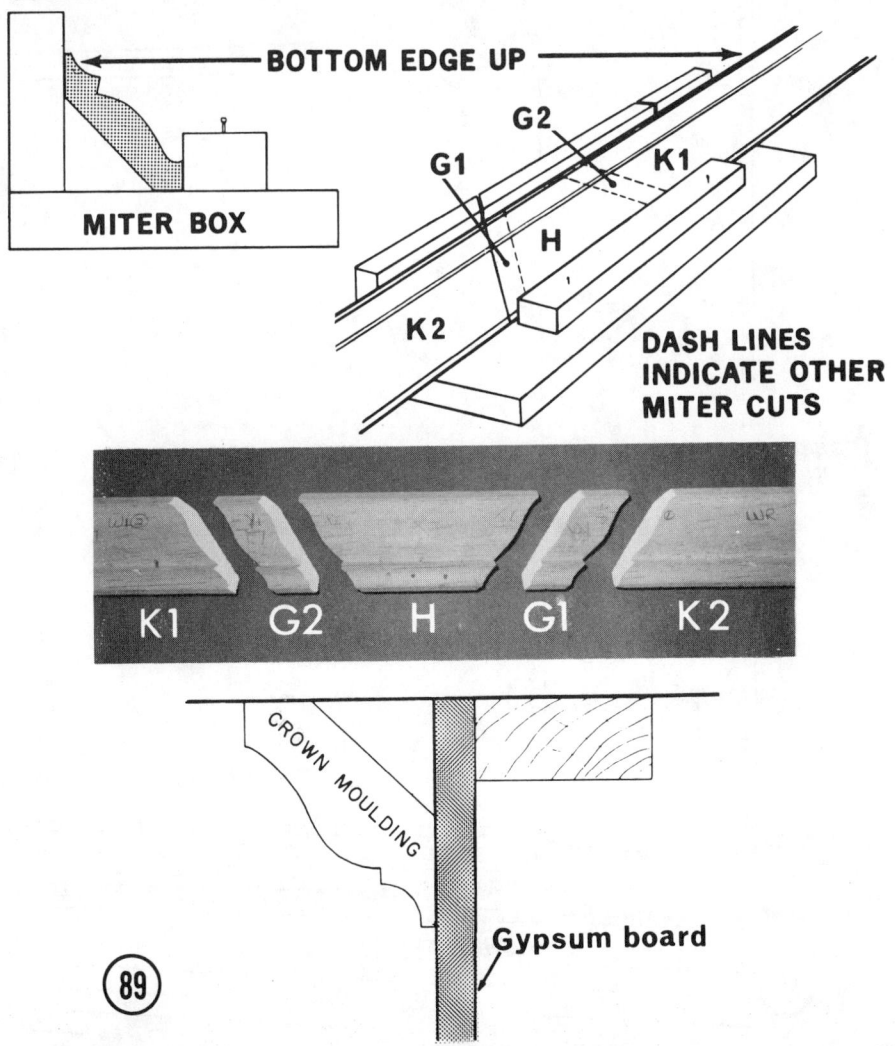

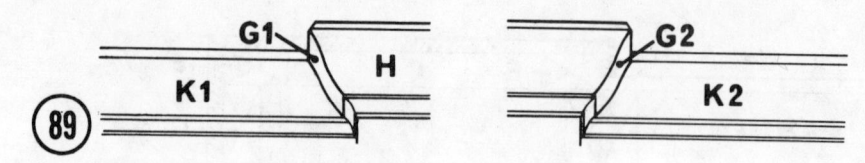

Nail in position with 3 penny finishing nails.

Apply baseboard and shoe molding, Illus. 90.

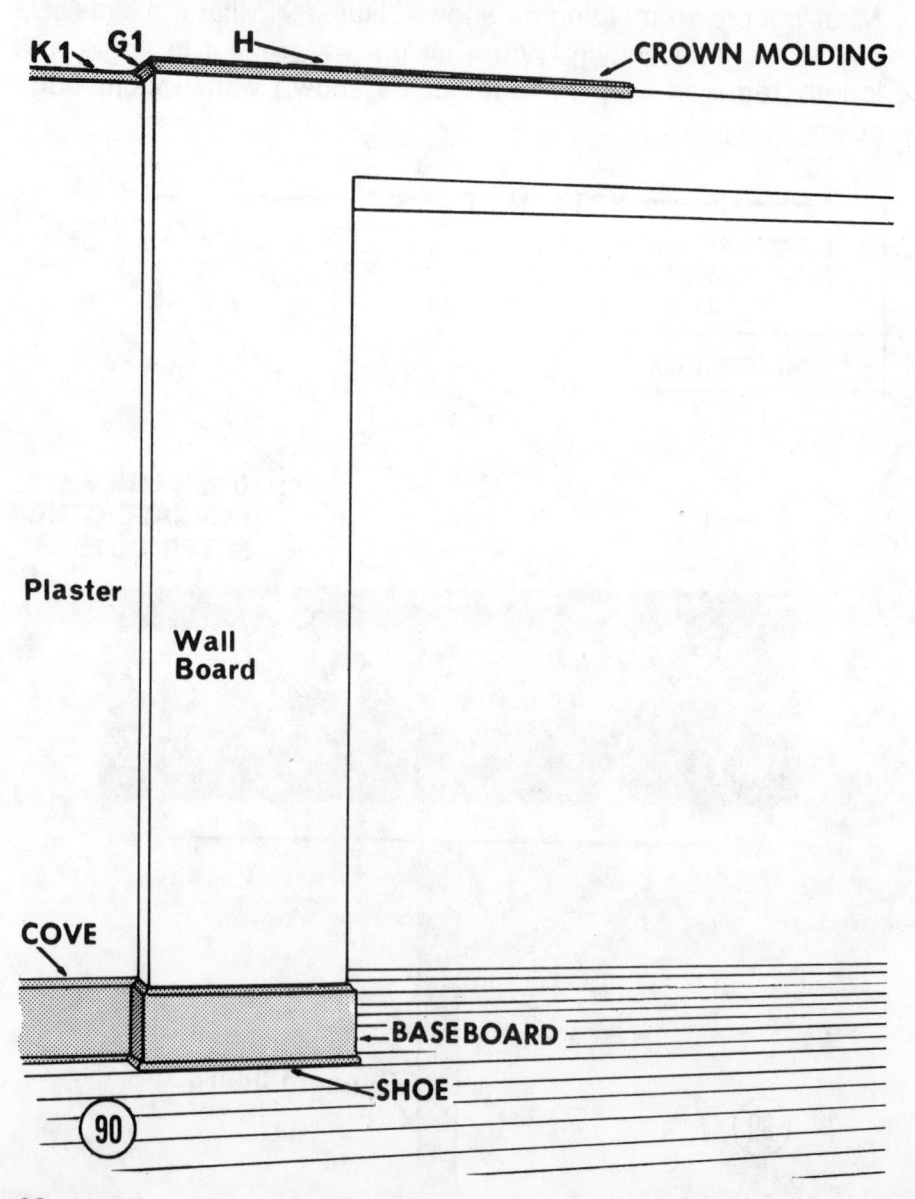

CONCRETE BLOCK WALL

If codes require replacing a store front or garage door opening with a concrete block wall, Book #697 Forms, Footings, Foundations, Framing provides much helpful information. It explains how to lay and cut blocks to size required, where to use special blocks, Illus. 91, for a wood or steel sash; how to build a 2 x 4 or 5/4 x 6 window buck, Illus. 92, to size window or door requires. Nail A to B, B to C.

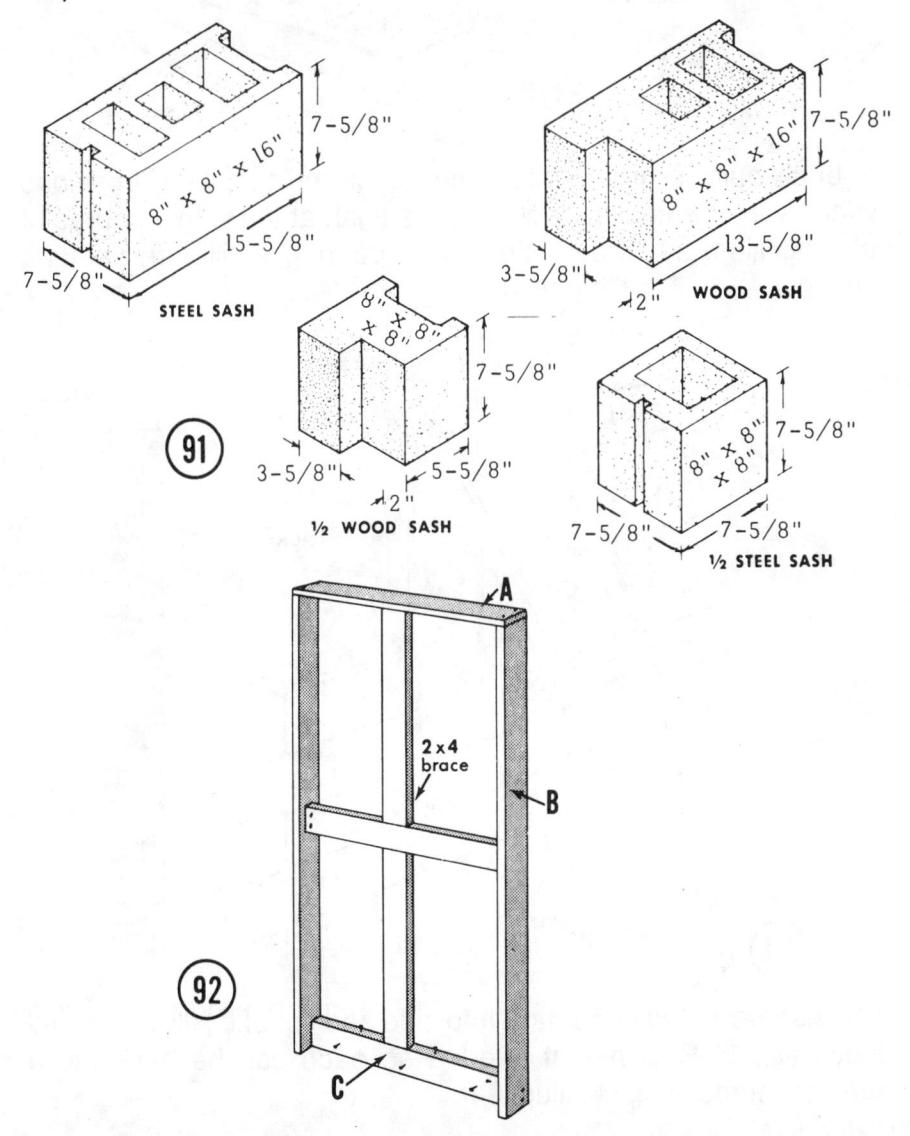

89

If you need to cut a block use a chisel, Illus. 93. Draw a line on block. Place block on a level surface or on a flat bag of sand. Strike chisel with hammer working your way along drawn line.

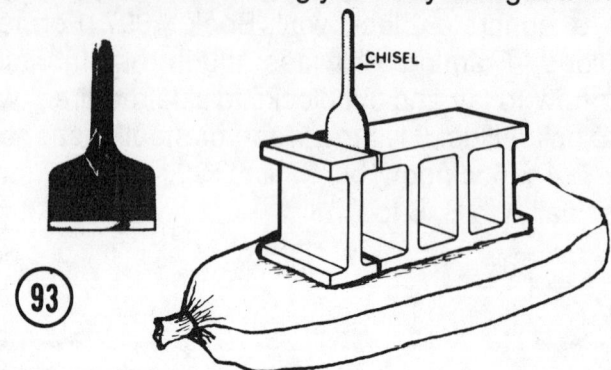

A buck built to size window manufacturer suggests, positions window in opening so buck finishes flush at top with a course of blocks, Illus. 94. It also simplifies "pouring a sill" after setting window.

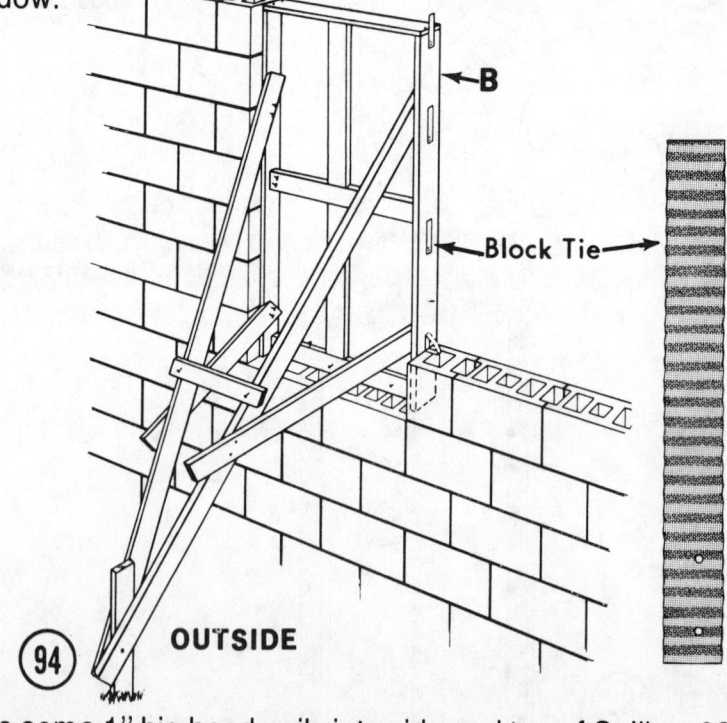

Drive some 1" big head nails into side and top of C, Illus. 92. Nail block ties to B at height needed so each can be bent into a mortar course in block, Illus. 94.

Square up buck. Level, plumb and brace buck in position, Illus. 94. Ruffle up and push balls of newspaper into cores in top course where sill is to be poured.

After laying blocks to height buck requires, remove braces and place window in buck, Illus. 95. Nail through casing into buck. Test open window.

Wire reinforcing in this mortar bed

(95)

Allow ¼" or spacing that window manufacturer suggests between block and buck. Be sure to bend ties down into each or every other mortar joint as you lay each course of block. Fill joint between block and buck or between block and window frame with non-hardening calking.

If you can't purchase a precast concrete sill, build a sill that finishes flush with face of blocks, Illus. 96. Use ¾" plyscord for a form inside and outside. Plane top edge to angle required. Support form in position with 2 x 4 legs A, and angle braces to stakes. Nail form temporarily to inside edge of buck. Don't drive nails all the way. Drill holes and use a twisted wire tie and 1 x 2 spreaders to hold sill form together and apart, Illus. 97. Mix one part portland cement to three parts sand for a mortar mix. Use color cement that matches blocks. Remove spreader as you fill form. Work mortar up under window sill and pack it in. Trowel finish sill to pitch shown. Allow sill to set at least four days. Cut wire and remove form. Recut wire, plaster over end. If you want the sill to project over face of block, place a 1 x 4 or thickness needed to project amount desired, Illus. 98. Nail plyscord form to back edge of buck. Don't drive nails all the way. Brace plyscord form in position.

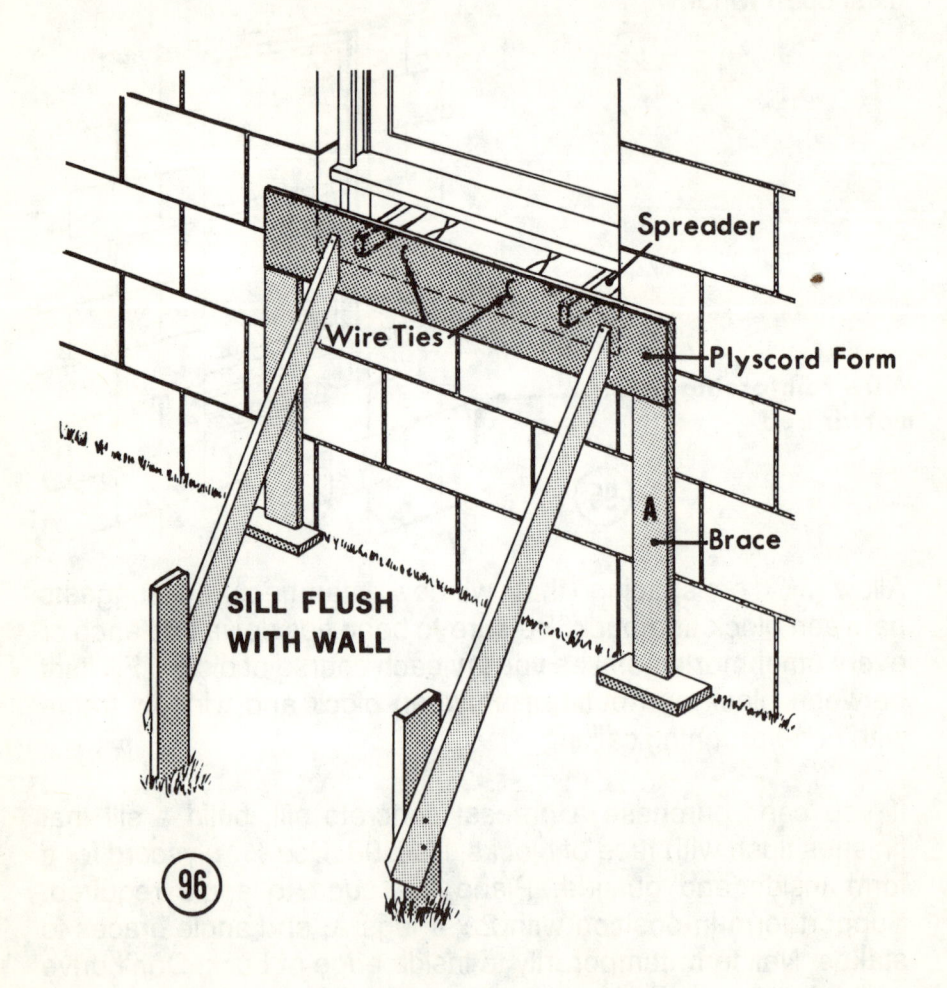

96

Spreader
Wire Ties
Plyscord Form
Brace
SILL FLUSH WITH WALL

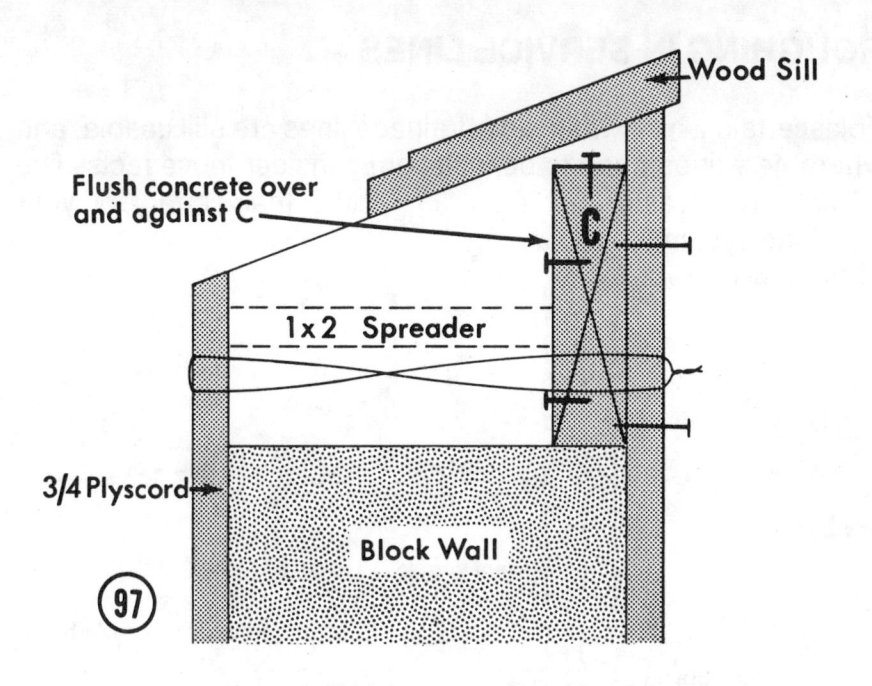

- Wood Sill
- Flush concrete over and against C
- 1 x 2 Spreader
- 3/4 Plyscord
- Block Wall
- C

(97)

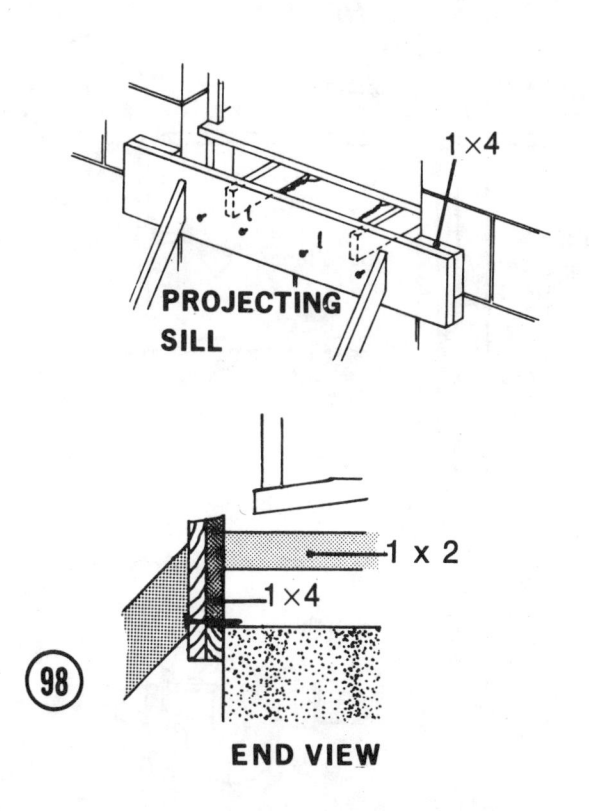

1 × 4

PROJECTING SILL

1 × 2
1 × 4

(98)

END VIEW

93

ROUGHING IN SERVICE LINES

To ascertain which waste and drainage lines are still usable, and where new lines need to be installed, consider these facts. The 4" cast iron waste line, Illus. 99, is the main artery of your plumbing system.

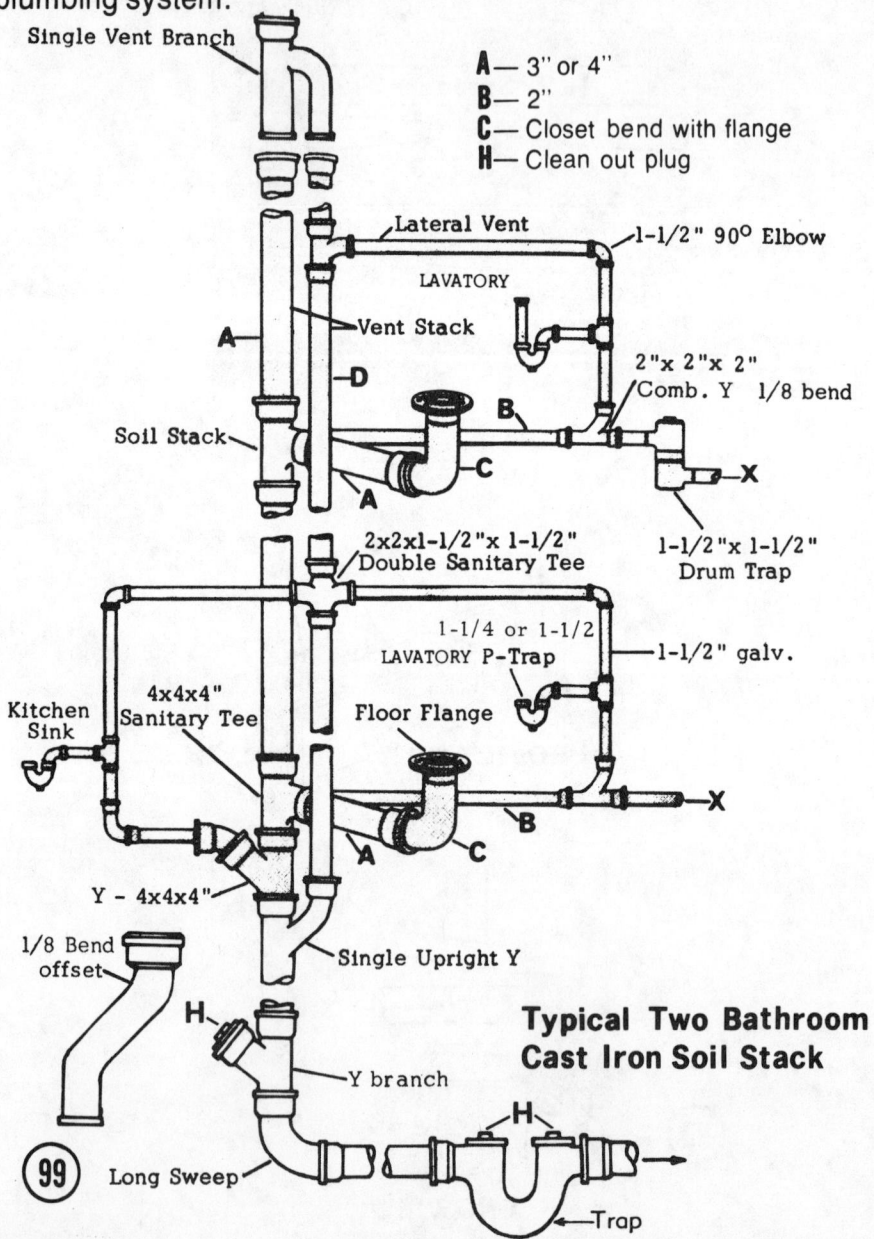

A — 3" or 4"
B — 2"
C — Closet bend with flange
H — Clean out plug

Typical Two Bathroom Cast Iron Soil Stack

(99) Long Sweep

Each toilet is connected directly to this line with 4" cast iron or 3" copper or plastic, Illus. 100. A kitchen sink, lavatory and bathtub are connected with 1½ or 2" galvanized, copper or plastic drainage lines. The 4" waste, and all drainage lines, are connected to vent lines of equal size, Illus. 99, or size local code permits. Local codes specify size of waste, drainage and vent lines. These specifications usually equal or surpass those of the national plumbing code.

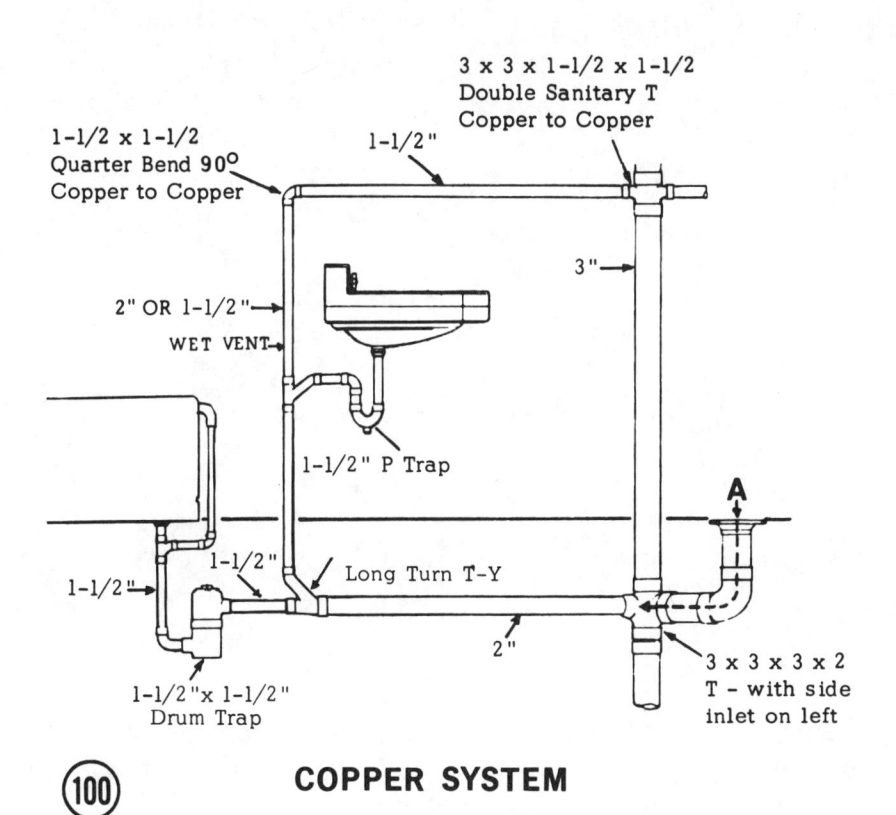

COPPER SYSTEM

95

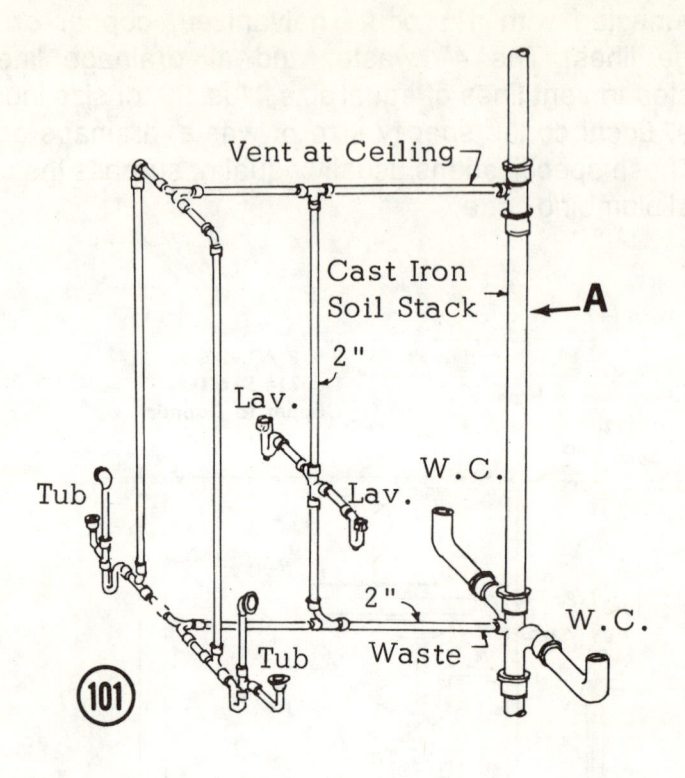

Rehabilitating a building to provide living space for one, two, three, four or more families, each with a kitchen and one or more bathrooms, only requires duplicating installation of the needed waste, drainage, vent and supply lines, end to end on one floor, Illus. 101, or one over one, Illus. 102, on as many floors as required. Installing a 4" waste line, also called soil line, up to a second, third or fourth floor, then running the vent line through the roof, doesn't require any more skill than making a one story, one family house installation. Both necessitate installing fittings exactly where the kitchen and bathroom fixtures require same.

CAST IRON

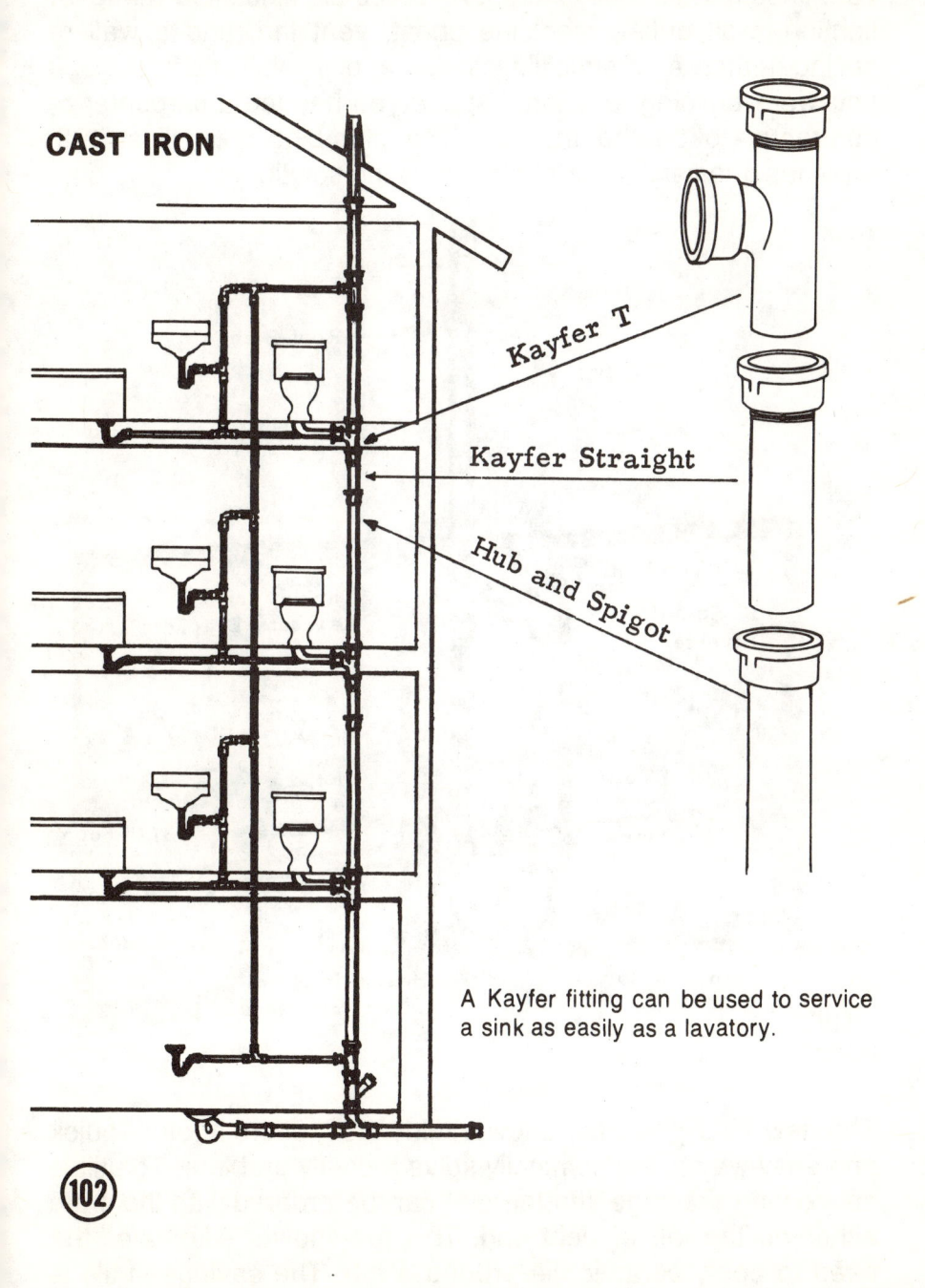

Kayfer T

Kayfer Straight

Hub and Spigot

A Kayfer fitting can be used to service a sink as easily as a lavatory.

(102)

Up to a short time ago installing a bathroom was considered a big deal. A plumber had to rough in waste, drainage, supply and vent lines, then set all fixtures. An electrician installed wiring for lighting, wall outlet, medicine chest, vent fan, and a wall or ceiling heater. A ceramic tile installer applied wall and floor tile. If you were building additional space you needed a carpenter or contractor to do the framing. The plumbing wall, Illus. 103, provides one very important labor saving solution.

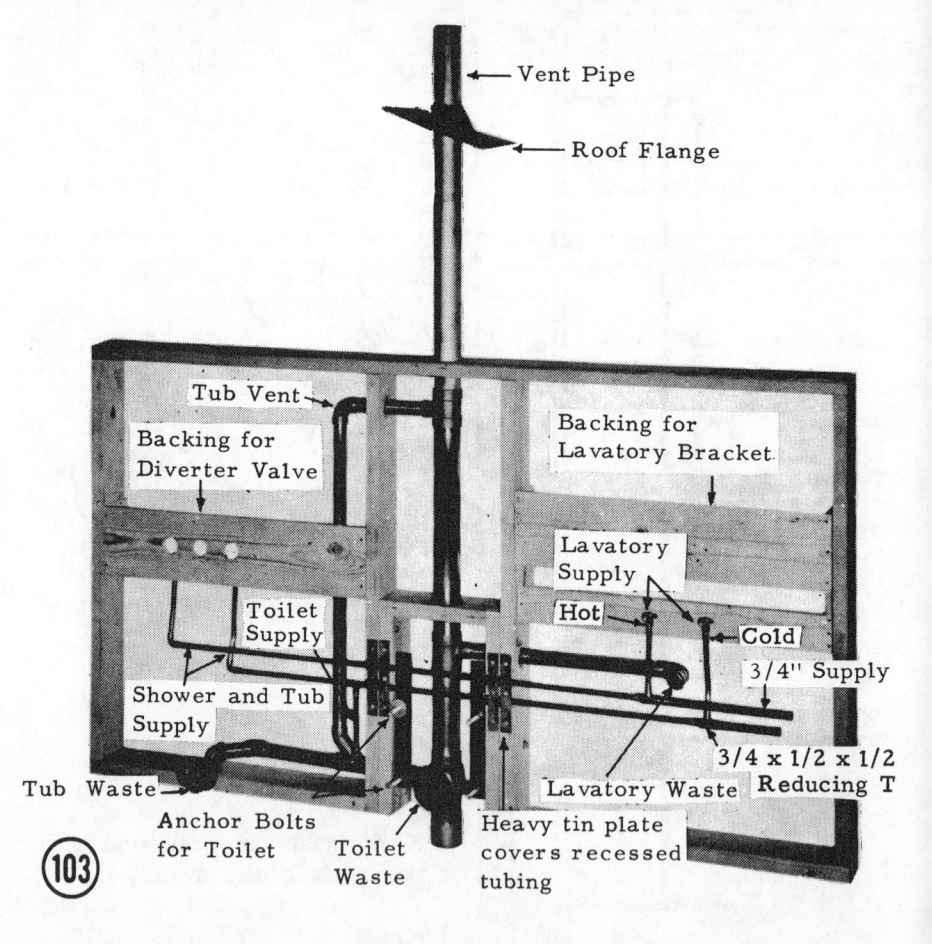

The new fiber glass tub-shower, Illus. 104, offers another quick and easy way to economically solve a costly problem. To utilize an existing drainage line the unit can be ordered with the drain either on the left or right end. This tub-shower eliminates the need to apply ceramic tile around a tub. The savings in tile is substantial. Everyone willing to follow simple directions can do most of the work. The plumbing connections, made by a licensed plumber, can be accomplished in a minimum of time. This permits inspection and approval required for an occupancy permit. See page 128 for complete directions covering installation of the tub-shower.

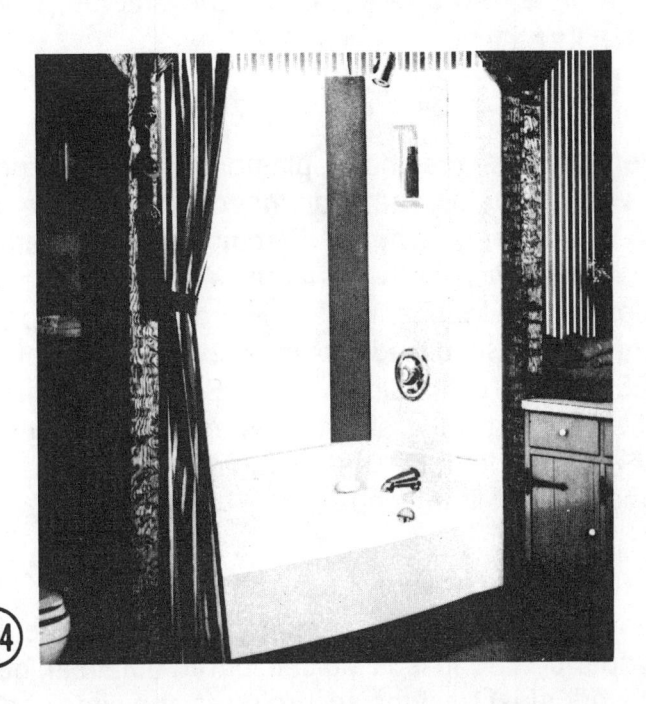

(104)

When it comes to plumbing, wiring and heating, consider hiring a pro who works alone. If you can find the time and he allows you to help, you learn much about a trade plus a higher return for every hour you pay. Most pros are real good Joes who will be happy to have you help. If they resent your assistance, make yourself scarce, or hire someone compatible. There's always another capable of doing what needs to be done, willing to work at a rate you can afford to pay, who doesn't resent your helping.

While codes require plumbing and electrical work be done by those licensed to do the work, drilling holes and snaking wire or pipe isn't difficult or prohibited by code.

99

The plumbing, electrical and heating lines are as important to a house as blood vessels are to a body. Installing new ones is a sound investment. The actual cost for materials and fixtures is small compared to the time required to install. Since anyone who can operate an electric drill and saber saw can cut openings in a floor or wall, considerable savings can be effected by doing what needs to be done. But do only the work codes permit.

Mail order houses, electrical, plumbing and heating supply retailers will estimate what you need and provide a layout showing what goes where. Electrical supply stores will recommend a service entry panel, size cable and receptacles that meet the Underwriters' requirements. Book #694 Electrical Repairs Simplified provides considerable information. Book #682 How To Install An Extra Bathroom contains over 200 illustrations that take all the mystery out of an installation. Book #675 Plumbing Repairs Simplified contains over 800 illustrations of cast iron, copper and plastic.

If you have a friend who has done any plumbing or electrical work, he'll tell you roughing in isn't difficult, but to obtain an occupancy permit all work must be done according to the code, and where specified, by those licensed to do the work.

Only inspection will determine whether you need to install a new 4" waste or 1½ or 2" drainage line. Not much happens to cast iron waste lines except be stopped up. If a joint leaks or smells, you might trace the problem to a sagging floor joist and a loosened joint. Hub and spigot cast iron, Illus. 105, is joined by inserting the spigot end as far down the hub as it will go. This is usually 3". Oakum is driven in with a calking iron, Illus. 106, and tamped tightly around the spigot. Melted hot lead is poured in to a depth of 1". When cool, the lead is tamped down with a calking iron and hammer. All vertical joints are joined in this manner.

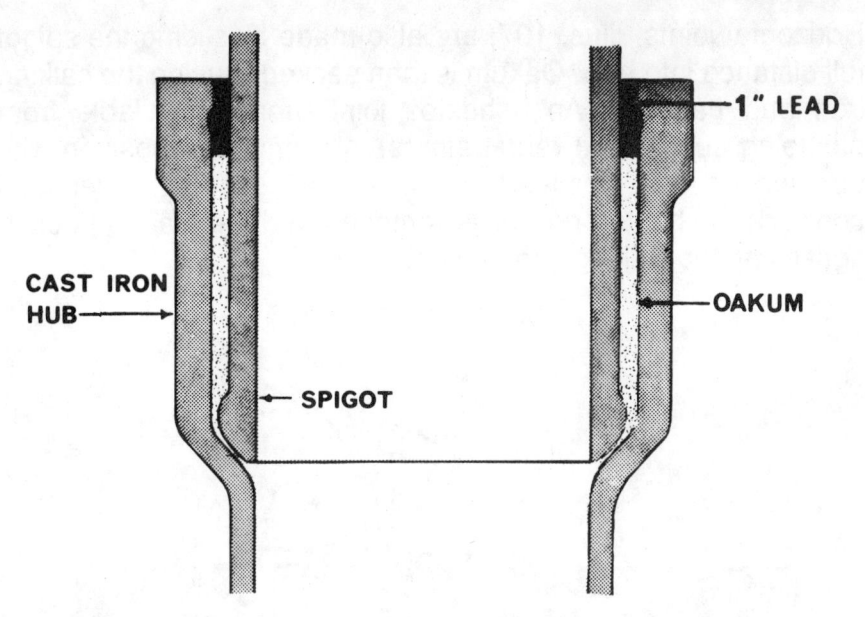

1" LEAD

CAST IRON HUB

OAKUM

SPIGOT

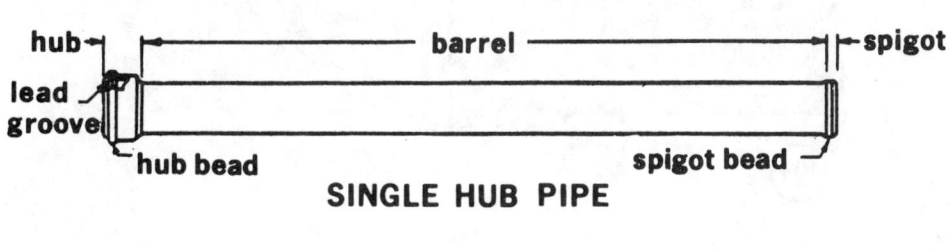

hub — barrel — spigot
lead groove
hub bead — spigot bead

SINGLE HUB PIPE

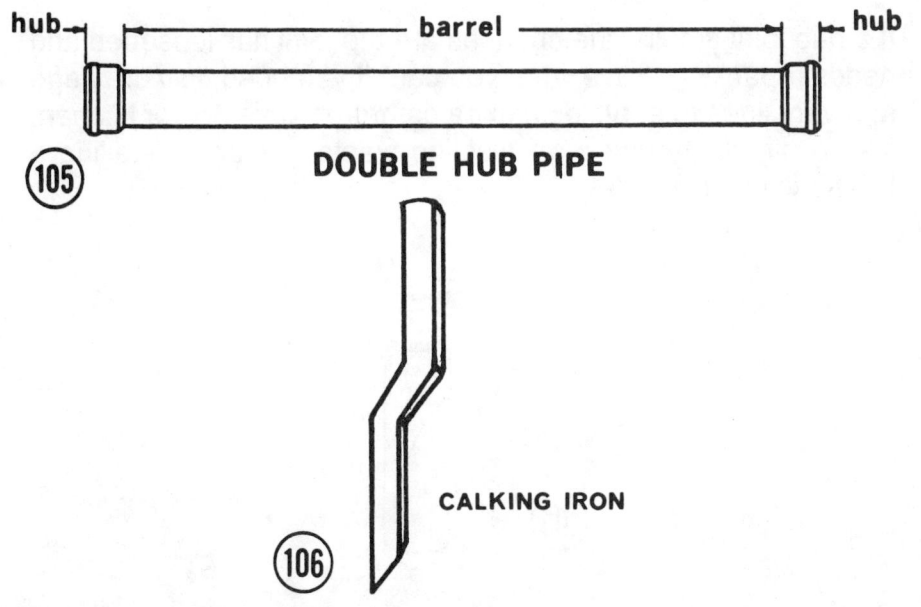

hub — barrel — hub

DOUBLE HUB PIPE

(105)

CALKING IRON

(106)

101

Horizontal joints, Illus. 107, are also made by sliding the spigot full distance into hub. Oakum is then packed in using the calking iron and hammer. An asbestos joint runner, available from plumbing supply and rental stores, is clamped in position with opening on top. Hot lead is poured into opening. After lead cools, the asbestos runner is removed and the lead is packed tight using the calking iron and hammer.

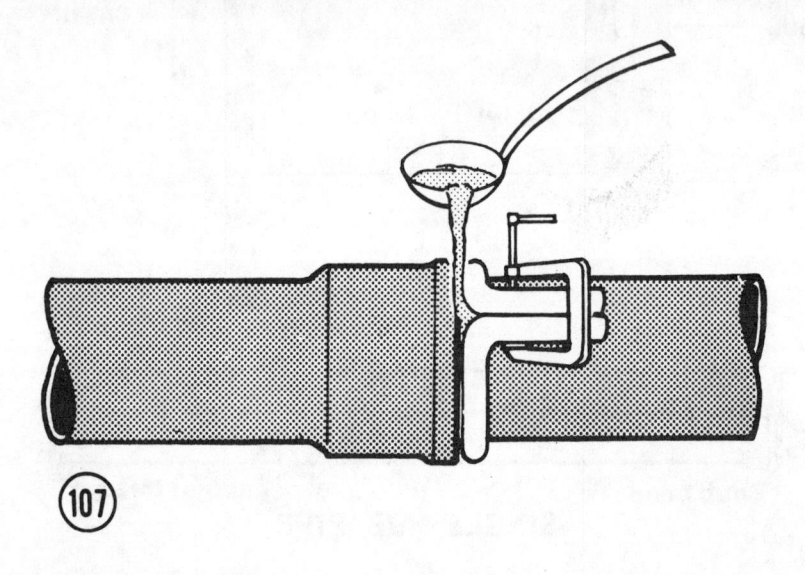

(107)

If a hub joint smells, the chances are the joint has loosened and needs repacking. Save what you can. If you need new drainage and vent lines to service an extra bathroom, lavatory, or kitchen, it's no big deal cutting an existing waste line and installing a Kayfer fitting, Illus. 108.

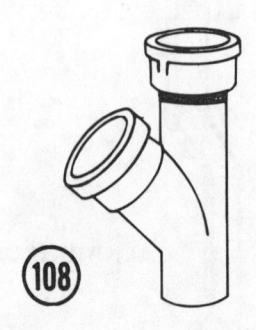

(108)

Visualizing direction, pitch, and fittings required to run a 3 or 4" waste line to a sewer connection can be simplified by using a six foot folding rule and a 1 x 2 by length needed. If you need help figuring bends, lengths, etc., stiffen a garden hose with wire cut from coat hangers. Straighten hanger wire. Tape wire to outside of hose, Illus. 109. After setting closet bend and nipple in position, Illus. 110, place hose to nipple and run hose to sewer connection. Make bends in hose comparable to fittings required.

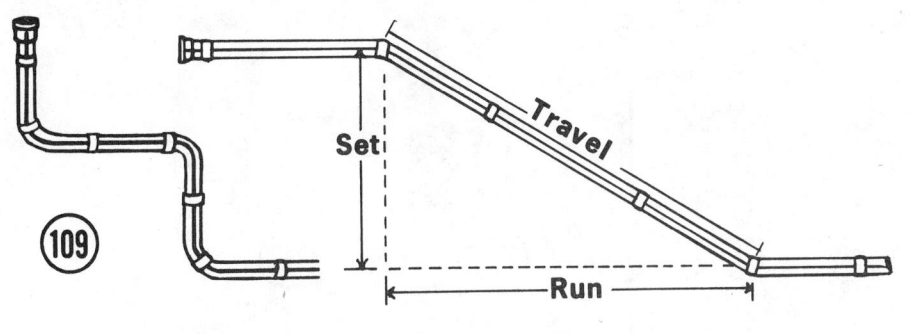

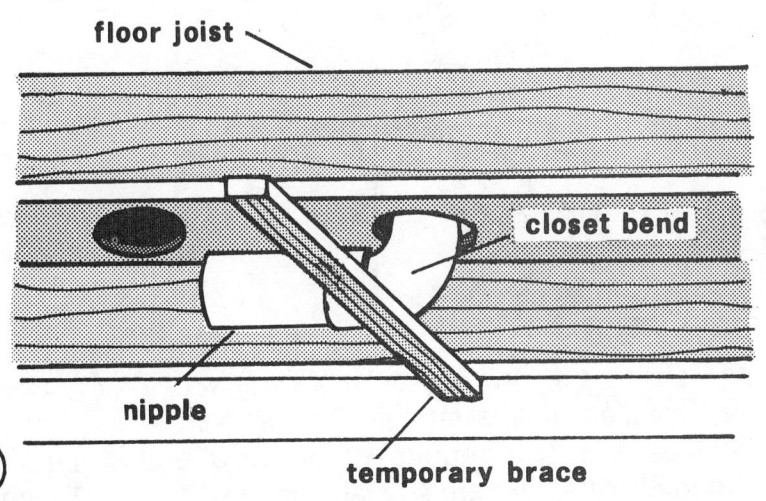

The slope of a sewer line is important. It can be vertical or any horizontal angle that pitches ¼" or more to a foot. This visualization provides an idea as to the length of pipe and fittings your installation requires. When you discuss installation of drainage and waste lines with a plumber, Department of Health, or building inspector, and they mention Set, Run and Travel, Illus. 109 indicates what each means.

The Kayfer fitting, Illus. 108, 111, 112, 113, simplifies making a connection to an existing, vertical sewer line. A Kayfer is like a regular fitting with one important exception; the hub at top is threaded. These threaded hub fittings are available in a Y branch, Illus. 114, or tee, Illus. 111. Also in 12" straight lengths, Illus. 112; and tapped straight lengths, Illus. 113. The Y Branch comes in: 3 x 3 x 2"; 3 x 3 x 3"; 4 x 4 x 2"; 4 x 4 x 3"; 4 x 4 x 4".

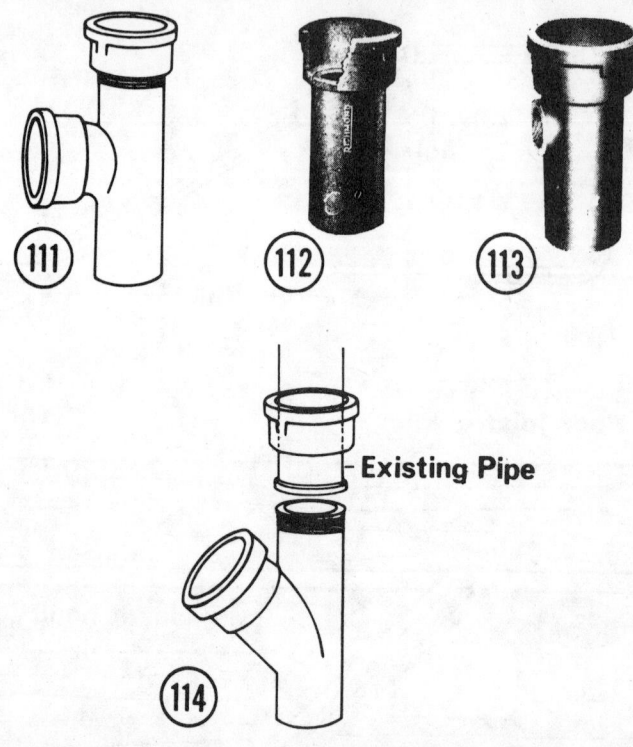

Existing Pipe

Illus. 115 shows a 4 x 4 x 4" Kayfer Y fitting with a 4 x 3" copper adapter, installed over a straight Kayfer. Note 4 x 3" copper adapter, Illus. 116. This permits connecting 3" copper, plastic or cast iron to 4". Adapters are available for 2 x 1½", 3 x 2" and for every other size needed. When making up fitting, apply Tape Dope to threads and only turn up threaded hub two or three threads. Calk joint with oakum and hot lead as with hub and spigot.

After making up Kayfer fitting, paint exposed threads with muriatic acid.

4x4x4" Kayfer Y

Kayfer straight length

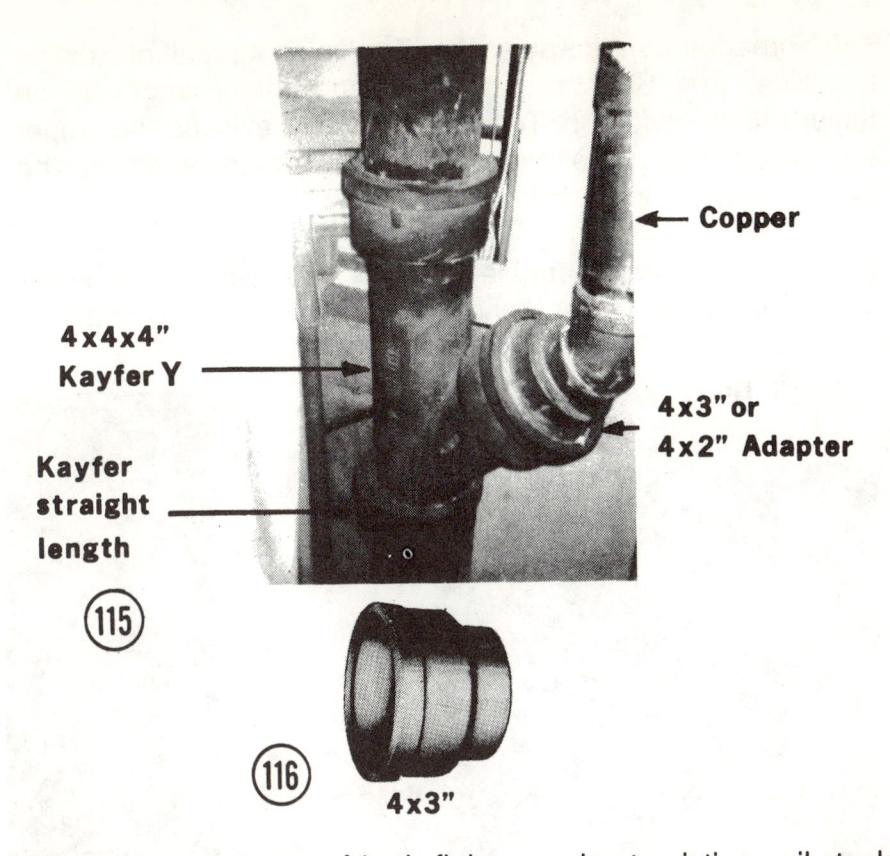

← Copper

4x3" or 4x2" Adapter

(115)

(116) 4x3"

Always measure run of both fittings and cut existing soil stack amount required, just above a hub, Illus. 117. Remove cut length. Wet a large clean rag, and stuff it into stub of pipe remaining in hub. Apply heat using one or two propane torches. When lead softens, pull stub of pipe out of hub, remove oakum calking, clean hub.

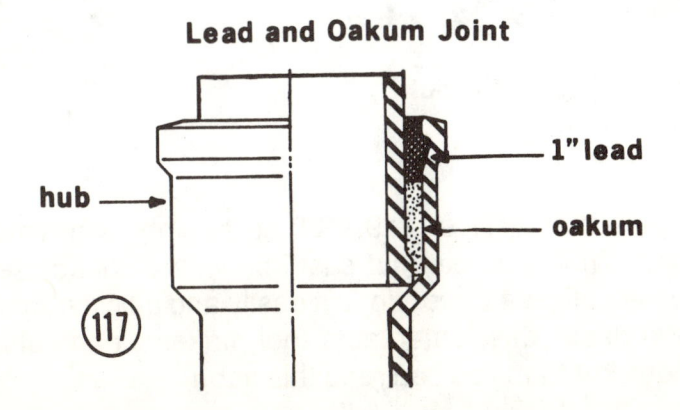

Lead and Oakum Joint

hub →

1" lead

oakum

(117)

Slide threaded hub of Kayfer Y or Tee up on top half of existing line, Illus. 114. Slide threaded hub on straight length up on spigot end of Kayfer Y or Tee. If you have cut existing line proper length, you will have to practically spring both Kayfer fittings and the hub and spigot nipple in position.

Illus. 118 shows how a double Y, 4 x 4 x 2 x 2" was installed over a 4 x 4 x 4" single Kayfer Y and short length of hub and spigot.

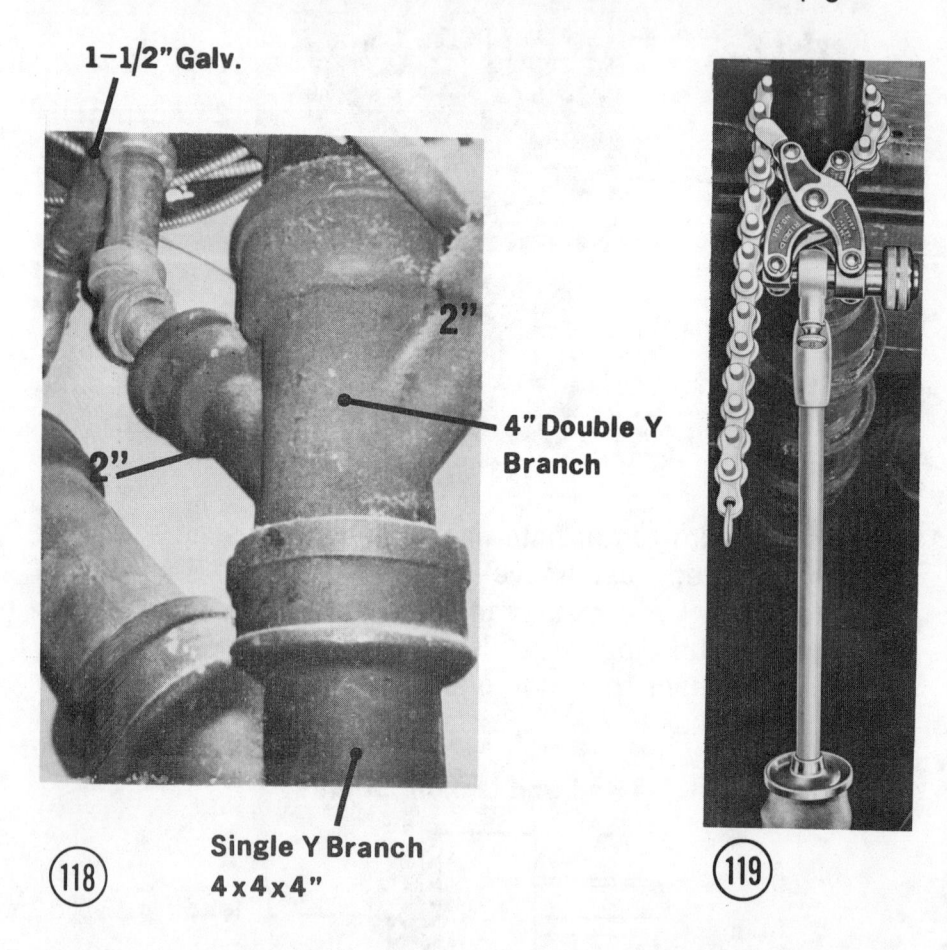

118 — 1-1/2" Galv., 2", 2", 4" Double Y Branch, Single Y Branch 4 x 4 x 4"

119

The soil pipe cutter, Illus. 119, 120, is an important time and labor saver. While you can cut cast iron with a cold chisel and hammer, the soil pipe cutter does it easily and quickly. Available on a rental basis, this remarkable tool makes clean cuts in 4" cast iron quicker than you can read this page.

CUTTING WHEEL — **ADJUSTABLE KNOB** — **CHAIN HOOK**

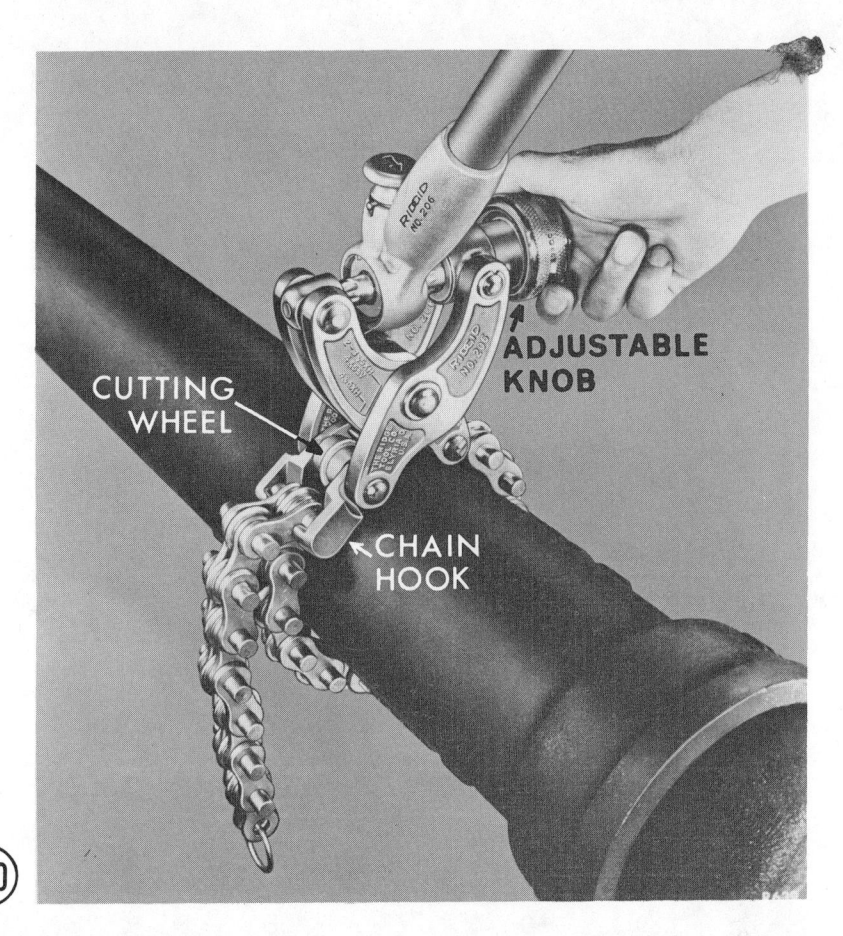

(120)

In some buildings you still find waste lines serviceably sound even though sections may be stopped up. Open a cleanout plug, Illus. 121, and run a snake through, Illus. 122. This will help pinpoint and release stoppage. If needed, rent an electric snake and test each line. Use plenty of water to make certain no joints leak or smell.

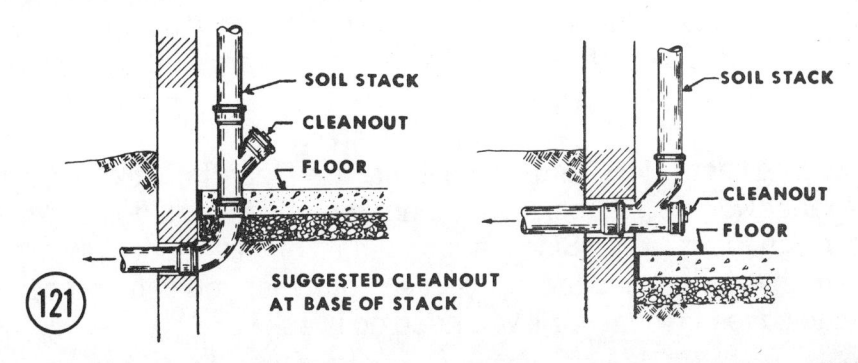

(121) SOIL STACK — CLEANOUT — FLOOR — SUGGESTED CLEANOUT AT BASE OF STACK

SOIL STACK — CLEANOUT — FLOOR

107

(121) CLEANOUT CONCRETE GRADE
IN THE LINE   AT END

SNAKE or SEWER ROD   **ELECTRIC SNAKE**

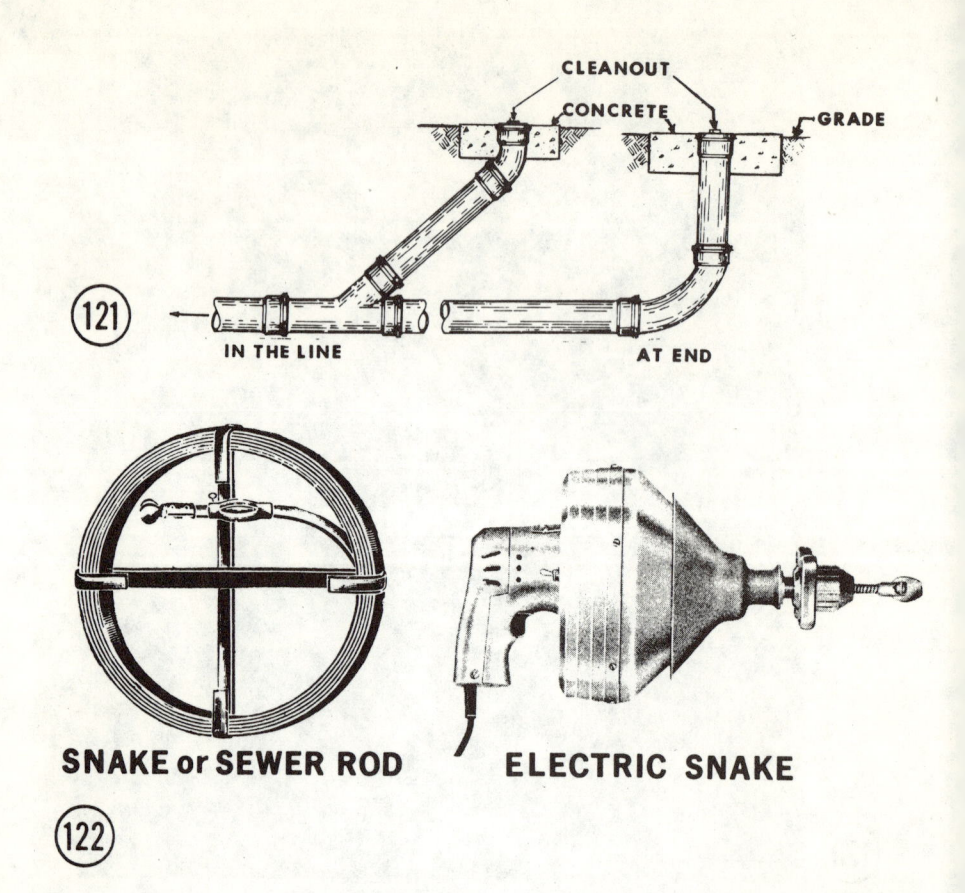

(122)

Sizable savings on plumbing and electrical work can be effected by preparing each area. Since all skilled trades charge by the hour, if you can halve the time on the job, you save accordingly. Opening up a wall between two studs, Illus. 123, to facilitate running waste, vent and supply lines; or opening up a floor, Illus. 124, to simplify installation of a closet bend for a toilet, heating or air conditioning ducts, is work you can do. Knowing what goes where and when, like learning to play billiards, is something everyone can pick up fast.

Building inspectors and those from the Department of Health invariably enforce rules when amateurs attempt doing work consigned to pros. Since a good half of this work concerns carpentry, many inspectors will tell you what you can and can't do to save big money. All you need do is ask.

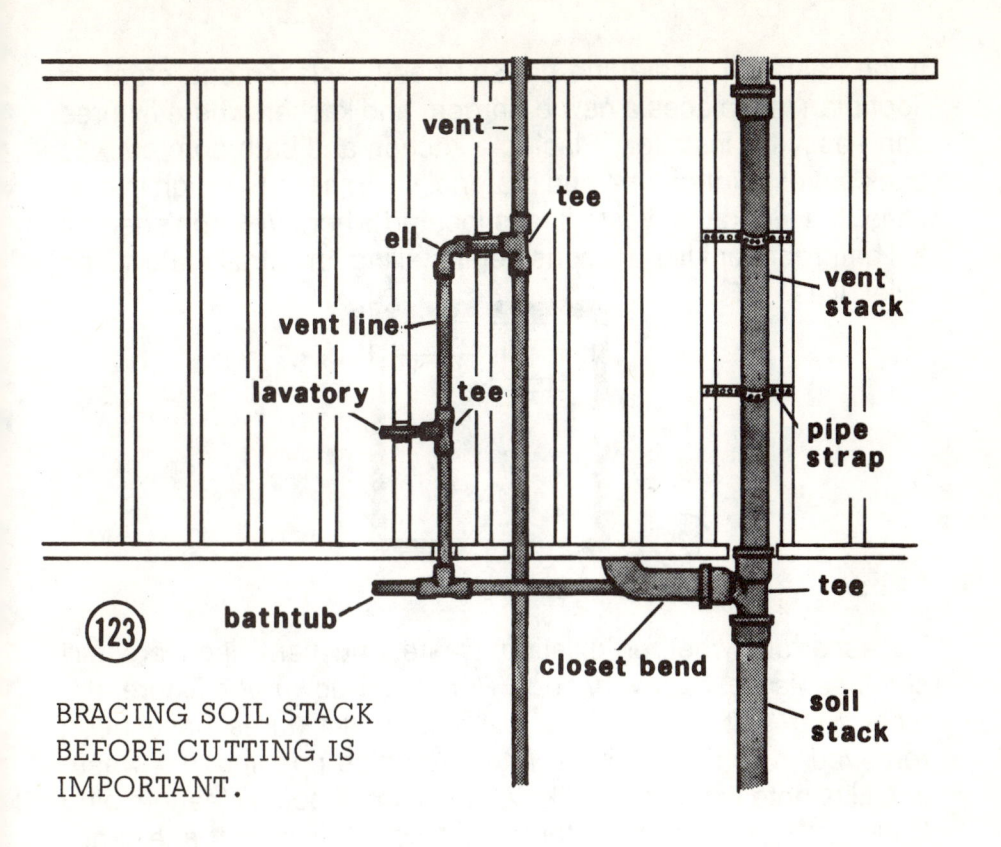

(123) BRACING SOIL STACK BEFORE CUTTING IS IMPORTANT.

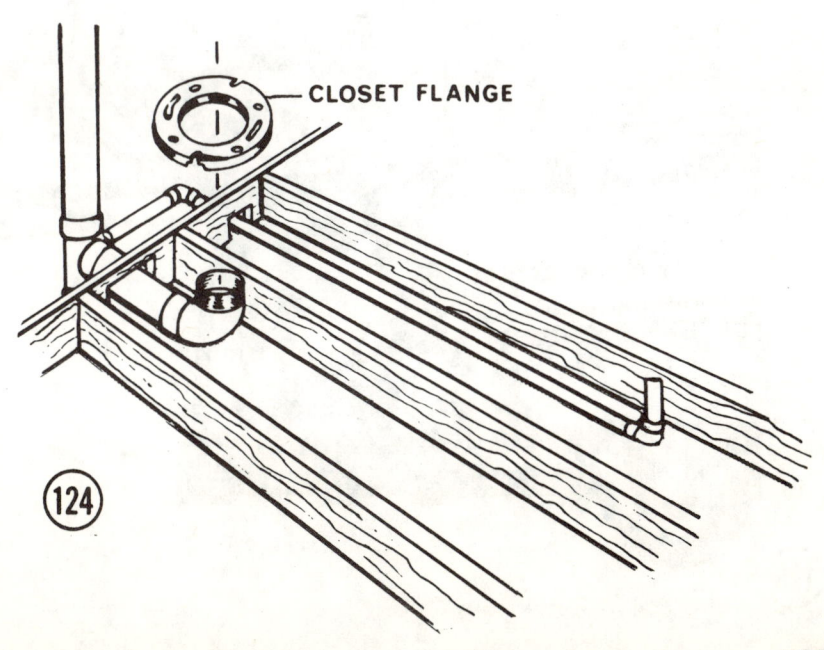

(124) CLOSET FLANGE

109

If the cast iron waste line doesn't need replacement, create a floor plan that places a new bathroom and kitchen where fixtures can easily be installed. Placing a kitchen and bathroom back to back saves a lot of time and material if you need to rough in new lines. If a workable waste line is located where you don't need a full bathroom or kitchen, consider installing an extra lavatory and toilet, Illus. 125.

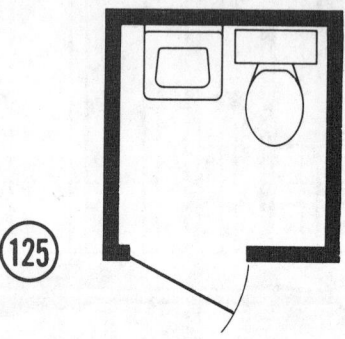

To ascertain whether existing waste and vent lines are still serviceable, test at every floor. Run water down one fixture at a time. Start with those in a basement. If fixtures have been removed, run a water hose into each pipe opening. If a waste line fills, note whether it leaks at any joint. Open a cleanout plug H, Illus. 126, to release water into a plastic bag or garbage can.

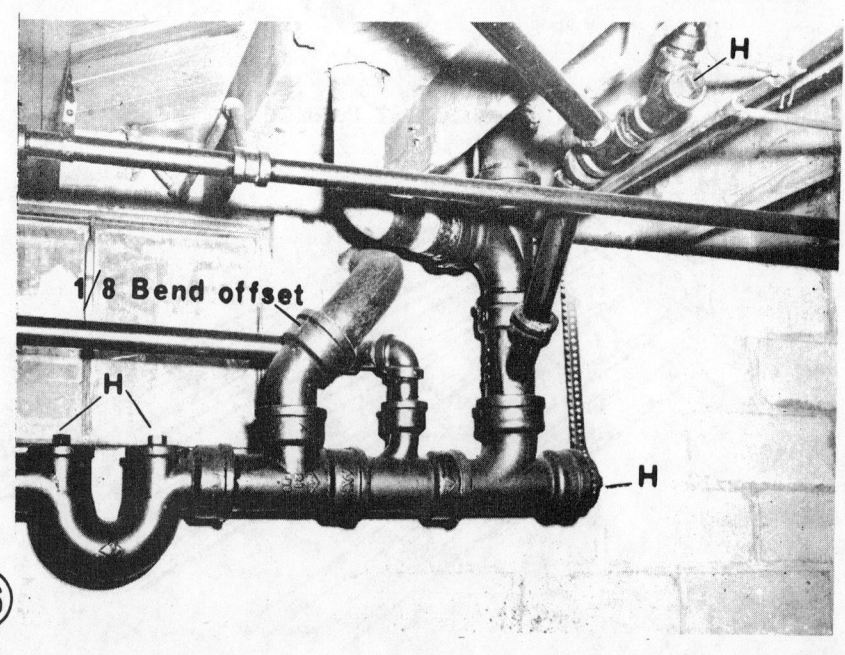

If a main waste line serving all floors is open, and the line between a house trap, Illus. 99, and sewer is stopped, run a snake through the cleanout plug.

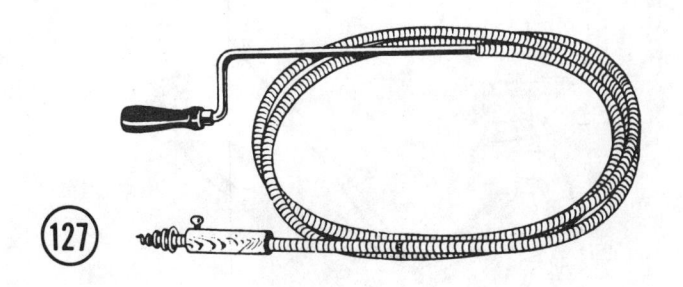

(127)

Test each workable toilet. If clogged, use a closet auger, Illus. 127, 128, 129, to see if you can loosen up stoppage. Vandals frequently throw anything handy down a toilet. Straighten out a coat hanger, and slip on a cord carrying handle, Illus. 130, then make a hook or eye at the end. By twisting this you can frequently catch and pull out rags, paper, even dislodge small objects.

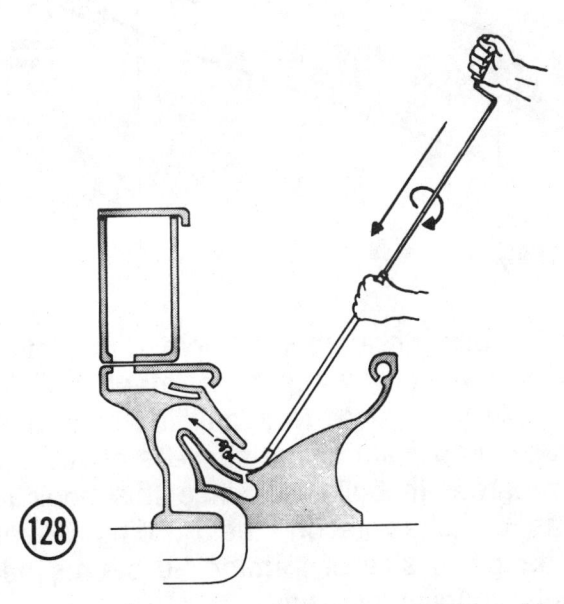

(128)

(129)

CORD CARRYING HANDLE

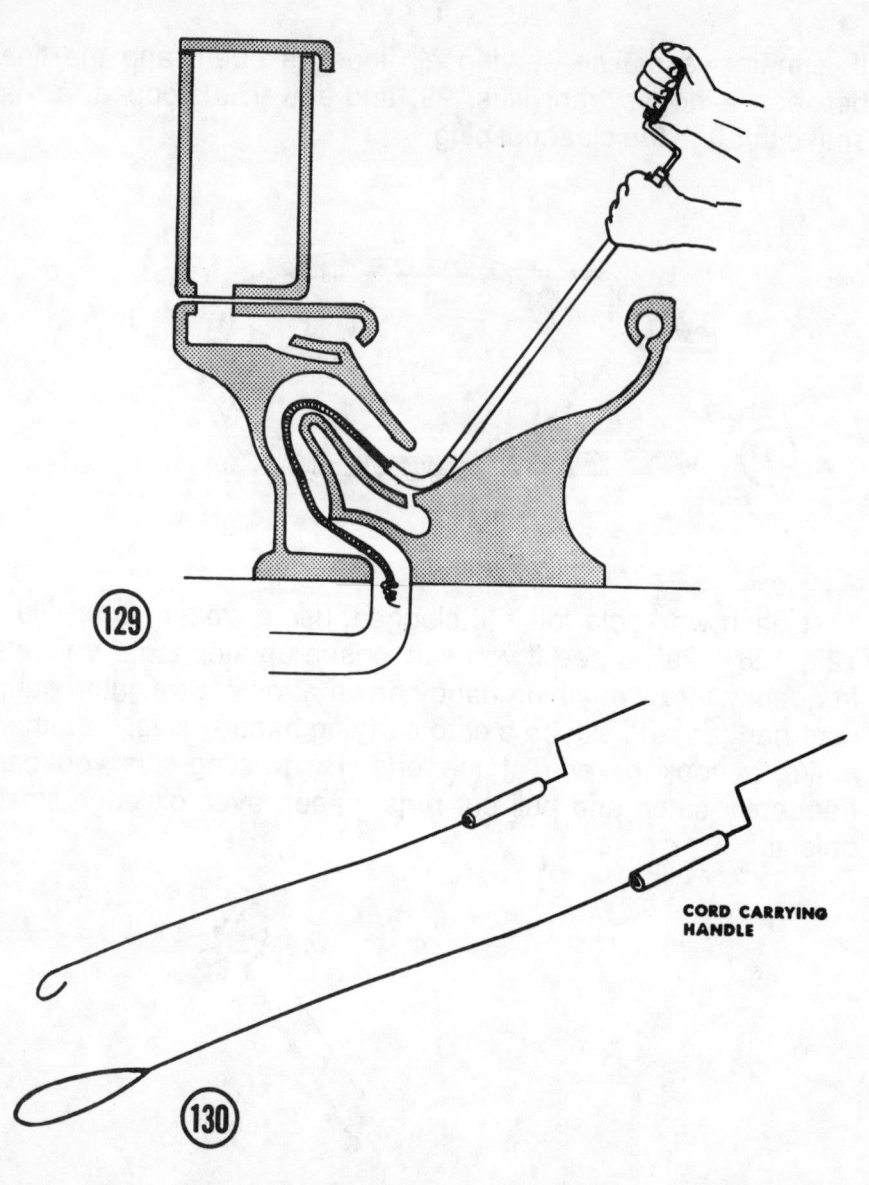

(130)

Regardless of the size or number of rooms or apartments you want to rehabilitate, all work must meet building code requirements. How you relate to a building or department of health inspector is important to the success of your job. It can also lead to a career in building. Since this book illustrates important areas of rehabilitation, the building inspector can indicate any change in size of framing he deems necessary, also stud and joist spacing, etc., etc.

Framing for a new kitchen or bathroom must be installed before running supply, waste and vent lines. Use 2 x 6 for shoe, plate and studs for a partition wall containing 4" waste lines, Illus. 123.

If you need to install a 4" cast iron waste line in a wall studded with 2 x 4, nail 1 x 2 or 2 x 2 furring to the shoe, plate and studs, Illus. 131, to provide width a cast iron waste line requires. 3" copper or plastic waste lines can be installed in an existing 2 x 4 wall.

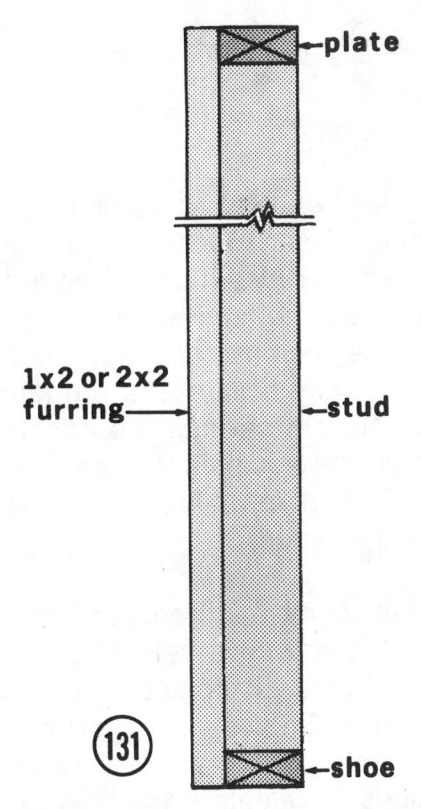

Check all floors to make certain each is level. If joists need to be raised, loosen brackets holding soil line to joists. Inspect line for leaks at each joint. Look for water stains, odor and wood rot. If a joint in wall shows surface stain or odor, open up the wall. Make a careful inspection. Have someone keep an eye on all usable waste, vent and supply lines before and during the time it takes to jack up floor joists. If a waste line is strapped to a sagging joist you could loosen a joint if you raise it too far.

113

Leaks around a vent line going through the roof can usually be corrected with a calking gun, Illus. 132, or with double-faced self sealing roofing squares mentioned on page 42.

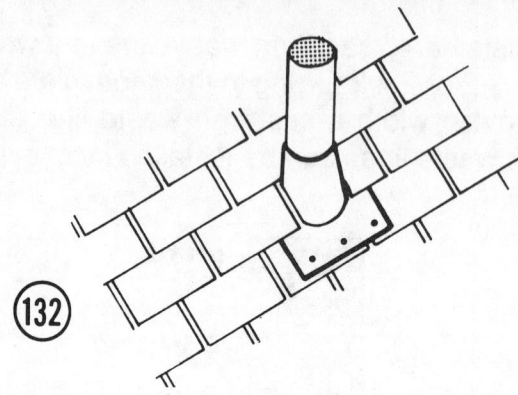

Before calling in a plumber, electrician or heating contractor, learn the "word game." Read Books #675 and #682 listed on inside cover. When you match parts needed with pictures that identify part, and become familiar with procedure required to repair existing service lines or install new ones, you begin to talk sense that saves many dollars. If a pro knows you know what needs to be done, big savings are effected. When you purchase pipe, fittings and equipment, then use a heavy duty saber saw, Illus. 24, to open up walls and floors where required, substantial savings are effected.

Level with the plumber. Ask his advice. Let him tell you why he likes or dislikes the plan you have selected for a new kitchen, bathroom, extra lavatory, etc. Listen and note what he says and how he presents his facts. One day soon you may be the expert telling some other homeowner how a house should be rehabilitated. Consciously evaluate everything you do, think and say. These are your entrance exams into a new way of life. A new career if you decide to go into business.

To obtain expert opinion as to where gas, electric, water and radiant heating supply lines should be installed, draw a plan of each floor. Indicate overall width, length and ceiling height. Indicate windows and doors, size of each room, present location of hot and cold water and waste lines, exact location of a kitchen sink, laundry tub, toilet, lavatory and bathtub. Show these floor plans to the gas or electric company home economist. Their experts will give you some of the best remodeling advice available—and it's free. Some will make a personal inspection to confirm their suggestions.

The location selected for an additional bathroom or new kitchen should be determined by two factors. If existing waste and vent lines are serviceably sound, you save a considerable sum connecting to them. If they are beyond repair, or located so you can't install a kitchen and bathroom conveniently, consider roughing in new lines. If this decision is made, use plastic instead of cast iron. If codes require cast iron, get permission to install no-hub cast iron, Illus. 133. This is easy to install and takes half the time.

No-hub cast iron pipe and fittings are available in the same assortment and same sizes as hub and spigot cast iron. All you do is cut pipe to length required, slip a neoprene gasket in position, Illus. 133, over end, slip the stainless steel collar in position. The fitting or pipe to be joined, is inserted in gasket, bolts on collar tightened, and you have a joint that will last as long as cast iron or stainless steel, Illus. 134. Besides being easy-to-join, it's remarkably quiet. The neoprene gasket tends to deaden noise immeasurably.

Illus. 105 shows two lengths of 4" cast iron hub pipe. Both come in 5' and 10' lengths. One is called single hub, the other double hub. The outlet end of single hub pipe is called a spigot. If you have to cut a length of hub pipe, always use pipe with double hubs. This permits using both pieces. Connecting hub and spigot, or hub to a cut end, requires oakum calking and hot lead, Illus. 105.

To make a connection to EXISTING VERTICAL CAST IRON, note Illus. 123, brace stack above and below piece you want to remove. Cut and remove a length just above a hub, Illus. 117. Apply heat from a propane torch and remove stub, lead and oakum. Install a Kayfer tee and straight length, hub and spigot, Illus. 102.

To make a connection to EXISTING HORIZONTAL SOIL LINE, note Illus. 126. An ⅛ Bend offset, Illus. 135, or any combination of fittings, can be used to angle over to existing line. Remove length of barrel, replace with a Kayfer tee or Y, plus a Kayfer straight length, plus a length of hub and spigot. Three fittings simplify springing replacements in position.

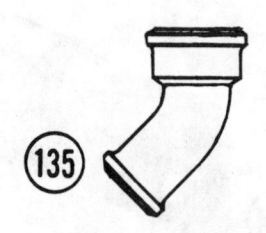

To add a new soil line or make a new connection to an existing one, draw chalk lines to indicate location, then saw through flooring and subflooring between floor joists. Since you will also have to install cats and backerboards for lavatory and tub controls, Illus. 136, remove plaster from entire wall. This simplifies roughing in plumbing, wiring and heating pipes, as well as duct work for a ventilating fan. It also permits nailing the framing a lavatory, tub and toilet requires, Illus. 137.

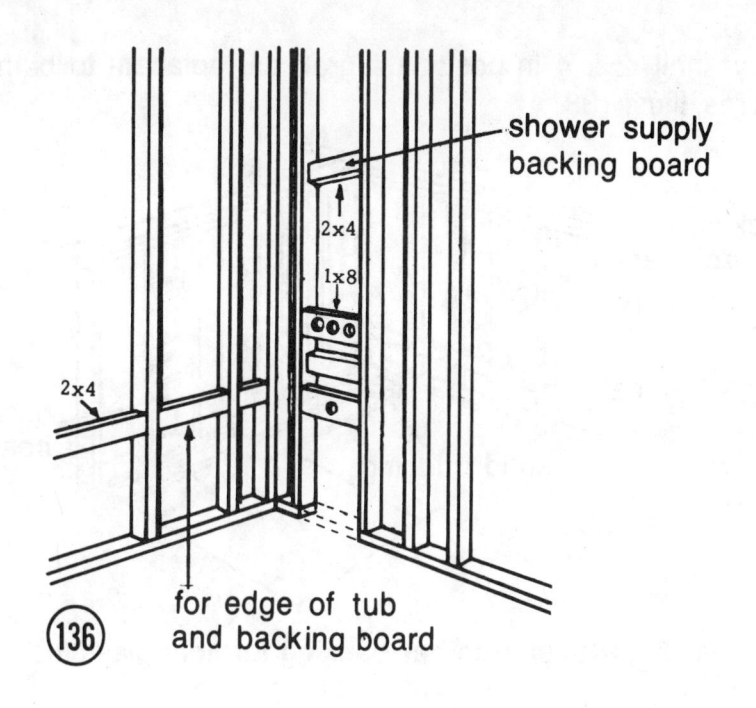

shower supply backing board

2x4

1x8

2x4

(136) for edge of tub and backing board

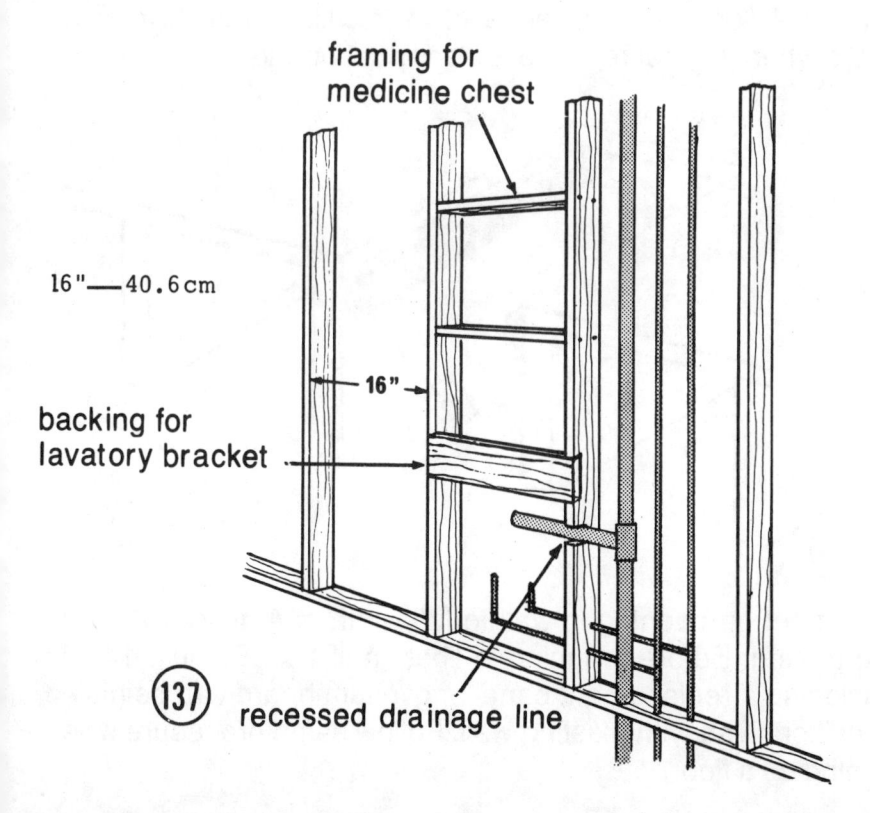

framing for medicine chest

16"——40.6cm

16"

backing for lavatory bracket

(137) recessed drainage line

117

Always nail 2 x 4 in position a grab bar adjacent to bathtub requires, Illus. 138.

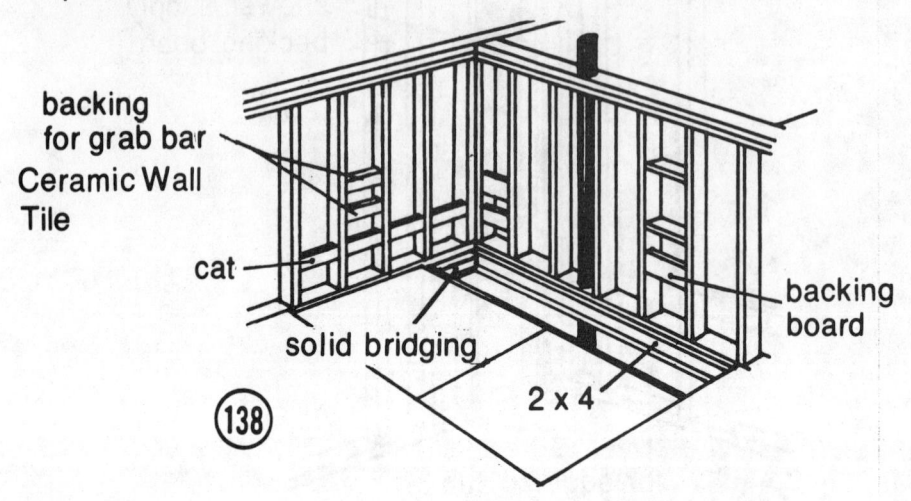

Figure 138: backing for grab bar Ceramic Wall Tile, cat, solid bridging, 2 x 4, backing board

See Illus.167,168 for grab bar backing for fiber glass tub.

Nail 1 x 2 flush with top edge of joists, Illus. 139, to provide nailors when you get ready to replace subflooring.

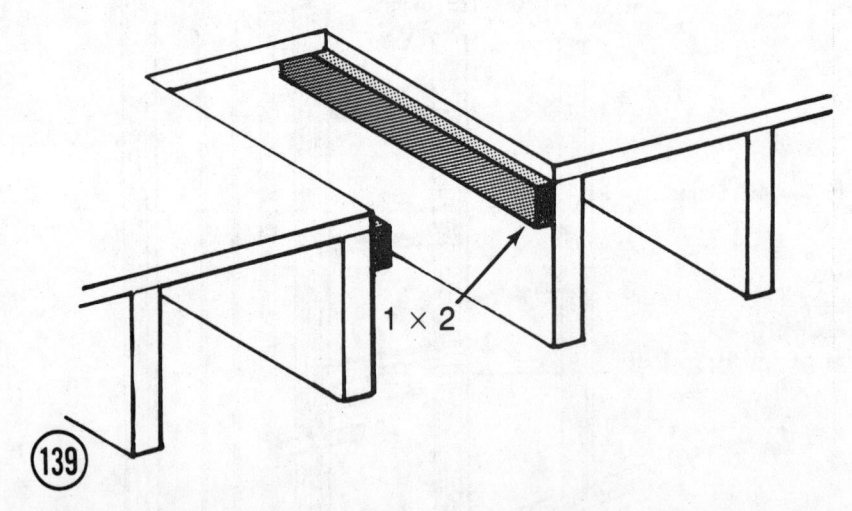

Figure 139: 1 x 2

Always cut an opening in wall to full width of A, Illus. 140, from stud to stud. Before roughing in lines, nail 1 x 2B, Illus. 141, in position so a replacement panel of gypsum board can be nailed in position flush with existing wall. Follow same procedure when opening up a floor.

Shower

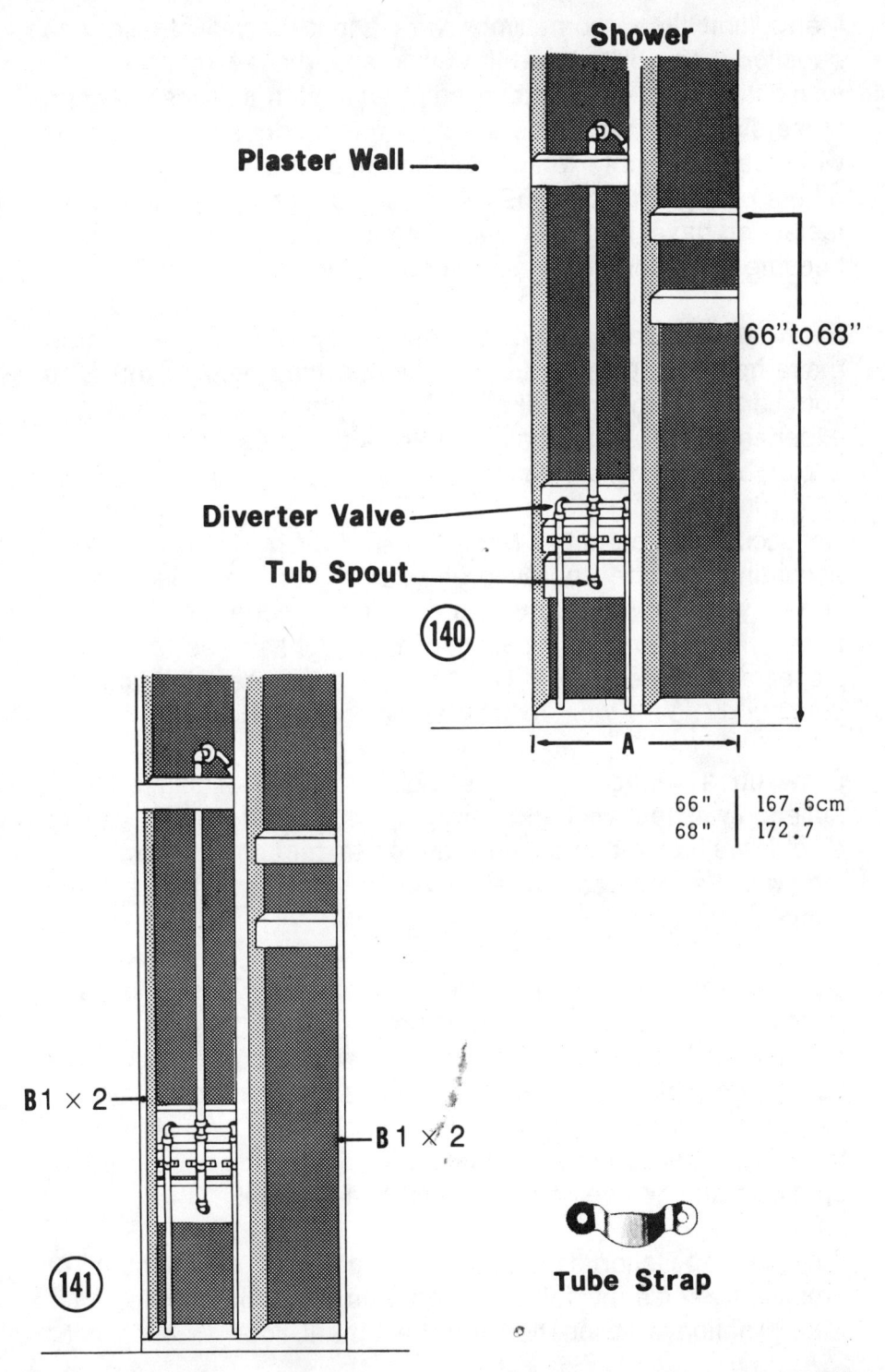

Plaster Wall

Diverter Valve

Tub Spout

(140)

|— A —|

66" to 68"

| 66" | 167.6 cm |
| 68" | 172.7 |

B 1 × 2

B 1 × 2

(141)

Tube Strap

119

Many "first time" home improvers and especially those who question their ability to do the work, spend a few months going to night school. They attend adult education classes covering those subjects that cause them the most concern. The time is well spent not only for what is learned, but also because of others one meets. Because some people grasp certain trades faster, or have had previous experience or association, they become whiz kids on wiring, plumbing, heating, air conditioning.

Each attends class to pick up more know-how. Since most of these homeowners can use your spare time help as much as you can use them, make a deal. Help them and you get experience, while their help can economically solve installation of plumbing, wiring or heating.

An occupancy permit will only be granted if all work is done according to code approved standards. For this reason make certain you follow a manufacturer's and/or code recommendations when making an installation. You might also ask a building inspector whether he will O.K. an occupancy permit if you and your buddy do the work exactly as the code specifies.

Draw up a wiring diagram showing location of all new wall outlets, switches, wall and ceiling lights. Locate where a gas or electric wall oven and counter range, refrigerator and ventilating fan will be located, where counter outlets will be most convenient.

Use colored chalk to indicate location of a tub, toilet and lavatory. Do the same in planning a kitchen, locating hot air registers or hot water baseboard radiation. When you discover how much a plumber, electrician or heating contractor pays his men per hour to measure and prepare a floor or wall prior to roughing in service lines and fixtures, you see the need to make openings and get the house ready for each trade.

Every rehabilitation job contains a different combination of problems, so it's difficult to suggest an exact procedure. After waterproofing a foundation and basement floor, leveling floor joists or replacing rotted timbers, it's usually necessary to start roughing in service lines. This is always done before laying any subflooring or patching any cracked plaster on walls or ceilings.

Always remove damaged finished flooring in any area selected for a bathroom or kitchen. This permits nailing exterior grade plywood over subflooring after roughing in service lines has been completed. The plywood provides a smooth base for ceramic or asphalt tile, linoleum or indoor/outdoor carpeting. The application of plywood and tile necessitates removing door and saddle, Illus. 142.

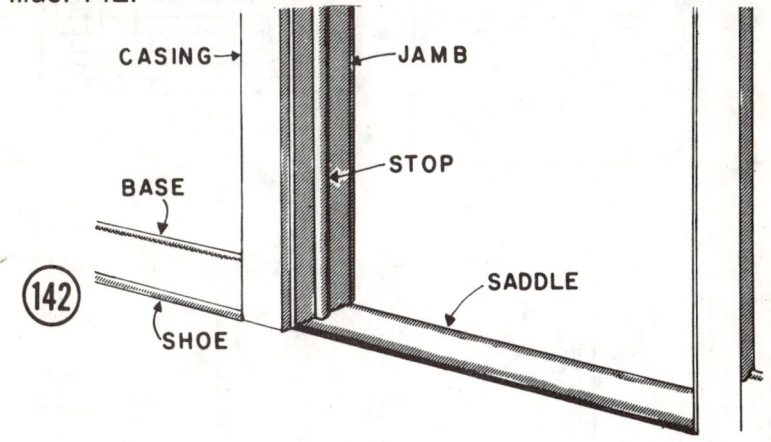

If existing finished floor is in good condition but contains a build up of paint, crud, etc., sand smooth and either refinish or prepare it for linoleum, asphalt tile or carpeting. Pull hinge pins to remove a door. Remove stops and pry up saddle. After new floor has been installed, install a new saddle, one designed for floor covering selected, Illus. 143. Saw bottom of door to accommodate new saddle.

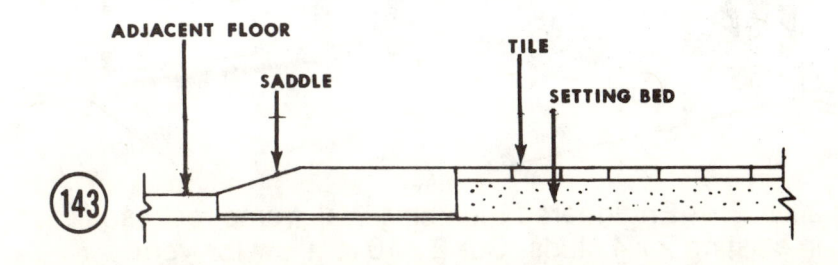

Locating a bathroom and kitchen back-to-back, Illus. 144, or a bathroom and lavatory back-to-back, or two bathrooms, Illus. 145, effects a considerable savings.

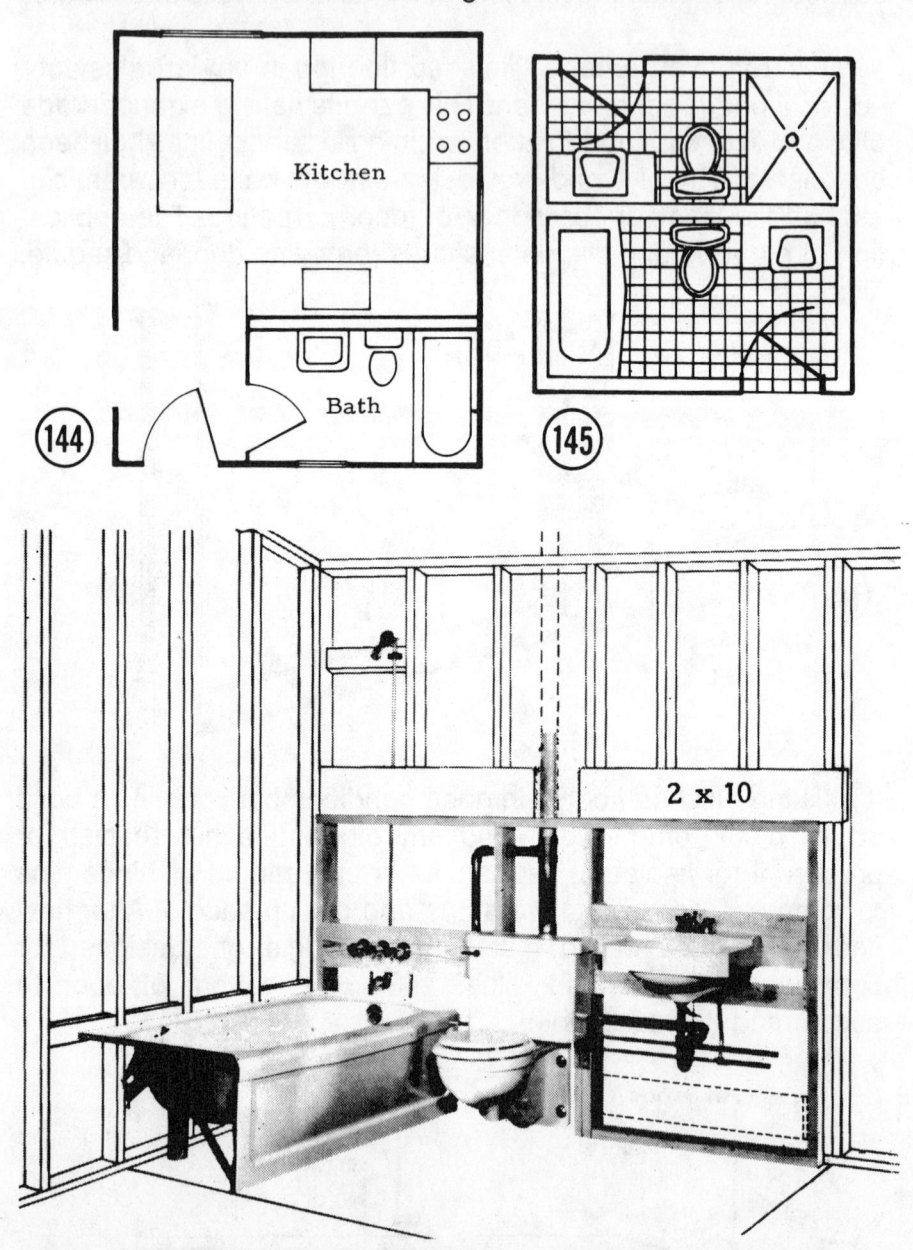

(144)

(145)

(146) 2 x 6 Pre–Engineered Plumbing Wall frame recessed in existing 2 x 4 studs. Cut 2 x 10 to allow for vent.

The preassembled plumbing wall, Illus. 103, framed at the factory in 2 x 6, greatly simplifies installation of an extra bathroom; bathroom and kitchen; two bathrooms; or a bathroom and lavatory. These come in a wide assortment of assemblies. Order what you need. The plumbing wall can be purchased separately or complete with a tub, wall hung toilet and lavatory that drain into wall inlets, Illus. 146. This unit only requires drilling four holes; one for a 3" waste line, one for a 3" vent line, plus two 1" holes for copper supply lines. While some wall units are shipped with a roof flange for vent line, all below floor connections, tubing and fittings, must be purchased locally.

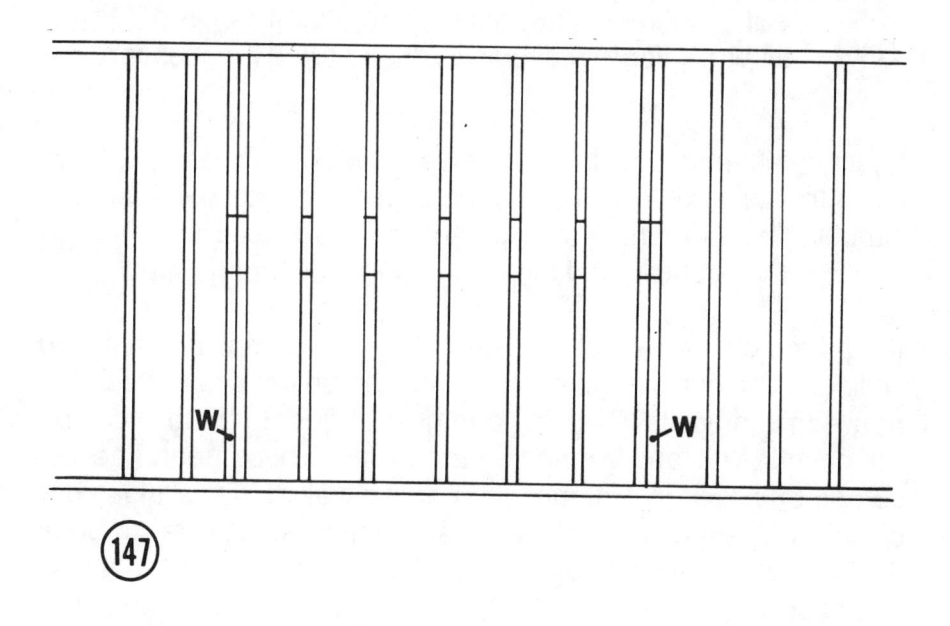

(147)

To install this time and labor saving unit, it's necessary to frame in an 88", or size opening unit requires, Illus. 147. Only open up subflooring if you need to run new supply lines and/or heating ducts. Place a 2 x 10, cut to length unit requires, across studs in position shown, Illus. 147. Mark studs. Nail extra studs W in position. Saw and chisel 1½ x 9¼" notch in each stud. Spike the 2 x 10 to studs except Y, then saw studs off flush with bottom edge. Saw and remove shoe, Illus. 148.

123

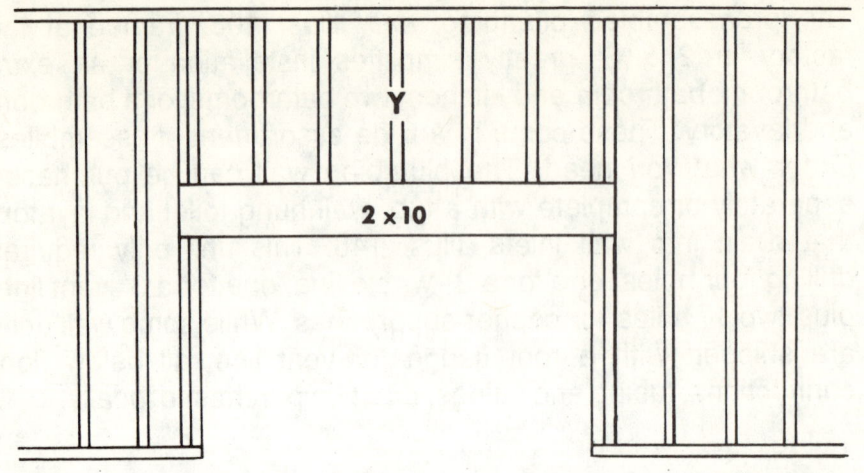

148 Nail all studs except Y to 2 x 10. Cut through 2 x 10 to allow for vent. Move and renail stud Y if necessary.

Position plumbing wall in opening. Check with level. Locate holes for soil and vent stack in exact position required. Remove plumbing wall. Cut hole through subflooring for soil line, through ceiling for vent stack, and through framing for supply lines.

If a plumbing wall is being installed over a room with a finished ceiling, a 90° quarter bend, Illus. 149, can be used to run soil line between floor joists. By using another 90° quarter bend, it can be run down a wall and connected to soil line in basement. The line can be enclosed in a dummy wall or in a wall-to-wall sliding door closet. Since closets are always in short supply, read Book #634 How to Build Storage Units. It tells how to build every kind you need.

149

To simplify installation of 90° quarter bend, sweat 3" nipple to A, Illus. 150, prior to placing plumbing wall in position. This simplifies connecting to 3" copper line when wall in is position.

A — Connect to 3" Soil Stack
B — 3" Vent
C — 3/4" Water Supply
D — Bathtub Drain
E — 1/2" supply to Bathtub Diverter Valve
F — Backing for Diverter Valve
G — 1-1/2" Bathtub Vent
H — Backing for Lavatory Bracket
J — Lavatory Waste
K — Lavatory Supply
L — Backing for Lavatory Supply
M — Toilet Waste
N — Studs Holding Toilet
O — Toilet Supply
P — 1/2 x 3/4" Reducer
R — Tee - 3 x 3 x 1-1/2"

Copper tubing and fittings are installed in position at factory.

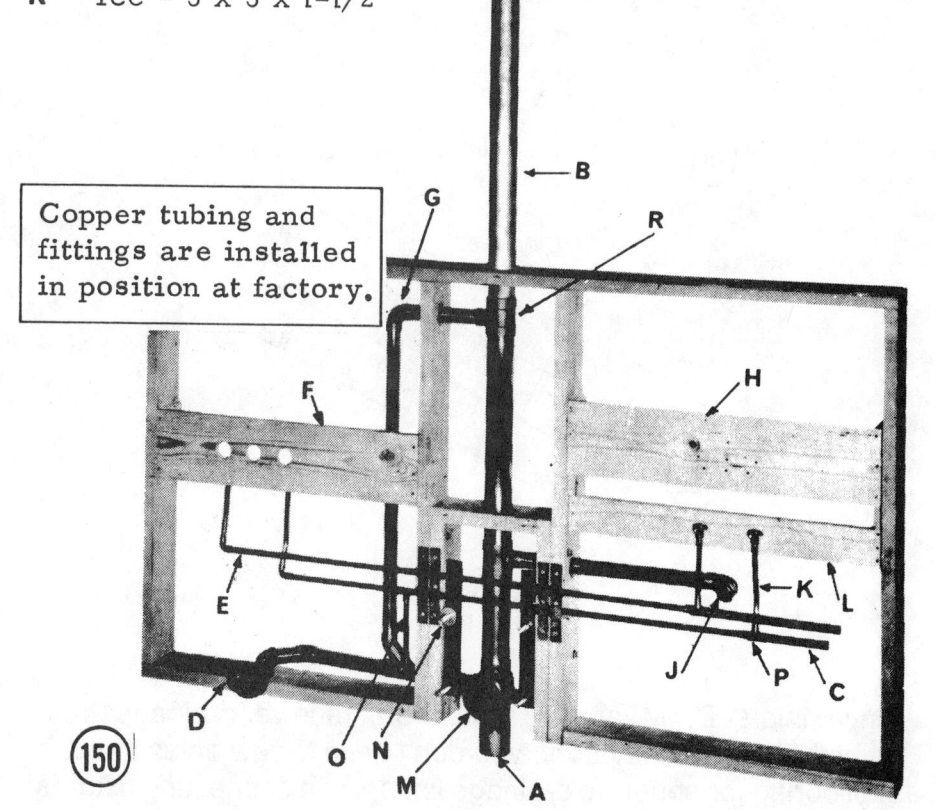

125

Replace plumbing wall in position, check with level. Shim with shingle if necessary. Nail frame to studs, to floor joists and to 2 x 10. To locate hole in roof for 3" vent pipe, drop a plumb bob down from ceiling to center of opening for vent. Drilll a hole to size vent pipe requires. Using a plumb bob, locate center of vent as it goes through the roof, drive a nail through roof to indicate exact position, Illus. 151. Remove nail and cut a hole to size vent pipe requires, Illus. 152.

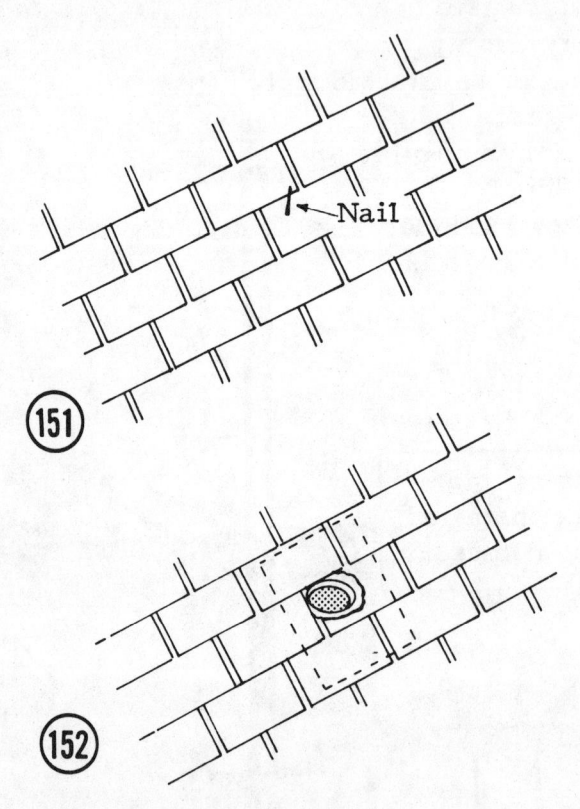

(151)

(152)

Since inlets D, M and J, Illus. 150, receive drainage from bathtub, toilet and lavatory, you don't have to saw holes through subflooring for separate drainage lines when connecting fixtures to a plumbing wall. Book #682 provides detailed directions covering installation of the plumbing wall and all fixtures.

APPLY INSULATION

After roughing-in all plumbing, electrical and heating lines, and having made provision for air conditioning if same is to be installed, insulate all outside walls and between rafters, or between floor joists if same are exposed in an unused attic space. Where outside wall studs are exposed, staple rock wool batts vertically between studs. Place the foil side facing in, Illus. 153. This reflects the warm air. To fully evaluate the need for insulation, consider this simple fact. Heat constantly moves from warm to cooler areas. A thickness of insulation determined by the serverity of the cold, is required to stop this movement.

(153)

All single glass windows permit warm air to escape. Double glazed windows containing a ¼" dead air space between panes, provide more resistance to the transmission of heat than an 8" concrete block wall. An outside wall containing exterior sheathing and siding, with gypsum or plywood paneling inside,

127

will lose between 200 to 250% more heat than the same wall with 3½" of rock wool insulation. The foil side should always face in. This reflects the heat back inside while the rock wool batt seals out cold.

Where inside walls are plastered or covered with gypsum wallboard or wall paneling, install loose insulation. This can be blown in between the studs by working inside the attic. Or have a commercial installer pipe in a liquid foam that expands and fills area between studs.

Always install 2 to 3½" thick rock wool batts between studs where waste drainage and supply lines are run in outside walls. Pack the insulation between the pipe and outside wall.

REPLACING OBSOLETE FIXTURES

The four piece fiber glass tub-shower, Illus. 154, comes in two 60 lb. cartons that can be carried through most narrow doorways. The tub is one piece. The two ends and back lock together in vertical and horizontal channels, Illus. 155. The manufacturer provides a tube of sealant. This is placed in a sealant channel. When the two ends and back wall are placed in position, the sealant provides a waterproof joint while clips, Illus. 156, supplied by manufacturer, lock corners together. The result is a 60 x 32 x 72" tub-shower that can be installed anywhere a drain, supply, vent line and framing permit.

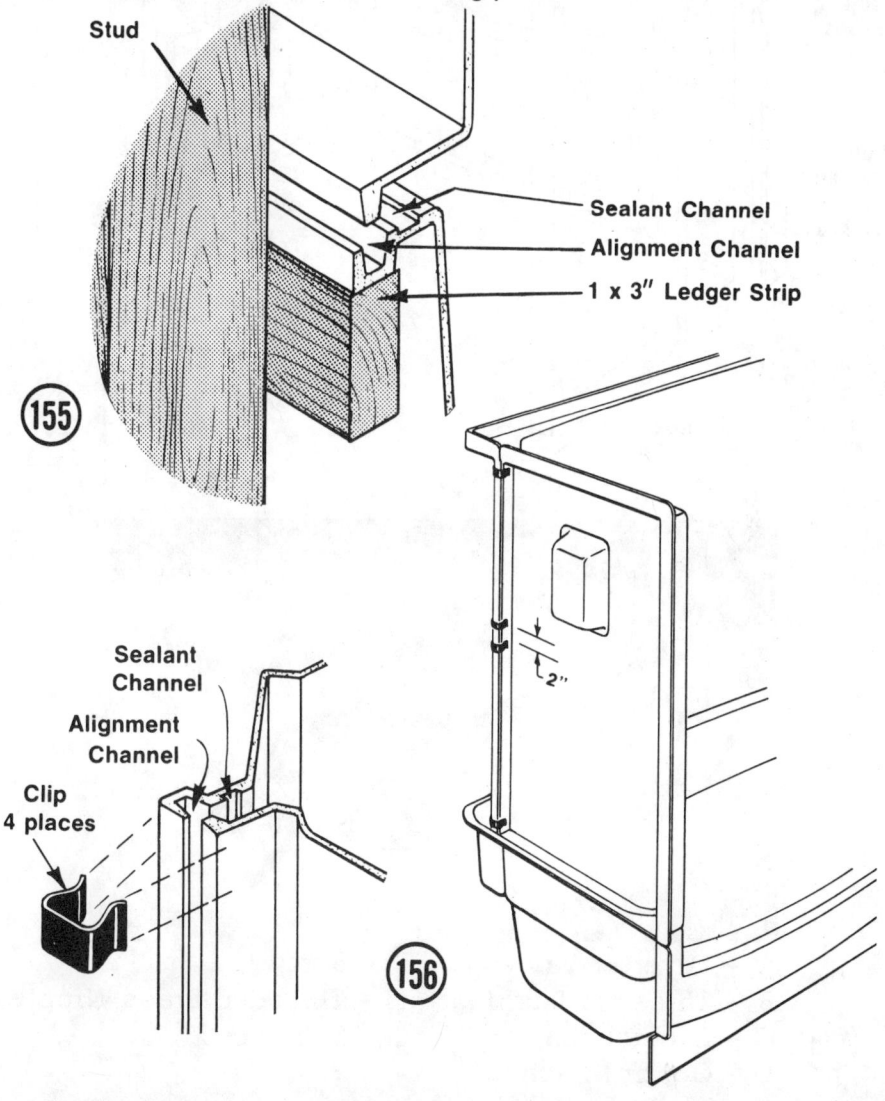

2x4 Blocking B FLUSH WITH INSIDE EDGE OF STUDS

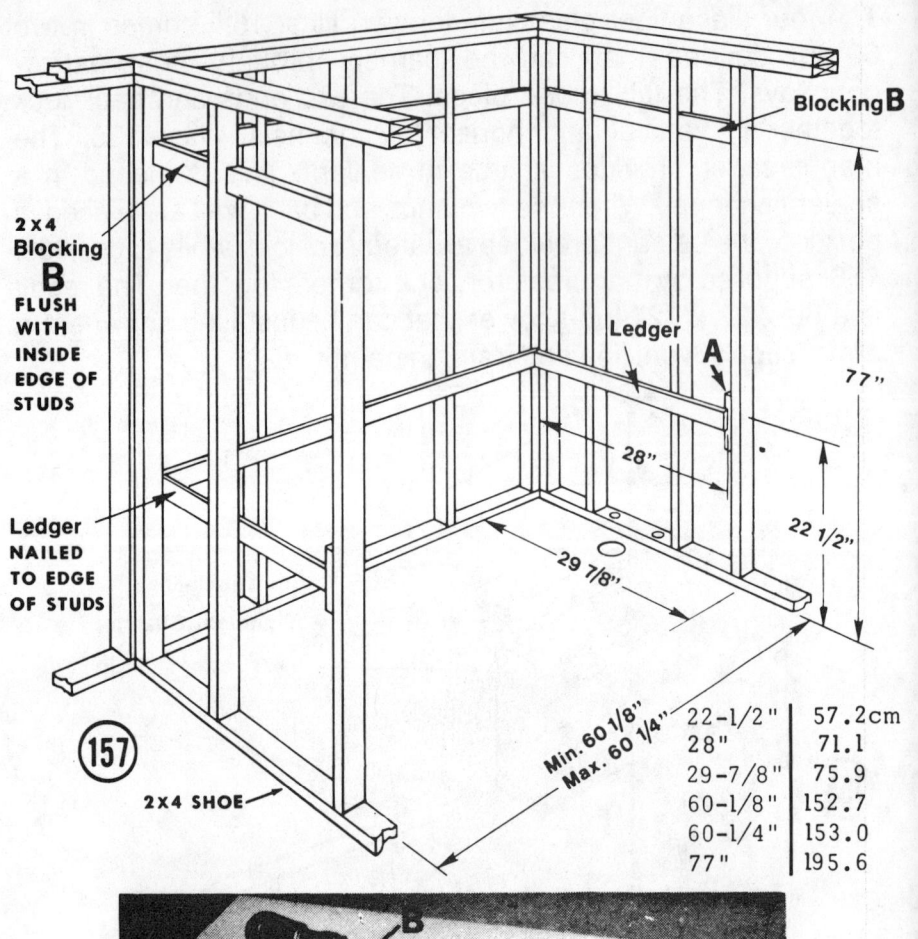

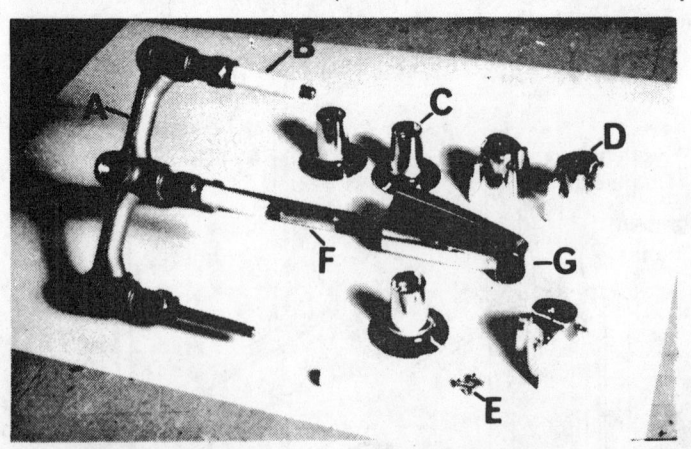

Ledger NAILED TO EDGE OF STUDS

Blocking **B**

Ledger

77"

28"

22 1/2"

29 7/8"

Min. 60 1/8"
Max. 60 1/4"

2x4 SHOE

22-1/2"	57.2 cm
28"	71.1
29-7/8"	75.9
60-1/8"	152.7
60-1/4"	153.0
77"	195.6

(157)

(158)

A - Diverter Valve
B - Threaded Bushing
C - Escutcheon
D - Control Knob
E - Screw
F - Threaded Brass Nipple
G - Tub Spout

This tub and shower requires framing in exact position noted, Illus. 157. After framing is completed, one man can install the tub and walls in less than a hour. Always read and follow tub manufacturers directions.

To remove an existing tub, remove controls, escutcheon, spout, Illus. 158, 159. Cover drain with a rag.

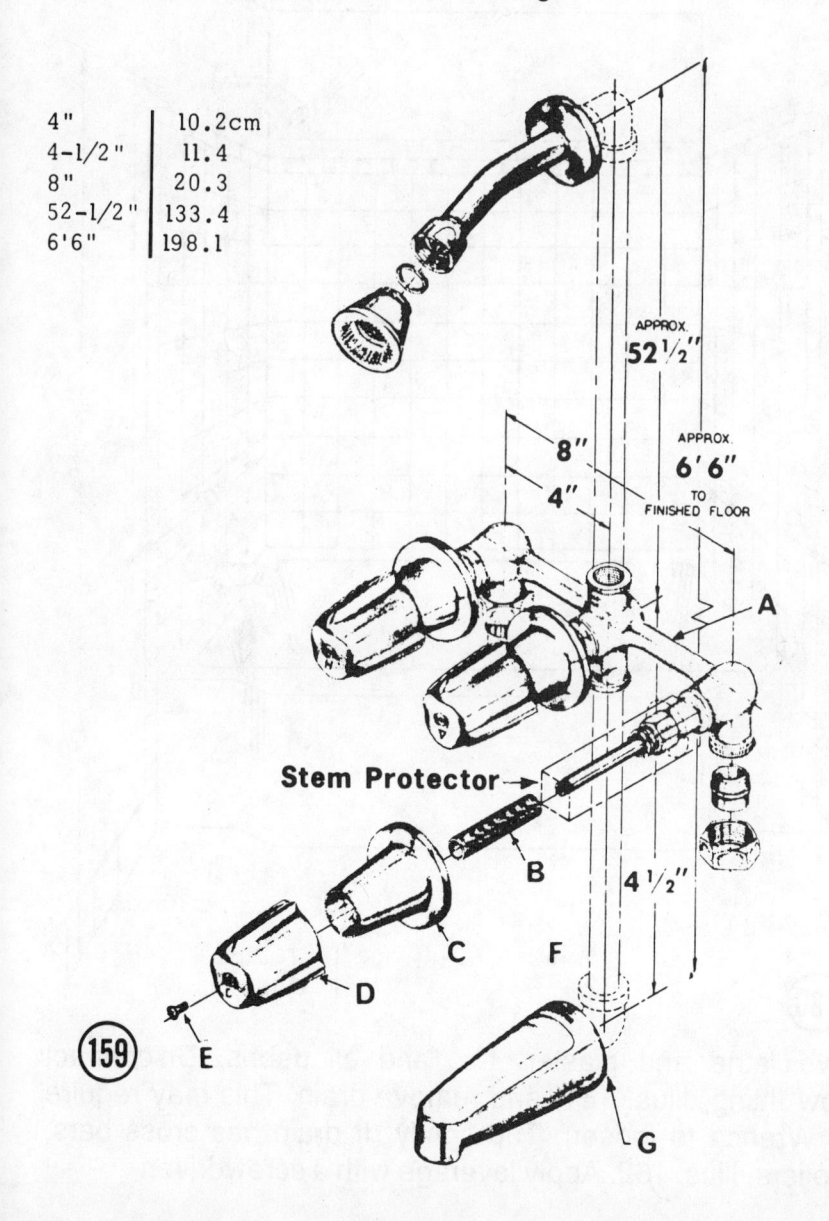

4"	10.2cm
4-1/2"	11.4
8"	20.3
52-1/2"	133.4
6'6"	198.1

131

Using a 4' level, draw lines 77" from sublfoor, Illus. 160, 30" from back wall. Using a keyhole or saber saw with a blade capable of cutting through ceramic tile, saw through lathe and plaster along drawn lines, BUT DO NOT CUT STUDS.

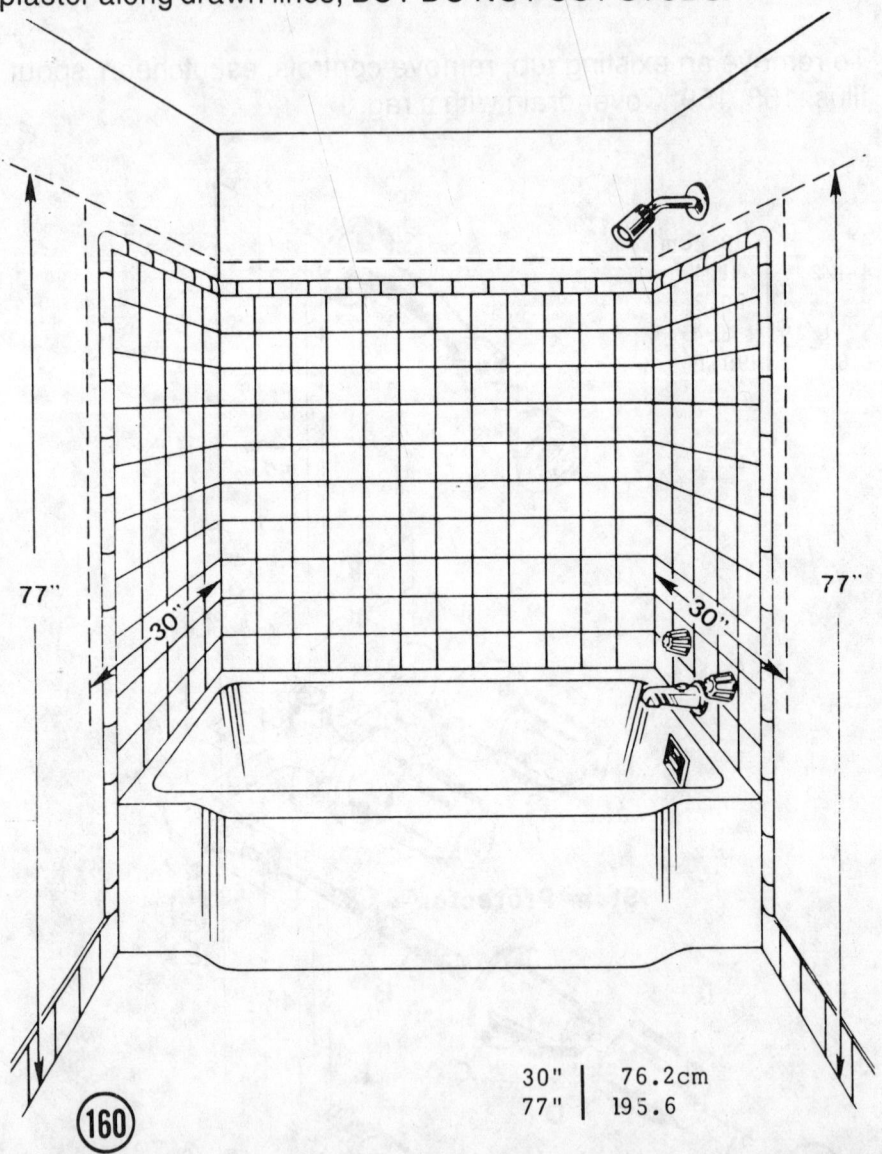

(160)

| 30" | 76.2cm |
| 77" | 195.6 |

Remove lathe and plaster, tile, and all debris. Disconnect overflow fitting, Illus. 161, and remove drain. This may require Liquid Wrench to loosen. Tap lightly. If drain has cross bars, insert pliers, Illus. 162. Apply leverage with a screwdriver.

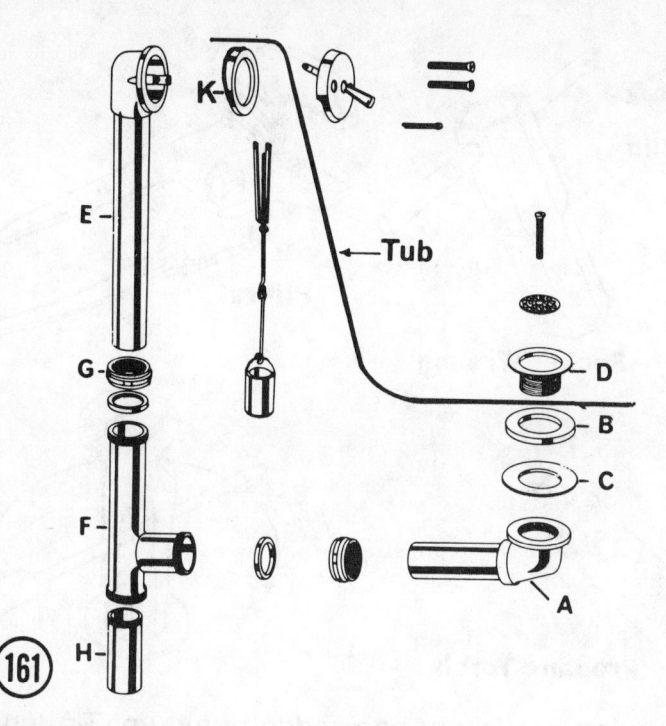

(161)

PLUMBING EQUIPMENT, TOOLS

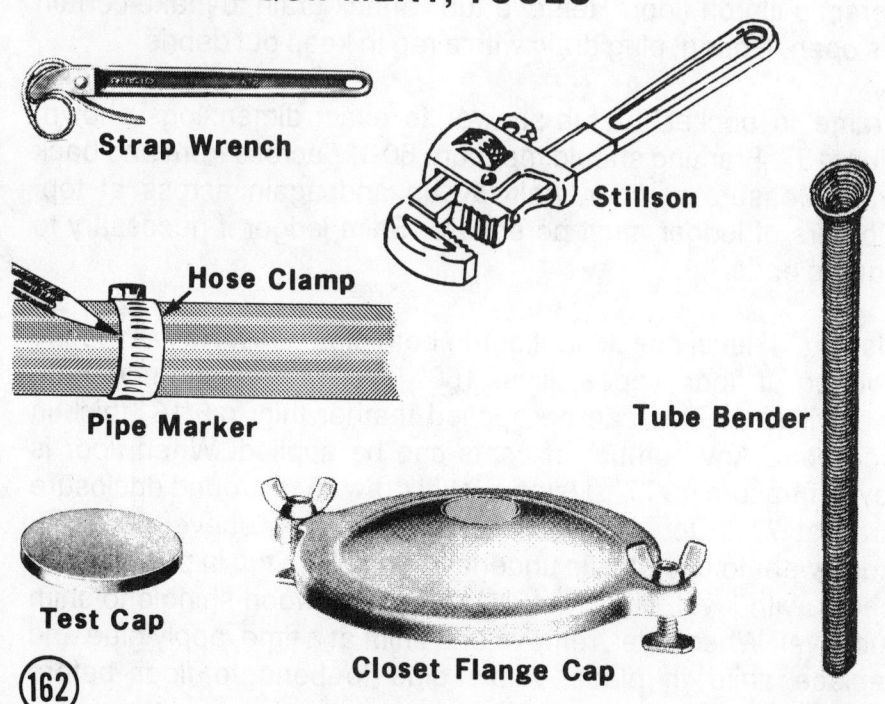

Strap Wrench

Stillson

Hose Clamp

Pipe Marker

Tube Bender

Test Cap

Closet Flange Cap

(162)

133

Aviation Clip

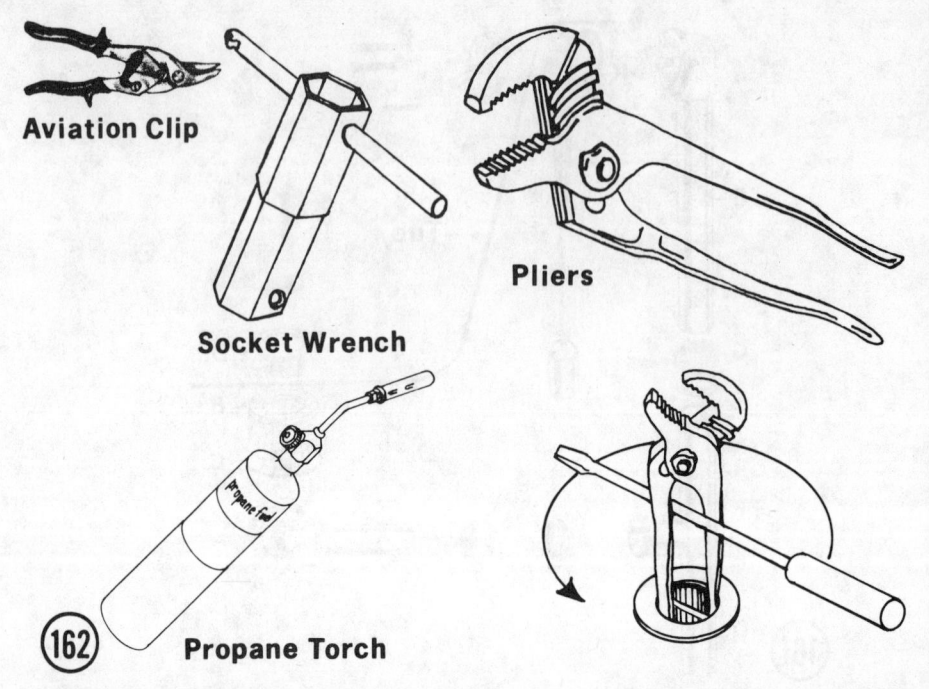

Socket Wrench

Pliers

(162) **Propane Torch**

Use a wrecking bar to pry back edge of tub up. Tip tub over ceramic tile on floor. Remove tub. Check drain to make certain it's open. If open, plug drain with a rag to keep out debris.

Frame in pocket for tub-shower to exact dimensions shown, Illus. 157. Framing should measure 60-1/8" across front and back wall. Measure at floor, halfway up and again across at top. Corners of ledger must be square. Shim ledger if necessary to square ends.

Using a 4' level check subfloor in both directions. Nail any loose flooring. If floor slopes, Illus. 163, level with plastic underlayment, Illus. 51. This can be applied feather thin to 5/16" thick in one coat. Any number of coats can be applied. When floor is level measure up 77". Using a level draw lines around enclosure area at 77". Double check height. If floor is uneven and you don't want to use plastic underlayment, place tub in position and check with level, Illus. 164. Use pieces of wood shingle to shim tub level. When level, remove one shim at a time, apply glue and replace shim in place. Allow glue to bond to floor before removing tub.

⑯₃ ⑯₄

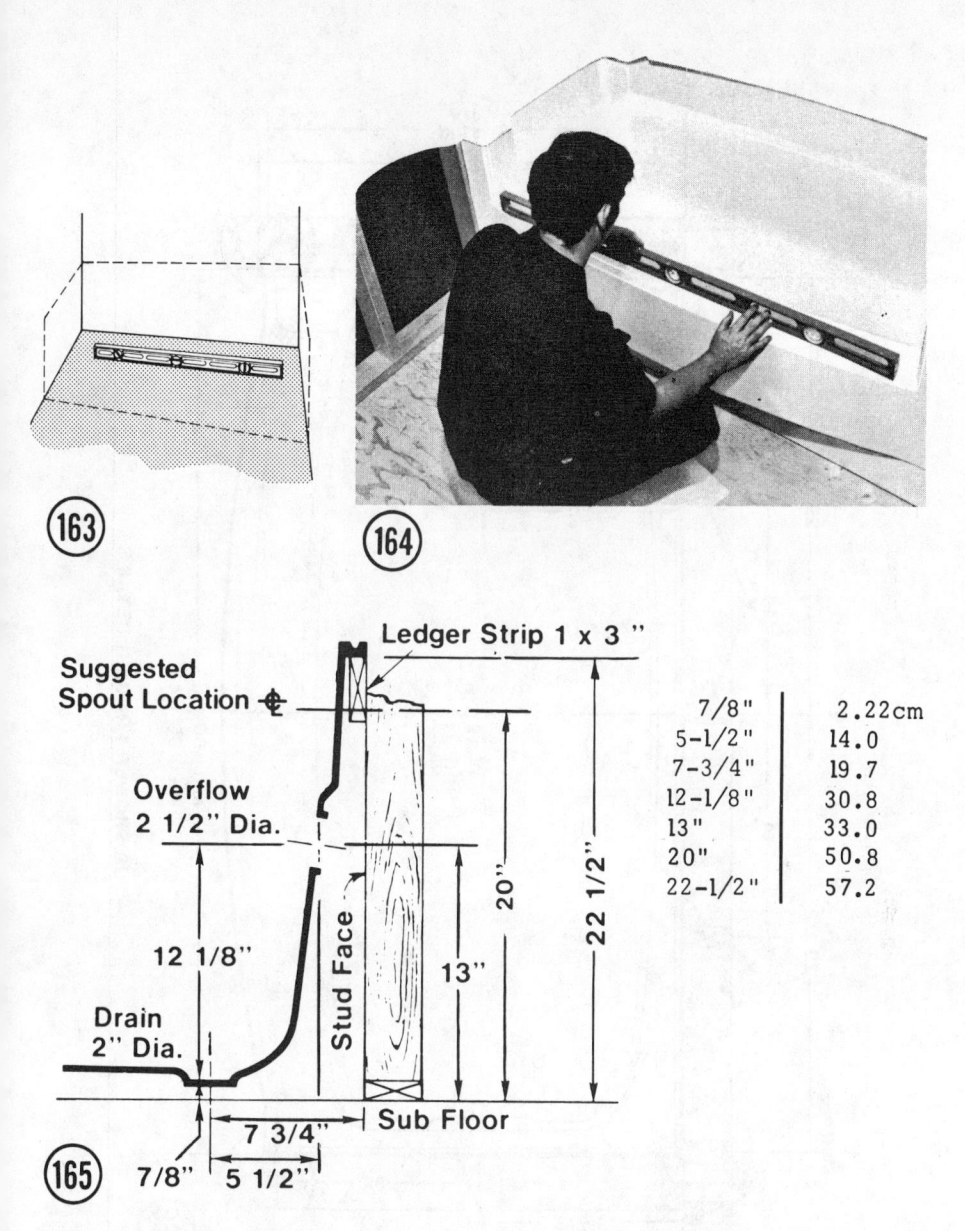

⑯₅

Suggested Spout Location ℄

Overflow 2 1/2" Dia.

12 1/8"

Drain 2" Dia.

Ledger Strip 1 x 3"

Stud Face

20"

13"

22 1/2"

Sub Floor

7 3/4"
7/8" 5 1/2"

7/8"	2.22 cm
5-1/2"	14.0
7-3/4"	19.7
12-1/8"	30.8
13"	33.0
20"	50.8
22-1/2"	57.2

To simplify installation the center of the tub drain should be 7-¾" from end wall framing, Illus. 165, and 13-⅞" from rear wall, Illus. 166. Draw dimensions on floor. Place tub in position. If existing framing doesn't measure this distance, remove tub and nail 1 x 2 or strips of plywood, use thickness required, to edge of shoe, studs and plate. Replace tub. The tub, drain and supply lines must be in position indicated, Illus. 166.

TUB SHOWER FRAMING DETAILS

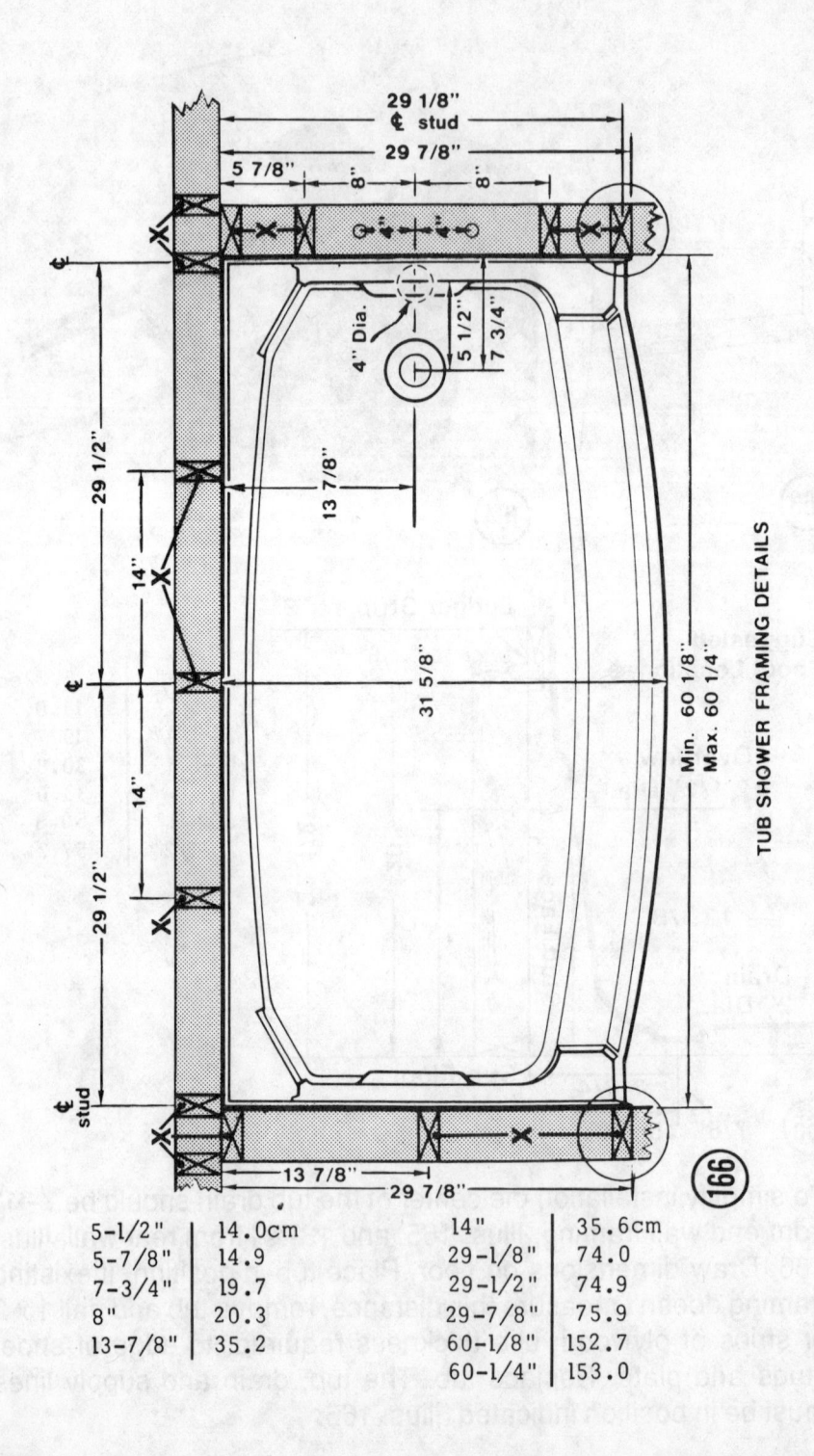

(166)

5-1/2"	14.0cm	14"	35.6cm
5-7/8"	14.9	29-1/8"	74.0
7-3/4"	19.7	29-1/2"	74.9
8"	20.3	29-7/8"	75.9
13-7/8"	35.2	60-1/8"	152.7
		60-1/4"	153.0

136

Tub drain requires a 4" diameter hole in subfloor, 13-⅞" from studs, 2¼" from a line drawn through center of holes for supply lines. Holes for supply lines should be 4" from center as noted, Illus. 166.

Nail extra studs X, Illus. 166, in position indicated, to provide framing needed. Nail 2 x 4A to studs, Illus. 157, at height indicated. Nail 1 x 3 ledger B in position, 22½" from subfloor. Draw a level line 22½" from subfloor and nail back ledger first. Then nail end ledgers to studs and to A. End ledgers should not be longer than 28".

Nail 2 x 4 blocking B between studs, Illus. 157. Draw a level line 77" from subfloor and nail studs to B. Keep B flush with edge of studs.

If you want to install a grab bar, nail a 2 x 4 to studs, Illus. 167, at height desired. Nail 2 x 4 securely to three studs for a horizontal grab bar. Nail two 2 x 4's across three studs if you want to install a vertical grab bar, Illus. 168.

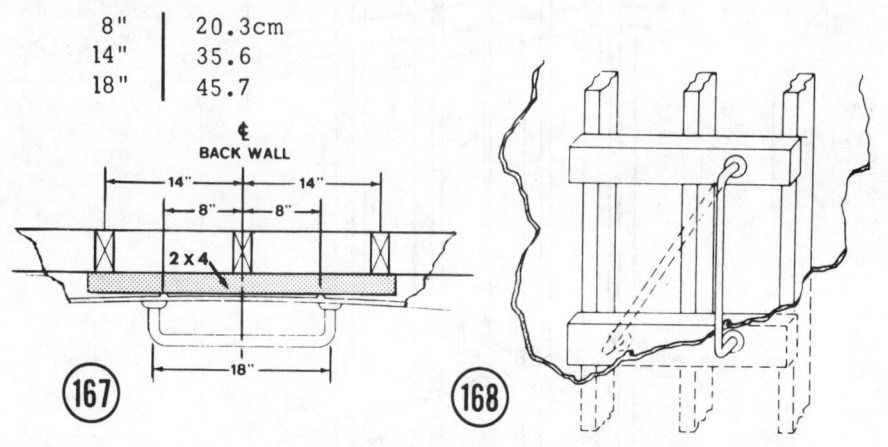

8"	20.3cm
14"	35.6
18"	45.7

Since you have to drill holes through wall of tub-shower, you can locate grab bar where desired. Reinforcing ribs, molded into the back wall, 8" on either side of a vertical center line, provide added strength grab bar requires. Grab bar may also be installed on end walls by nailing 2 x 4 in position required. Nail backerboards in position required, Illus. 169.

Nail studs to 2×4 or 2×6 backerboard in position grab bar requires.

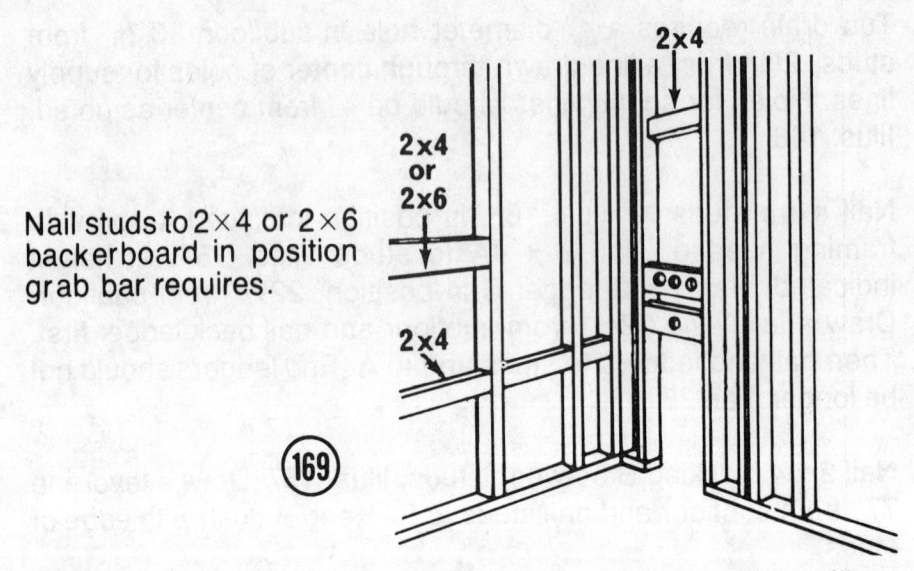

(169)

Rough in supply lines, Illus. 170, using soft copper tubing. Illus. 159 indicates position. Do not strap tubing to backerboard at this stage.

2"	5.1cm
22-1/2"	57.2
28"	71.1
29-7/8"	75.9
77"	195.6

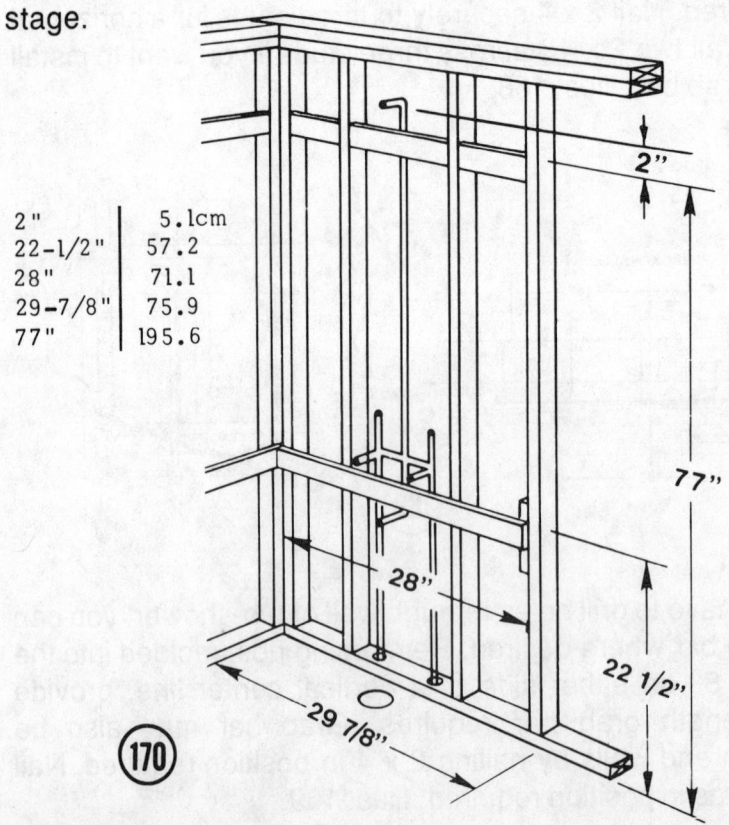

(170)

The diverter valve, Illus. 171, is connected to hot and cold supply lines, shower outlet and tub outlet in position shown, Illus. 159.

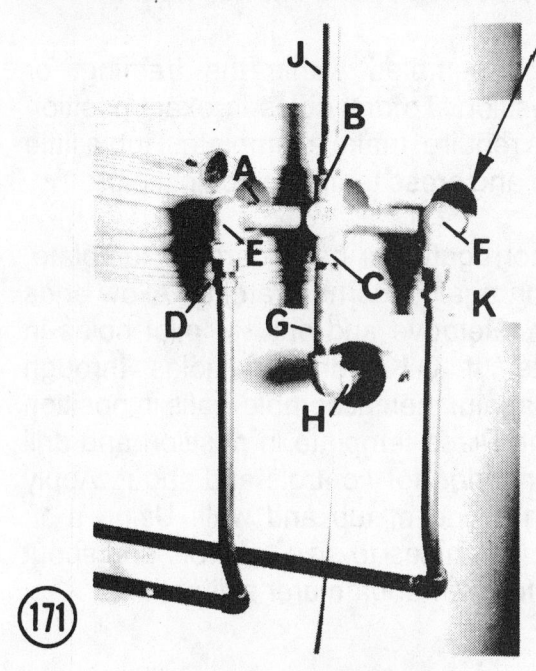

Drill 2" holes in backerboard in position Diverter Valve requires.

A — Diverter Valve
B — Shower Outlet
C — Tub Outlet
D — Male Adapter
E — Cold
F — Hot
G — Brass Nipple
H — Brass Ell
J — Shower Line
K — Female Coupling

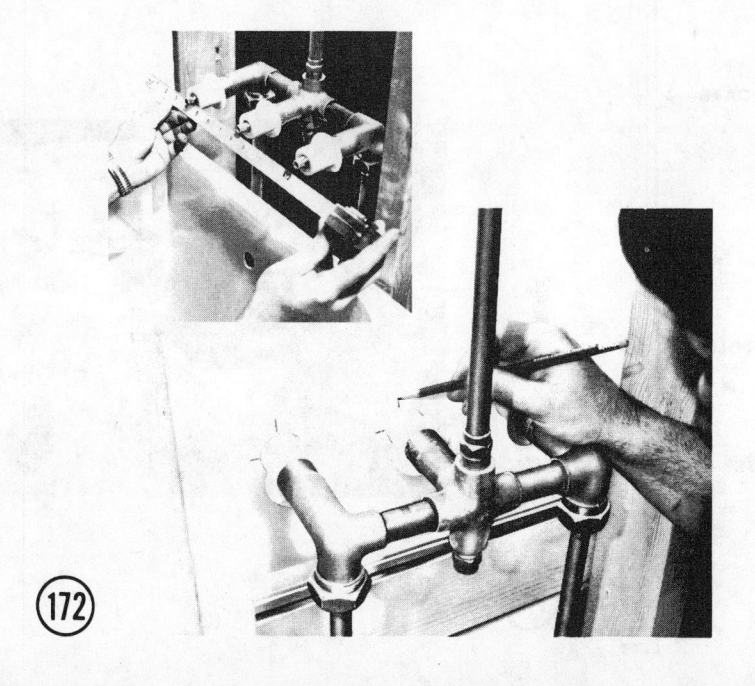

Illus. 172 indicates position of installed shower wall. This measures 1 5/8" from stud. Allow amount needed for escutcheons when cutting pipe for controls, spout and shower head.

The tub-shower can be assembled within the framing, or outside, then slide into position. To drill holes in exact position shower, spout and controls require, make a template. Rub a little chalk on edge of each pipe and press template against pipe.

Use a 24 x 84" piece of corrugated or hardboard for template. Place it squarely in position against corner framing. Allow ends of pipe to imprint position. Remove and drill 1/8" pilot holes in center. Replace template. If O.K., drill 1" holes through template. Check template again, then assemble walls in position on tub. Do not use sealant. Place template in position and drill 1/8" pilot holes in position needed for controls and spout. Apply masking tape to finish on inside of tub and wall. Using a 1" spade bit, or 1" hole saw, drill holes to size controls and spout require, Illus. 173. Always follow manufacturer's directions.

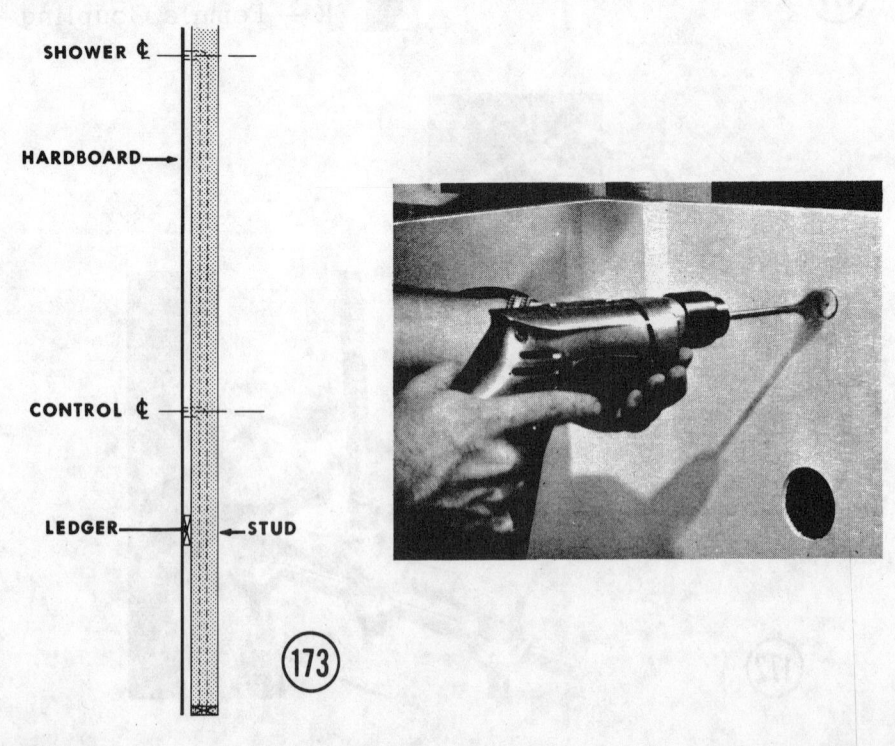

If studs are exposed and you can assemble the unit in place, position tub and check with level. Leave the tub protector in place so you can stand in tub without marring finish. Note: ledge on tub should rest evenly on ledger strip all the way around.

Assemble overflow tee, Illus. 161, 174. The tub is designed to use a standard 16" adjustable drain and overflow fitting. Apply non-hardening putty or equal sealant to recess in tub, Illus. 165. With gasket B and metal washer C in position shown, Illus. 161, on underside of tub, make up fitting by screwing D into A. Depending on fitting, you can usually turn D with handle or nose of pliers, Illus. 162. Wipe away excess sealant when D is firmly seated.

(174)

Drainage control and overflow pipe E, Illus. 161, fastens to tub with two screws, and to F with a slip joint compression nut and washer G in position shown. The thinnest part of beveled rubber washer K is normally placed down. Since manufacturers frequently make design changes, always follow directions manufacturer provides. Screw nipple H into F using a strap wrench, Illus. 162. You can also wrap adhesive tape around H and tighten with a pair of pliers or a stillson wrench, or fasten a pipe clamp to H. Use pliers on clamp.

The tub-shower has both alignment and sealant channels, Illus. 156. Follow manufacturer's directions and apply sealant manufacturer provides, Illus. 175, in sealant channels. Do not put sealant in an alignment channel. Keep this clean.

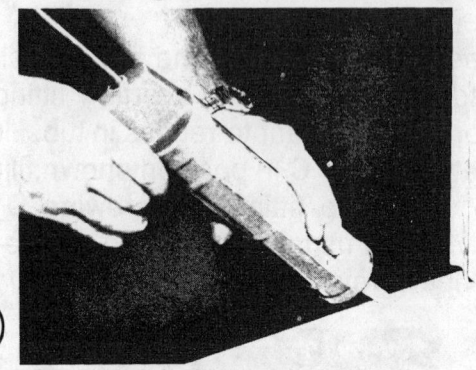

(175)

If framing on back and end walls is accessible, apply a continuous ⅛" bead of sealant in horizontal sealant channel. Place back wall in position and seat wall securely in alignment channel.

Apply a ⅛" bead of sealant to vertical sealant channel farthest from plumbing wall. Apply sealant to horizontal sealant channel on this end. Position this end wall and seat securely in both horizontal and vertical joints. Do the same for end wall on plumbing end.

Fasten corners with clips provided, Illus. 156. Use 4 clips in position indicated, Illus. 172. 2 clips 2" apart at center, one clip at top and bottom. Using a wet cloth wipe away excess sealant.

(176)

Exerting downward pressure, Illus. 176, nail wall with big head #6 galvanized roofing nails through holes at corners. If you question your nailing skill, use a piece of aluminum or hardboard to protect finish while nailing, Illus. 177.

Nail end panels in position. Start nailing at back wall. Make certain nails keep all joints tight. If nailing pulls a joint open, use shims. Drive nails into mid points of end panels. Nail back wall starting at center. Fasten vertical nailing flange at front. Wipe away excess sealant with a wet cloth. Fasten the tub apron nailing flange to studs starting at top and working down.

If back corners of recess are not accessible, do this. Install tub as previously described. Apply sealant where required and assemble end walls to back wall. Apply sealant to channel on tub. Position assembled wall sections on tub. Nail flanges as previously described.

Calk all openings around valve and spout with water resistant sealer, Illus. 178. Your tub-shower dealer sells a mildew resistant sealer that may be used to seal external seams.

(178)

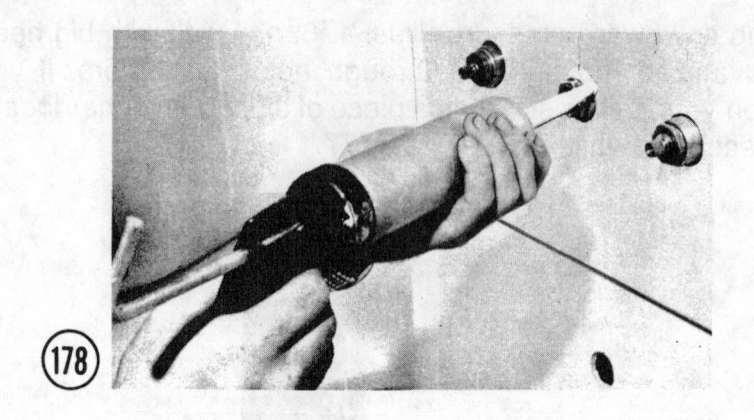

Because this material forms a skin fast, then becomes difficult to smooth, make a practice run before applying. Only apply an 8 or 10" length bead at a time. Wipe smooth with your finger, Illus. 179. Remove excess. If you apply masking tape to both sides of each joint, you can do a better job.

(179)

To finish installation from top of wall enclosure to ceiling, nail ⅛" furring strips to studs, Illus. 180. Apply water resistant sealer to top edge of wall. Apply ½" gypsum board with factory finished paper bound edge down against tub enclosure. Leave a ¼" sealant joint between edge of wallboard and enclosure. Nail wallboard to studs. Drive first course 1¼" above enclosure wall. Follow tub-shower manufacturer's directions to clean up unit. Apply controls, spout, shower head. Fasten supply lines to backerboard with pipe clamps or strap.

144

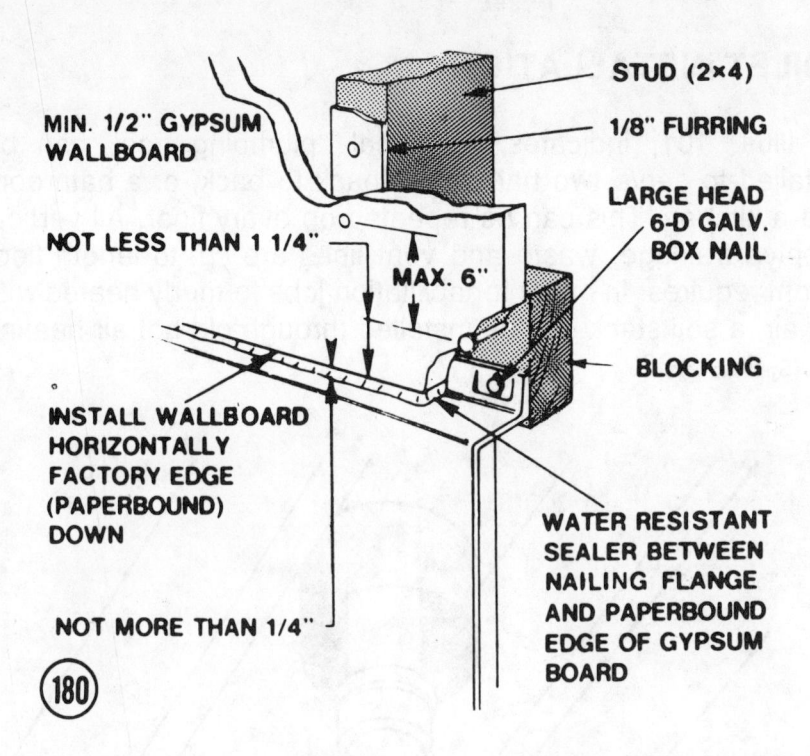

MIN. 1/2" GYPSUM WALLBOARD

STUD (2×4)

1/8" FURRING

NOT LESS THAN 1 1/4"

MAX. 6"

LARGE HEAD 6-D GALV. BOX NAIL

BLOCKING

INSTALL WALLBOARD HORIZONTALLY FACTORY EDGE (PAPERBOUND) DOWN

NOT MORE THAN 1/4"

WATER RESISTANT SEALER BETWEEN NAILING FLANGE AND PAPERBOUND EDGE OF GYPSUM BOARD

(180)

The tub opening is 57 ¾". Shower enclosures may be installed with self tapping screws, molly fasteners or toggle bolts.

To service a tub trap and diverter valve, install an inspection panel in wall backing up plumbing, Illus. 181. Dash lines indicate position of a removable plywood or hardboard panel. Screw or hinge panel in position. Cut panel full width of two studs by 26" high.

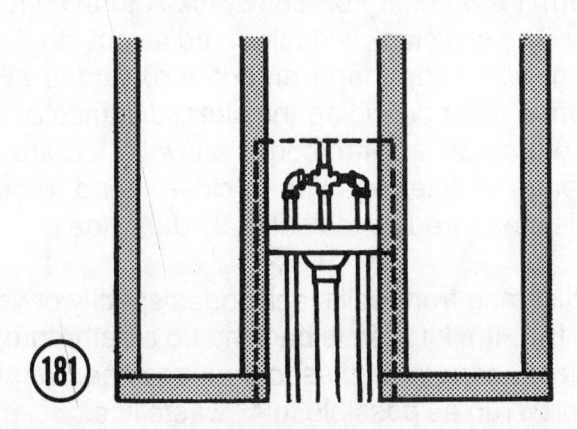

(181)

145

TOILET INSTALLATION

As Illus. 101, indicates, a typical "plumbing tree" can be installed to serve two bathrooms back to back, or a bathroom and a kitchen. This can be repeated on every floor. All vertical supply, drainage, waste and vent lines are cut to length floor height requires. In many rehabilitation jobs formerly heated with hot air, a soil stack can be installed through old hot air heating ducts, Illus. 182.

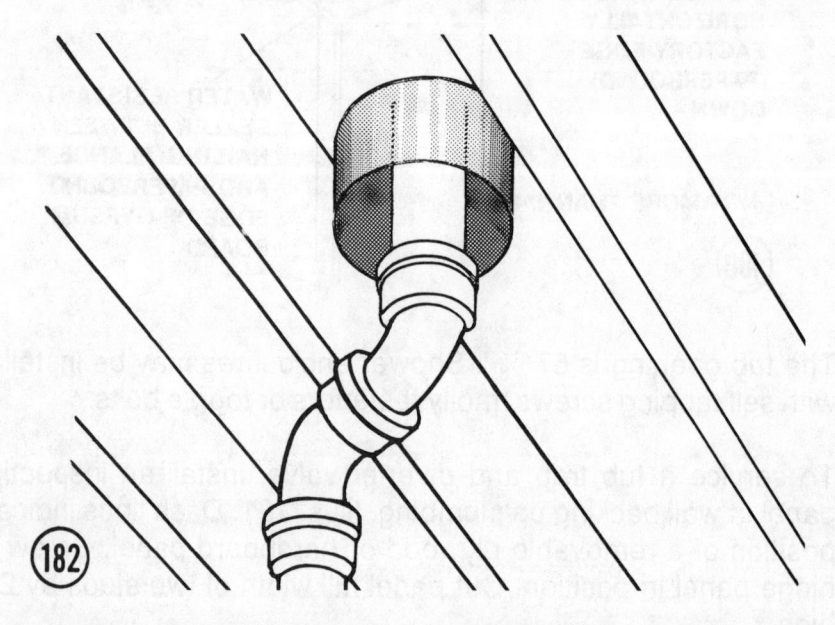

(182)

Most codes permit a 4" cast iron soil stack A to accommodate up to six toilets. The soil stack is designated a vent stack when it passes the point where drainage enters line. Codes allow the soil stack to vent a toilet providing the lineal distance of A, Illus. 100, is not more than 36". Some codes allow 72". Distance A is figured from center of inlet opening in closet bend to center of soil stack, and is measured as indicated by dash lines.

Position toilet distance from soil stack codes specify or vent it as shown in Illus. 183. If a kitchen is backing up a bathroom, run 2" or 1½" galvanized, copper or plastic drainage line from kitchen sink with as short a run as possible to 4" waste line.

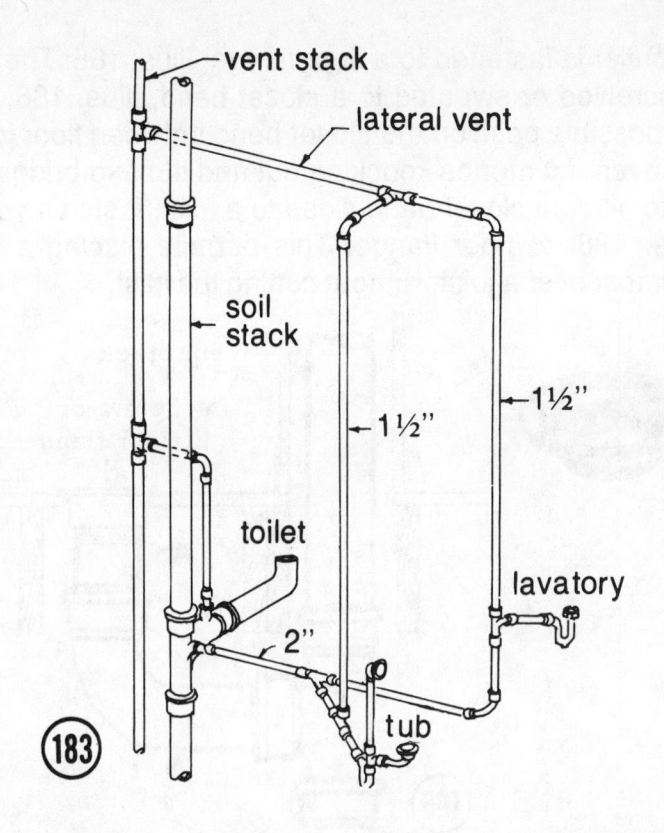

(183) Diagram showing vent stack, lateral vent, soil stack, toilet, lavatory, tub with 1½", 1½", and 2" pipe labels.

Most toilets are positioned distance from a finished wall the toilet manufacturer specifies. If ½ or ⅝" vinyl covered gypsum board is nailed to studs, and ceramic tile is applied, measure 13" from studs. Illus. 184 indicates 12" to center of waste outlet.

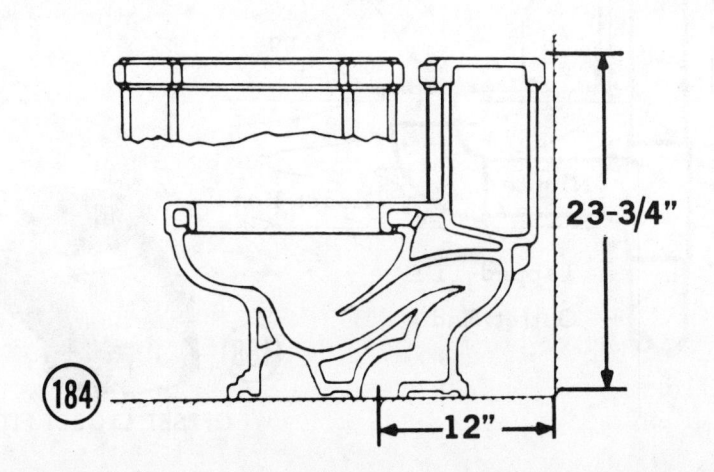

(184) Toilet side view: 23-3/4" height, 12" to center of waste outlet.

147

The toilet outlet is fastened to a floor flange, Illus. 185. The floor flange is screwed or sweated to a closet bend, Illus. 186, 187. Wherever possible position the closet bend between floor joists, Illus. 186, even if it means knocking out and moving bridging. If you need to place a closet bend close to a joist, fasten an offset fitting, Illus. 188, to floor flange. This permits placing a toilet close to, almost over a joist, without cutting the joist.

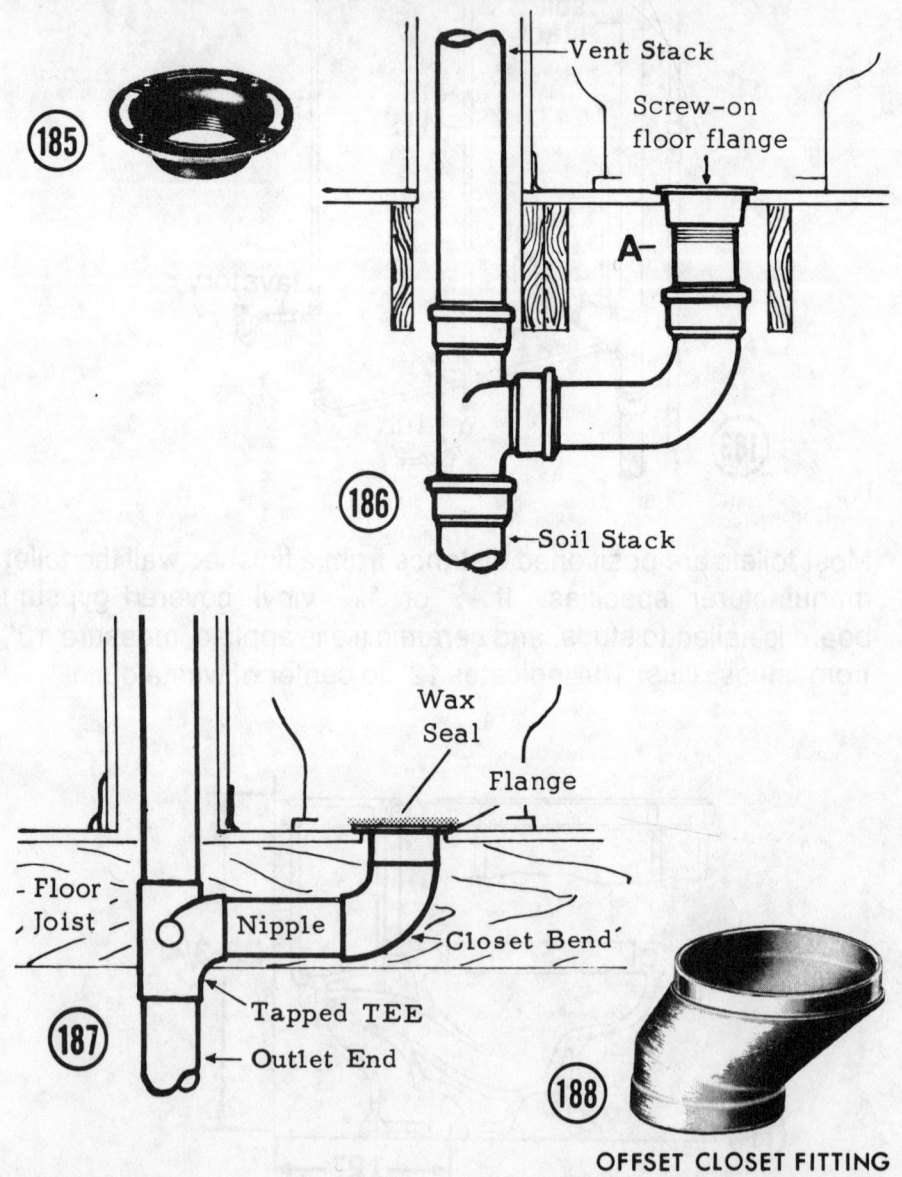

OFFSET CLOSET FITTING

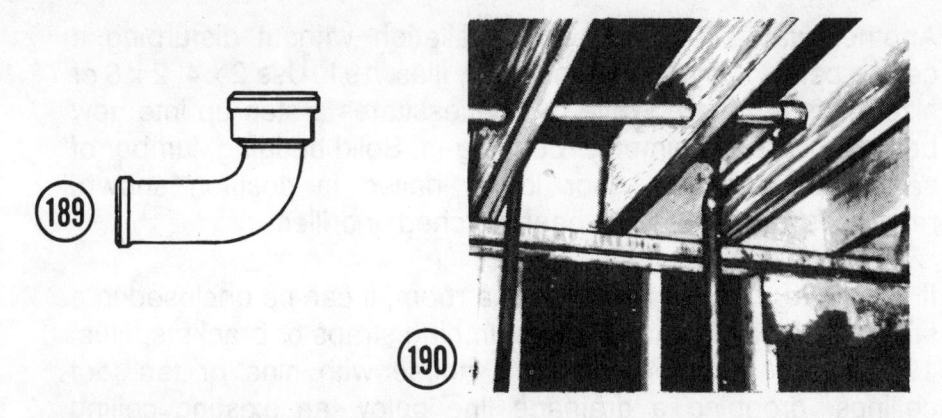

If closet bend is placed at right angle to floor joists, Illus. 186, use a nipple and a long ¼ Bend, Illus. 189, to soil line. While this doesn't present any problem in a first floor installation over a basement, it does present a problem on upper floors. If codes permit connecting a closet bend to 3" copper, or plastic, the 3" line can be installed through holes drilled in joists, Illus. 190.

Cast iron closet bends can be screwed to a floor flange, others can be calked with oakum and lead.

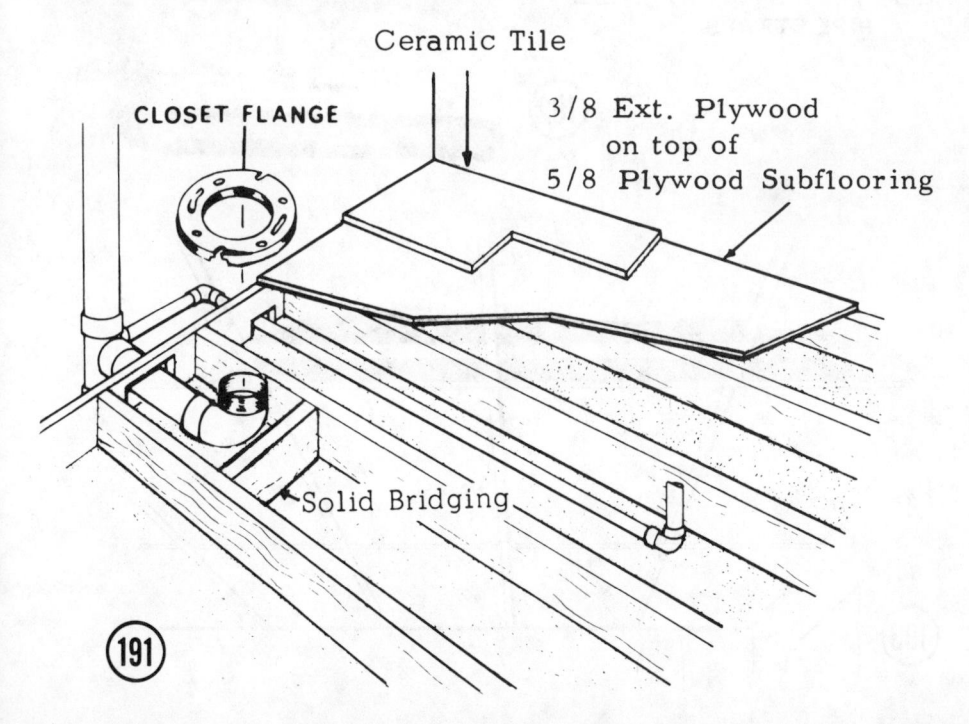

149

Another way of making an installation without disturbing a ceiling below is by raising the floor, Illus. 191. Use 2 x 4, 2 x 6 or size joists required. While this necessitates a step up into new bathroom, it does simplify roughing-in. Solid bridging, lumber of same dimension as floor joists, nailed in position shown, reinforces joists that have been notched or drilled.

If you have to run a line across a room, it can be enclosed in a storage wall and braced with plumbing straps or brackets, Illus. 192. If you are modernizing a house with nine or ten foot ceilings, dropping a drainage line below an existing ceiling simplifies installation. The pipe can then be concealed behind a suspended ceiling, Illus. 193.

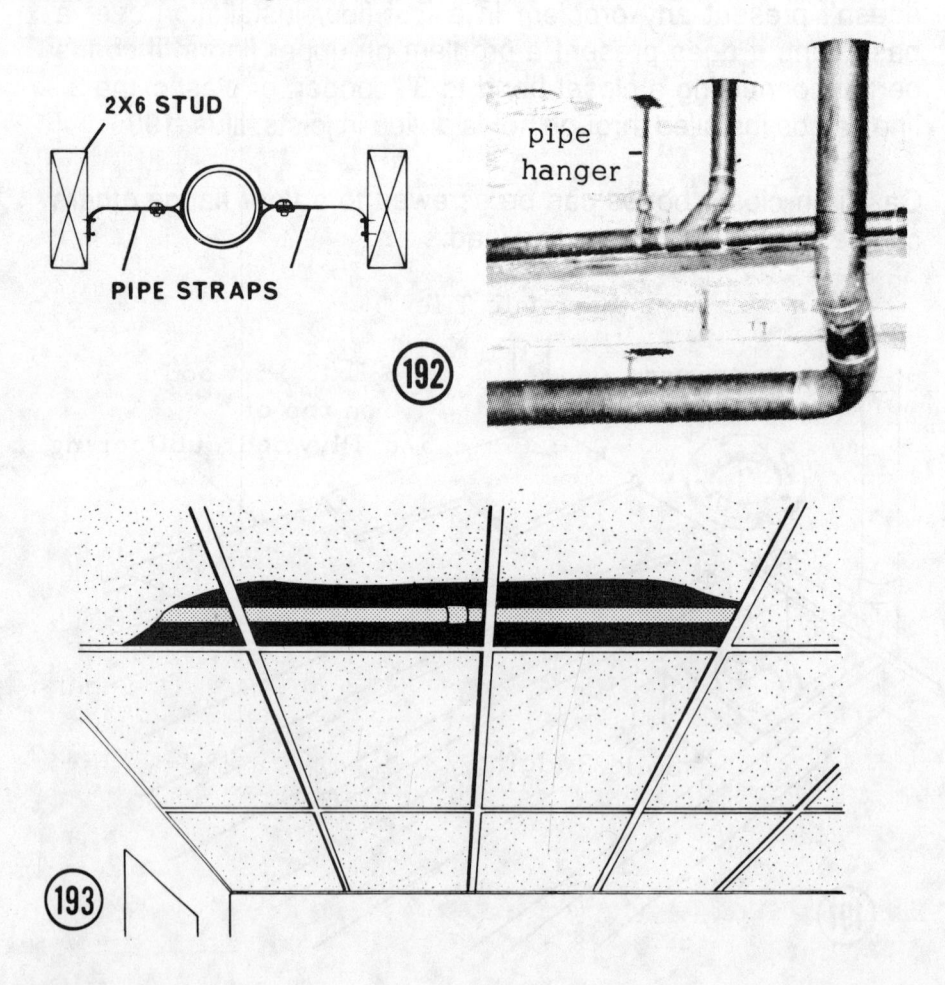

Complete kits containing fittings required for waste, drainage and vent lines are avalable in cast iron, galvanized, copper and plastic, Illus. 17, from many plumbing supply retailers.

Since every installation contains a different set of problems, it's difficult to estimate how much time it will take to rough-in. Study Illus. 99. Estimate how many fittings you require to run line A to toilet. Count the number of joints. Practice making no-hub or oakum and lead connections. Check time for making one, and you can judge how long it will take to rough-in all needed.

By plugging opening in a fitting with a large rag, your lines will be kept operable after each day's work.

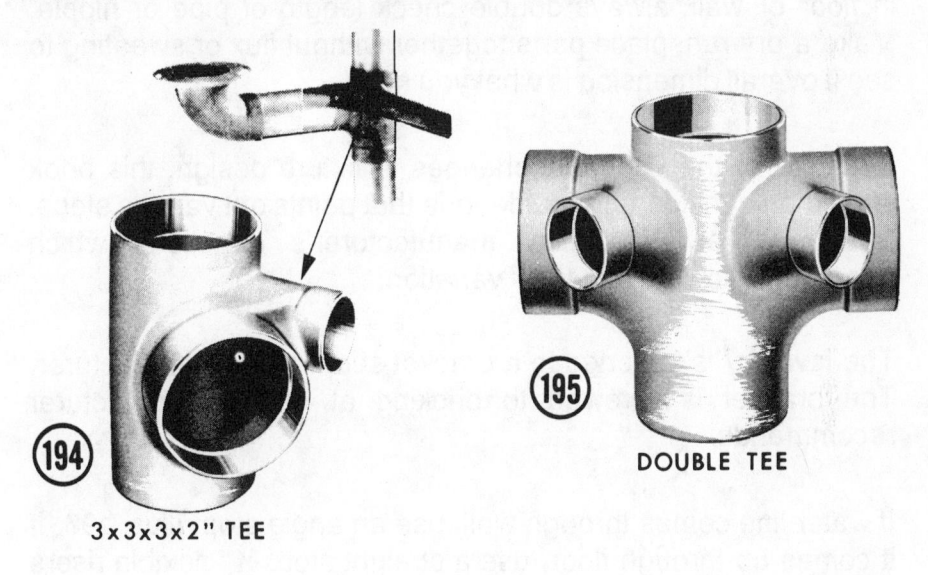

3x3x3x2" TEE

DOUBLE TEE

Fittings are available with side inlets, Illus. 194; on one, or both sides. To determine what hand fitting you require, place fitting in position shown. If the side inlet appears on the right, it's a right hand fitting. Illus. 194, shows a 3 x 3 x 3 x 2 tee with right hand inlet. Tees are available with two 1¼, 1½ or 2" side inlets, plus two 3" inlets for closet bends. With this one tee you can serve two toilets.

Illus. 195, shows a double T that serves two toilets and two 2" branch lines.

Fittings simplify joining various kinds of pipe, cast iron, galvanized, copper or plastic. Each kind can be connected to other size pipe with necessary adapters. Illus. 116 shows a 4 x 3" adapter. This is being used to connect 4" cast iron pipe hub to 3" copper. Adapters are available in various sizes from 4 x 3", 4 x 2", 4 x 1½", etc.

LAVATORY INSTALLATION

Due to the many variations that normally exist in roughing-in, i.e., thickness of lumber or plaster, bulge in plasterboard, slope in floor or wall, always double check length of pipe or nipple. Make a dry run, place parts together without flux or sweating to see if overall dimension is what you need.

Because of the continual changes in fixture design, this book should be considered a guide, one that points out various steps. You must always follow manufacturer's directions which frequently allow for a ½ to 1" variation.

The lavatory is fastened to a bracket supplied by manufacturer. The bracket is screwed to backing at height manufacturer recommends.

If water line comes through wall, use an angle stop, Illus. 196. If it comes up through floor, use a straight stop. ⅜" flexible risers are easy to bend.

Many lavatories contain a 1¼" drain and tailpiece, Illus. 196A, that connects to a 1½" P Trap with a compression fitting. Actually this fitting is no more than a 1½" threaded nut with a 1¼" hole in top. A nylon or lead compression ring, compresses when nut is tightened to make a watertight joint. This is called a 1½ x 1¼" compression joint adapter. The P Trap empties into 1½" drainage line that is also connected to a slip joint compression fitting.

⅜" riser

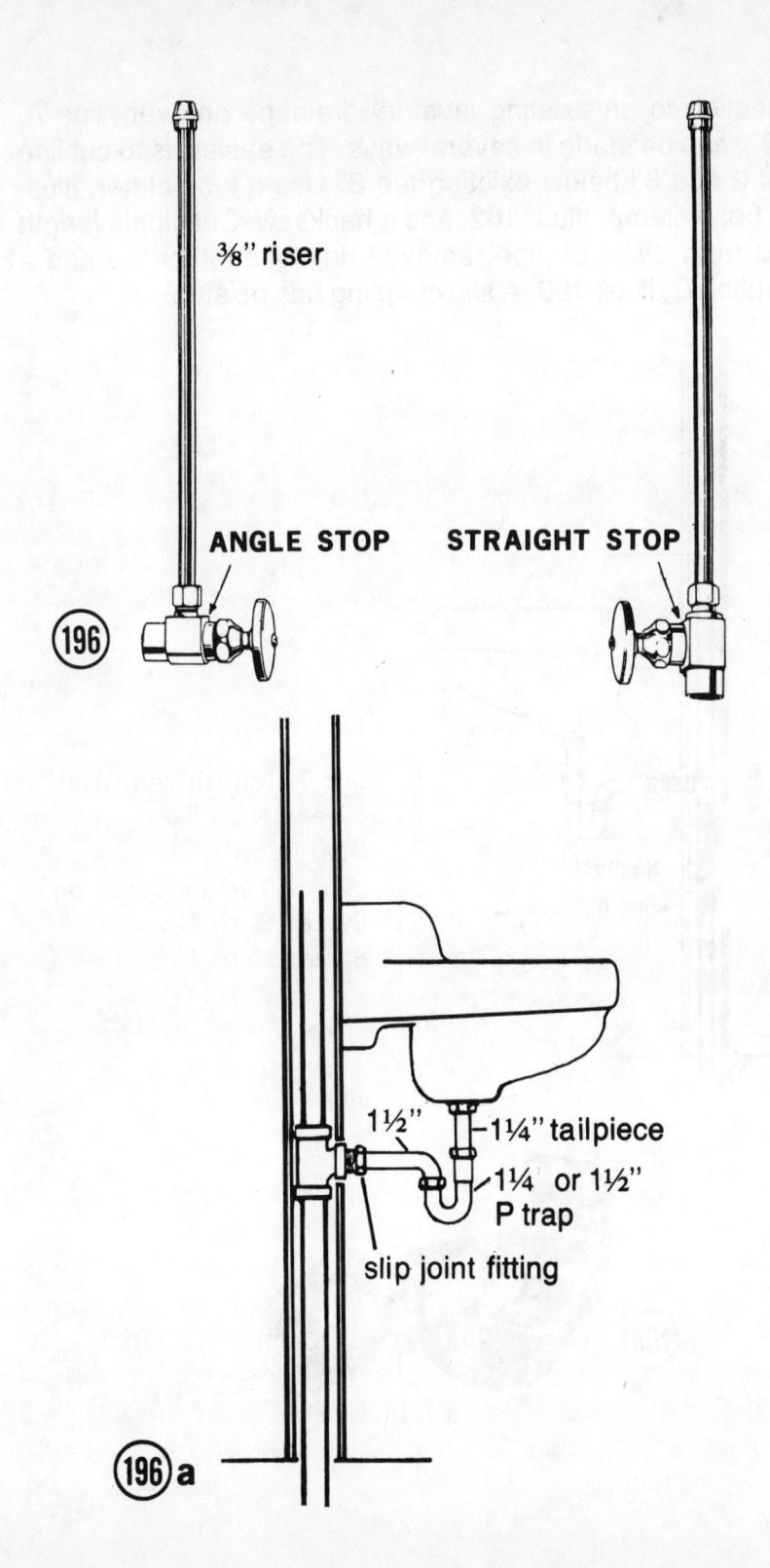

ANGLE STOP   STRAIGHT STOP

(196)

1½" —1¼" tailpiece
      1¼ or 1½"
      P trap
slip joint fitting

(196)a

153

A connection to an existing lavatory drainage and vent line A, Illus. 197, can be made in several ways. The easiest is to cut line A about 2 and 8" below existing tee B. Use a tube cutter, Illus. 198, or hose clamp, Illus. 162, and a hacksaw. Cut nipple length required from piece of pipe removed. Install another tee and a slip coupling C, Illus. 199. A slip coupling has no stop.

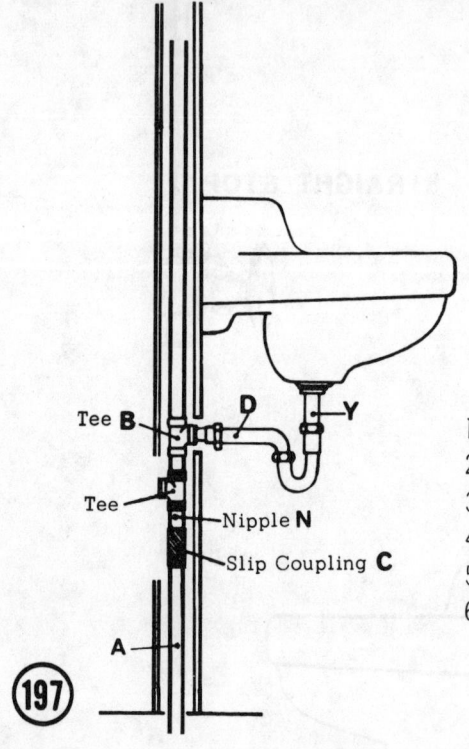

1. Cut N length required
2. Sweat N to Tee
3. Slip C on A
4. Sweat Tee in position
5. Sweat C to N
6. Sweat C to A

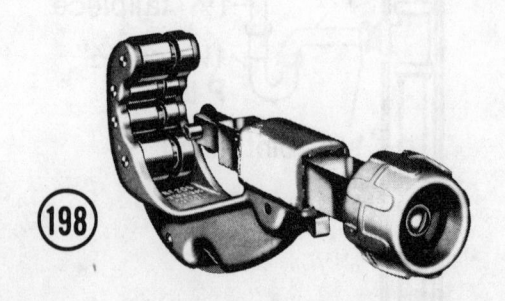

154

1-1/2"
C
|← 2-1/4" →|
Copper to Copper

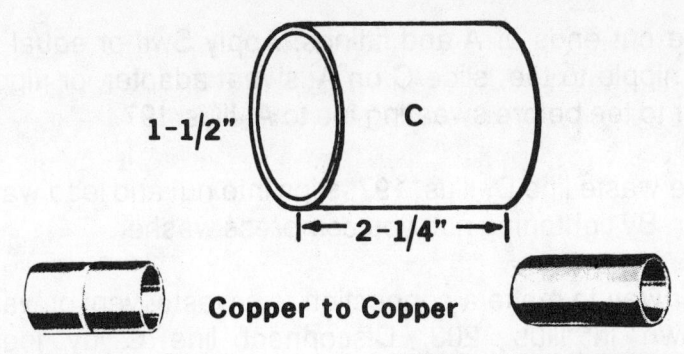

COUPLING WITH STOP   **COUPLING WITHOUT STOP**

(199)

If necessary to extend connection outside of finished wall, cut a nipple to length required, Illus. 200. Sweat tee to nipple. Sweat a coupling with slip joint connection to nipple. This permits connecting chrome or brass pipe to fixture drain.

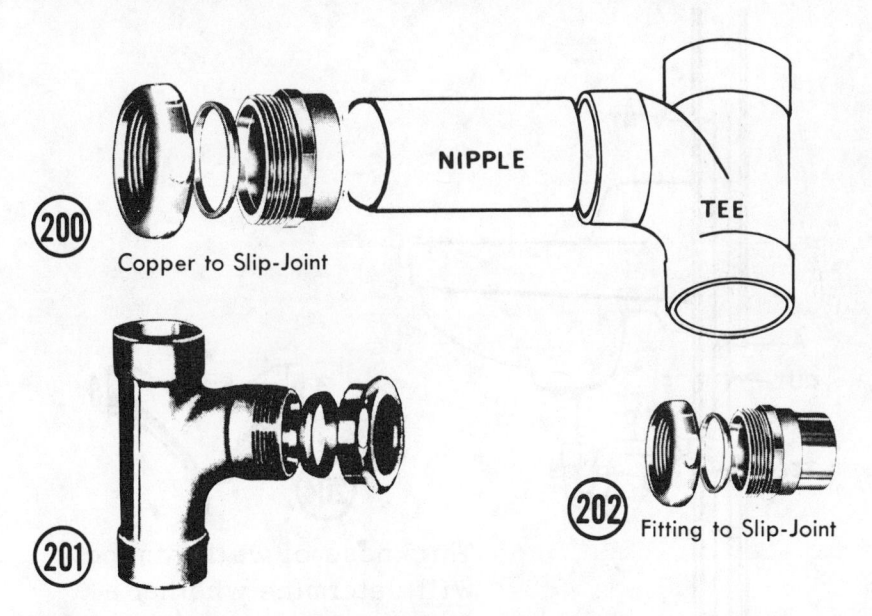

(200) Copper to Slip-Joint

NIPPLE   TEE

(201)

(202) Fitting to Slip-Joint

You can also use a trap tee, Illus. 201, or a regular tee with a fitting slip joint adapter, Illus. 202. In this case the adapter is sweated to tee. These alternates are mentioned because your retailer might be out of stock on one item and an unskilled sales clerk won't known about substitutes.

Prepare cut ends of A and fittings. Apply Swif or equal solder. Sweat nipple to tee, slide C on A, sweat adapter, or nipple and adapter to tee before sweating tee to A, Illus. 197.

Chrome waste line D, Illus. 197, slips into nut and lead washer in adapter. By tightening nut, you compress washer.

Another way to make a connection to a waste, vent or water line is shown in Illus. 203. Disconnect line C by loosening compression nuts B. Cut line A 6" above tee. Apply heat and remove tee, nipple and/or slip joint adapter from tee. Prepare ends of line A for solder. Install a Double Long Turn T-Y, Illus. 204. While this fitting will project beyond most plasterboard walls, use a nipple if same is required. Join line with a slip coupling and nipple as shown, Illus. 205.

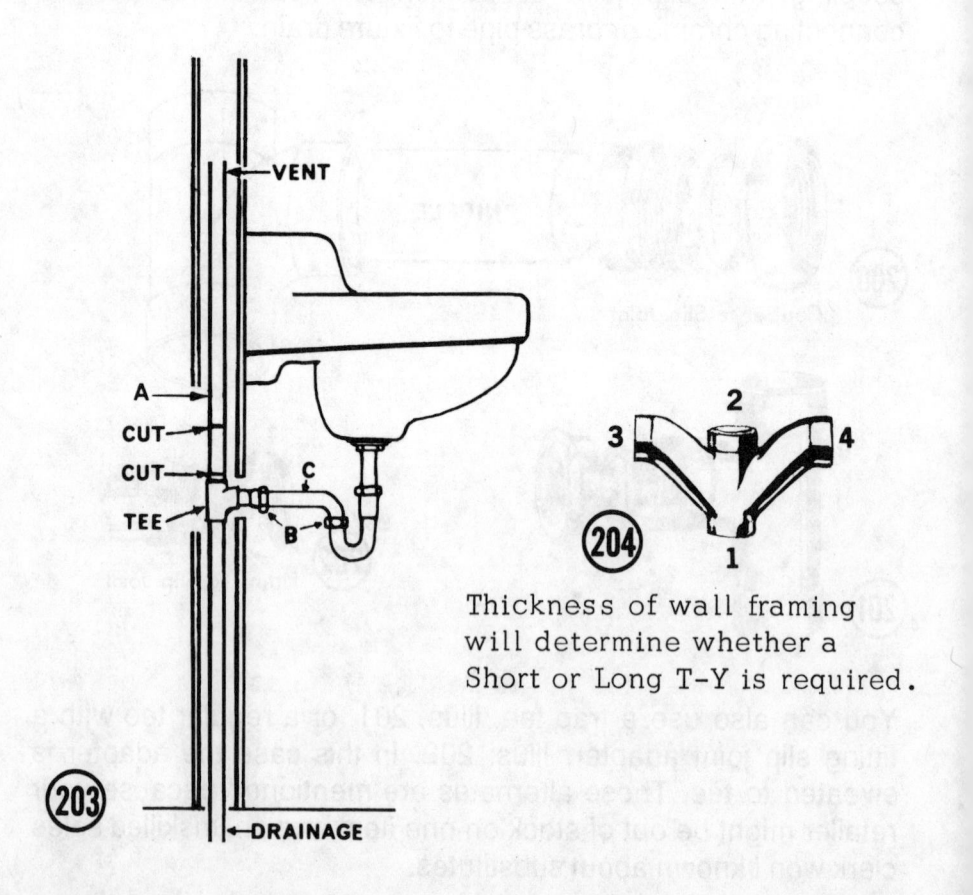

Thickness of wall framing will determine whether a Short or Long T-Y is required.

NIPPLE

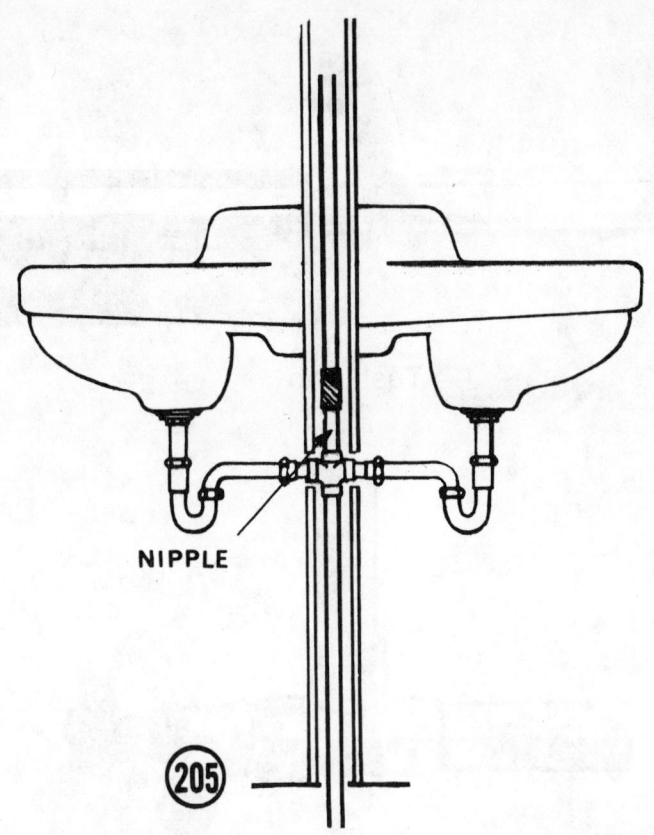

(205)

Using a tee, slip coupling, and a nipple, you can make a connection to water, vent or drainage line.

After installing waste, vent and supply lines, make a test. This requires temporarily plugging end of all openings with a cap, Illus. 206. Both screw or sweat caps are available at your plumbing supply dealer. Attach a male or female boiler drain, Illus. 207, anywhere to new line. Attach a hose and watch for water or air leaks. You can also rent an air tank with a pressure gauge. If it holds, you have done an excellent job. If it fails, use soap and water to find leaky joint. Heat joint to take it apart. Remember to dry, clean and prepare parts as you would any new connection.

Most fixture manufacturers supply fittings, nipple and stop valve. Apply Tape Dope to threads of nipple and fasten into tee. Screw stop valve to nipple and ⅜" flexible riser to tank.

(206) Test Cap

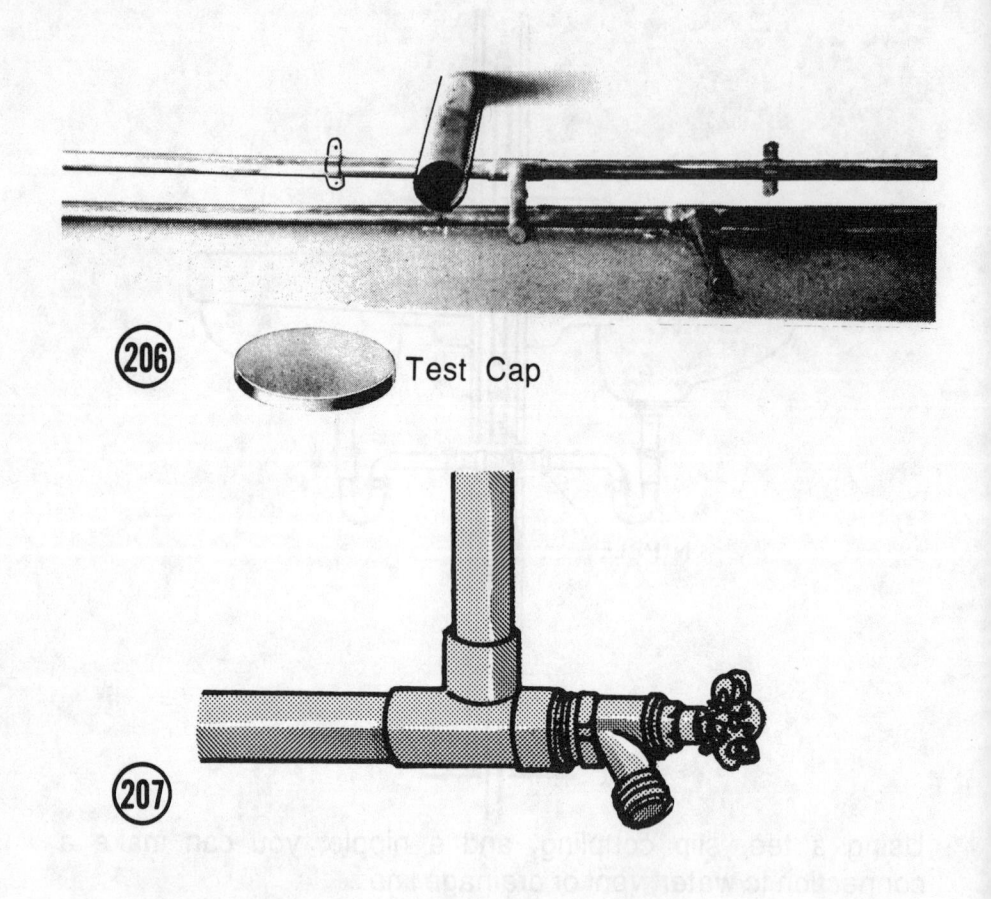

(207)

Manufacturers usually pack directions with their fixture. These provide exact roughing-in dimensions, size holes to drill, distance lavatory stands off floor on legs supplied, etc. If possible, borrow and study installation directions before buying the fixture. In this way you have a chance to find out everything you need to know.

If you want to make more than a small bend in ⅜, ½, even ¾" tubing, use a tube bender, Illus. 162. Just insert tubing in flexible size bender pipe requires.

To connect an additional lavatory alongside an existing one, use a three way stop valve, Illus. 208. This has a ½" supply inlet that feeds two ⅜" flexible risers.

158

(208) ½" inlet — ⅜" to fixture — ⅜" to fixture

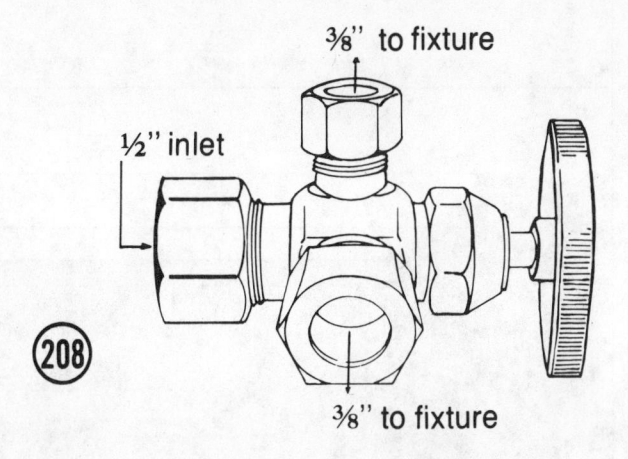

To supply a lavatory, or other fixture, at some distance from an existing one, use ⅜" copper tubing and flare fittings. To make a flare fitting, cut tubing length required. Remove burrs with a knife. Slip a flare nut A, Illus. 209, over end of tubing. The end of tube is placed flush with top face of flaring tool. The flaring tool handle is screwed down to make flare. When end is flared, the nut is fastened to fitting required. A wide selection of flare fittings are available.

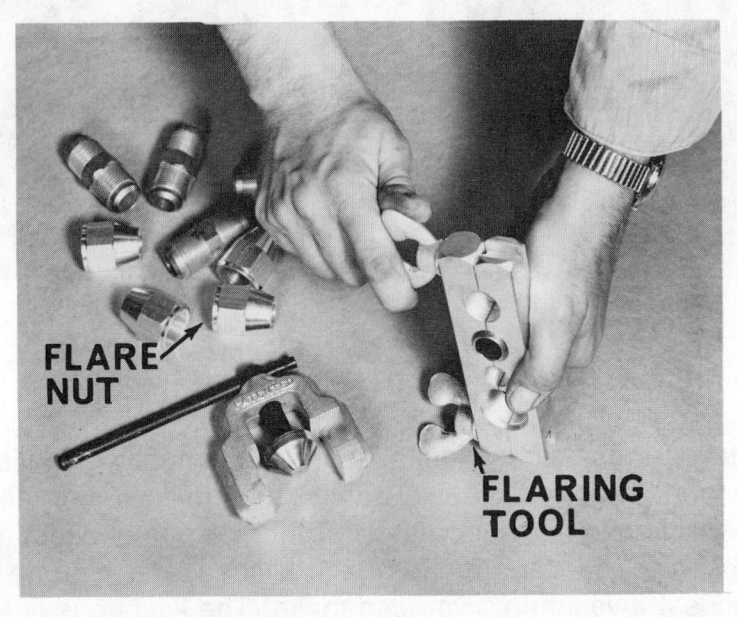

(209) FLARE NUT — FLARING TOOL

TO MODERNIZE A KITCHEN

To transform a kitchen into a labor-saving machine, that's fun to use and a delight to live with, is not difficult nor need be expensive. No special creative skill or carpentry experience is required to plan and modernize a kitchen, and it's one of the soundest investments you can make. The kitchen is one room that sells, or stops the sale of more houses, than any other.

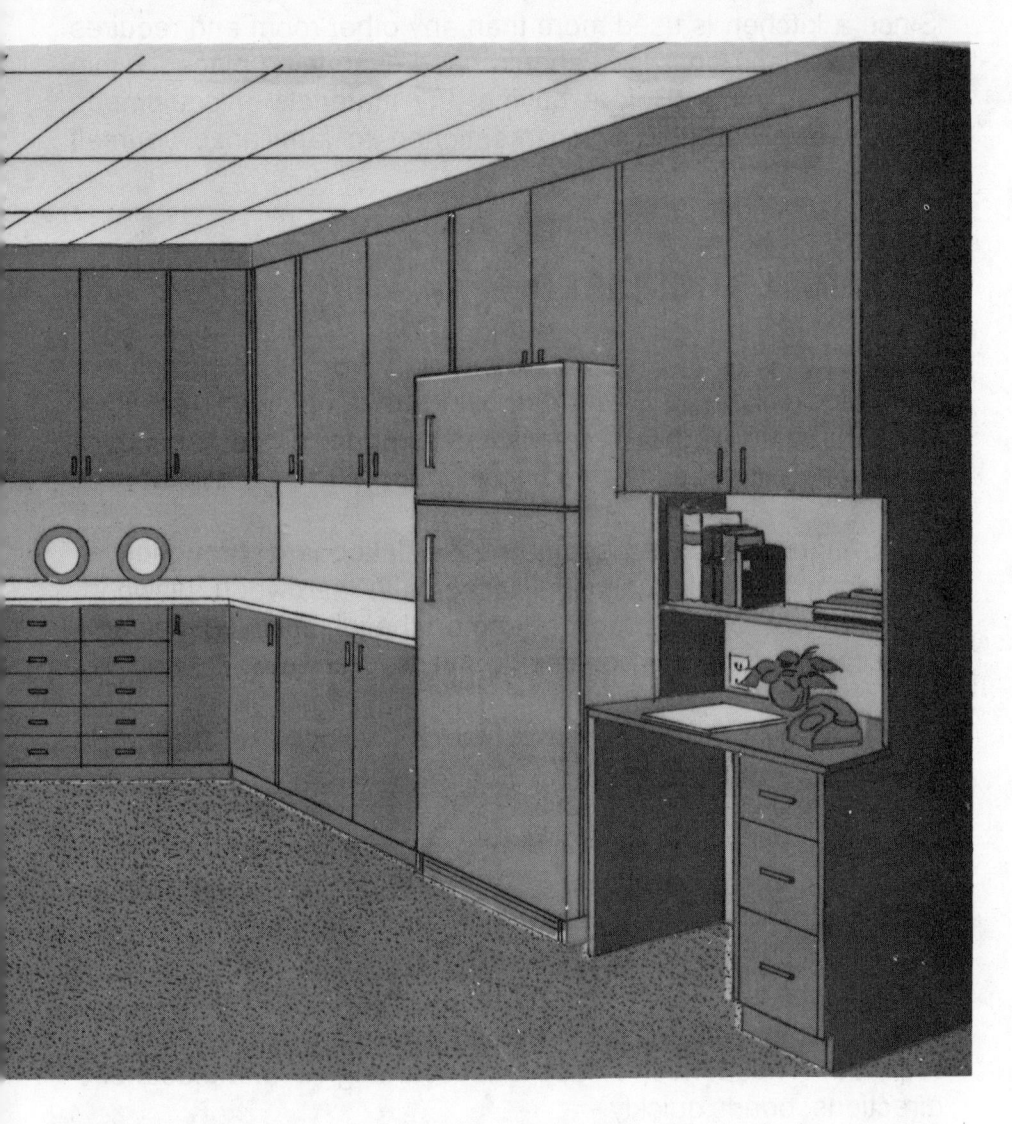

Since kitchens vary in size, shape, location of waste and supply lines, windows and doors, place a check mark alongside those paragraphs and illustrations that refer to your kitchen. This will permit ready reference when you start actual work. While this book contains many of the basic modernization plans and procedures described in Book # 658, How to Build Kitchen Cabinets, it differs in cabinet design and construction. The cabinets built according to procedure outlined in this book can be painted or constructed with prefinished hardwood plywood.

Since a kitchen is used more than any other room and requires more time and energy, it should have everything placed within convenient reach. Before buying any materials or equipment, note each illustration when mentioned to familiarize yourself with general procedure.

MATERIALS REQUIRED.

Base and wall cabinets can be built from ¾" thick fir or hardwood veneered plywood or flakeboard, or a combination of ½" flakeboard and ¼" prefinished plywood. Since flakeboard does not warp, we suggest using it for doors and countertops.

If you plan on painting cabinets, use flakeboard throughout. If you want to build cabinets faced with hardwood plywood, cabinets that require practically no on the job finishing, and only an occasional waxing, you can do it in several ways.

   1. Buy ¾" prefinished hardwood plywood, or hardwood veneered flakeboard, or

   2. Use ½" flakeboard with ¼" prefinished hardwood plywood. While this takes more time, it costs considerably less for materials.

New panel adhesives permit bonding ¼" prefinish to ½" flakeboard with professional results assured. No nails or skill is required. The adhesive, applied according to manufacturer's directions, bonds quickly.

A paper thin matching wood veneer tape, available at your plywood dealer, can be glued to all exposed ¾" edges. Where a ¼" prefinished plywood edge is exposed, this can be finished with matching Putty-Stik.

Since flakeboard does not warp, we recommend its use for doors and countertops that are to be covered with plastic laminate.

The key to building cabinets comparable in quality to those installed by custom cabinet installers, lies in using the same materials in the same manner.

SELECT THE PLAN THAT SUITS YOUR NEEDS

Illus. 210—A kitchen along one wall.

Illus. 211—A kitchen on facing walls.

Illus. 212—An L-shaped kitchen.

Illus. 213—The popular U.

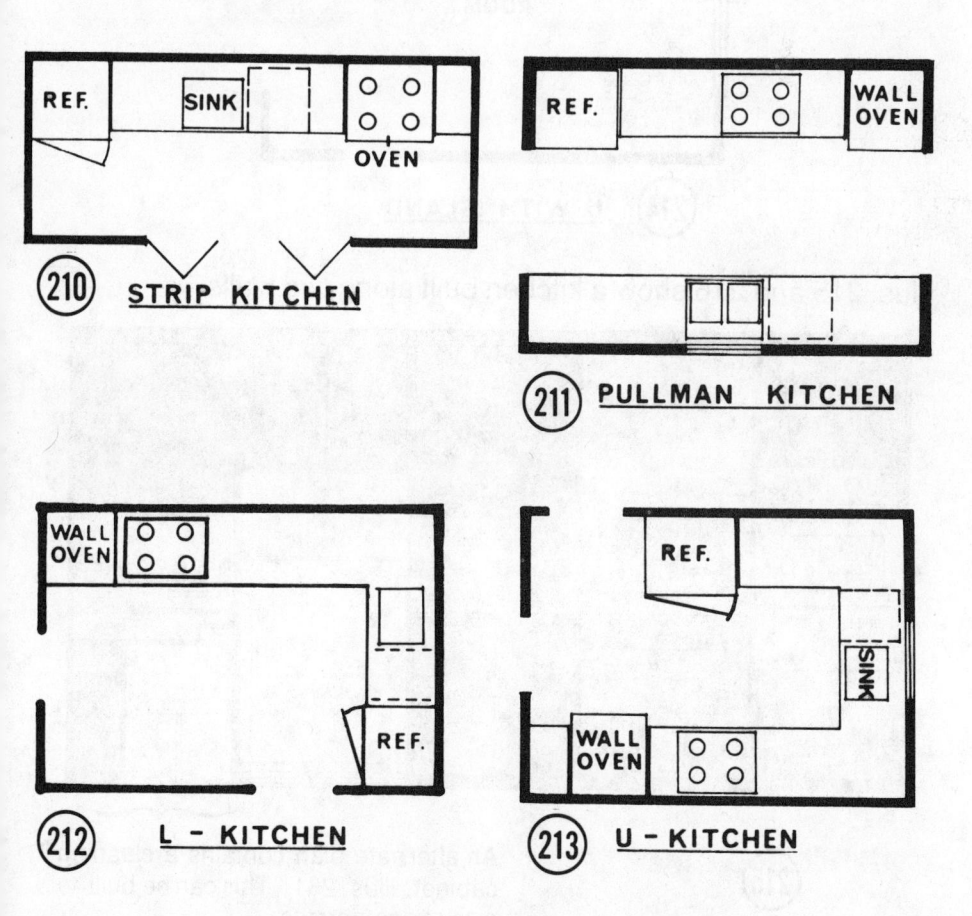

(210) **STRIP KITCHEN**

(211) **PULLMAN KITCHEN**

(212) **L - KITCHEN**

(213) **U - KITCHEN**

Illus. 214—Another U with island.

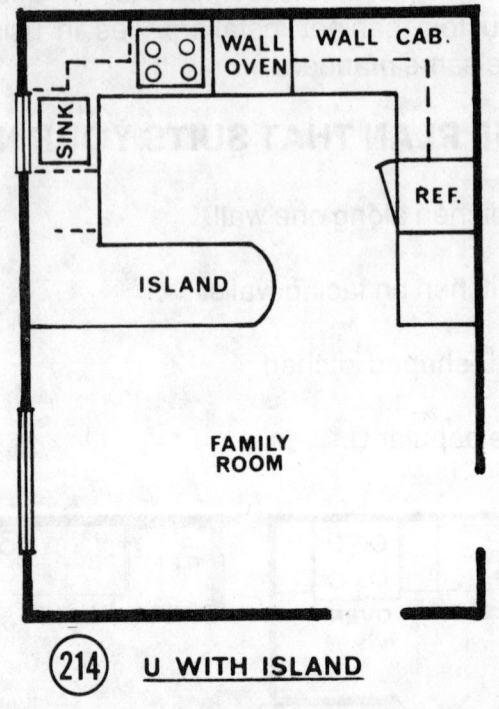

(214) U WITH ISLAND

Illus. 215 and 216 show a kitchen built along two walls.

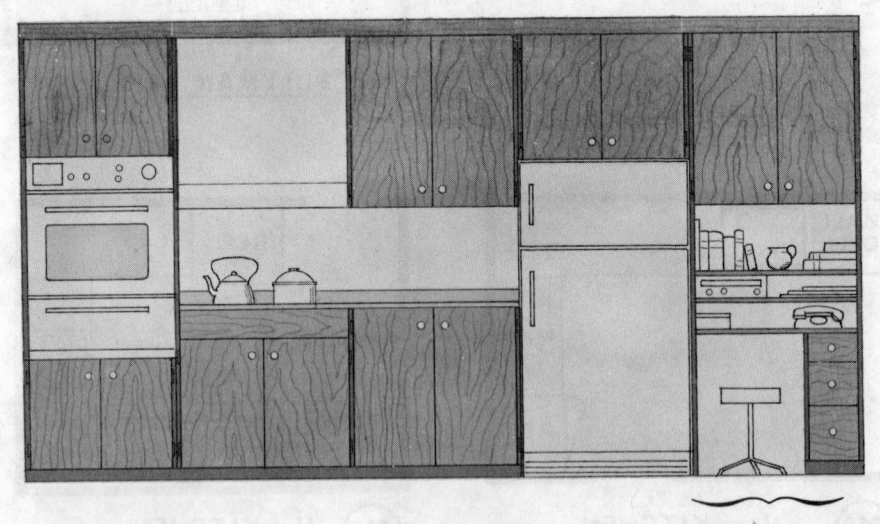

(215) An alternate plan contains a cleaning cabinet, Illus. 281 This can be built to size space permits.

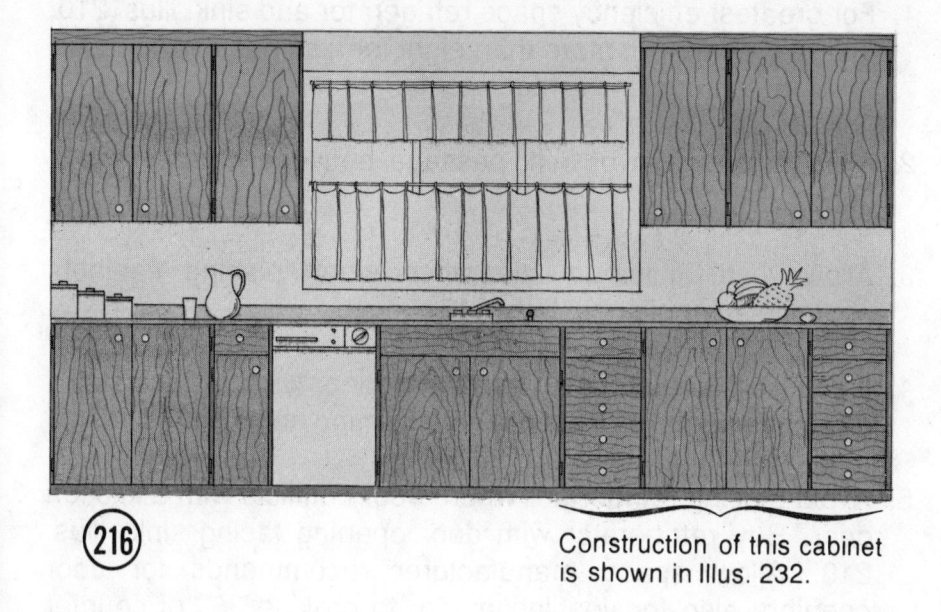

(216) Construction of this cabinet is shown in Illus. 232.

A gas or electric wall oven can be installed in corner, with a counter range adjacent. If space permits, a desk can be placed in position shown. Illus. 216 shows facing wall of this room with sink in position indicated.

If you want to build a kitchen along one wall, Illus. 215, the desk could be eliminated. The refrigerator would be moved into this area, the sink would be installed in counter. Counter space should be provided on both sides of sink and between range and oven.

BASIC PLANNING

When building a kitchen along two facing walls, allow a center aisle of not less than four foot width.

Proper distance between appliances is important for two reasons; when too far apart you take too many unnecessary steps; when too close, there isn't enough counter space. If you relocate refrigerator, sink and range, follow these recommendations:

1. For greatest efficiency space refrigerator and sink, Illus. 210, four feet apart, not more than eight feet; sink and range, four to six feet; range and refrigerator four to ten feet.

2. Allow a minimum of 3 ft. passage between cabinet and a door.

3. Allow 4 ft. minimum clearance when placing cabinets opposite an appliance, Illus. 213.

4. If you want to remove an existing door or window, or install a new one in another location, note framing on page 75.

5. Avoid placing refrigerator where door conflicts with a kitchen door. Buy refrigerator with door opening facing sink, Illus. 210. Allow space manufacturer recommends for door opening, also for ventilation. Try to provide 36" of counter space on door opening side of refrigerator, Illus. 214 (Never less than 15").

6. Provide counter space on both sides of sink and range.

7. While sinks are traditionally placed beneath a window, a counter under window is just as handy. Never place range beneath a window.

BASE AND WALL CABINET MEASUREMENTS

Base cabinets are 24" in depth, Illus. 217, while countertop measures 25". Allow 15" to 18" between wall cabinet and countertop. Follow range manufacturer's recommendations when placing cabinets over range.

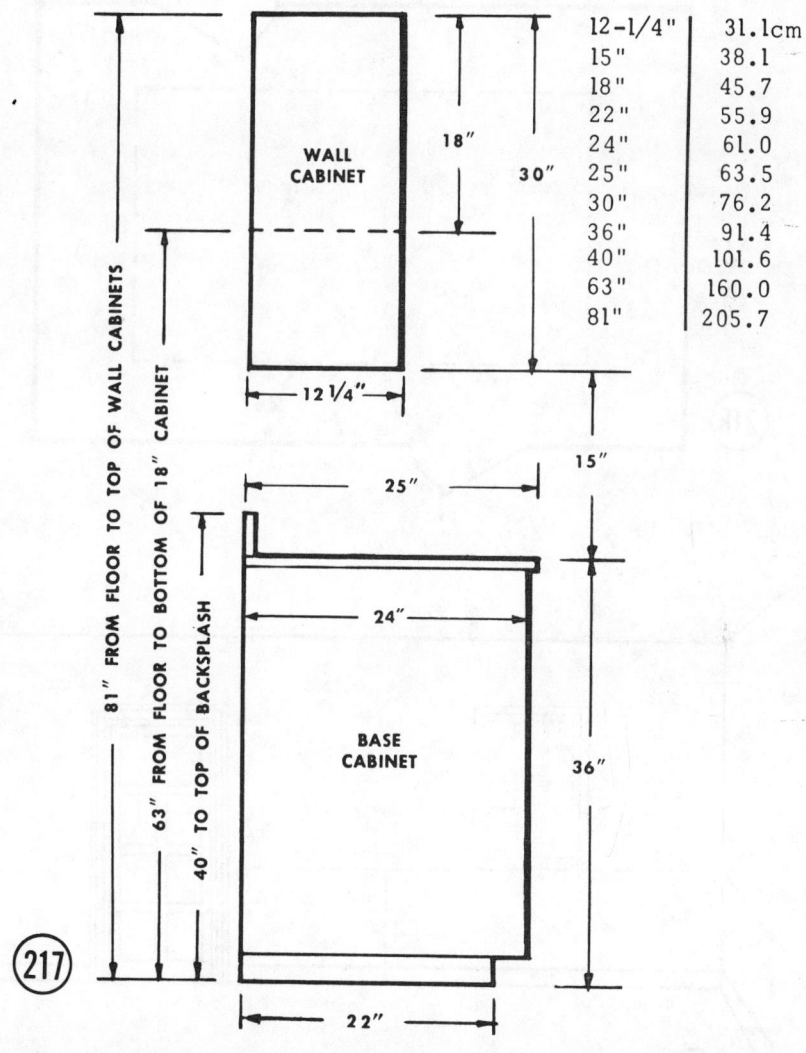

12-1/4"	31.1cm
15"	38.1
18"	45.7
22"	55.9
24"	61.0
25"	63.5
30"	76.2
36"	91.4
40"	101.6
63"	160.0
81"	205.7

217

While most base cabinets, sinks and cabinet ranges stand 36" high, some manufacturers build these 30" to 32". This is a more convenient height for a small person. Install countertop range and wall oven at height manufacturer recommends.

Draw a rough floor plan of your kitchen on any piece of paper, Illus. 218. Draw a double line to indicate windows. Indicate doors and direction they swing. Now measure entire kitchen, Illus. 219. Indicate each measurement. Take measurements at counter height (three feet from floor).

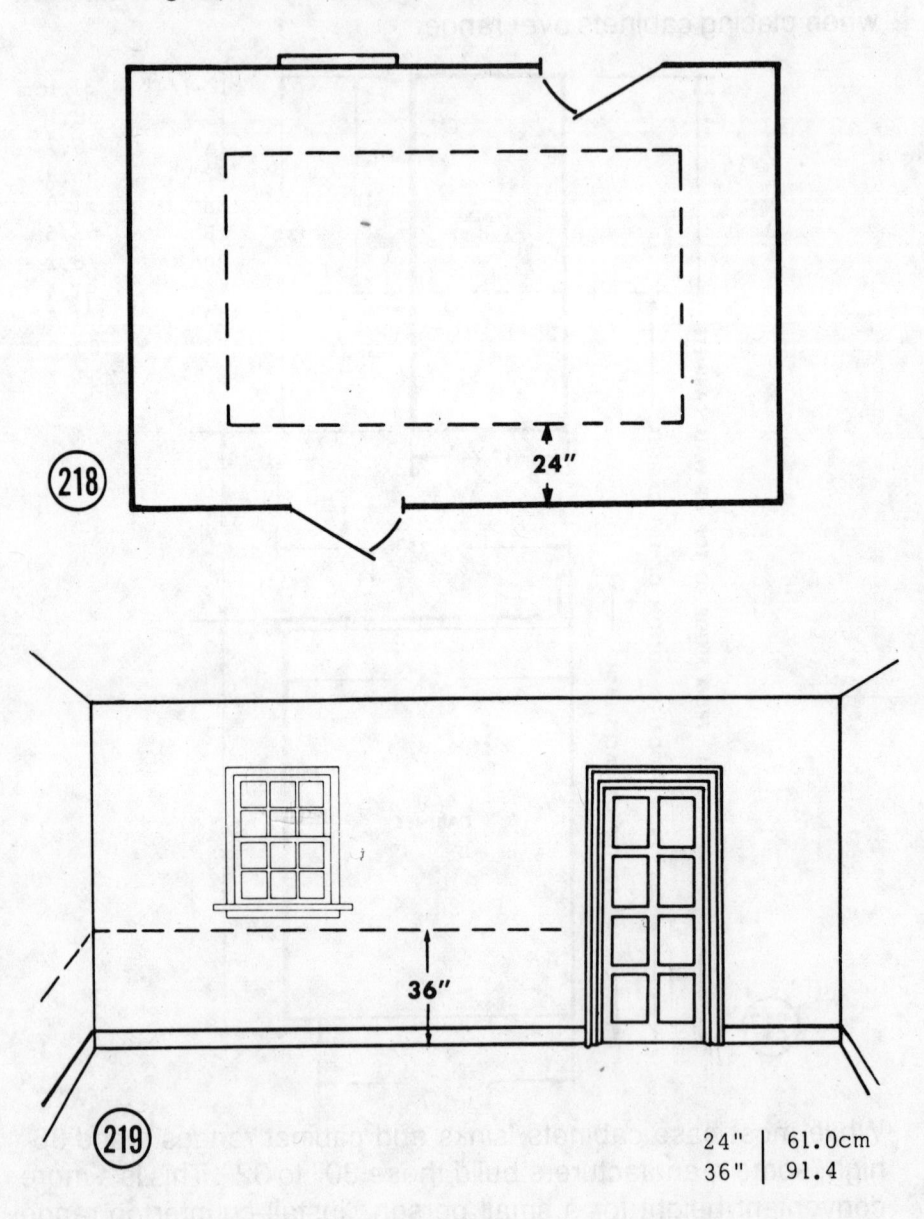

(218)

24"

(219)

| 24" | 61.0cm |
| 36" | 91.4 |

168

Measure wall from a corner to edge of casing—B, Illus. 220. Measure across window (or door)—C. If you don't plan on relocating a range, sink or refrigerator, measure space from corner to each piece of equipment. These measurements are needed to figure actual area available for cabinets and equipment.

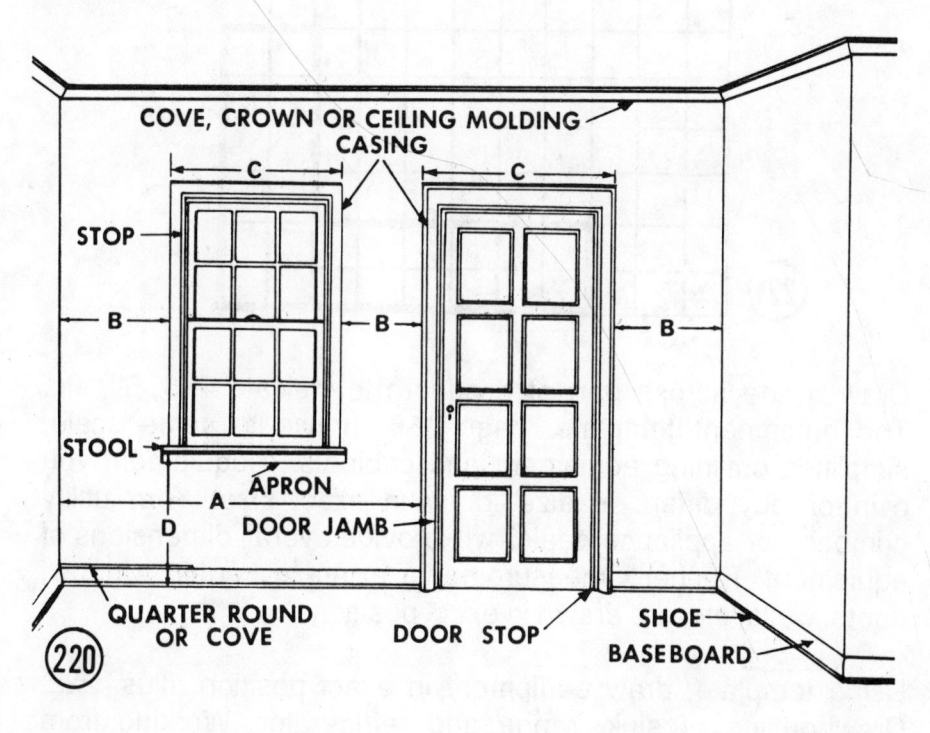

Mark size and location of sink, range, refrigerator, radiator, floor or wall registers, chimney, and other protrusions. A radiator and register can be concealed without impairing its efficiency.

Counters can be cut to fit around a chimney, pipe, etc. If a new sink is to be installed under a window, check distance D, Illus. 220.

Window sill should be at least 40"; if it's less than 40", it's still possible to install equipment by following directions. Note Illus. 228, 229. Next double check all measurements; does B plus C equal A?

Draw floor plan on ruled paper, Illus. 221, page 255. Allow each square to indicate one foot of floor space. If a wall measures 12 ft., the same wall drawn on ruled paper would be 12 squares.

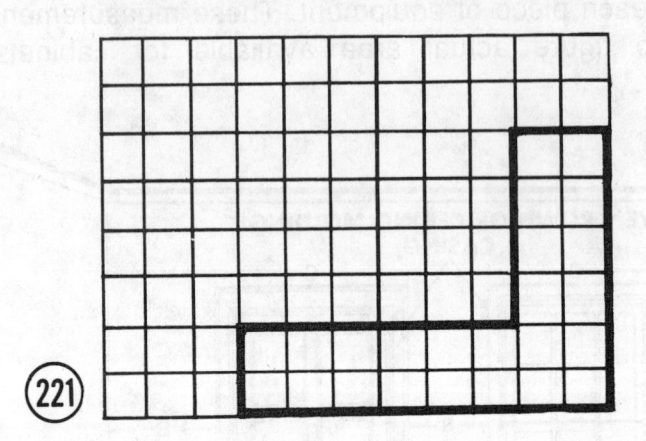

(221)

Draw a line across part of a square to indicate 4, 5, 6", etc. The equipment template, page 256, drawn to same scale, simplifies outlining equipment and cabinets. If equipment you own or buy differs in size, draw in exact size. Your utility company or appliance dealer will provide overall dimensions of equipment. Recheck measurements to make certain window, doors, walls, etc. are drawn in exact position.

Using template, draw equipment in exact position, Illus. 222. Draw outline of sink, range and refrigerator. Working from corner of room, fill in space with base cabinets.

To further check measurements, add width of each cabinet. Total should equal space available. You can build base and wall cabinets to size required by following directions on page 178.

If you plan on installing a new sink, dishwasher, disposal or large hot water heater, or moving present sink to a new location, get estimates from two reliable plumbers. Show the plumber a floor plan so he can estimate exact amount of material required. Ask him to price materials separately from labor. In this way you will know how much he's charging for materials, and for labor. It will also encourage you to do more of the work.

(222)

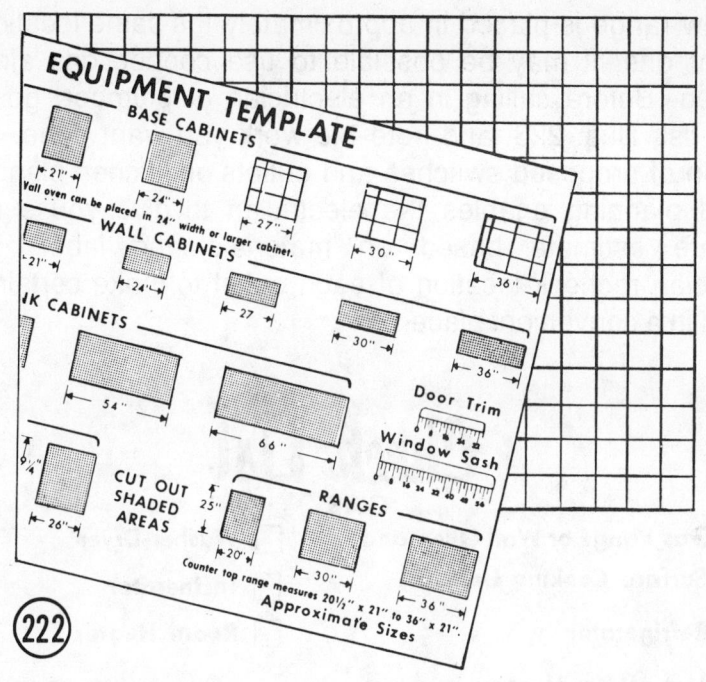

If plumber suggests moving sink slightly to right or left to save fittings or labor, follow his suggestion providing it does not interfere with the efficiency of your plan. If a dishwasher, and/or washing machine is to be installed, ask the plumber if your present hot water heater and waste line is adequate. If a disposal is to be installed, call the local building inspector for information concerning size of waste line local codes require, before buying equipment.

ADD NEEDED OUTLETS

A modern kitchen requires many wall outlets, ample lighting, separate service lines for automatic dishwasher and disposal. A heavier line is required for an electric range. Moving a range to a new location need not be costly. Actual expense can be figured by cost of additional gas pipe or electric cable, plus time required to install. In most cases a new range, wall oven, refrigerator, clothes dryer, large hot water heater, or furnace complete with air conditioning, can be connected to your present service lines. Read Book #694, Electrical Repairs Simplified, for additional information.

If a new range is placed in approximately the same location as present one, it may be possible to use connections already installed. Before calling in an electrician or plumber, go over check list, Illus. 223, and note the work you want done. Mark location of proposed switches and outlets on kitchen plan. This careful planning enables the electrician to give you a more accurate estimate based on materials and labor. Have electrician recheck location of each outlet to make certain it is placed in a convenient place.

Check List

GAS

- ☐ Gas Range or Wall Oven and Surface Cooking Unit
- ☐ Refrigerator
- ☐ Hot Water Heater
- ☐ Washer-Dryer
- ☐ Incinerator
- ☐ Room Heater

ELECTRIC

- ☐ Kitchen-overhead light
- ☐ Light over Sink
- ☐ Lights under Wall Cabinets
- ☐ Island Outlet
- ☐ Outdoor flood light
- ☐ Ventilating fan
- ☐ Air Conditioner *

Wall Outlets for:

- ☐ Refrigerator
- ☐ Washing Machine *
- ☐ Home Freezer *
- ☐ Clock
- ☐ Coffee Maker, Knife Sharpener, Mixer, Toaster, Radio, and similar kitchen appliances.

110 volt separate circuit wiring for:

- ☐ Dishwasher   ☐ Disposer   ☐ Ironer

220 volt, 3 wire service for:

- ☐ Washer-Dryer   ☐ Electric Range or Wall Oven and Surface Cooking Unit

(223)

*Separate circuit advisable

If you plan on installing an air conditioner, be sure a separate line is included.

Visit your local utility company. Tell them what new appliances you plan on adding. They can advise whether your present service line is adequate. Remember—additional equipment adds a heavier load. Never overload.

Call the telephone company. Ask them to run a line to your kitchen.

BUY APPLIANCES

Take your plan to an established appliance dealer. While appliances can be purchased at almost any price, the cheapest is seldom the best. A reliable dealer who sells at established prices will help you get satisfaction if anything goes wrong. Get exact dimensions of each piece of equipment selected. Recheck layout to make certain each piece fits space planned.

PREPARE ROOM

Next prepare the room by removing everything possible. Wall space should be cleared. If you plan on installing a new sink, range or refrigerator, don't disconnect anything until you have new equipment ready for immediate installation.

The easiest way to build base cabinets is to remove the baseboard within area of cabinets. Use a pry bar, remove nails. Reuse baseboard to finish any exposed base after cabinets are placed in position. Patch holes in plaster with patching plaster. Sand patch smooth.

If wall is rough, plaster loose or badly cracked, cover entire wall with ½" or heavier gypsum board, or ¼" prefinished hardwood paneling.

GENERAL PROCEDURE

Kitchen modernization follows this procedure: 1. Remove old floor covering. 2. Rough in plumbing, wiring, heating, lighting, gas, and telephone lines. 3. Cover walls with panelboard if needed. 4. Install cabinet type sink, dishwasher and floor model range. 5. Build base and wall cabinets. 6. Cover countertops with plastic laminate. 7. Install drop-in counter sink and/or range, dishwasher, wall oven. 8. Cover wall area between base cabinets. (This can be done before installing base and wall cabinets or after.) 9. Build header, Illus. 278, if same is required. 10. Paint, wallpaper, or install hardwood panels. 11. Lay finished floor. 12. Install refrigerator.

Book #615 provides complete instructions for laying asphalt or vinyl tiles. Book #606 explains how to lay ceramic tile.

CHECK FLOOR

If floor requires recovering, remove old floor covering. Nail down loose boards. If floor is rough, sand smooth. If too rough, or springy in spots, cover entire floor with ⅜, ½ or ⅝", exterior grade plywood. Use thickness that eliminates spring. Nail panels every 4" along edges, every 6" along floor joists. Use 6 penny common nails.

If floor is firm, but uneven, or slopes, you can fill and smooth low spots with latex floor underlayment. This can be spread from a feather edge to 5/16" thick in one coat, Illus. 51. Any number of coats can be applied. It dries to a hard base. Follow manufacturer's directions for applying underlayment selected. It is important both from operation and appearance that floor be level.

To determine whether floor has any high point along its outer edge, check with a four foot level at various points, Illus. 224. When you find the highest point, measure up 40", Illus. 225. Using a level as a straight edge, Illus. 226, draw a line around room at 40". Now measure down from this line to floor at various points. If you find any point less than 40", you didn't start measuring from the highest point. Start over and draw a new line, 40" from the highest point. This line now represents top edge of a 4" high back splash on base cabinet. If you build base cabinets or a back splash to some other height, draw line at this height.

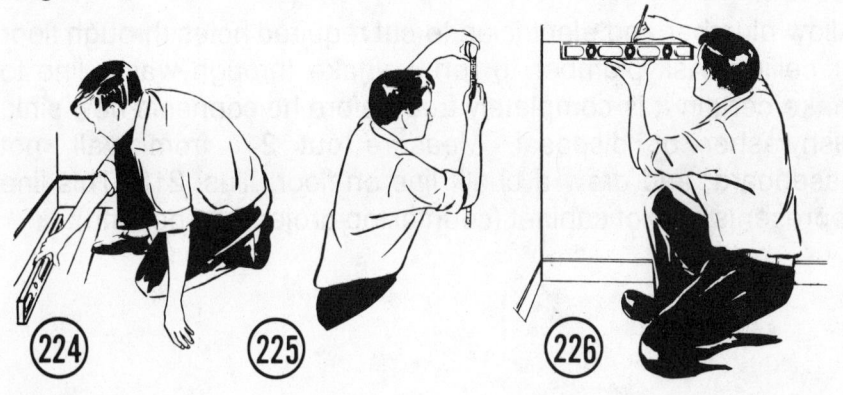

Next measure up 81" from same high point on floor. Using a level, draw a line around room. This line represents top of wall cabinets. Wall cabinets can also be installed to 84", or to ceiling if desired.

Double check your plan by drawing an outline of each cabinet and piece of equipment full size directly on wall. Use a piece of chalk or crayon, Illus. 227. Work carefully. When you draw outline of each cabinet, use a level to insure drawing vertical and horizontal lines correctly.

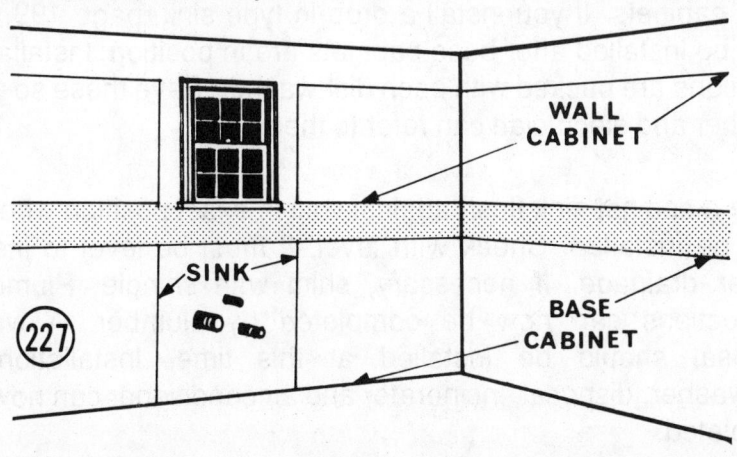

Locate and label each outlet directly on wall in exact spot you want it. If sink is to be moved, outline new location on wall and floor. This eliminates any question as to location of waste and water lines. This full size planning shows electrician and plumber exactly where to rough in wiring, plumbing and gas line.

Allow plumber and electrician to cut required holes through floor or ceiling. Ask plumber to run a snake through waste line to make certain it is completely free before he connects new sink, dishwasher or disposal. Measure out 24" from wall, not baseboard, and draw a chalk line on floor, Illus. 218. This line represents face of cabinet (countertop projects 1" beyond).

INSTALL SINK OR DISHWASHER SINK, RANGE

The first piece of equipment to install is a cabinet sink or combination dishwasher sink. This should be installed before base cabinets. If you install a drop-in type sink, page 199, this must be installed after base cabinets are in position. Installation directions are packed with each dishwasher. Save these so your plumber and electrician can refer to them.

Place a cabinet sink flush against wall in exact position where it is to be installed. Check with level. It must be level to insure proper drainage. If necessary, shim with shingle. Plumbing connections can now be completed by plumber. A waste disposal should be installed at this time. Installation of dishwasher, disposal, incinerator and air conditioner can now be completed.

HOW TO HANDLE A LOW WINDOW

If you have a double hung window, lower than 40", here's what to do. Remove window apron, Illus. 228. Cut side window trim off at 40" height. Saw sill off flush with wall. Cut three pieces of aluminum storm window channel to length required and screw in position. Slide a piece of frosted glass or plastic in place, Illus. 229. If window has handles on bottom rail, remove, and replace same on side. The window will now slide behind frosted glass when in closed position. If you install a dishwasher sink standing more than 40", cut trim back to height required.

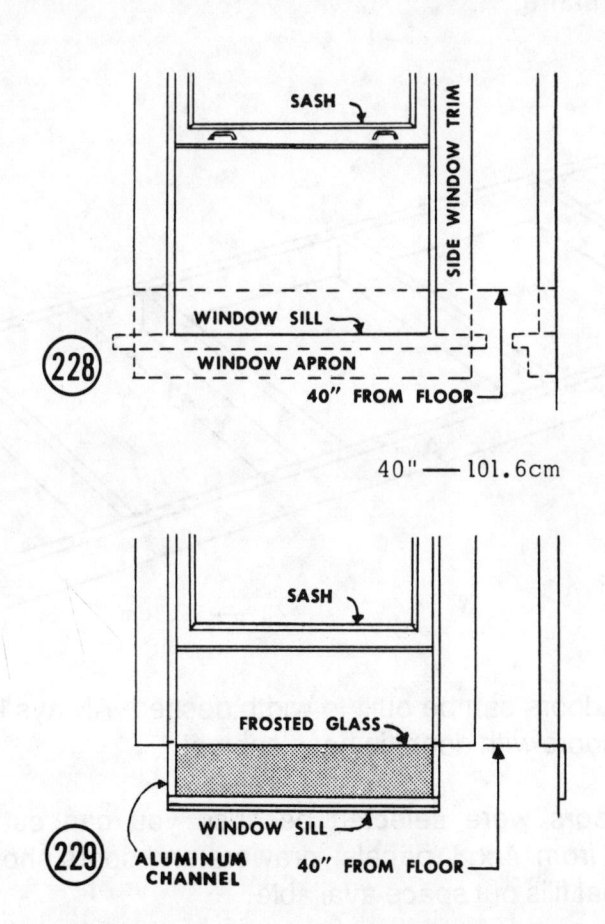

40" — 101.6cm

BUILD BASE CABINETS

Since surfaced lumber varies in width and thickness, we figured a 1x2 as measuring ¾ x 1½"; a 1x3 as measuring ¾ x 2½". We figured plywood and hardboard thickness indicated.

Remove shoe molding and baseboard, Illus. 220, within area of base cabinets.

Measure space available for a base cabinet and build base, Illus. 230. Lay out base cabinets with drawers and doors where your plan requires same.

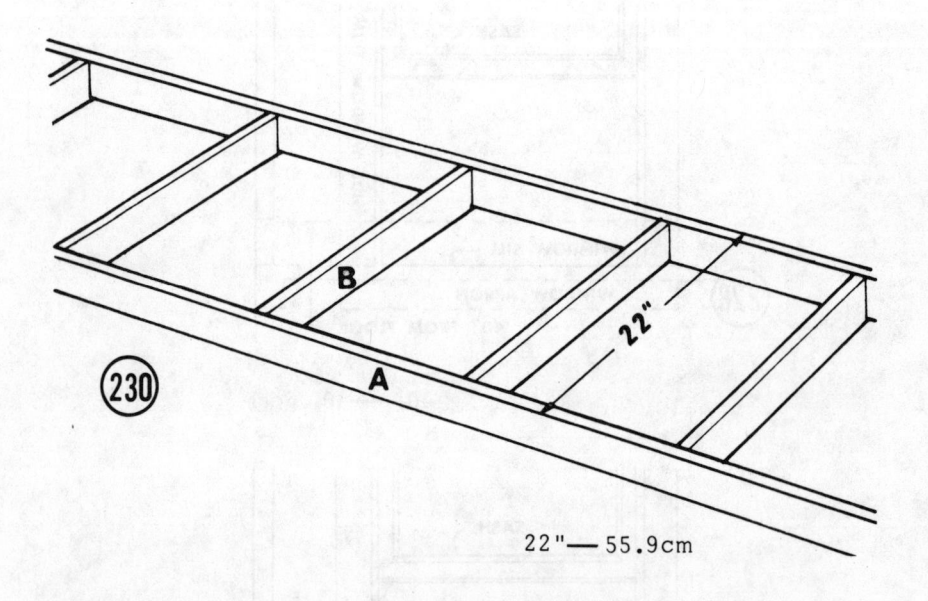

22"— 55.9cm

Drawers and doors can be built to width desired. Always line up wall cabinet doors with doors in base cabinet.

While 16" doors were selected because you can cut them economically from 4 x 8' panels, drawers and doors should be built to size that fills out space available.

To simplify construction, directions show how to build base cabinet, Illus. 216, 231, 234.

Cut two A, Illus. 230, from 1x3 to length required. Cut cross-framing B, 1 x 3 x 20½", or length required to maintain 22" overall.

Space B—16" apart, or locate same under an end D, or partition E, or DD. Apply glue and nail A to B with two 6 penny finishing nails at each joint.

Place assembled base in position. Check with level lengthwise and crosswise. If necessary to level base, do so with a piece of shingle, then toenail base to floor with 6 penny finishing nails.

Cut ¾" plywood for floor C—24" x length of base, Illus. 231.

Cut ends D, ¾ x 31⅞", Illus. 231. Cut partition E, ¾ x 23½ x 31⅞", Illus. 232, 233. Use ¾" plywood. Note: Partition E is cut ½" less in width than D, and is notched at top to receive 1x2-G.

Cut partition DD—¾ x 24 x 31⅞". Partitions DD and E are notched at top to receive G.

Partition E is spaced where required for drawers or shelves. If you prefer one 32" shelf, you can eliminate E.

Follow this construction when building a base cabinet with drawers and shelves, Illus. 216, 232, 234.

Cut two outer ends D. Do not notch top. Notch DD and E to receive G. Cut ⅜" plywood, 2 x 30¼" for drawer stops H, Illus. 231. Glue and brad H in position to D. Cut ⅜ x 1⅜ x 22" drawer guides F. Using a square, locate and draw lines on D to indicate position of F. Glue and screw F in position with 1" No. 6 flathead wood screws.

Cut partition E from ¾" plywood, 23½ x 31⅞". Notch top where shown to receive 1x2-G. Partition E is optional.

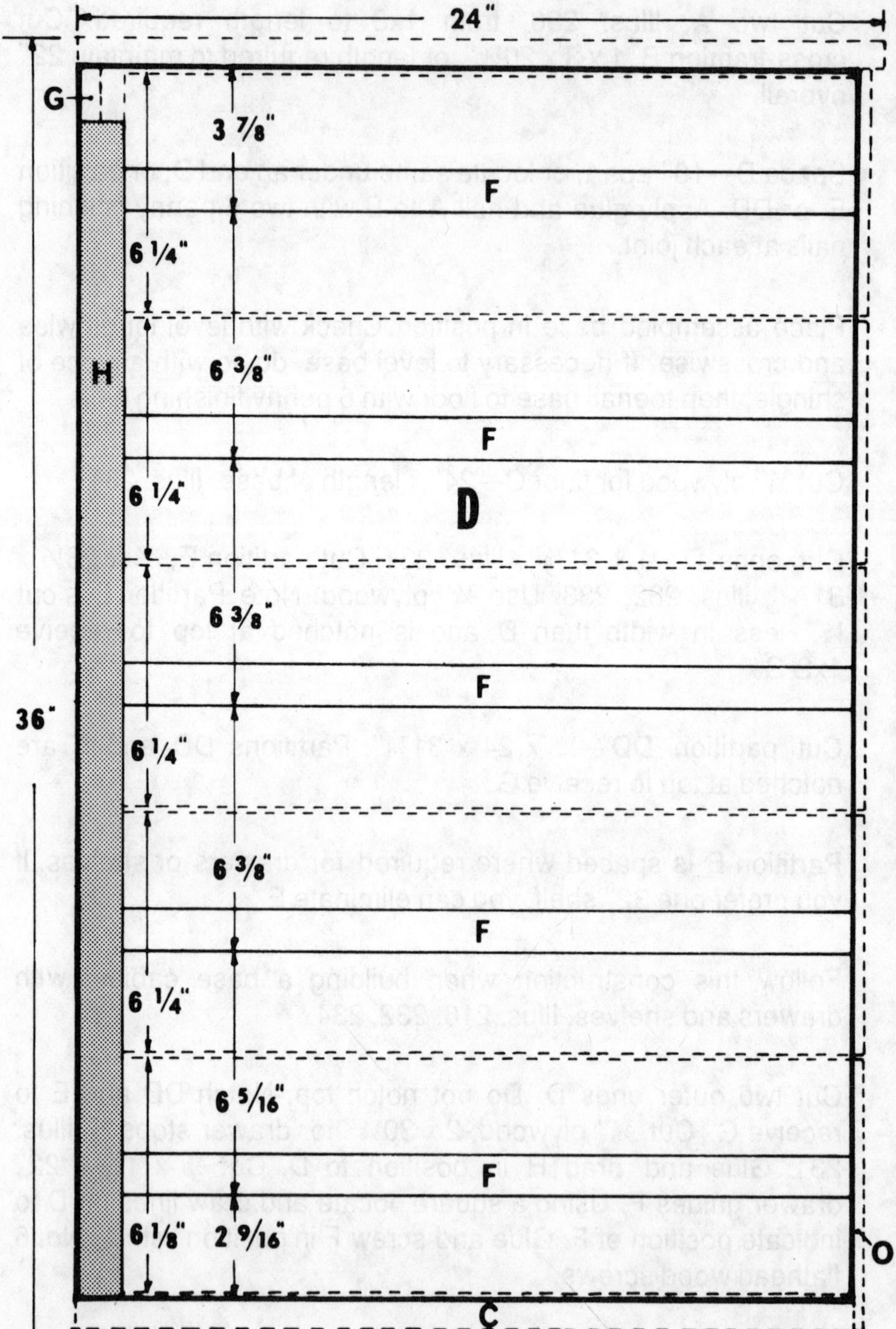
24"
G
3 7/8"
F
6 1/4"
H
6 3/8"
F
6 1/4"
D
6 3/8"
F
36"
6 1/4"
6 3/8"
F
6 1/4"
6 5/16"
F
6 1/8"
2 9/16"
O
C
A
231
B
A

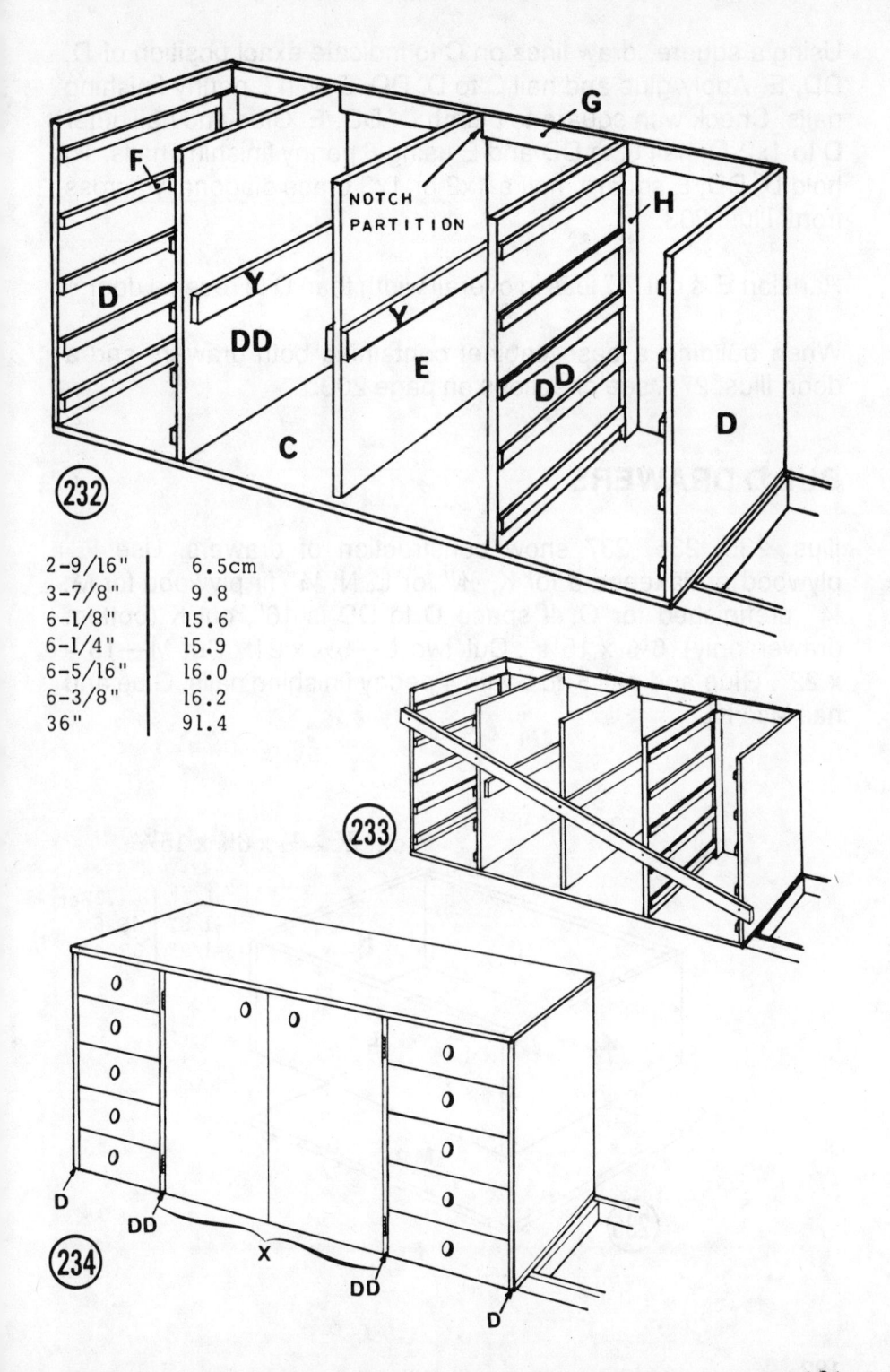

2-9/16"	6.5 cm
3-7/8"	9.8
6-1/8"	15.6
6-1/4"	15.9
6-5/16"	16.0
6-3/8"	16.2
36"	91.4

181

Using a square, draw lines on C to indicate exact position of D, DD, E. Apply glue and nail C to D, DD, E with 8 penny finishing nails. Check with square to plumb D, DD, E. Glue and nail outer D to 1x2-G; nail G to DD and E using 6 penny finishing nails. To hold D, DD, E square, nail a 1x2 or 1x3 brace diagonally across front, Illus. 233.

Partition E is cut ½" less in overall width than D to receive door.

When building a base cabinet containing both drawers and a door, Illus. 271, see directions on page 203.

BUILD DRAWERS

Illus. 235, 236, 237 show construction of drawers. Use ½" plywood or flakeboard for K, ⅜" for L, N; ¼" fir plywood for M; ¼" prefinished for O. If space D to DD is 16", cut K (bottom drawer only) 6⅛ x 15⅛". Cut two L—6⅛ x 21". Cut M—15⅛ x 22". Glue and nail K to L with 4 penny finishing nails. Glue and nail M to KL.

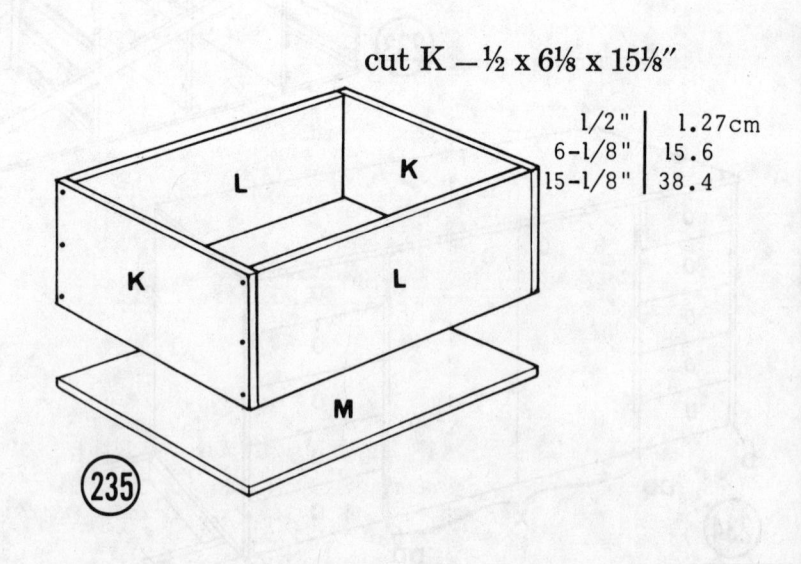

cut K — ½ x 6⅛ x 15⅛"

1/2"	1.27cm
6-1/8"	15.6
15-1/8"	38.4

(235)

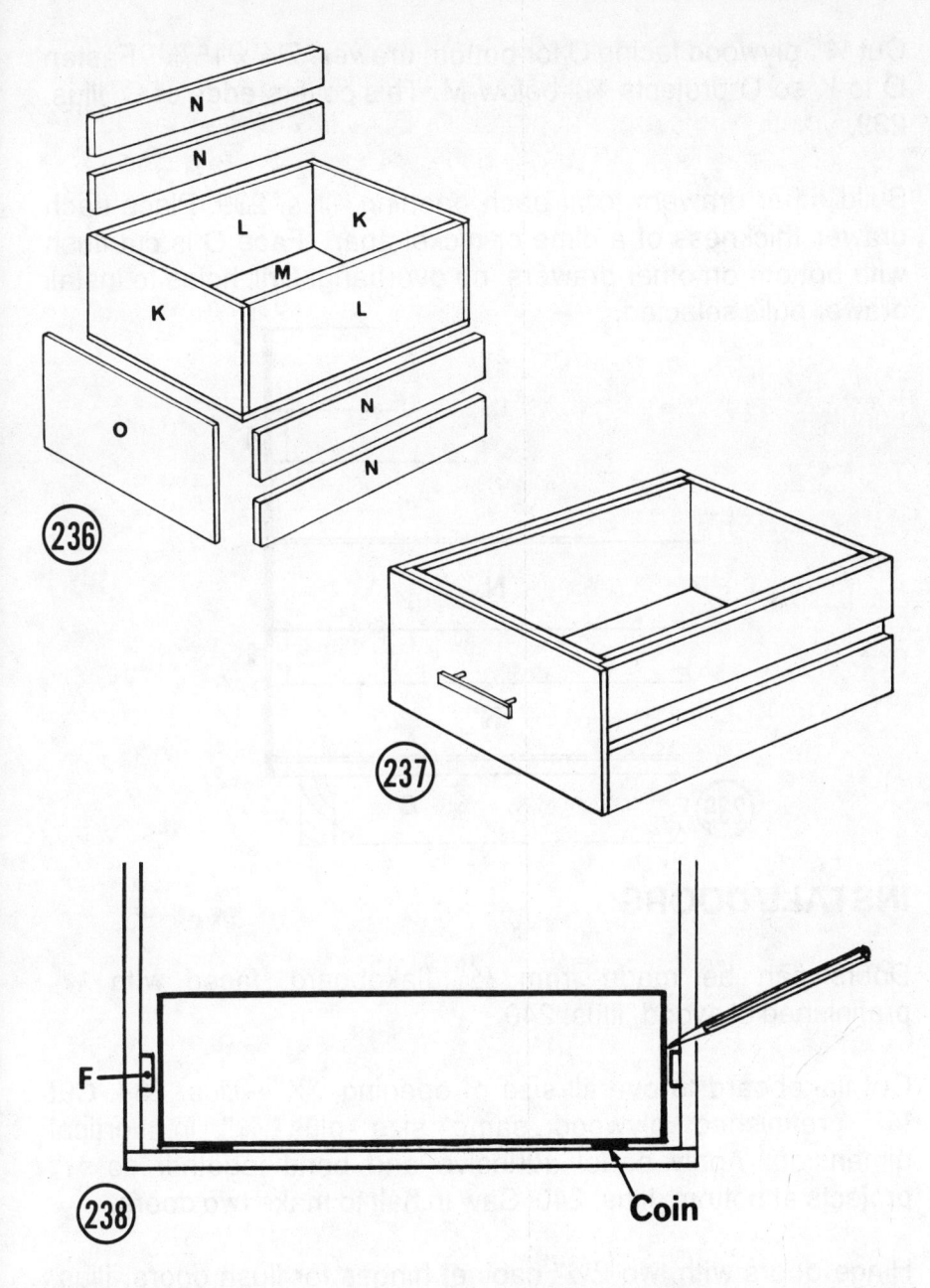

Cut N—2½ x 22". Place bottom drawer KLM on four dimes, one in each corner. This raises drawer up about 1/16". Place drawer halfway in position. Mark position of F on L. Fasten N to L so there's about 1/16" clearance between N and F. Sandpaper or plane F so drawer slides freely, Illus. 238, 239, 272.

183

Cut ¼" plywood facing O for bottom drawer, 7⅛ x 15⅞". Fasten O to K so O projects ¾" below M. This covers edge of C, Illus. 239.

Build other drawers to fit each opening, Illus. 239. Place each drawer thickness of a dime or nickel apart. Face O is cut flush with bottom on other drawers, no overhang. Drill holes to install drawer pulls selected.

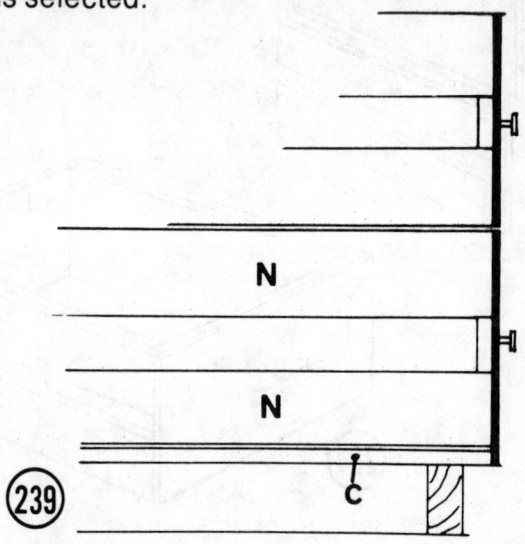

INSTALL DOORS

Doors can be made from ½" flakeboard, faced with ¼" prefinished plywood, Illus. 240.

Cut flakeboard to overall size of opening, "X"—Illus. 234. Cut ¼" prefinished plywood same size plus ¾" in vertical dimension. Apply panel adhesive and bond together so ¾" projects at bottom, Illus. 240. Saw in half to make two doors.

Hinge doors with two 2½" cabinet hinges for flush doors, Illus. 240.

Mortise edge of door full thickness of closed hinge, Illus. 241. Fasten hinge to D, 2½" down from top, 2½" up from bottom, Illus. 242.

½" ¼"

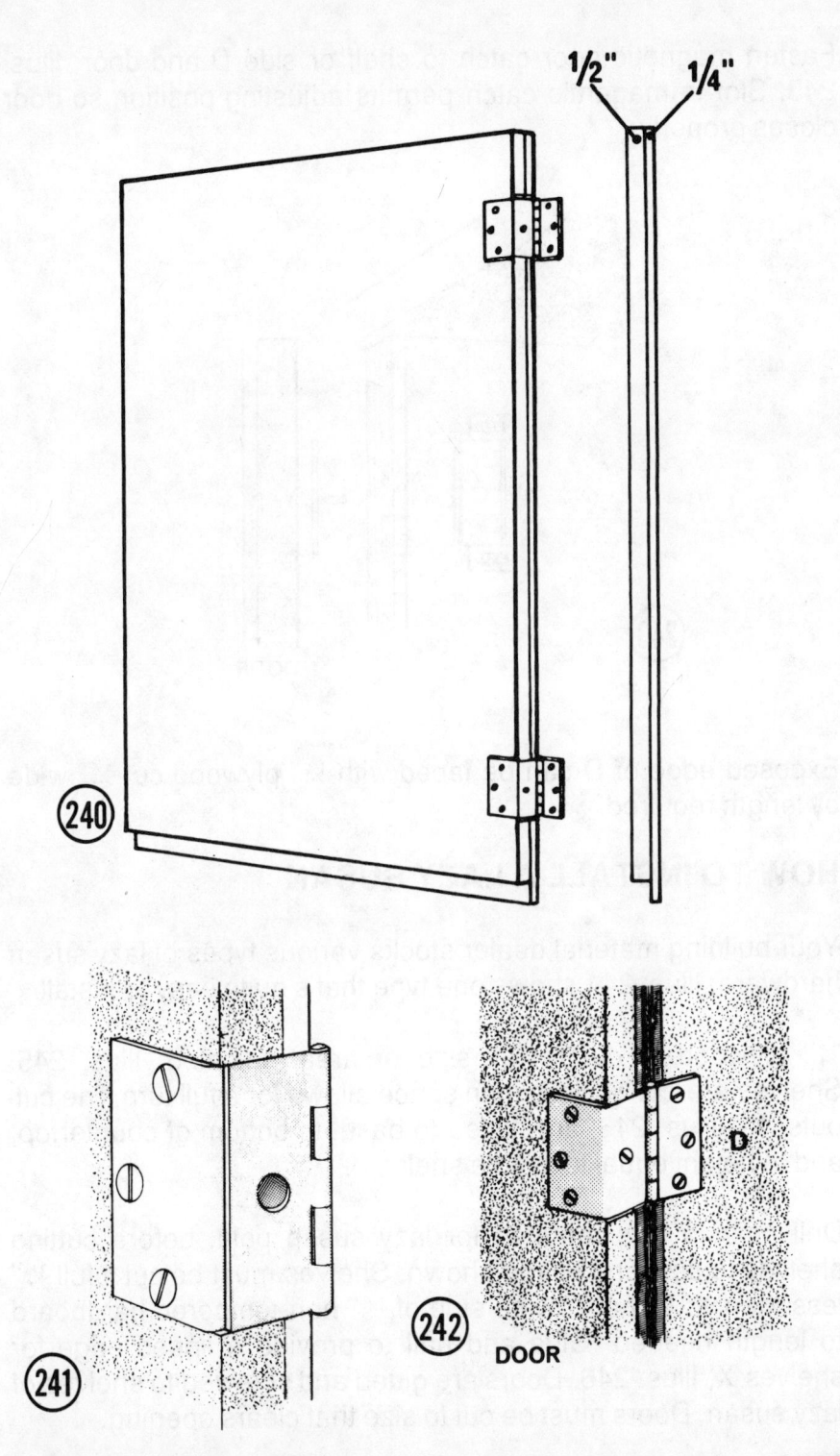

240

241

242 **DOOR** D

185

Fasten magnetic door catch to shelf or side D and door, Illus. 243. Slot in magentic catch permits adjusting position so door closes properly.

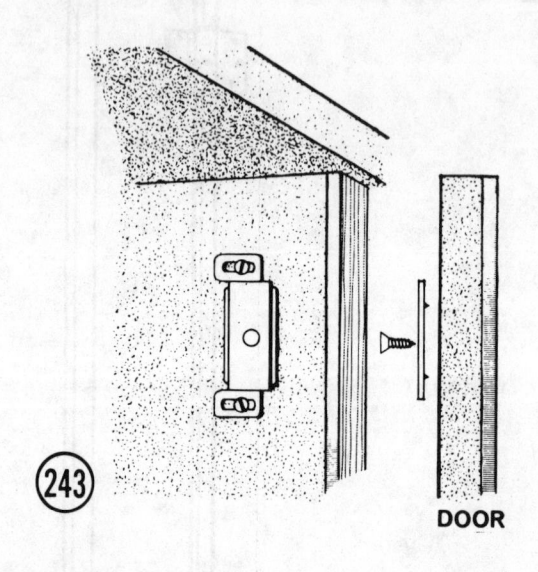

Exposed edge of D can be faced with ¼" plywood cut ¾" wide by length required.

HOW TO INSTALL A LAZY SUSAN

Your building material dealer stocks various types of lazy susan hardware. Illus. 244 shows one type that's quite easy to install.

¾" plywood is cut to full size of area indicated, Illus. 245. Shelves are cut ¾" less than space allows for a full turn. The cutouts, X—Illus. 246, are nailed to base, to bottom of countertop, and at height equal to middle shelf.

Drill hole to size required for lazy susan pole, before cutting shelves to size and shape shown. Shelves must be cut a full ¾" less than X. Cut a 1" wide strip of ⅛" non-tempered hardboard to length needed. Glue and nail to provide a lipped edge for shelves X, Illus. 246. Doors are glued and screwed to shelves of lazy susan. Doors must be cut to size that clears opening.

Top Guide Plate

245

¾"

¾" Plywood or Flakeboard

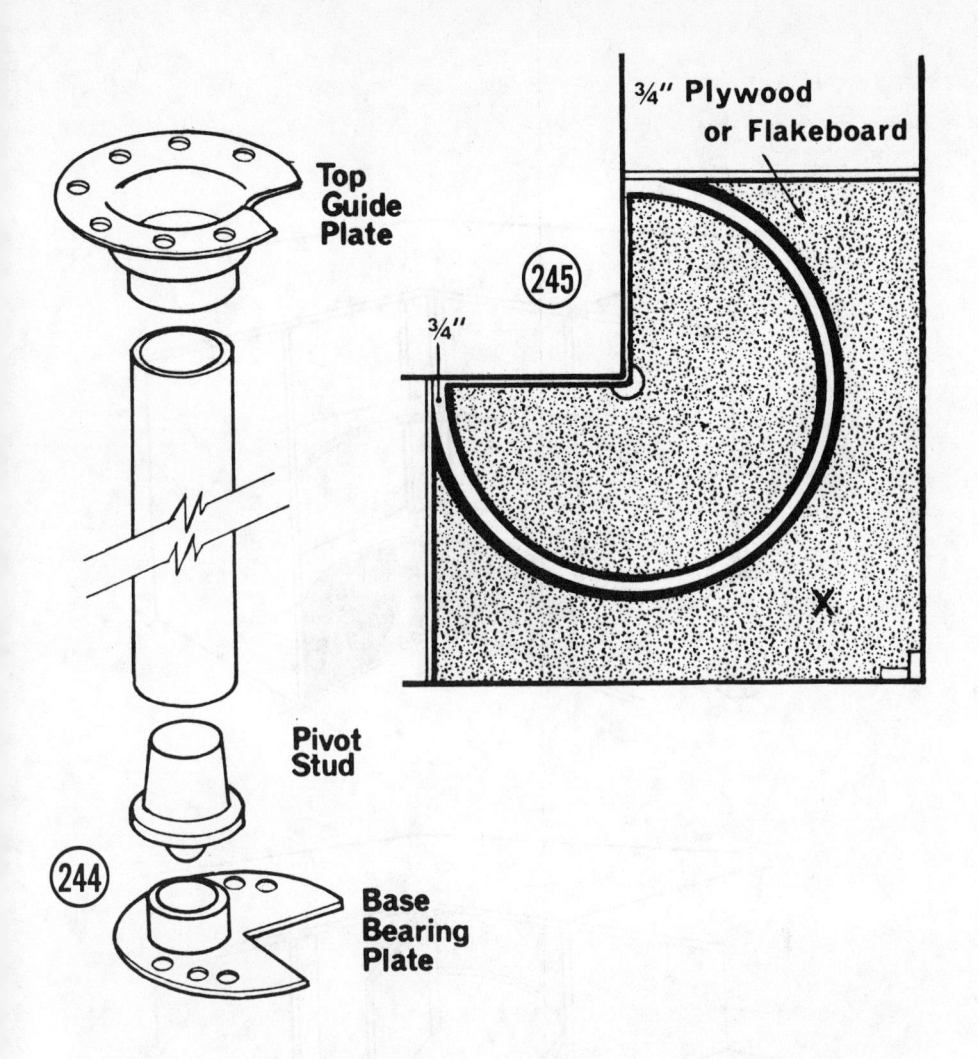

Pivot Stud

244

Base Bearing Plate

Shelf brackets, supplied by lazy susan manufacturer, are fastened to bottom face of shelf. The pole is installed, shelves secured to pole with set screw in shelf bracket; doors are then glued and screwed to shelves.

A top pole bracket is fastened to bottom of countertop. The pole is inserted in top bracket. The bottom pivot is placed in position, Illus. 244. The bottom plate is slipped into position and screwed to floor.

1" flexible metal or plastic edging can be fastened to shelves to provide a lipped edge, Illus. 247.

(246)

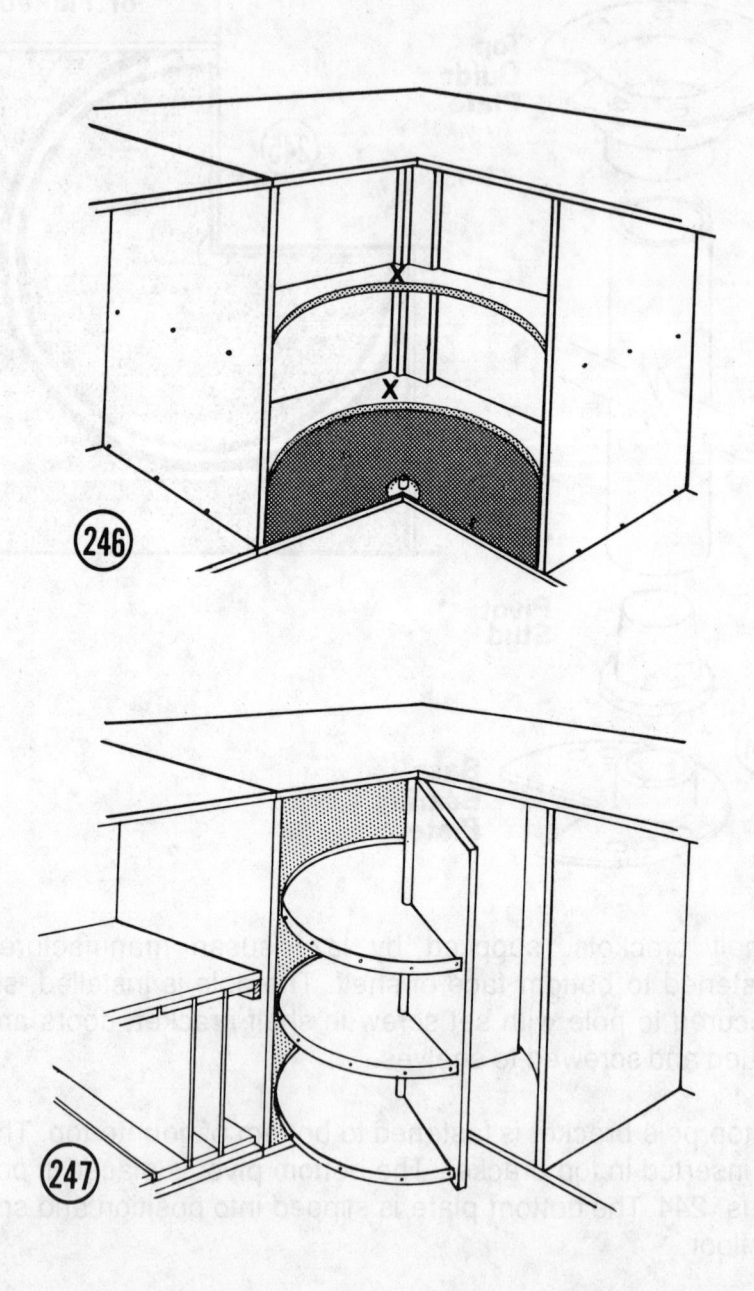

(247)

188

WALL OVEN CABINET

After deciding where a wall oven is to be installed, equipment selected, ask your electrician or utility company to run service line required. Manufacturer of equipment provides details concerning location of gas line or outlet box, how wall oven should be vented, height equipment should be placed, etc. Rough in vent and service lines before building cabinet.

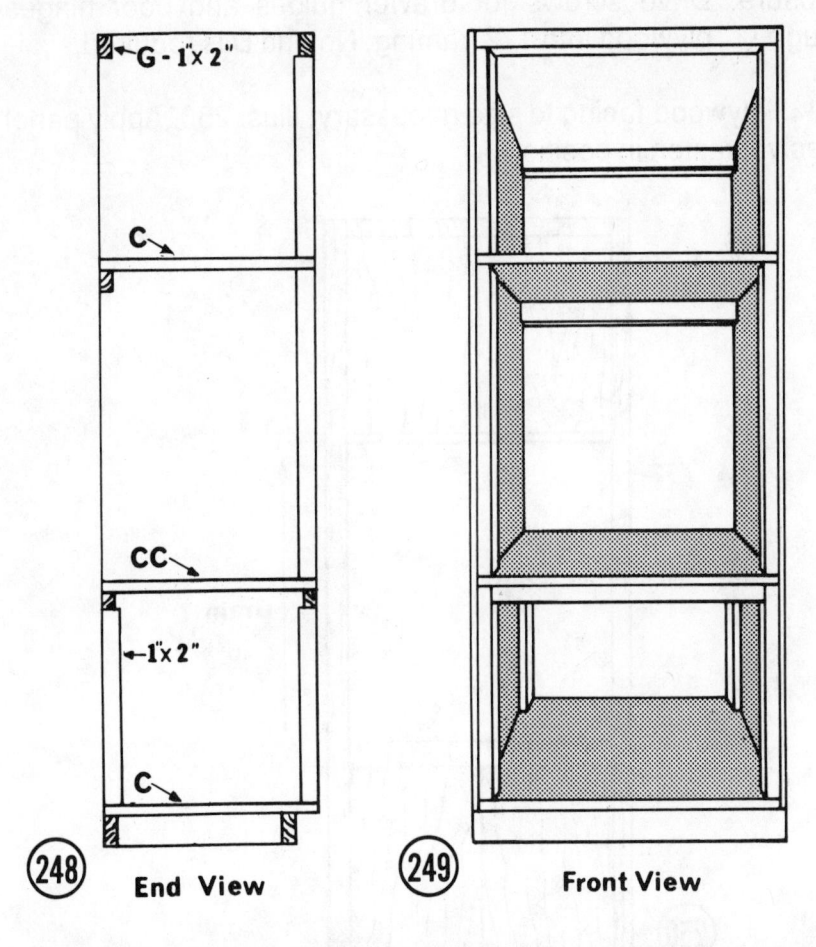

248 End View

249 Front View

Illus. 248, 249, 250 shows construction of a cabinet that will accommodate a wall oven. Sides are cut 24" wide (or width manufacturer recommends), by height of wall cabinets. Build 1x3 base as previously outlined for base cabinets. A wall oven enclosure can be built with ¼" plywood sides and front. Build

189

enclosure and front opening to size equipment manufacturer recommends. Use ¾" plywood for C and shelf CC. Use 1x2-G, in position noted, to fasten enclosure to wall and to support shelves CC. 1x2 is used to support four corners of CC. Doors can be cut to size required and hinged to 1x2 framing.

When a base cabinet butts against oven enclosure, Illus. 215, you can fasten drawer guides F directly to ¼" plywood wall oven enclosure. Drive screws for drawer guides and door hinges through ¼" plywood into 1x2 framing. No end D is required.

Cut ¼" plywood facing to size necessary, Illus. 250. Apply panel adhesive, fasten in position.

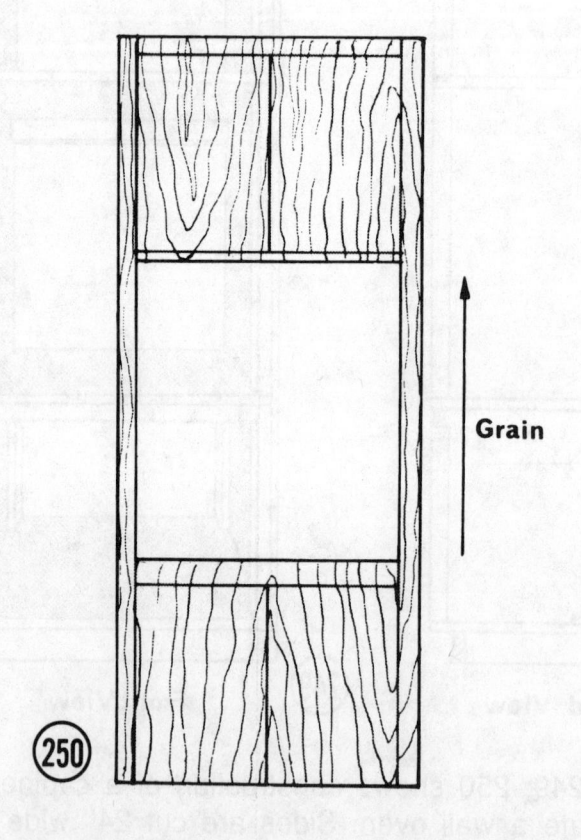

(250) Grain

Allow ¼" plywood on bottom doors to project over C, Illus. 240. Make doors for upper cabinet flush, no projection, Illus. 250. ¼" plywood covers all edges of C, CC and 1x2 framing.

REFRIGERATOR ENCLOSURE

No 1x3 base is required for a floor refrigerator. Install an electric outlet in position required.

Cut ¾" plywood for both sides to full width of refrigerator. Only the door projects beyond front edge. Nail sides to 1x2 cross framing G, Illus. 251. Nail sides to adjacent base cabinet.

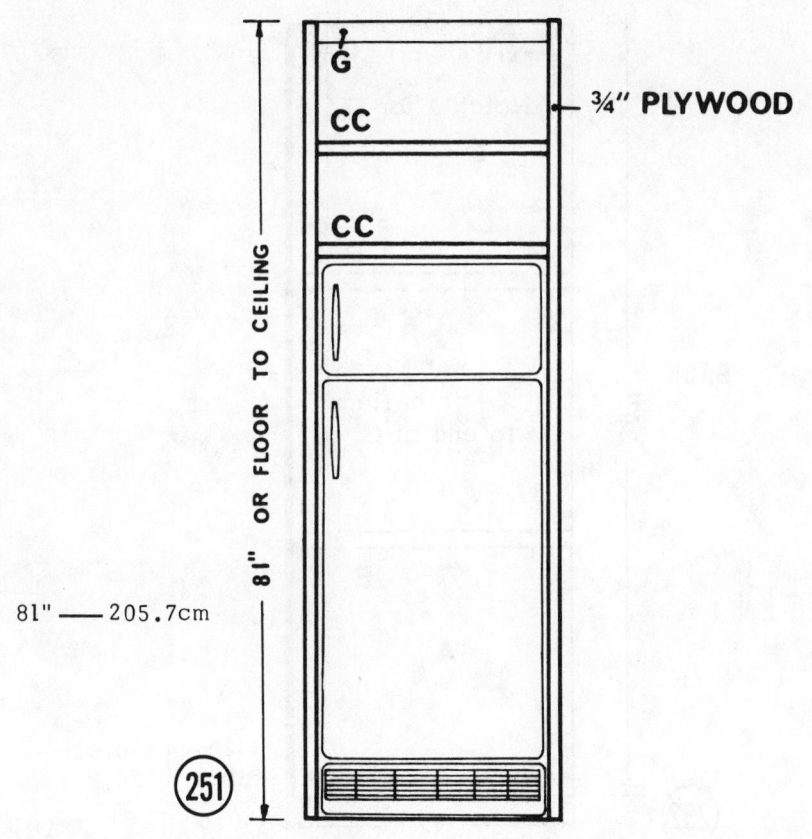

81" —— 205.7cm

If refrigerator is placed in an exposed end, build a 2x4 or 2x6 partition, Illus. 277. Cut ¼" prefinished plywood to size. Apply with panel adhesive. Miter cut matching ceiling trim, apply in position indicated. Do same with matching base, Illus. 220.

If you plan on installing a wall refrigerator, follow procedure outlined for a wall oven with these exceptions. Due to weight of unit, frame opening with lumber recommended by manufacturer.

HOW TO BUILD WALL CABINETS

Use ½" flakeboard for ends A and shelves B; 1 x 2 for G and shelf supports, Illus. 252, 253, 254. Cut A—12" by height desired. Notch top ends of A—1½", in position shown to receive 1x2 framing G. Bottom edge of D is notched ½" deep to receive bottom shelf. Decide what you want to store on shelves, then space ½" notches accordingly, Illus. 253.

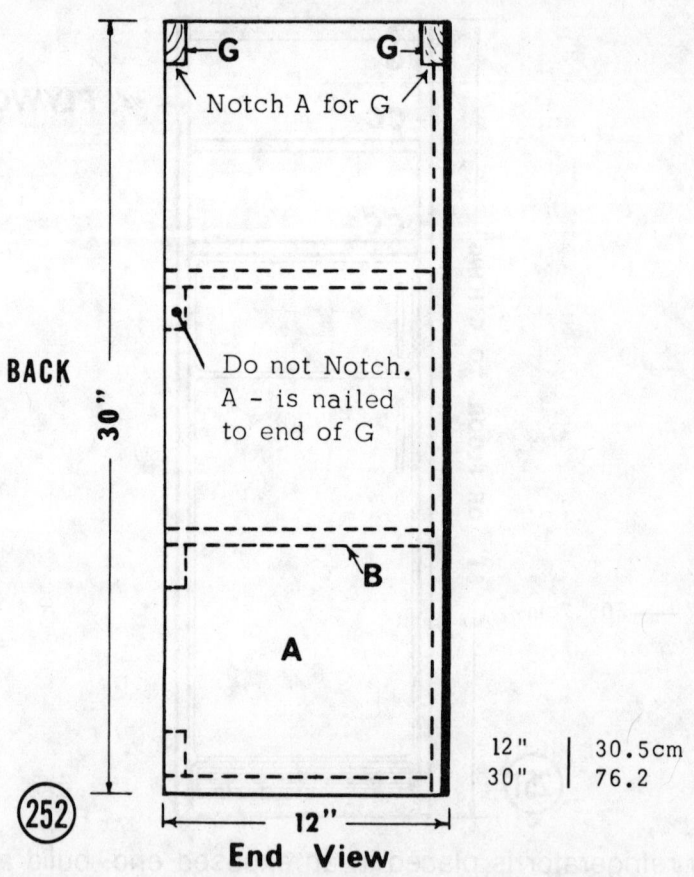

```
                G         G
           Notch A for G

   BACK
           Do not Notch.
           A - is nailed
           to end of G
   30"

                    B

           A

                              12"  | 30.5cm
                              30"  | 76.2
     (252)
              12"
           End View
```

Cut shelves B, Illus. 254, 11½" wide by length required. Position D to line up with D in base cabinets.

Apply glue and nail top G to A ; nail shelves to 1 x 2 supports flush with back. Nail A to shelf supports and to shelves. Check with square and hold in position with 1 x 2 brace nailed diagonally across front, Illus. 255, 233.

(253)

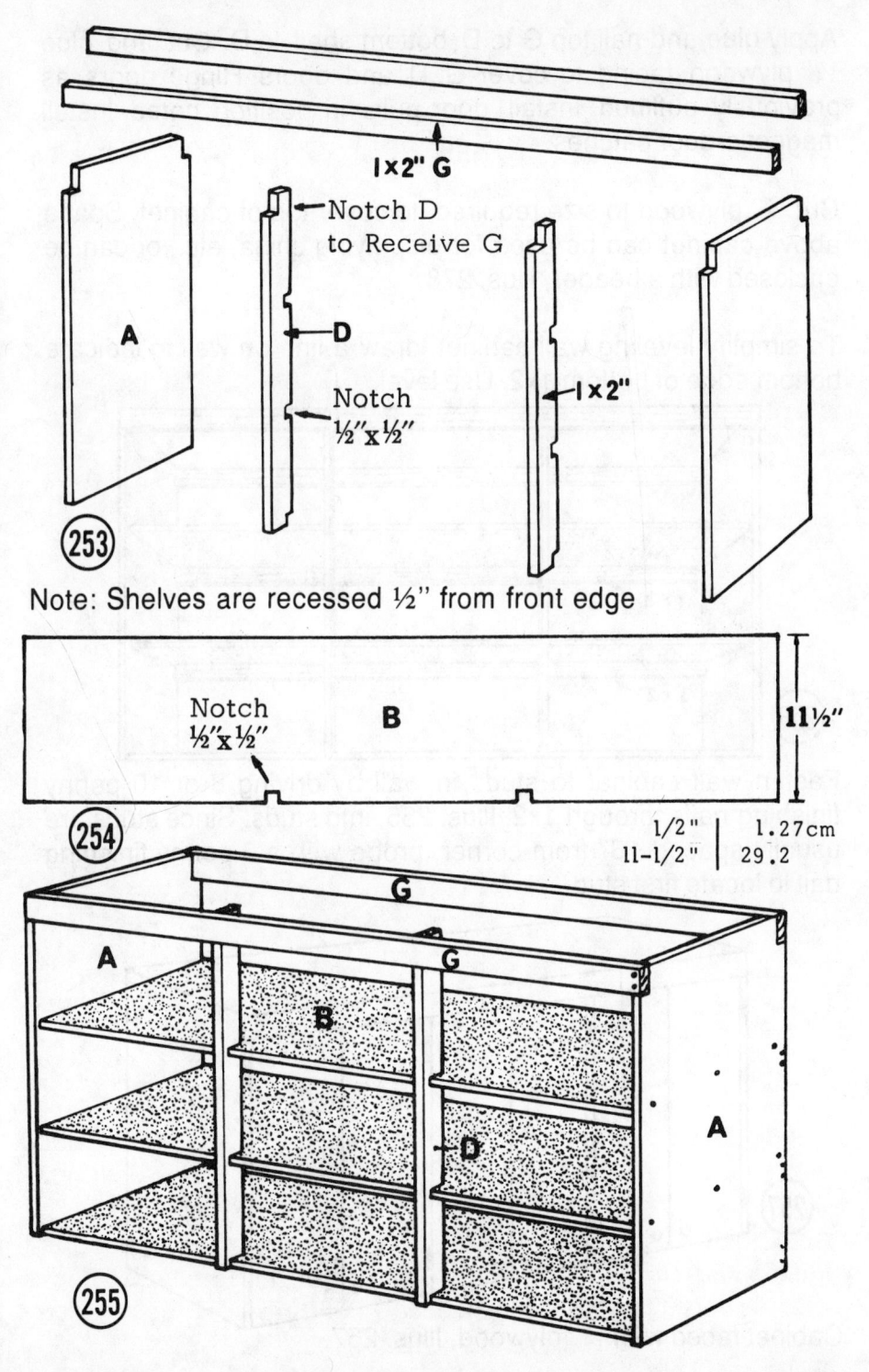

1×2" G

Notch D to Receive G

A

D

Notch ½"x½"

1×2"

Note: Shelves are recessed ½" from front edge

Notch ½"x½"

B

11½"

(254)

1/2"	1.27cm
11-1/2"	29.2

(255)

G

A

G

B

D

A

Apply glue and nail top G to D; bottom shelf to D. Cut and glue ¼" plywood facing to cover G, D and doors. Hinge doors as previously outlined. Install door pulls in position noted. Install magnetic door catches.

Cut ¼" plywood to size required, to cover top of cabinet. Space above cabinet can be used for displaying china, etc., or can be enclosed with a header, Illus. 278.

To simplify leveling wall cabinet, draw a line on wall to indicate bottom edge of bottom 1x2. Use level.

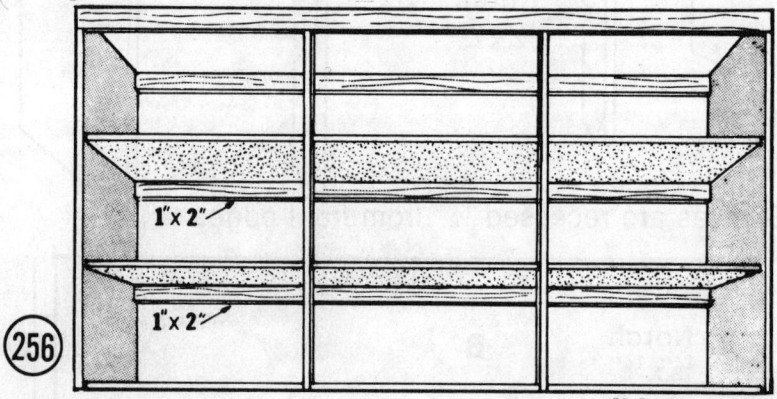

Fasten wall cabinet to studs in wall by driving 8 or 10 penny finishing nails through 1x2, Illus. 256, into studs. Since studs are usually spaced 16" from corner, probe with a 6 penny finishing nail to locate first stud.

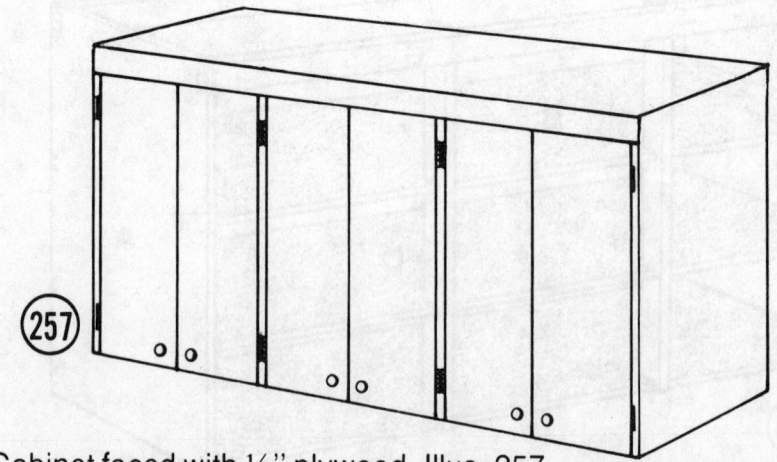

Cabinet faced with ¼" plywood, Illus. 257.

Illus. 258 and 259 show framing for a wall cabinet built in corner. All shelves are recessed ½" from face of D to receive ½" flakeboard doors.

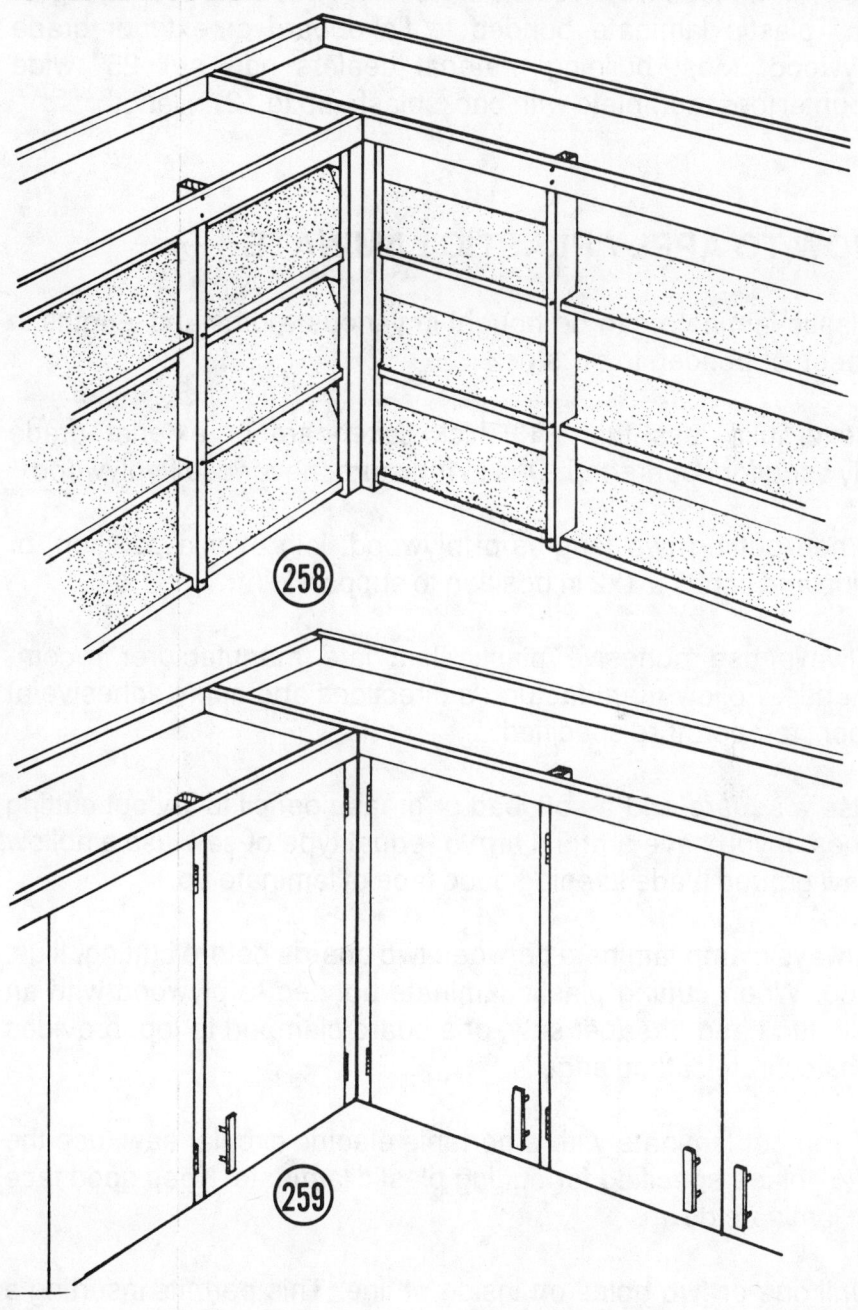

(258)

(259)

195

COUNTERTOP

Use ¾" flakeboard or exterior grade plywood for countertop or buy plastic laminate bonded to flakeboard or exterior grade plywood. Most building material dealers now sell 25" wide countertops, complete with backsplash, up to 12' in length.

HOW TO APPLY PLASTIC LAMINATE

Plastic laminate can be bought in various widths and lengths in sheet, or bonded to ¾" stock.

Never use less than ¾" thick flakeboard or exterior grade plywood for countertop. Due to moisture, never use fir plywood.

When butting two lengths of plywood, join over a partition, or glue and screw a 1x2 in position to support joint.

Always use adhesive plastic laminate manufacturer recommends. Follow manufacturer's directions and apply adhesive at room temperature specified.

Use a square and a soft lead or grease pencil to lay out cutting lines. If you have a radial arm or equal type of saw use a hollow saw ground blade keeping good face of laminate up.

Always clamp laminate between two boards before cutting, Illus. 260. When cutting plastic laminate bonded to plywood with an electric hand or saber saw, one board clamped to top, provides an accurate cutting edge.

If you cut laminate with a portable electric circular saw, use the 6½" blade specified for cutting plastic laminate. Keep good face of laminate down.

Drill one or two holes on inside of line. This permits inserting a keyhole or saber saw, Illus. 261.

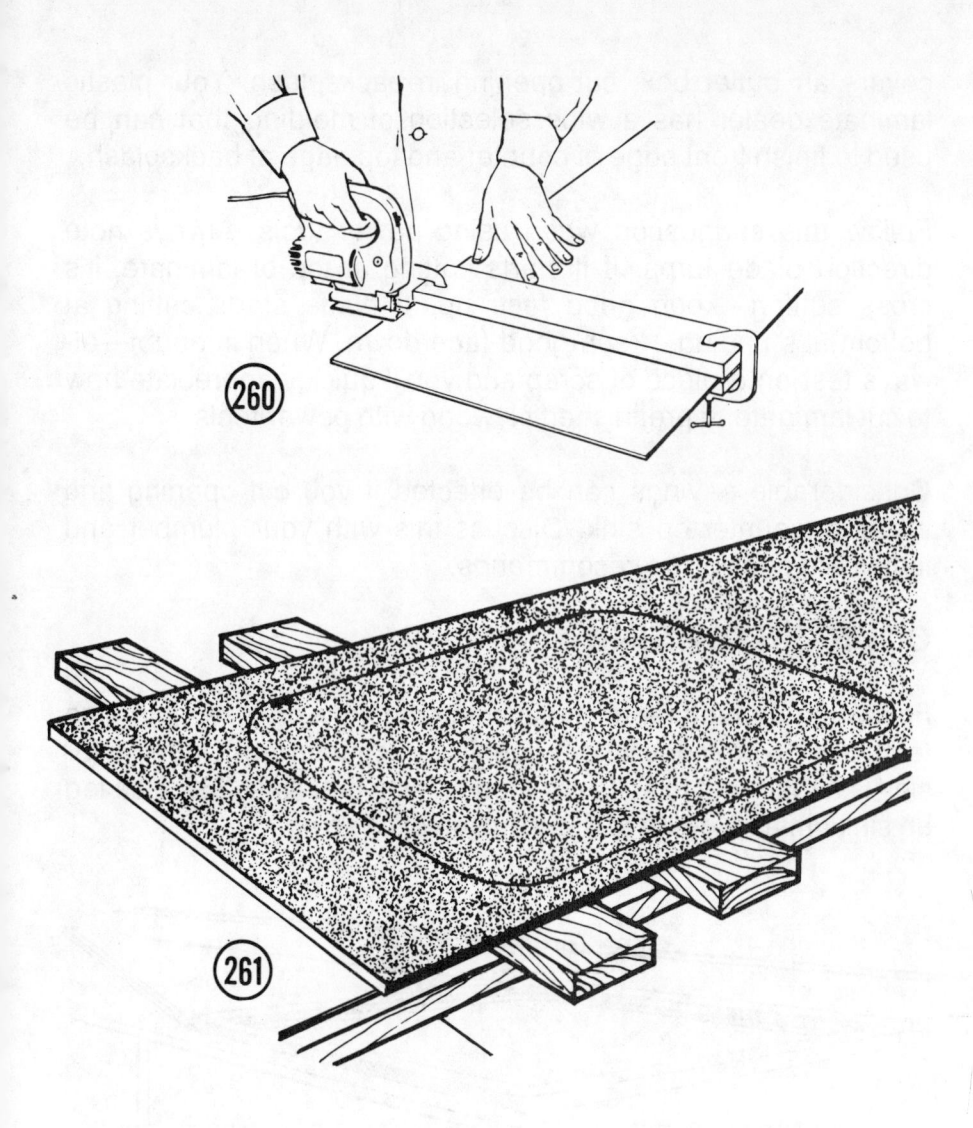

Plastic laminate can also be cut with a fine tooth crosscut hand saw or a keyhole saw. Keep good face up. Saw only on down strokes. To keep from clipping, clamp between two boards.

Always cut on outside of a line. This permits filing, planing or sanding edge to size required.

Use ¾" flakeboard or exterior grade plywood for backsplash. This is usually cut 4" in height. Glue and nail backsplash to countertop before applying plastic laminate. If backsplash covers an outlet box, cut opening in backsplash. Your plastic laminate dealer has a wide selection of molding that can be used to finish front edge of counter and top edge of backsplash.

Follow this suggestion when using power tools. Always note direction blade turns. If it starts cutting at top of laminate, it's cross cutting—keep good face up. If blade starts cutting at bottom, it's ripping—keep good face down. When in doubt—always test on a piece of scrap and you'll quickly appreciate how to cut laminate or prefinished plywood with power tools.

Considerable savings can be effected if you cut opening and install a countertop sink. Discuss this with your plumber and install it in position he recommends.

COUNTERTOP SINK

Follow manufacturer's exact dimensions, or use full size template he provides to cut opening in countertop. Opening for sink is usually cut to full size of leg on sink rim, Illus. 262. Use leg on sink rim as a guide to draw outline of opening.

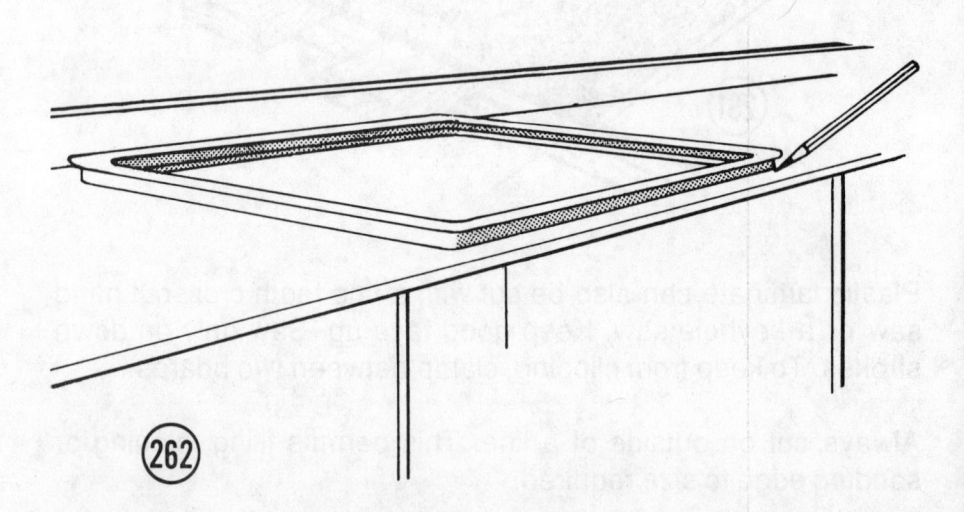

Place frame sink manufacturer supplies, in position on countertop. This is usually 2" from front edge. Use leg on sink frame, Illus. 262 as a template. Using a soft pencil, or a grease pencil, trace outside face of curved edges at four corners. Remove sink frame. Using a straight edge, connect corners. By drawing a thick line, the outer edge of line will be about 1/16" larger than frame leg. Saw opening along outside edge of line. This provides an opening with 1/16" clearance all around, Illus. 263.

Apply calking to top edge of opening, Illus. 263, to bottom surface of sink frame, and to both sides of leg on frame.

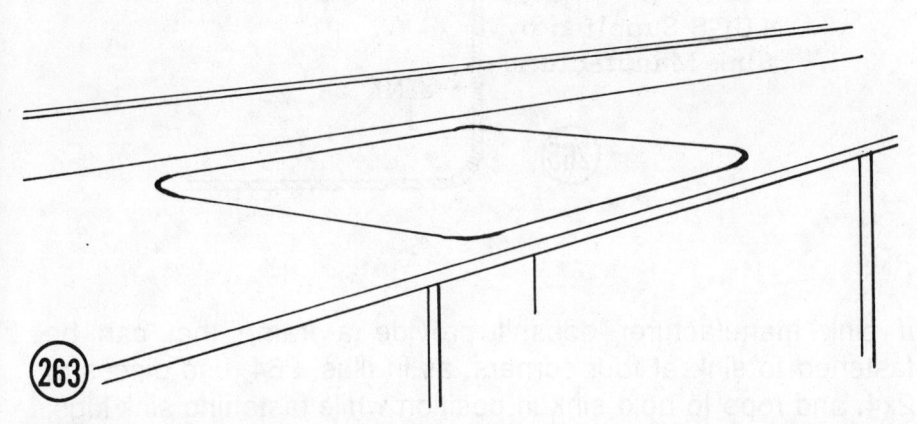

Place frame, leg up, on a flat surface. Place sink in position on frame. Fasten sink to frame with 4 corner brackets, Illus. 264. Fasten bolts securely. This locks sink to frame.

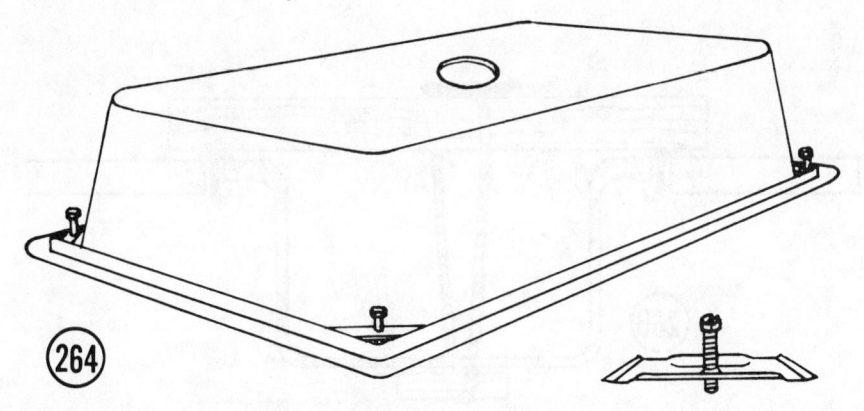

Now place sink and frame in opening and fasten frame to countertop with lugs, Illus. 265, spaced every 6 or 8". Tighten lugs evenly, with same pressure on each, until top of frame fits securely to countertop. Don't apply too much pressure or you will pull frame out of position.

SINK FRAME

LUGS Supplied by Sink Manufacturer

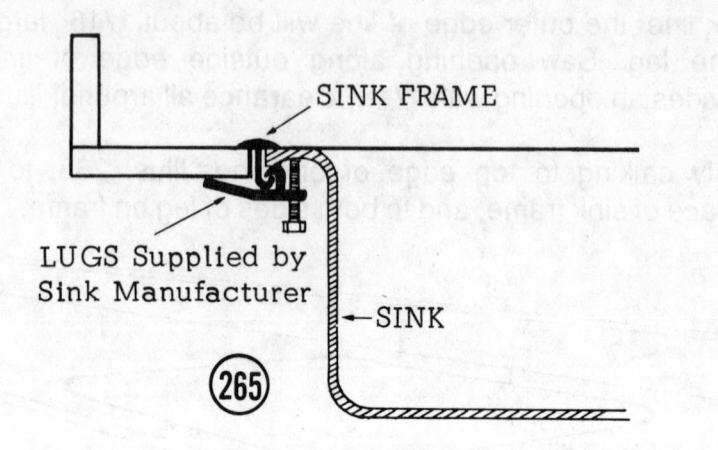

SINK

265

If sink manufacturer doesn't provide a frame that can be fastened to sink at four corners, as in Illus. 264, use pieces of 2x4, and rope to hold sink in position while fastening sink lugs, Illus. 266.

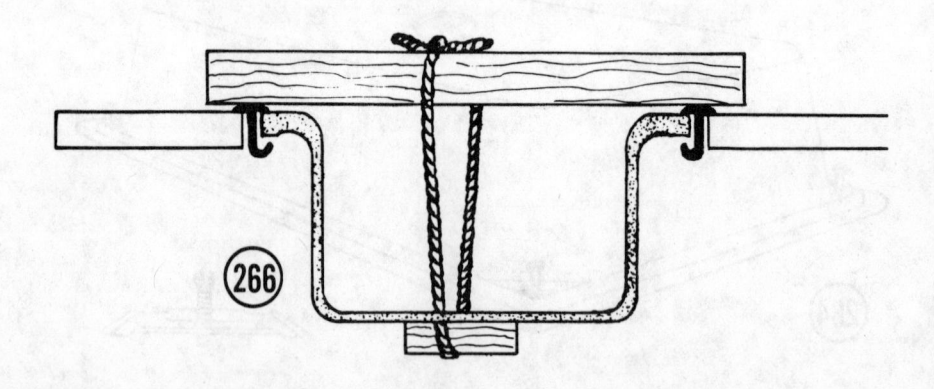

266

If faucets go through countertop, and not through sink, drill holes to size and position required by sink manufacturer.

COUNTER RANGE

Manufacturers provide a sketch or full size template for cutting opening in countertop. A saber saw with a blade containing 10 teeth to the inch, simplifies cutting. Allow counter space on both sides of range, Illus. 267, 268. Note, Illus. 25.

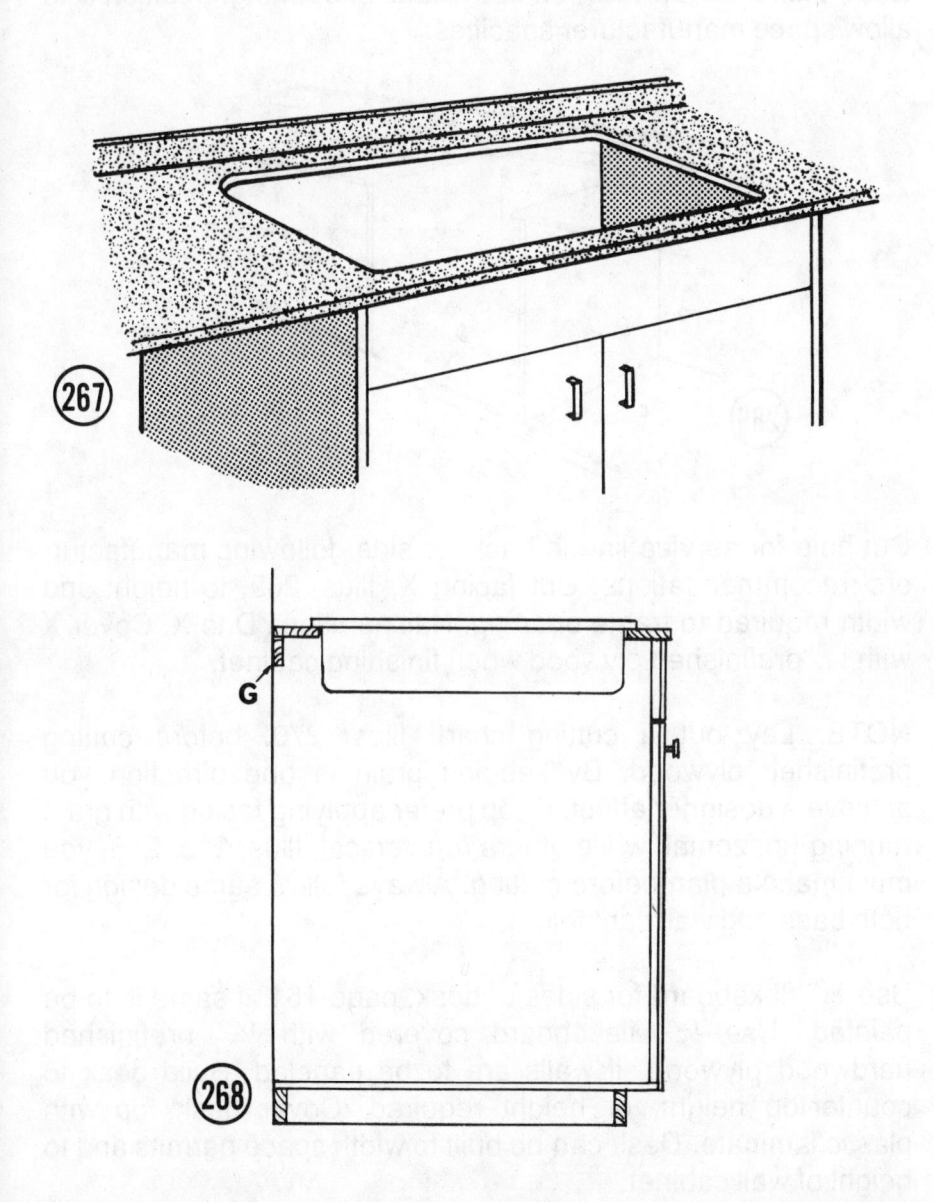

(267)

(268)

201

BUILT-IN RANGE AND OVEN

Many combination range and oven units can be installed by cutting countertop and cabinet to shape shown, Illus. 269. Cut countertop to size range manufacturer recommends. Since many units hang from flanges resting, or fastened to countertop, install a ¾" partition on both sides of opening. Position D to allow space manufacturer specifies.

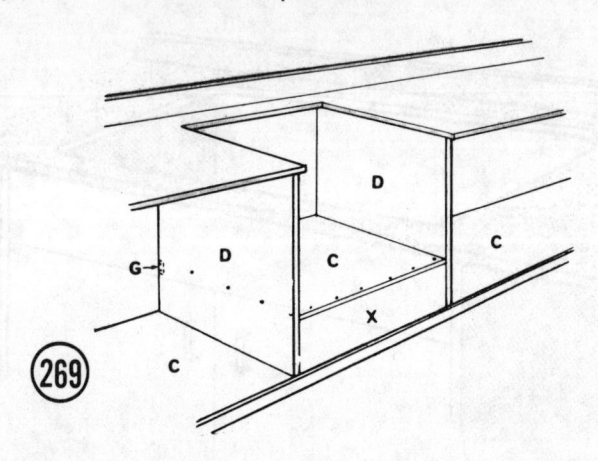

Cut hole for service line in back, or side, following manufacturers' recommendations. Cut facing X, Illus. 269, to height and width required to frame opening. Nail partitions D to X. Cover X with ¼" prefinished plywood when finishing cabinet.

NOTE: Lay out a cutting chart, Illus. 270, before cutting prefinished plywood. By keeping grain in one direction you achieve a designer effect. If you prefer applying facing with grain running horizontal, while others run vertical, Illus. 215, 216, you must make a plan before cutting. Always follow same design for both base and wall cabinets.

Use ¾" flakeboard for sides of desk, page 161, if same is to be painted. Use ½" flakeboard covered with ¼" prefinished hardwood plywood, if walls are to be paneled. Build desk to countertop height, or height required. Cover desk top with plastic laminate. Desk can be built to width space permits and to height of wall cabinet.

⌀—— 4' ——

O

DOOR

GRAIN

¼" PREFINISHED HARDWOOD PLYWOOD

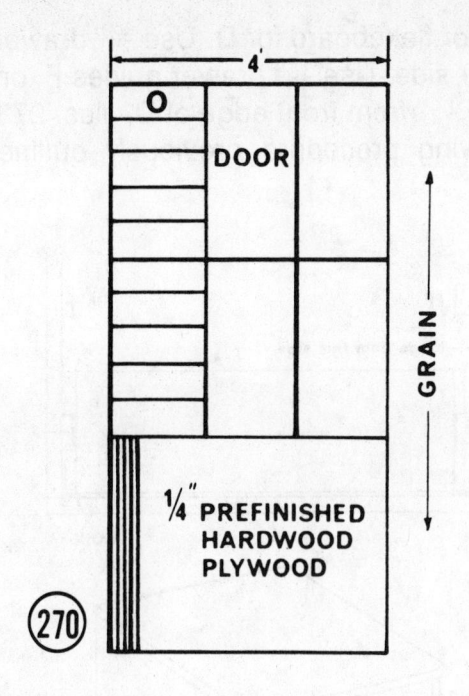

(270)

When building a base cabinet containing drawers, or trays, concealed by a door, Illus. 271, follow these directions.

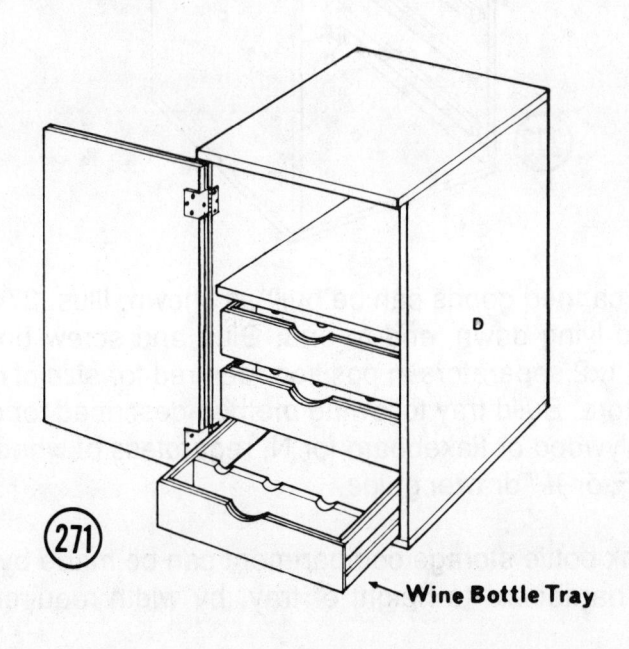

(271)

← Wine Bottle Tray

203

Use ¾" plywood or flakeboard for D. Use ¾" drawer guides FF, Illus. 272, on door side. Use ⅜" drawer guides F, on other side. Recess FF and F ½" from front edge of D, Illus. 273. Install FF, F, and H, following procedure previously outlined for base cabinet.

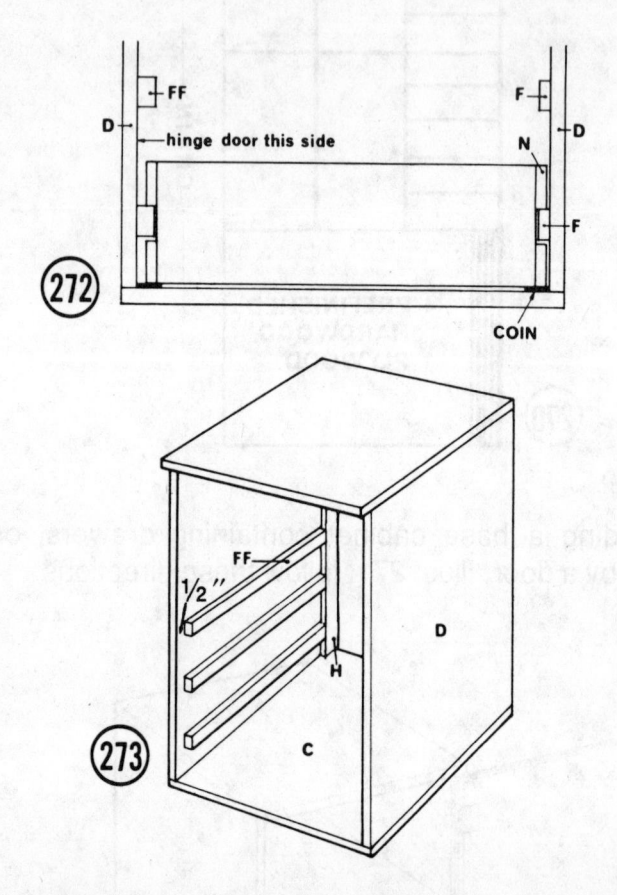

A tray for canned goods can be built as shown, Illus. 274. Cans are stored lying down, end to end. Glue and screw bottom of drawer to 1x2 separators in position required for size of can you want to store. Build tray following method described for drawer. Use ⅜" plywood or flakeboard for N, regardless of whether you use ¾" FF, or ⅜" drawer guide.

A soft drink bottle storage compartment can be made by cutting ⅛ or ¼" hardboard to height of tray, by width required, Illus. 275, 276.

(274) **Canned Goods Tray**

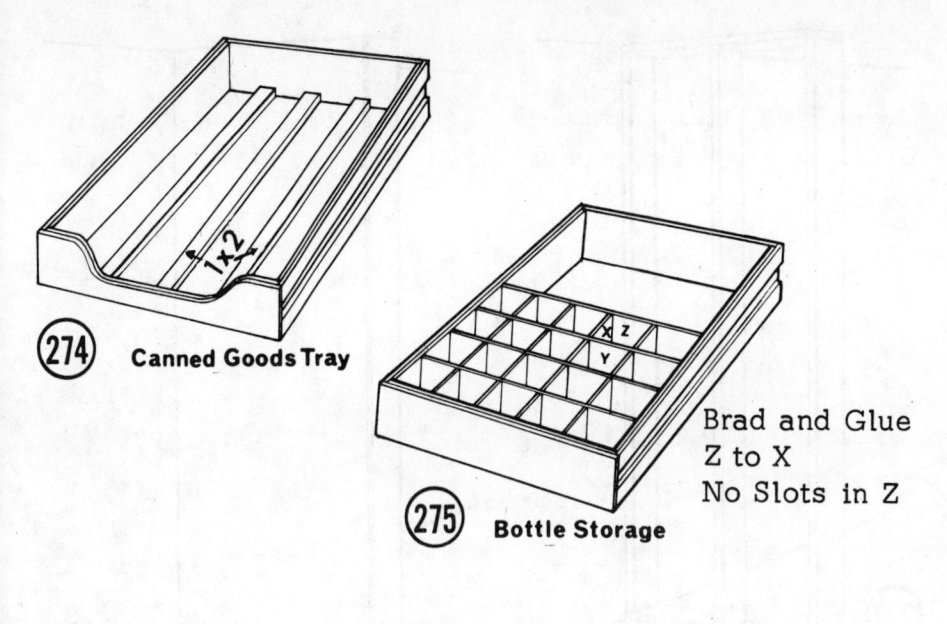

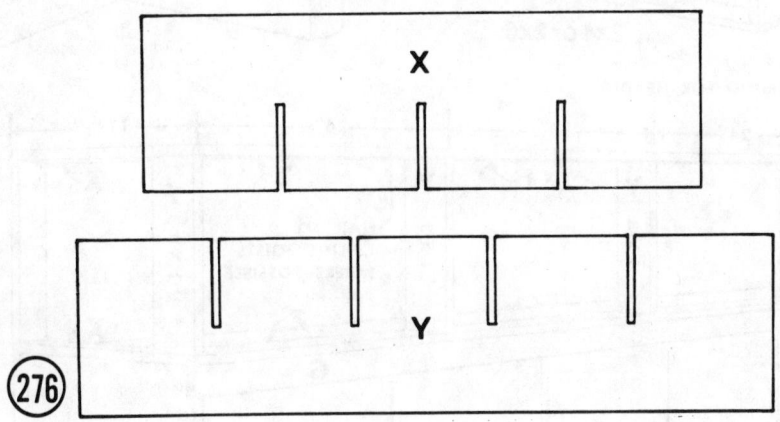

(275) **Bottle Storage**

Brad and Glue
Z to X
No Slots in Z

(276)

If refrigerator is placed in an exposed end, build a 2x4 or 2x6 partition, Illus 277. Cut ¼" prefinished plywood to size. Using panel adhesive, apply paneling. Miter cut matching ceiling trim, apply in position indicated. Do same with matching base.

Space above wall cabinets, in a room with a high ceiling, can be enclosed with a header, Illus. 278. Nail 1x3 to top of cabinet, another 1x3 to ceiling. Nail 1x3 studs, 24" on centers. Cover G and framing for header with one piece of ¼" prefinished plywood.

(277) 2x4 or 2x6

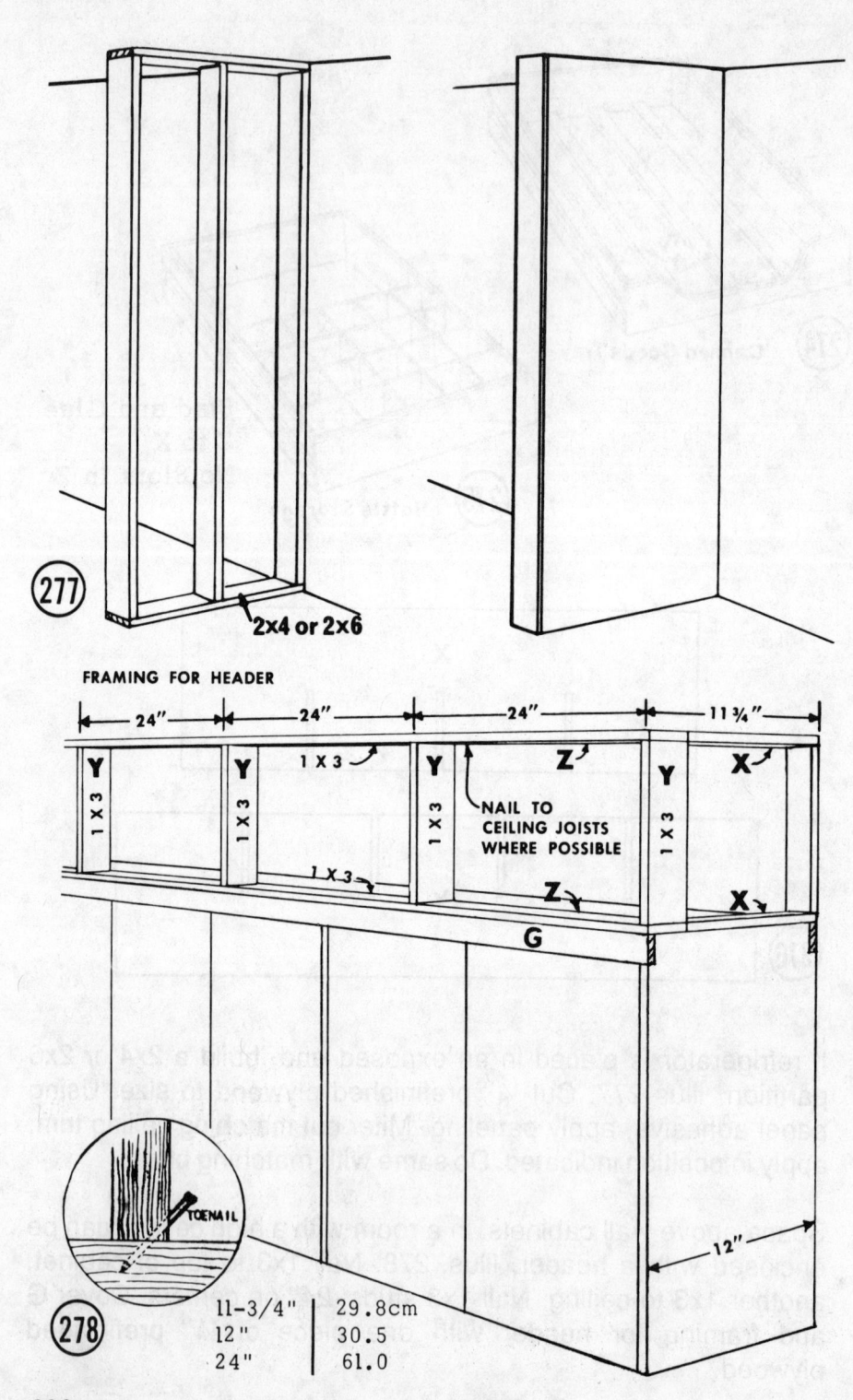

FRAMING FOR HEADER

24" — 24" — 24" — 11¾"

1 X 3 — Y — Y — Z — Y — X

NAIL TO CEILING JOISTS WHERE POSSIBLE

G

(278) TOENAIL

11-3/4"	29.8cm
12"	30.5
24"	61.0

206

BUILD PASS THROUGH

Illus. 279 shows wall framed for pass through between kitchen and dining area.

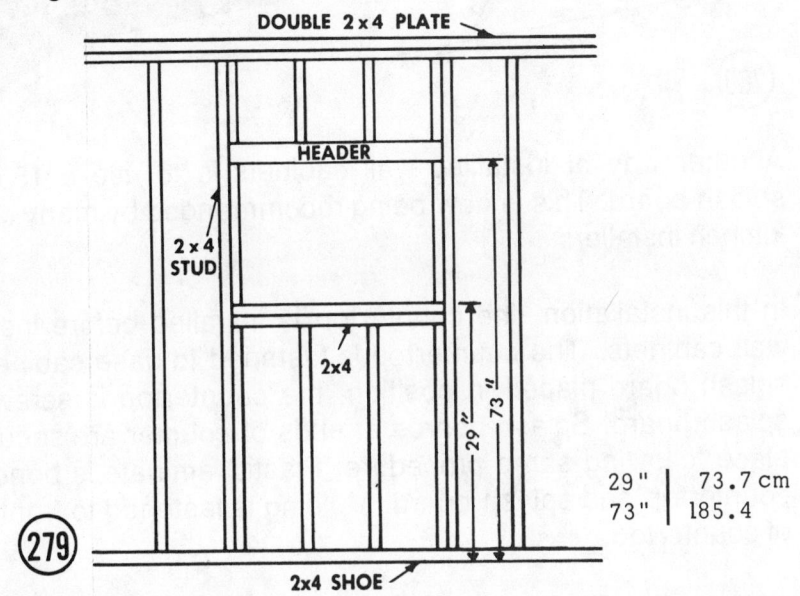

| 29" | 73.7 cm |
| 73" | 185.4 |

If there is a dumbwaiter in the house your insurance company will recommend framing it in and covering with gypsum wallboard, paneling, or base and wall cabinet.

HOW TO INSTALL ASSEMBLED CABINETS

Estimate size of space available following procedure previously outlined. Order cabinets to fit. Most manufacturers also sell "filler units" to fit odd size space.

Level up base cabinets as previously suggested. If shingle is required to level base cabinet, the base can be covered with matching floor tile, Illus. 280.

To simplify installing wall cabinets, draw a line. Use level, Illus. 226, at height that indicates bottom of wall cabinet. Nail a 1x2 temporarily along this line. This supports wall cabinet while being installed.

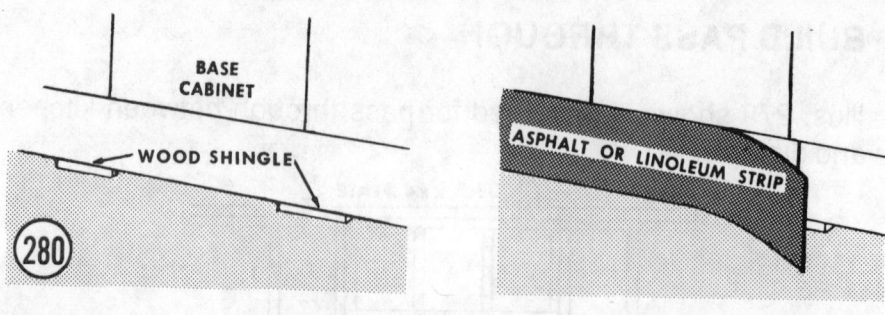

Another way of installing wall cabinets is to use a 15 or 18" splash board. This is now being recommended by many custom kitchen installers.

In this installation, the countertop is installed before installing wall cabinets. The countertop is fastened to base cabinet, the splash board placed in position, the countertop is screwed to splash board. Splash boards at ends of counter are secured in place following same procedure. Plastic laminate is bonded to countertop and splash board. Molding is fastened to front edge of countertop.

A free standing island can be built following base cabinet construction. Extend countertop 6, 8 or 10" on one or both sides, and/or exposed end. Cover back of cabinet with ¼" prefinished plywood or flakeboard.

A cleaning closet, Illus. 281, can be built to fit any space available. If doors are made to match those on wall cabinets, upper part can be used to store cleaners, polishers, etc., while lower part accommodates brooms, mops, pails, vacuum sweeper, etc.

WALL COVERING

After plumbing and electrical work has been roughed in, you can apply washable wallpaper or plastic wall covering on walls. Since the covering need only be applied to exposed area, use the best, it costs very little. Allow covering to overlap wall and base cabinet space 2". The outline of cabinets and equipment drawn on wall serves as a guide for applying wall covering.

The wall above top cabinets need not be covered. This can be enclosed by building a header above cabinets, Illus. 278. If no header is used, wall can be painted color of ceiling.

Since decorative ceramic tile is now in popular demand for use on countertops and on walls between base and wall cabinets, this can be installed after cabinets are in position. Complete, step-by-step directions for installing ceramic tile are provided in Easi-Bild Simplified Direction Book #606, How to Lay Ceramic Tile.

ELECTRIC EXTRAS

Range hoods are now available with electronic filters that eliminate need for duct work. While a ventilating fan on an outside wall seldom needs duct work, if duct work is required, run ducts through cabinet to header, then to outside wall, Illus. 278.

New automatic appliance centers can be installed in countertops or in walls. These offer a completely automatic power source containing timer, receptacle, retractable cords for coffee maker, toaster, mixer, iron, sharpener, etc. Each circuit is protected by a circuit breaker.

Switches for outside floodlights should not be overlooked when planning your kitchen. Provision for such light may be made now at little extra cost and the lights added later.

Magnetic switches on kitchen windows and door, plus an emergency alarm button to discourage burglaries, should be installed before paneling or wallpapering walls. See Book #695 How to Install Protective Alarm Devices.

Built in radio, television or intercom, available in convenient sizes and finishes, are now available for use in modern kitchens.

Heat sensitive fire alarms for the home are available. Install where manufacturer specifies in rooms containing a fireplace, range or oven. Make certain the burglary and fire alarm system selected carries the Underwriters Seal of Approval.

ADHESIVE SIMPLIFIES MODERNIZING REFRIGERATOR

You can transform old fashioned metal and wood kitchen cabinets, or a refrigerator, Illus. 282, into handsome, furniture type cabinets, by applying prefinished hardwood plywood.

If your refrigerator is in good working condition, but shows age, glamorize it in the following manner. First measure overall width, height and depth of refrigerator, Illus. 283. Place a piece of 1x2-A on face of refrigerator. Place a piece of ¼" plywood on top of 1x2. Place another piece of ¼" plywood on refrigerator door. If both panels are on same plane, cut 1x2-B length required. If panel on door projects beyond panel on A, cut 1x2-B length required so both panels are flush. Don't cover any ventilating grill.

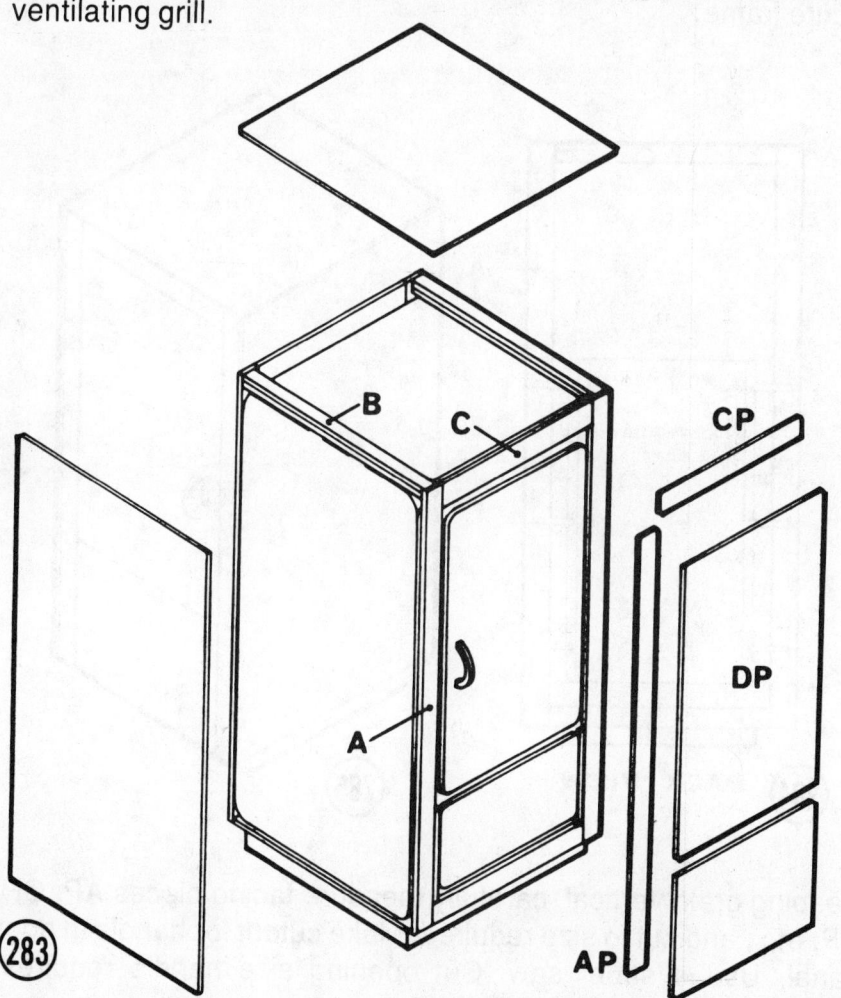

211

Apply glue and nail A to B with 6 penny finishing nails. Place in position on refrigerator. Allow outside edge of AB to project ⅛" from side of refrigerator. Cut 1x2 C length required. Apply glue and toenail C to AB in position shown. Check framing with square.

Test refrigerator door to make certain it moves freely. Position A-¼", or distance required, away from hinge to provide clearance hinge requires. Fasten back frame, Illus. 284, to refrigerator with plumber's strap. Remove screws in refrigerator to fasten strap in position. If refrigerator doesn't have any screws in the right position, fasten additional 1x2 across back to secure frame.

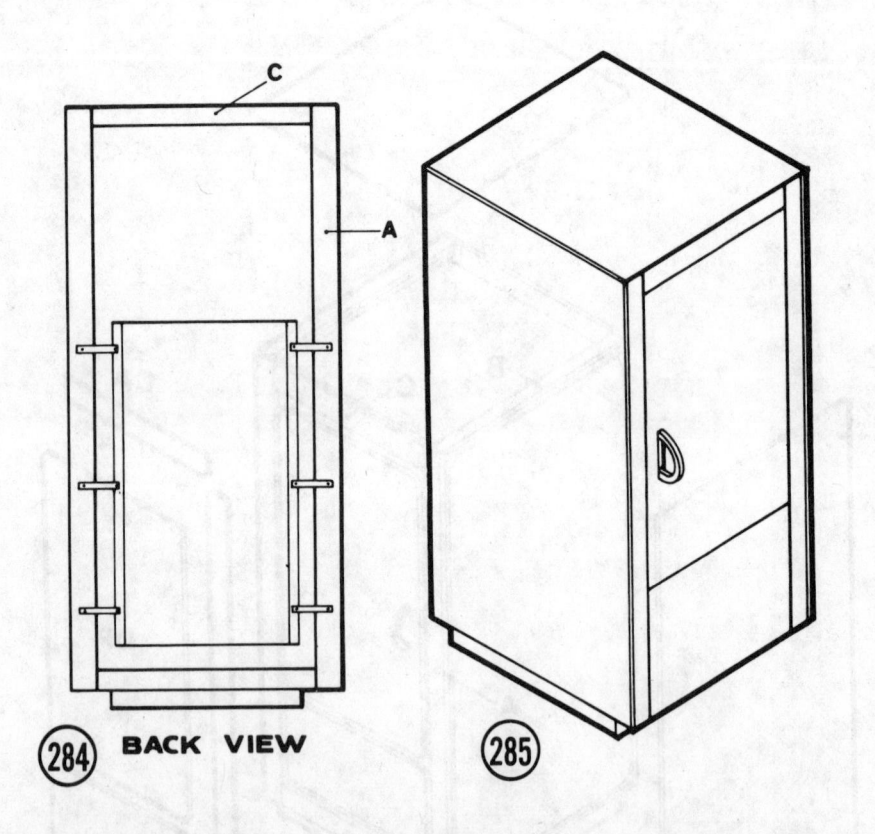

(284) BACK VIEW   (285)

Keeping grain vertical, carefully measure facing pieces AP, CP, DP, etc., and cut to size required. Make cutout for handle in door panel. Use a saber saw. Cut opening size handle requires.

Place panel in position to test handle. Sandpaper edges. Holding door panel in position, open and close door to make certain it doesn't bind on hinges.

You now have a square and level frame. Cut ¼" prefinished hardwood plywood to size required. Apply adhesive and fasten in position. Due to moisture content around most old refrigerators, panel adhesive or waterproof glue is recommended, Illus. 285.

Holding door panel in position, open and close door to make certain it doesn't bind on hinges. Door panel can be glued to door with epoxy. Use 1-1½" dabs of epoxy every 8 to 10", Illus. 286.

Cut top and side panels, glue in position. Edge of plywood can be finished with matching Putty Stik. If edge requires filling, use matching wood filler, Illus. 287.

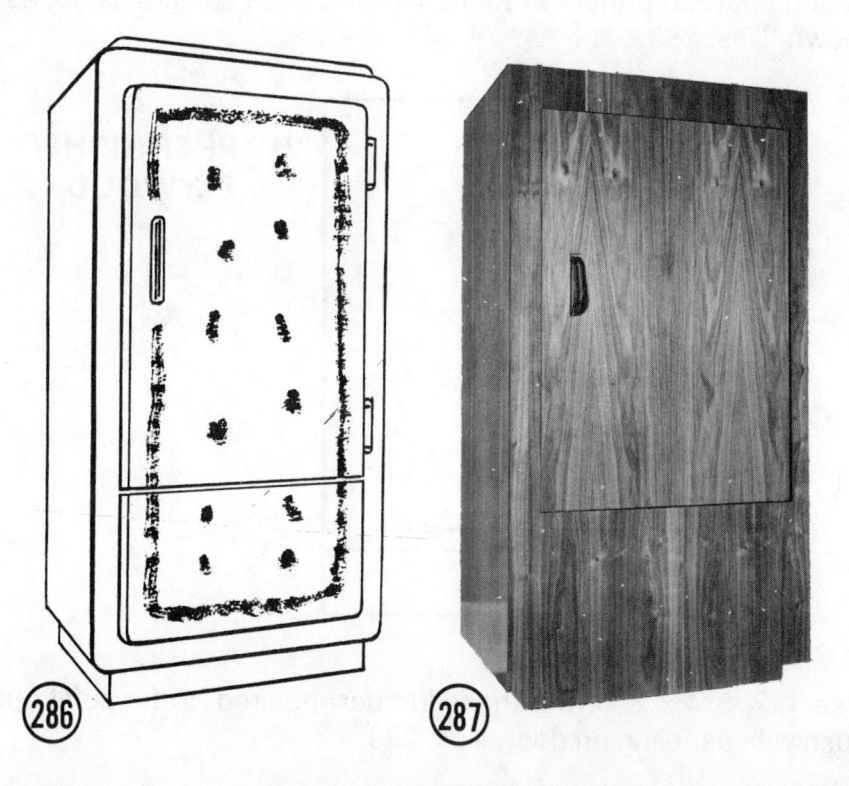

HOW TO MODERNIZE WOOD KITCHEN CABINETS

Remove ceiling molding, door hardware, any raised molding on door. Before cutting prefinished paneling, make a test using ¼" fir plywood. Cut panel to size door requires, cut a piece to cover adjacent post. Hold both parts in position, or use rubber cement to temporarily fasten panels in place. If door swings free, proceed with prefinished plywood. If door binds, try adjusting hinges to accommodate thicker door. If existing hinges can't be adjusted, test door with one continuous hinge, or two 5" pieces of continuous hinge, Illus. 291. If door still binds, use 3½" H-hinges.

If you plan on modernizing your kitchen cabinets with hardwood plywood facing, go all the way and apply panels to walls. First remove ceiling molding. Buy panels that equal floor to ceiling height. When cutting panels for wall cabinets, lay out your cutting chart so panel for soffit, wall and base cabinet, is cut as shown, Illus. 288.

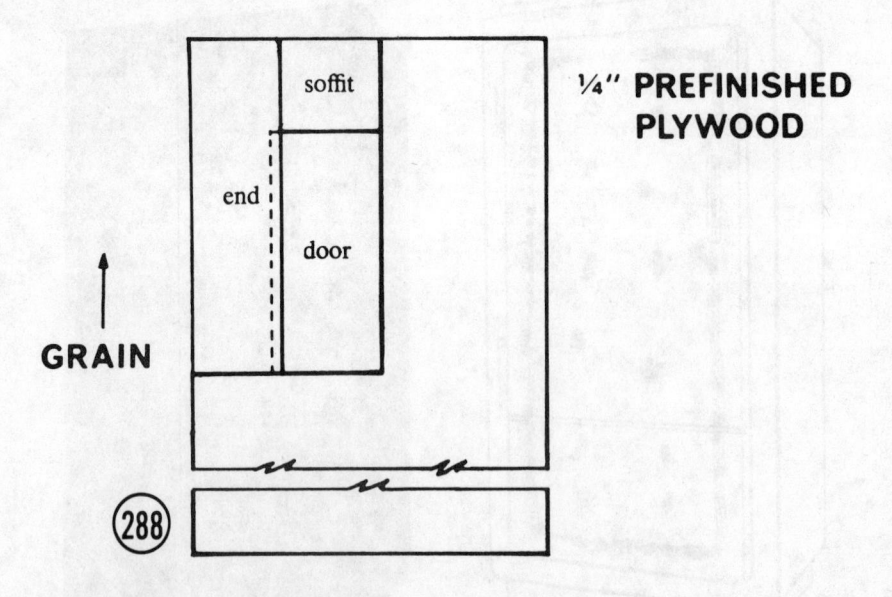

¼" PREFINISHED PLYWOOD

288

Use 1x2, 5/4 x 2, or thickness lumber required, to fur soffit out flush with paneling on door, Illus. 289.

(289)

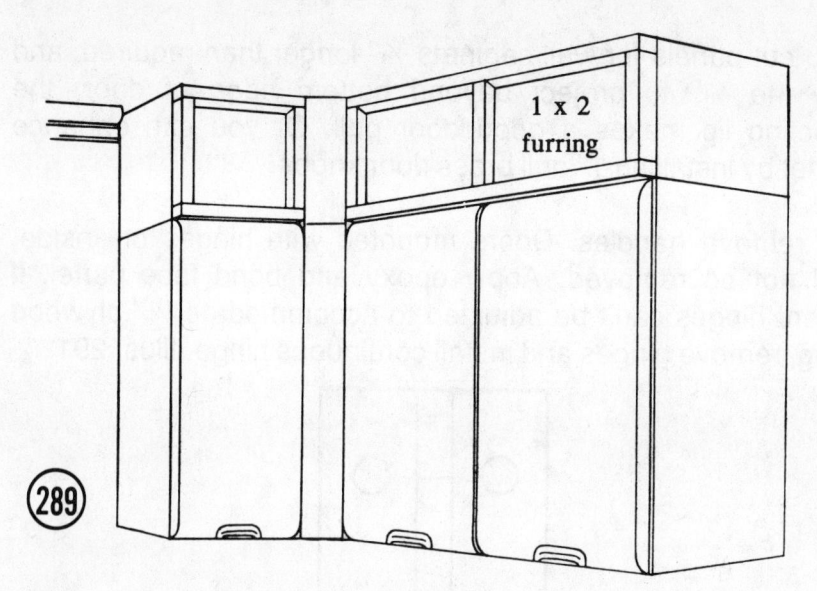

1 x 2 furring

Always cut plywood so grain runs vertically. A rough layout permits cutting panel with little waste.

If you want to cover both edges of a wood cabinet door with plywood, trim door down to size required, apply ¼" plywood strip A to both edges, Illus. 290.

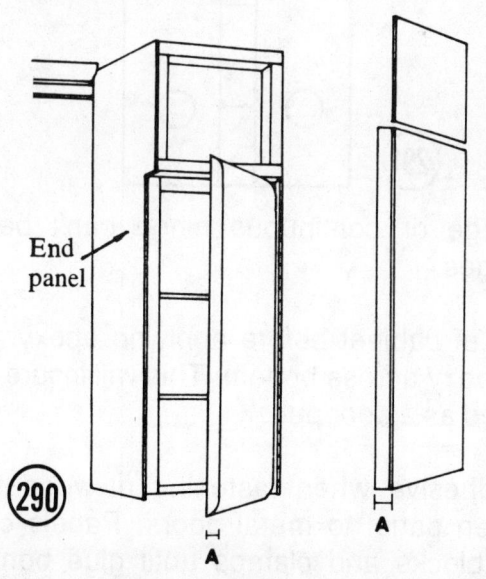

End panel

(290)

Cut END PANEL slightly oversize. Scribe to wall, cut to width required, then cut strip A for edge of door.

If you cut panels for wall cabinets ⅜" longer than required, and allow the ⅜" to project beyond bottom edge of door, the projecting lip makes a good door pull. Or you can enhance cabinet by installing 1" dull brass door knobs.

First remove handles. Doors mounted with hinges on inside, need not be removed. Apply epoxy and bond face panel. If present hinges can't be adjusted to accommodate ¼" plywood facing, remove hinges and install continuous hinge, Illus. 291.

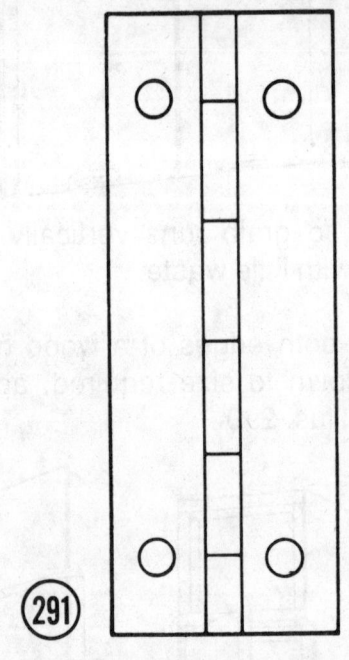

(291)

If original hinge or continuous hinge can't be used, apply colonial H-hinges.

Sand surface of cabinet before applying epoxy. Apply a 1" to 1½" strip of epoxy across bottom. This will insure extra strength when lip is used as a door pull.

Use panel adhesive when fastening plywood to wood. Use epoxy to fasten panel to metal doors. Panels can be held in position with blocks and clamps until glue bonds, Illus. 292. Follow panel adhesive manufacturer's directions. Some recommend applying plywood to metal with panel adhesive, Illus. 293.

292

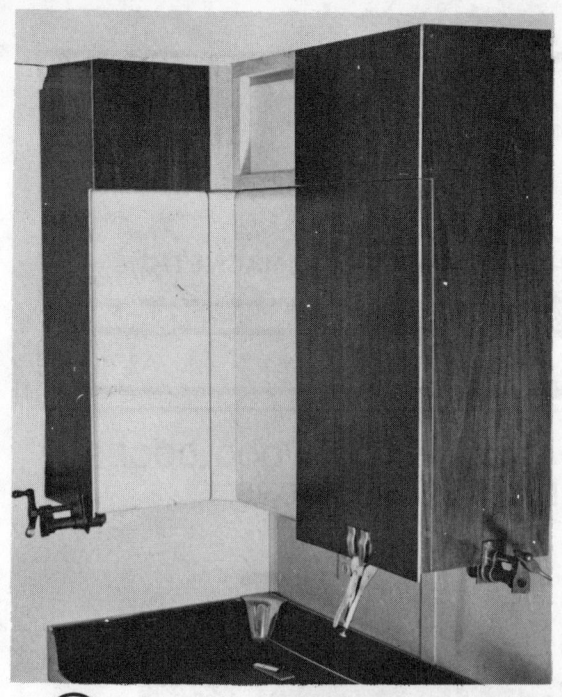

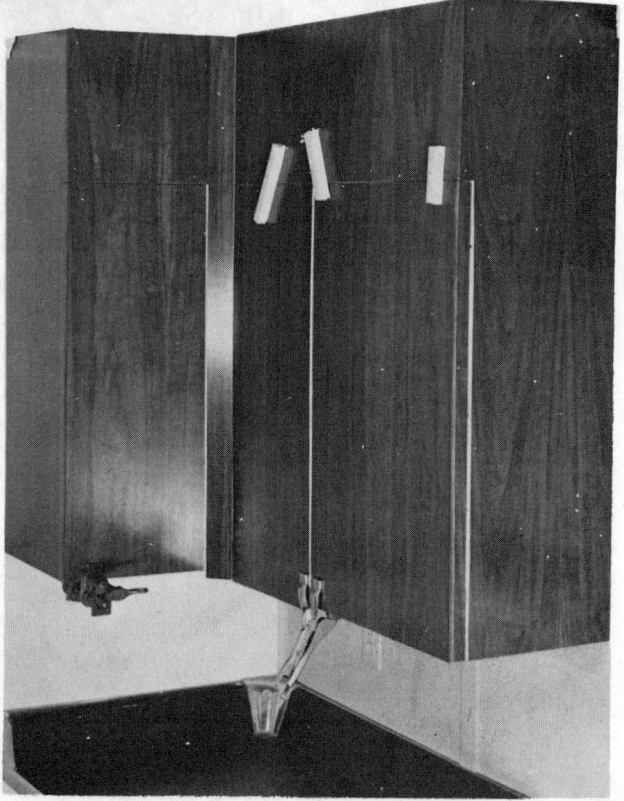

293

217

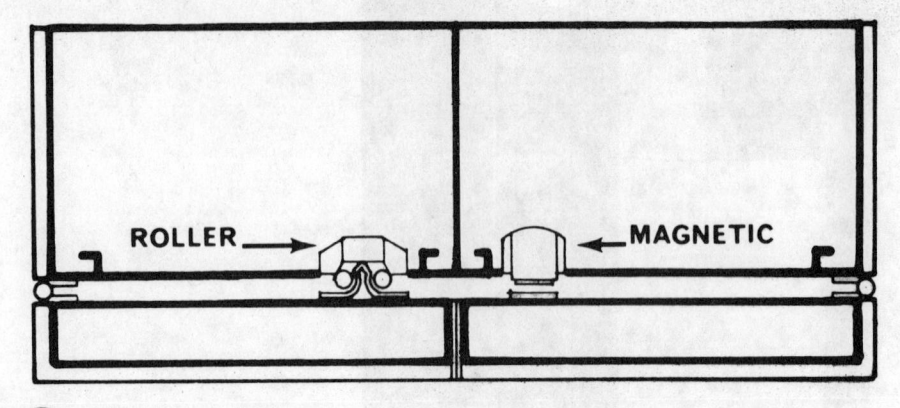

(294) USE MAGNETIC CATCHES ON WOOD DOORS, ROLLER CATCHES ON METAL DOORS.

218

Apply paneling to ends first. Cut panel width required to cover end of cabinet and edge of door. Scribe edge to fit against wall, then cut panel to size required, Illus. 290.

Install a magnetic door catch in position following manufacturer's directions, Illus. 293, 294. Stain edge of panel. Finish exposed edge of door with wood tape when space doesn't permit covering with ¼" plywood, Illus. 295.

Use 3" strips of hardwood plywood for ceiling trim, Illus. 296.

APPLICATION AT CEILING

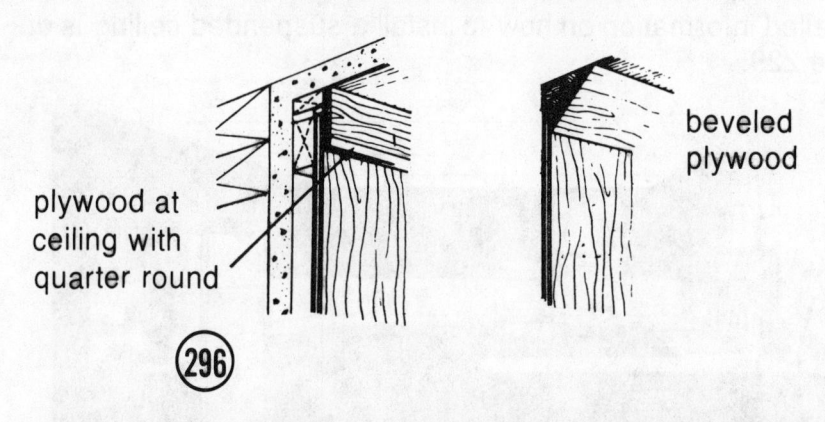

plywood at ceiling with quarter round

beveled plywood

(296)

Use panel adhesive when applying plywood to studs in new construction, over smooth, tight plaster or plaster board.

INSTALL CEILINGS

If an existing ceiling is beyond repair consider applying gypsum wallboard or decorative ceiling tiles. These can be bonded with adhesive if existing ceiling provides a tight level base. If ceiling is loose or damaged beyond repair, remove lathe and plaster and nail gypsum wallboard to joists.

If room height permits, consider installing a suspended ceiling, Illus. 297. This is easy to install and simplifies finishing a room with a level ceiling without a lot of leveling. A suspended ceiling should only be installed after wall paneling has been completed. Detailed information on how to install a suspended ceiling is on page 229.

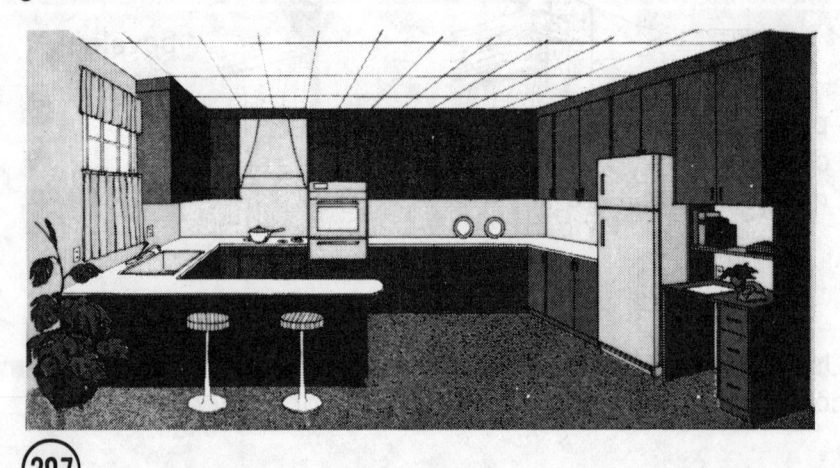

(297)

PANEL WALLS

If walls are beyond repair you can apply gypsum wallboard over a tight, plumb, lathe and plaster wall, or apply plywood or hardboard paneling. This can be bonded with adhesive or nailed.

Remove shoe molding, baseboard and crown molding, Illus. 298. With a straight 2 x 4 and a 4' level, Illus. 299, check walls at various points to make certain each is plumb. If plaster is loose, remove lathe and plaster.

221

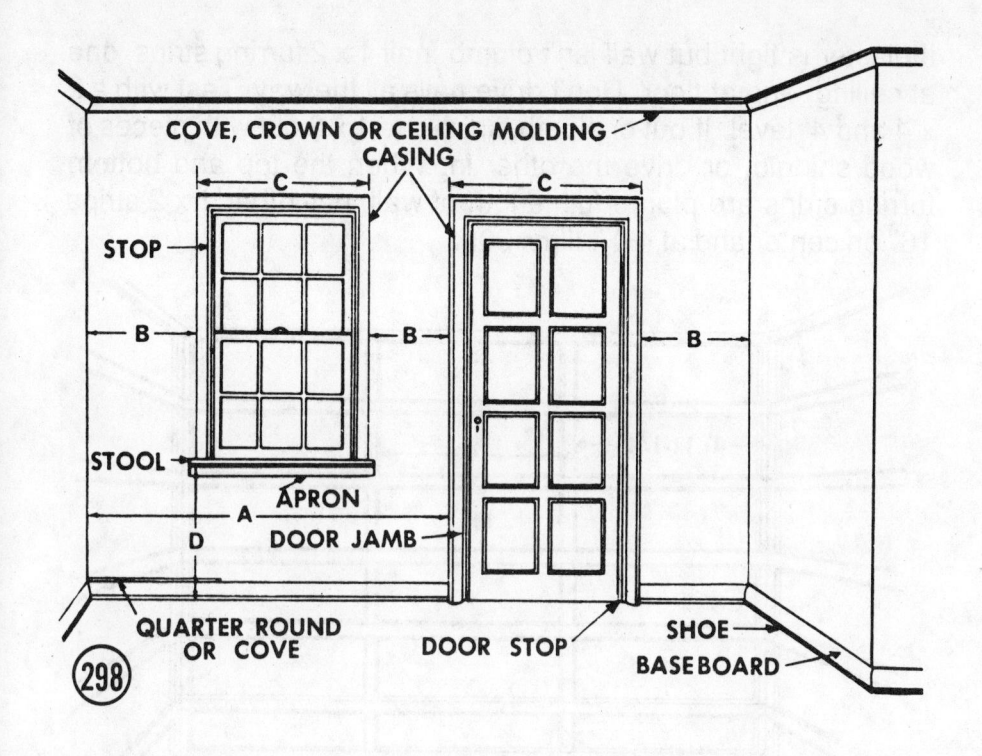

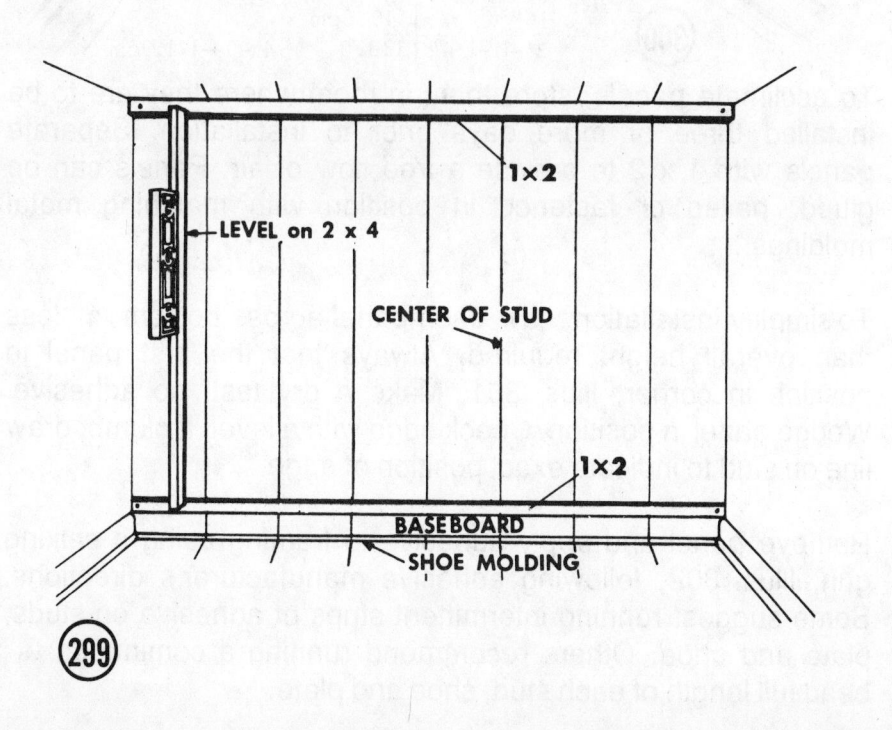

If plaster is tight but wall isn't plumb, nail 1 x 2 furring strips, one at ceiling, one at floor. Don't drive nails all the way. Test with a 2 x 4 and 4' level. If out of plumb, shim one 1 x 2 out with pieces of wood shingle, or drive the other in. When the top and bottom furring strips are plumb full length of wall, nail other 1 x 2 strips 16" on center and at 4'0", Illus. 300.

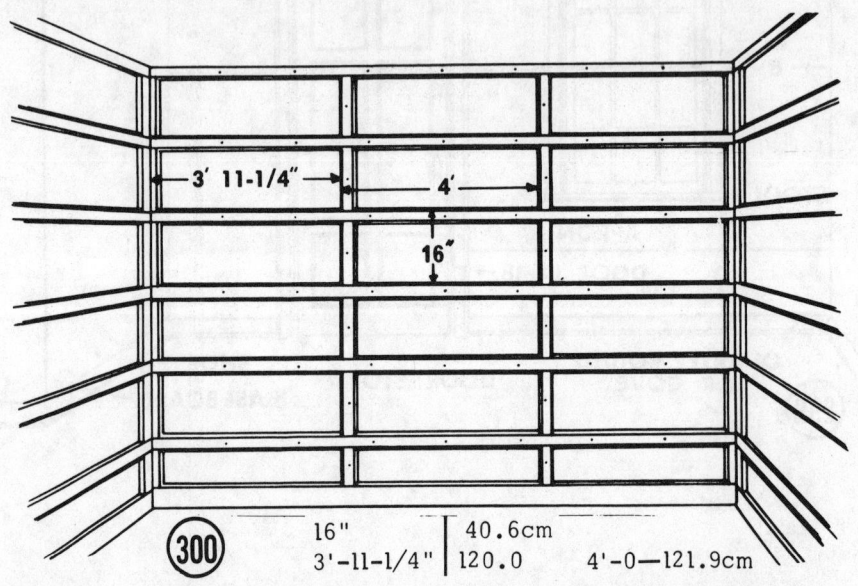

300
```
          16"      | 40.6cm
       3'-11-1/4"  | 120.0      4'-0—121.9cm
```

To acclimate panels, store them in room where they are to be installed three or more days prior to installation. Separate panels with 1 x 2 to provide a free flow of air. Panels can be glued, nailed or fastened in position with matching metal moldings.

To simplify installation, saw each panel across bottom ¼" less than overall height required. Always test the first panel in position in corner, Illus. 301. Make a dry test, no adhesive. Wedge panel in position. Check edge with a level. If plumb, draw line on stud to indicate exact position of edge.

Remove panel and apply adhesive to framing using a calking gun, Illus. 302, following adhesive manufacturer's directions. Some suggest running intermittent strips of adhesive on studs, plate and shoe. Others recommend running a continuous ⅛" bead full length of each stud, shoe and plate.

(301)

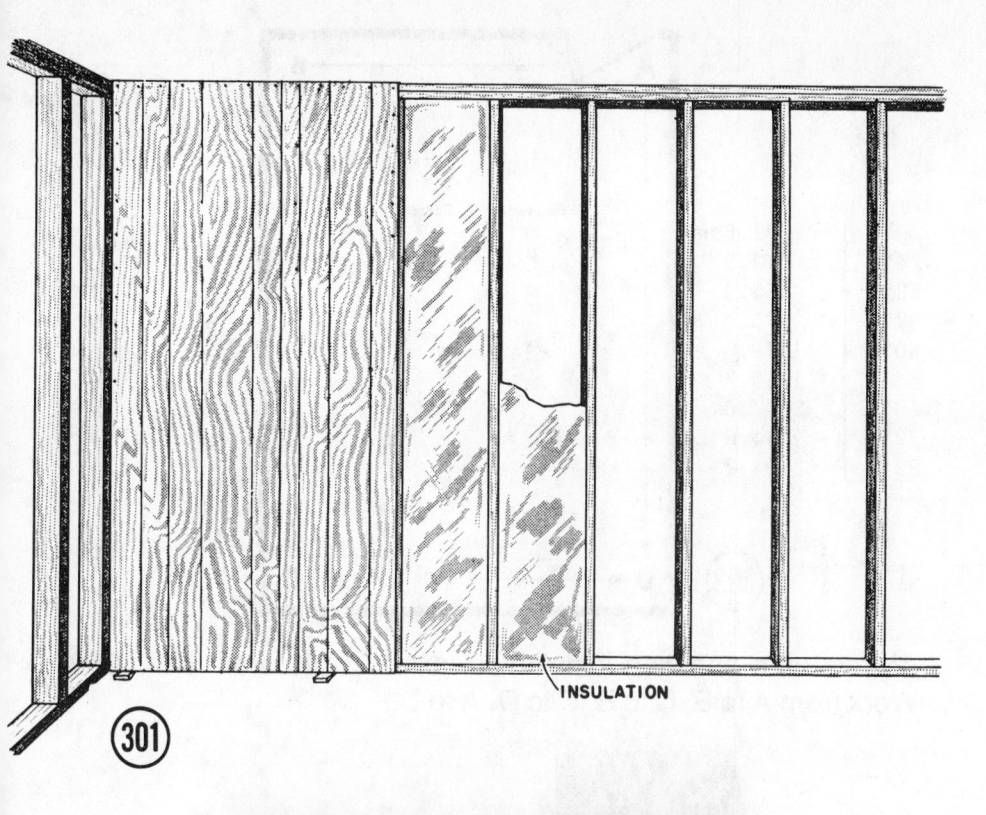

INSULATION

(302)

Panel adhesive greatly simplifies installation, but it should only be applied in temperatures ranging from 60° to 100°. Due to expansion, don't butt panels tight, allow 1/16", or amount plywood manufacturer or retailer suggests.

223

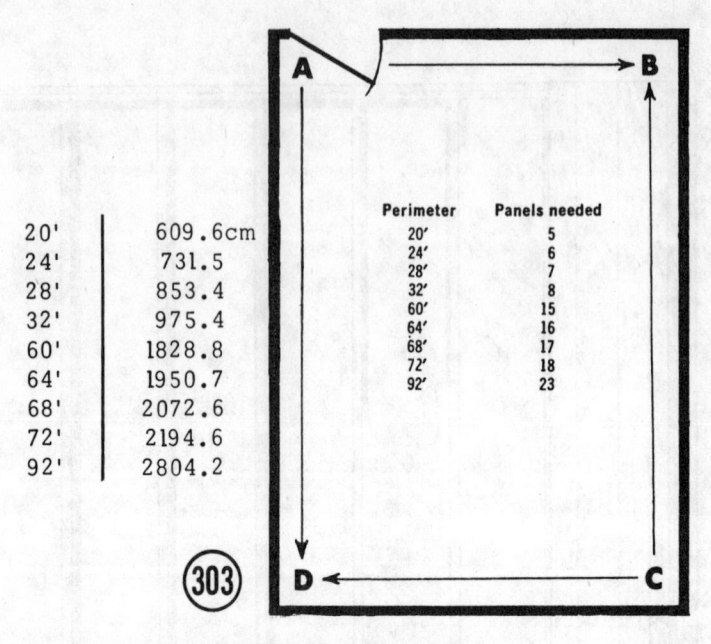

20'	609.6cm	Perimeter	Panels needed
24'	731.5	20'	5
28'	853.4	24'	6
32'	975.4	28'	7
60'	1828.8	32'	8
64'	1950.7	60'	15
68'	2072.6	64'	16
72'	2194.6	68'	17
92'	2804.2	72'	18
		92'	23

Always plan paneling installation in direction noted, Illus. 303. Work from A to B, C to B, C to D, A to D.

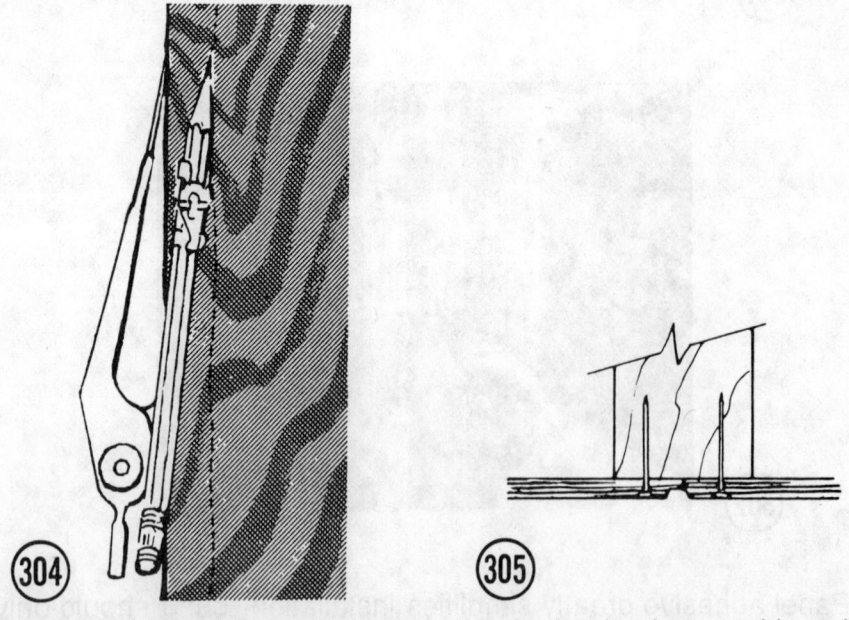

If the first panel in corner doesn't check plumb when positioned dry, hold it plumb with a couple of nails driven temporarily into top edge. When panel is plumb, scribe to corner, Illus. 304.

Keep point of scriber following corner, pencil on panel. A white charcoal pencil, available in art supply stores, will mark without damaging a prefinished panel. Remove panel and saw or plane edge to scribed line. Replace panel, check with level. When first panel checks plumb, remove and apply adhesive to studs, shoe, plate and to any cats between studs. If you prefer to nail panels, nail every 6" along outer edge, every 12" to intermediate studs. If grooved paneling is being installed, nail panel as shown, Illus. 305. Avoid nailing in grooves. Always match groove at joint over a stud.

First measure perimeter by adding width and length of room. For example, 12, 12, 16, 16 = 56 ft. Next convert according to chart, Illus. 303. If exact figure isn't shown, take next higher figure. For example, 24 + 32 = 56. 24 requires 6 panels; 32 requires 8; 6 + 8 = 14 panels. Add approximately 5% for waste. This estimator is designed for rooms having 7 ft. or 8 ft. ceilings. For higher ceilings, ask your dealer to estimate paneling required. Now deduct for doors, windows, fireplace area, etc. If you want to panel a door, do not deduct.

When a panel requires a cutout for part or all of a door, window, switch or outlet box; plumb panel in position on left side of window, door, etc., tight against ceiling. Draw top and botton line of opening. Measure distance to edge of previously installed panel A, Illus. 306.

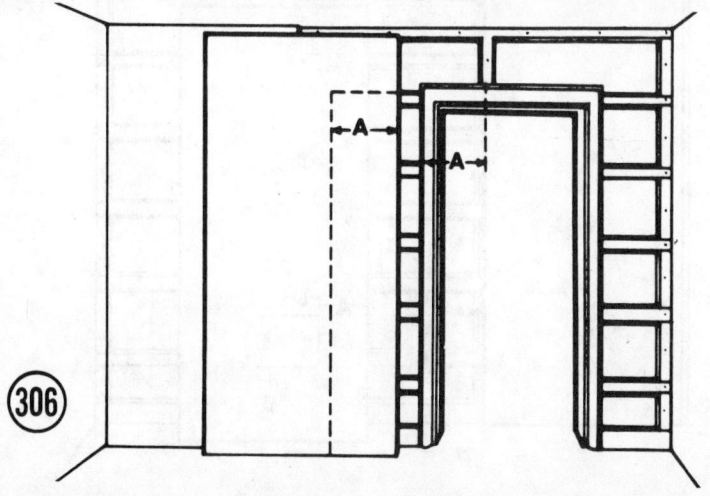

Drill a slot of ⅛" holes at diagonal corners on inside of line drawn for an opening, Illus. 307. This permits inserting a keyhole or saber saw.

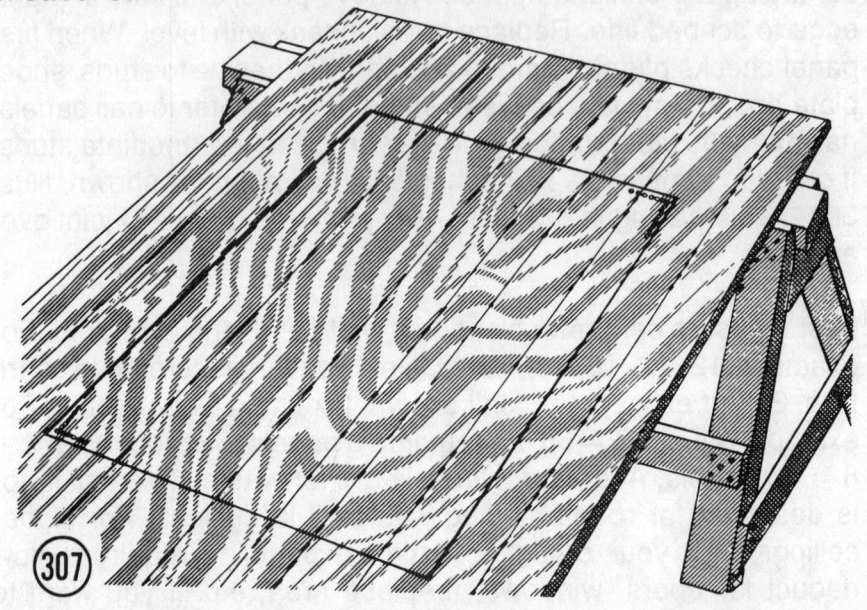

Carefully measure and cut openings for wall outlets, switches, etc. A, Illus. 308, indicates distance to edge of panel to edge of box. B, indicates distance from bottom of box to bottom of panel. C and D equal size of box.

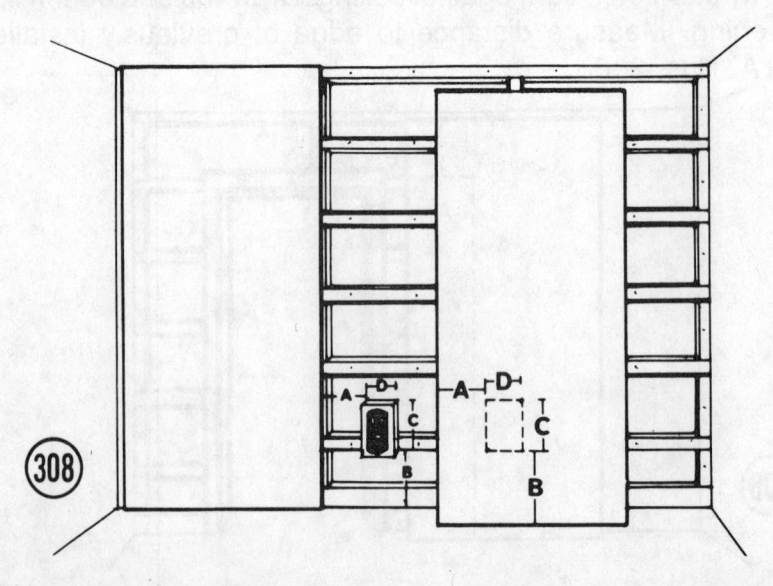

226

Drill ½" holes in position indicated, Illus. 309. Use a keyhole or saber saw to cut opening for box.

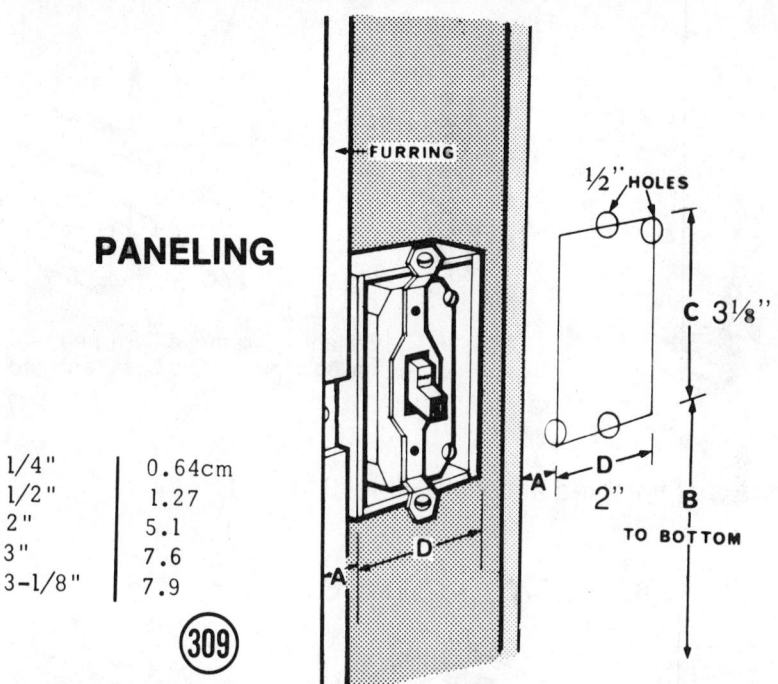

PANELING

1/4"	0.64cm
1/2"	1.27
2"	5.1
3"	7.6
3-1/8"	7.9

(309)

Where a ceiling height is over 8'0" you can use 8'0" panels by adding a base, Illus. 310. Use scrap pieces to fur out bottom.

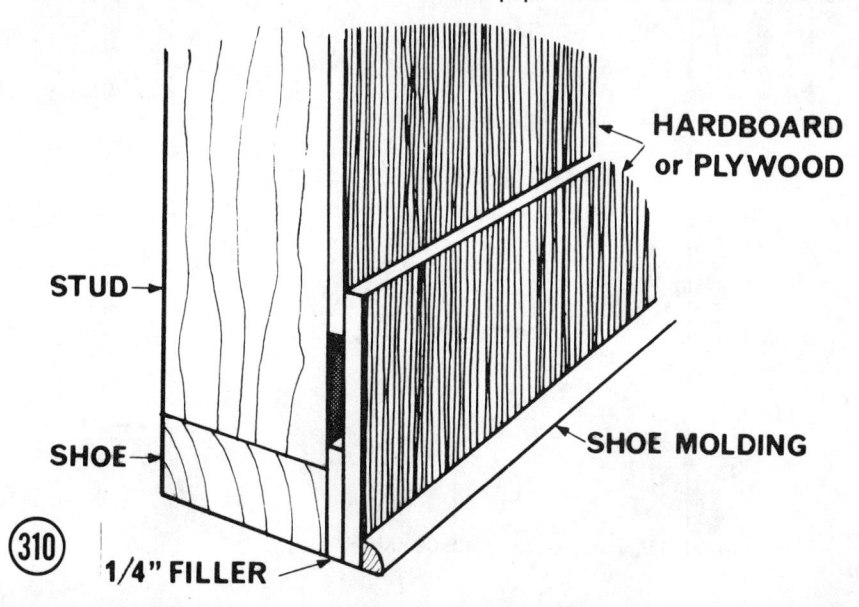

STUD

SHOE

(310) 1/4" FILLER

HARDBOARD or PLYWOOD

SHOE MOLDING

227

APPLICATION AT FLOOR

Apply quarter round at floor.

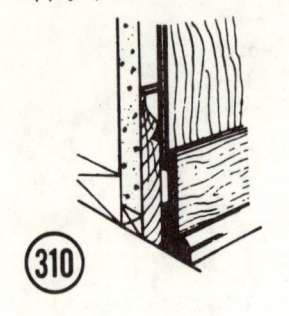

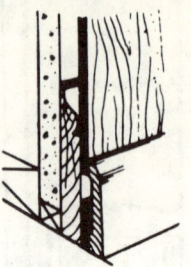

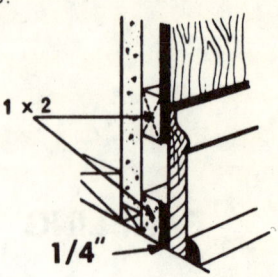

Panel over existing base.

1 x 2

1/4"

Baseboard removed. Furring nailed in place. Old base replaced.

(310)

Note method of finishing at ceiling, Illus. 311.

APPLICATION AT CEILING

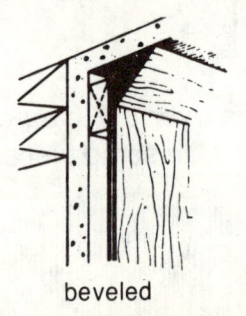

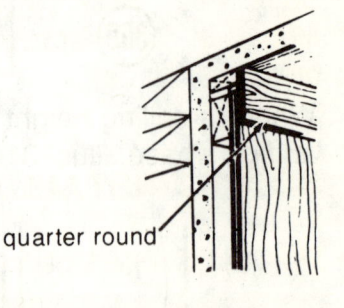

crown molding or cove

beveled

quarter round

(311)

MATCHING MOLDINGS

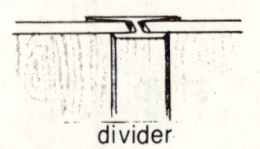

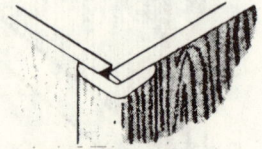

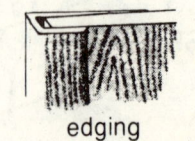

inside corner

inside corner or cove

divider

outside corner

outside corner

edging

(312)

228

Your lumber dealer can provide matching moldings, Illus. 312, that offer another way of installing hardwood panels. Start by fastening inside corner in position with lathe nails. Push panel into molding, then pull out approximately 1/16" as shown. Since molding holds edge, no edge nailing is required. Nail panels every 8" to studs, except where divider strip is to be installed. Butt divider strip against edge of panel, then pull away 1/16". Plumb with level and nail in position with lathe nails through exposed flange. Follow same procedure when installing outside corner.

Another way to install paneling is to butt panels at inside and outside corners, and cover joint with matching wood moldings. Matching casing molding is available for trimming around windows, doors and for use as ceiling trim. A matching base molding is also available. This should be nailed in position after finished flooring has been laid.

Book #605 How To Apply Paneling covers many additional steps. It also explains how to select and install matching moldings, etc., etc.

HOW TO INSTALL A SUSPENDED CEILING

Most suspended ceilings consist of three aluminum components—a prepunched wall angle, Illus. 313, main runner and cross tees, plus 2 x 2 or 2 x 4 ceiling panels.

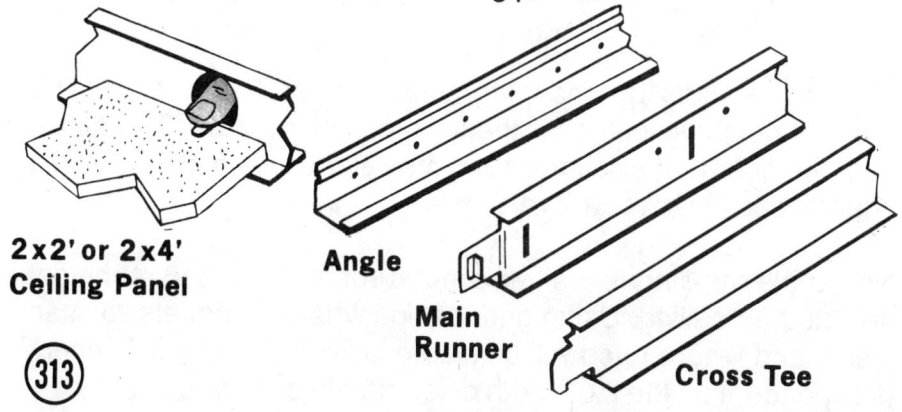

2x2' or 2x4' Ceiling Panel

Angle

Main Runner

Cross Tee

313

Prior to installing a dropped ceiling in rooms on a top floor, ascertain whether attic floor was insulated. If not, staple insulation between joists.

Using the grid on page 254, make a sketch to ascertain best way to run main runner and cross tees, Illus. 314. Does a 2 x 2 panel make a better looking ceiling than a 2 x 4 panel? Or should you cut border panels to one size and go clear round the room with this width panel? Using the layout chart, allow each square to equal one foot. Indicate all lighting panels, heat and air conditioning louvers. Clear plastic panels can be dropped into areas to provide lighting. Always plan lighting panels an equal distance from walls and each other. Fluorescent channel lighting should never be installed in ceilings less than 7'6" in height.

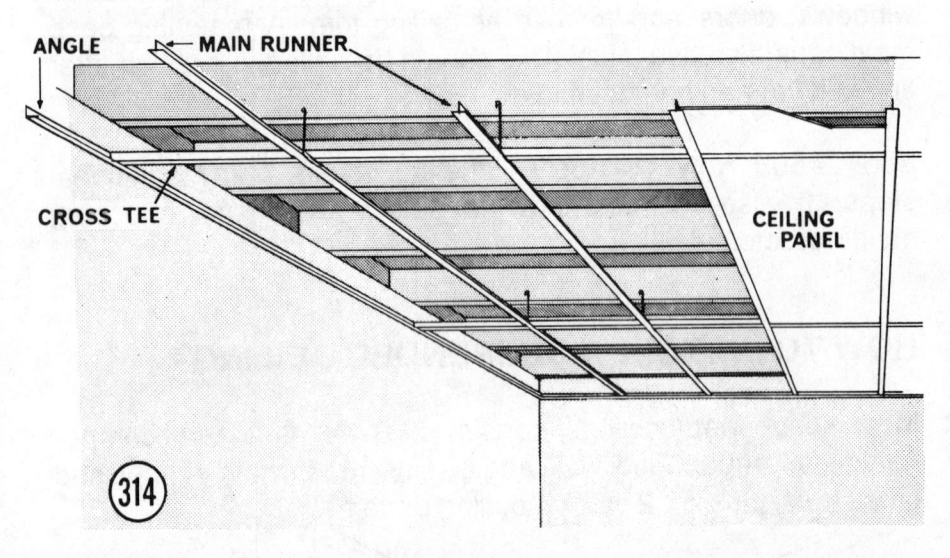

Installation starts by snapping a level chalk line clear around room at height selected for the finished ceiling, Illus. 315. Since both the floor and existing ceiling may slope, use a 4' level and a chalk line to establish a level line.

Nail angle molding to wall all around room, Illus. 316, at height selected for ceiling. Using grid, decide what size panels you can install and where each will be located. Position of main runners is dependent on the 2'0" width or length of each panel.

315

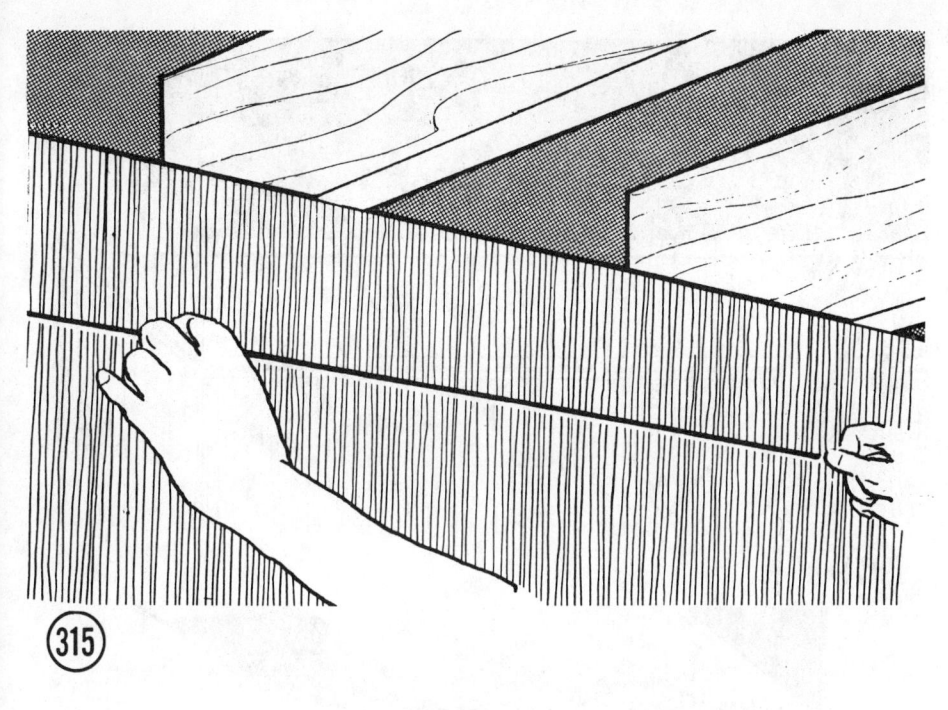

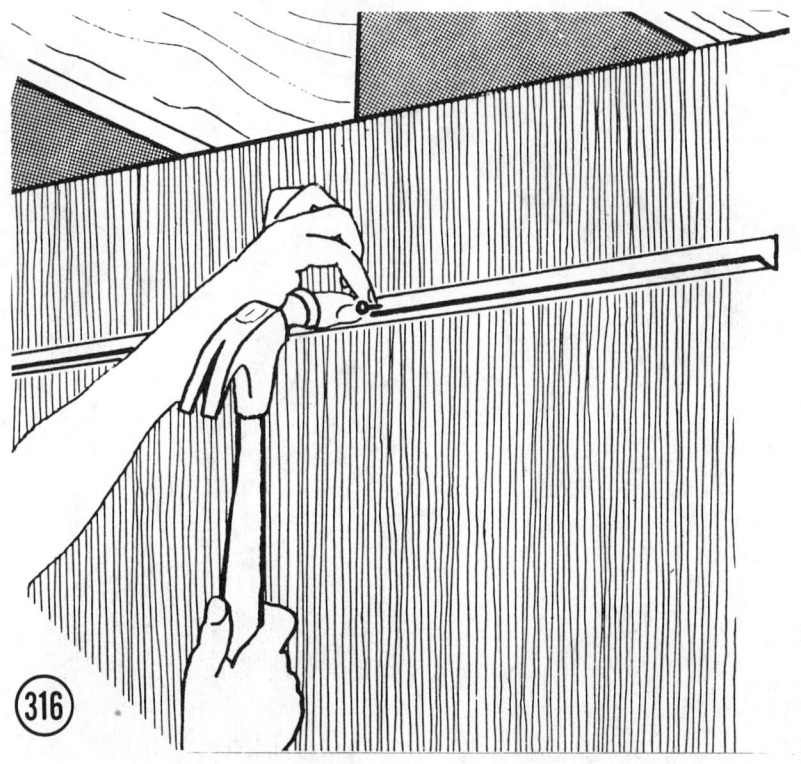

316

③17

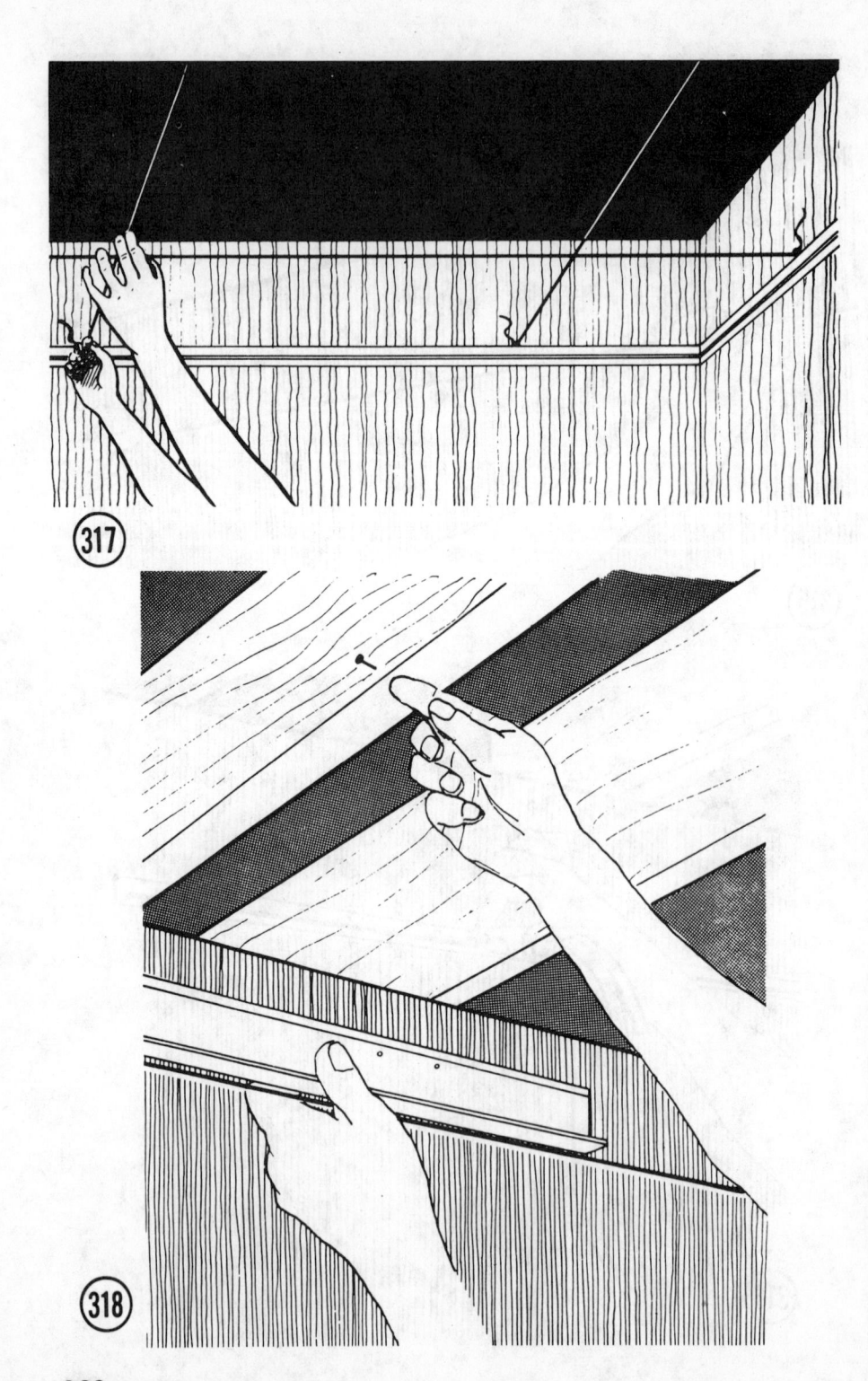

③18

Stretch guide lines from wall-to-wall angle in position selected for main runners, Illus. 317.

Main runners are hung from wires nailed to joists, Illus. 318, 319. All main runners must be level and at height equal to wall angle. When level, twist wire several times to lock in position. Main runners rest on wall angles. These can be spliced end to end to length needed following manufacturer's directions.

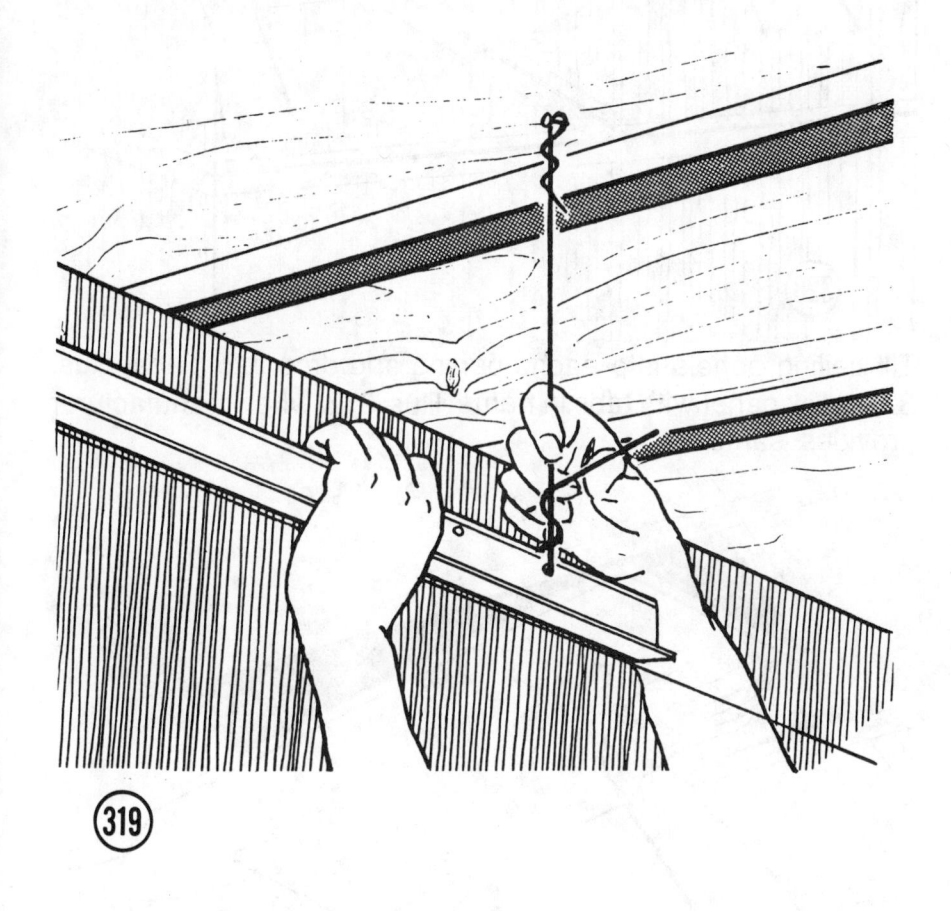

319

If you decide to cut border panels to a special size, use a linoleum knife or coping saw.

Insert cross tees into main runner, Illus. 320. Push down to lock together following manufacturer's directions. These are positioned to accommodate size tiles grid indicates.

(320)

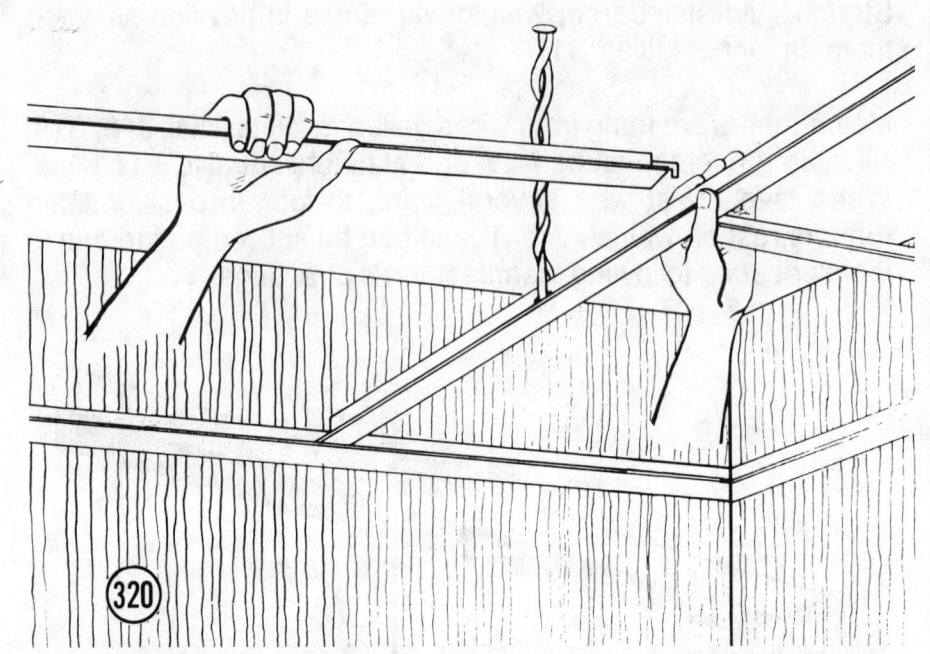

Tilt ceiling panels into each opening and drop into place, Illus. 321. Lock panel with tabs in frame, Illus. 313, when manufacturer provides same.

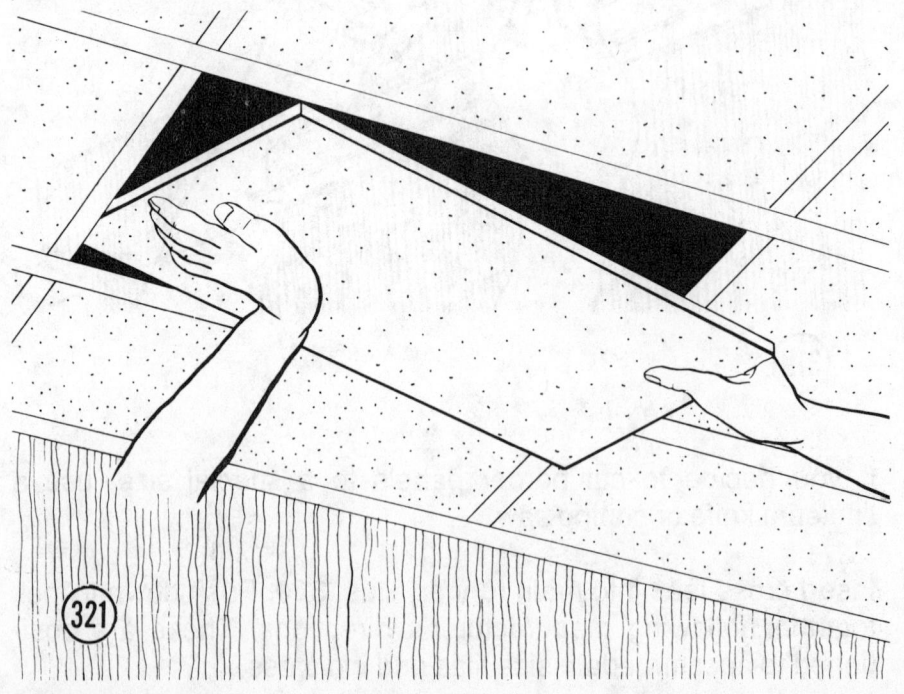

(321)

Drop lens panel, Illus. 322, in opening under fluorescent fixture. Book #694 Electrical Repairs Simplified provides considerable information covering the installation of fluorescent fixtures.

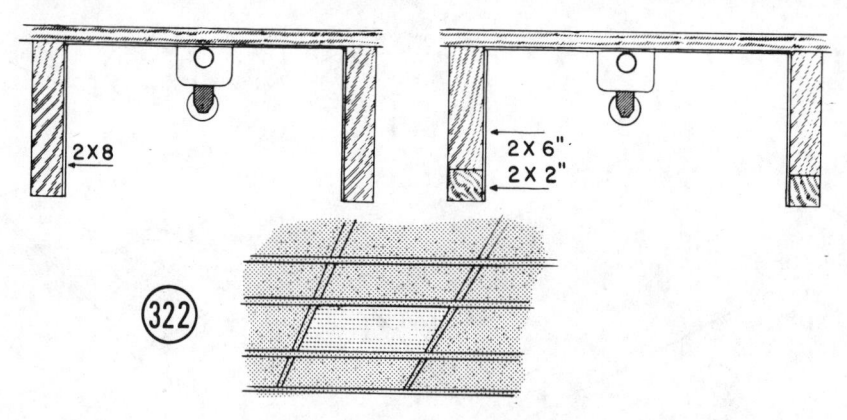

1 x 2 or 1 x 3 framing, Illus. 323, simplifies enclosing a duct away from a wall. Build frame to width required. Allow 2" space between duct and ceiling panels. Nail 1 x 2 A to joists. Cut 1 x 3 B to length required. Nail B to A, nail C to B.

If joists run parallel to duct, nail B to joists. Cover sides of frame with matching plywood panels, Illus. 324. Attach wall angle to framing and to wall,

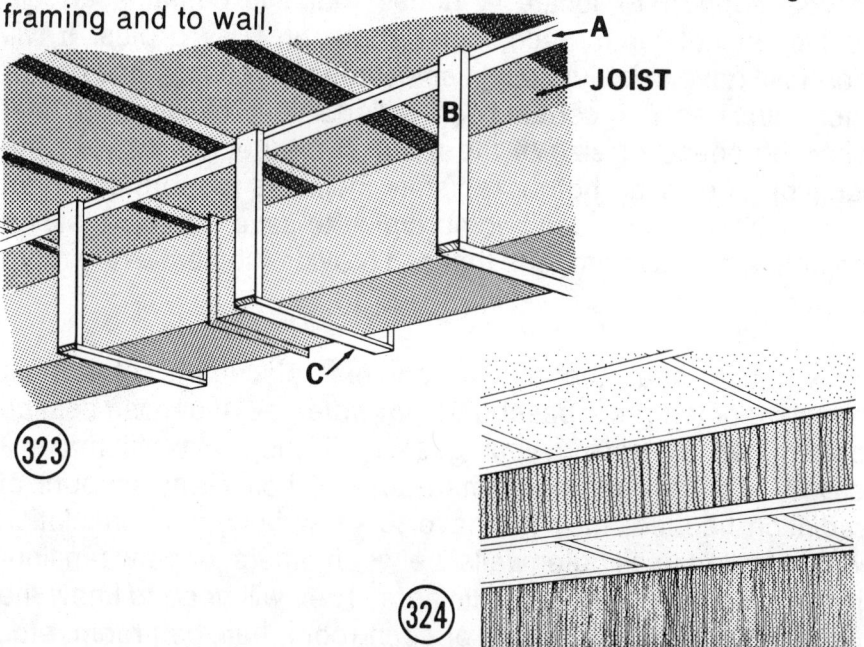

235

Cutouts for posts can be made with a utility knife, Illus. 325. Always make a full size cardboard template before cutting a ceiling panel.

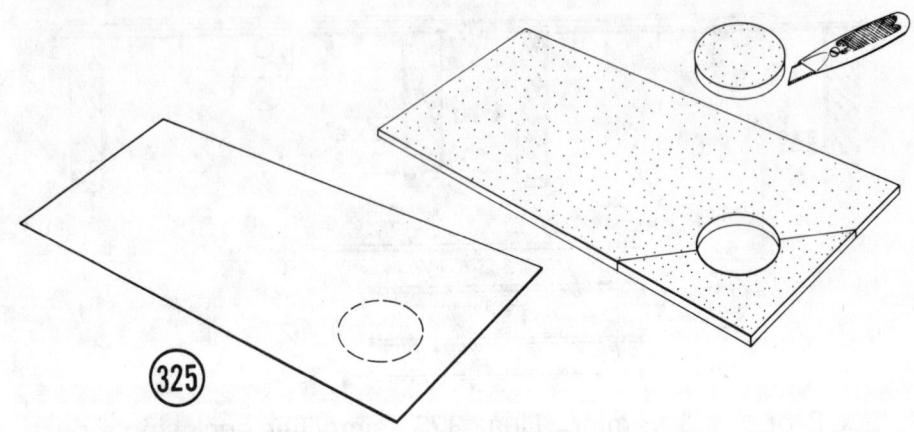

(325)

A pair of aviation snips or a fine tooth hacksaw, Illus. 162, simplifies cutting aluminum framing to length required.

HEATING TIPS

If you happen to locate a house that still contains an old fashioned hot air furnace, don't count on it as a plus. It will normally have to be junked. In some houses you may find one or more ducts serving certain floors still usable, providing you don't alter the shape or size of the room. If the duct is rusty, or the location of existing hot air registers indicates the former tenant liked a cold house, don't compromise to save money. Install a complete new system, one that can provide the heat every room requires.

How much heat the house requires, placement of hot air registers or length of baseboard hot water radiation, can best be determined by having your gas or oil supply house make a survey. To intelligently estimate size of boiler and amount of radiation needed, they will have to know how much insulation was installed in all outer walls, between rafters, or between floor joists in an open, unused attic area. They will need to know the full width, length and height of each room, hall, bathroom, etc., also the width and height of each window and outside door. Closets on outside walls will have to be included in the overall size of each room. Windows with single thickness glass lose heat faster than those with double thickness. Windows with double glass panes separated by ¼" air space provide the best resistance to heat. If you plan on installing a hot water or hot air system yourself, a heating supply retailer, or mail order company selling the complete package, needs all the the above information to intelligently appraise your needs. Since your gas or oil supplier has an important stake in you, ask them to double check the details the heating equipment retailer recommends. When sloppy estimates are used, you could end up with equipment that provides 200 to 300% more BTU's than you actually need.

Installing hot air ducts between studs and floor joists isn't difficult. All straight duct work, elbows and connectors, Illus. 326, can be purchased KD. All parts are numbered and placement of each is indicated on an installation plan. Installing each exactly where the equipment supplier specifies just takes time. Cutting all openings, installing duct work and registers, then repairing a wall or floor before applying wall paneling or floor covering, can effect big, big savings.

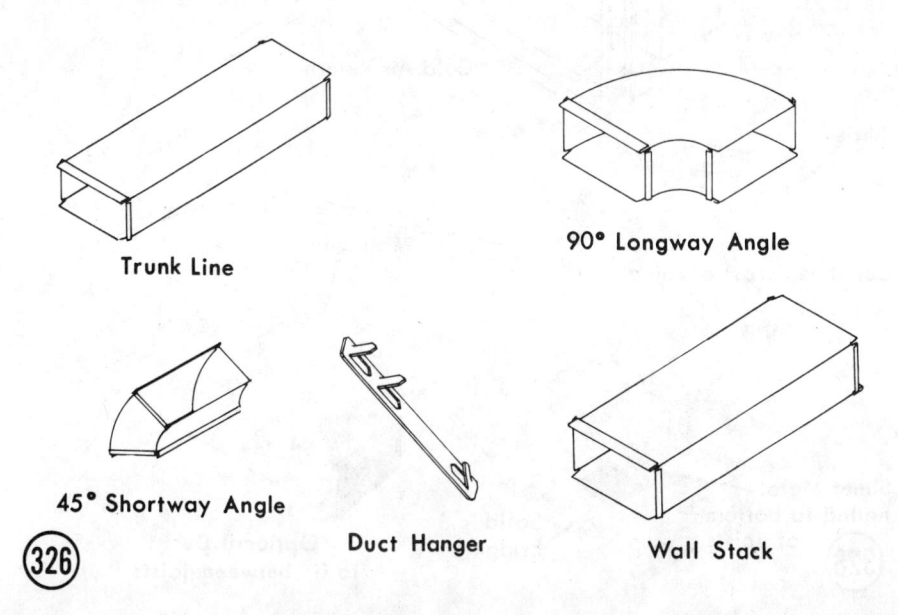

Trunk Line

90° Longway Angle

45° Shortway Angle

Duct Hanger

Wall Stack

(326)

237

90° Stack Elbow

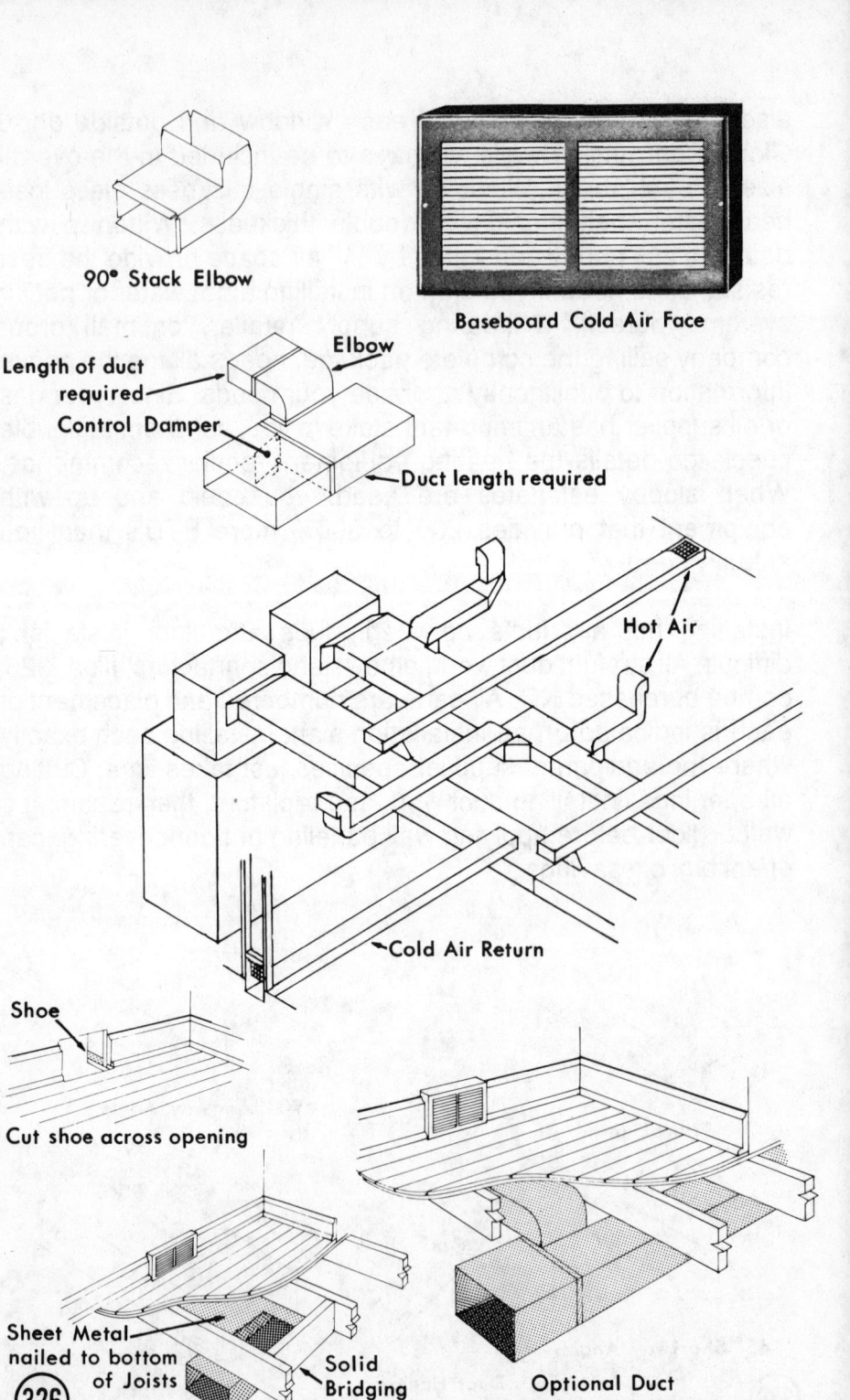

Baseboard Cold Air Face

Length of duct required
Elbow
Control Damper
Duct length required

Hot Air

Cold Air Return

Shoe
Cut shoe across opening

Sheet Metal nailed to bottom of Joists
Solid Bridging

Optional Duct to fit between joists

(326)

238

Where to install a straight duct, elbow or sleeve is determined by the size and shape of a room, placement of furnace and direction of floor joists. Always run your duct work between joists. One exception can be across a basement ceiling.

Installing a new hot water or hot air furnace and connecting it to an existing chimney, isn't difficult nor does it require any special skill. You must make certain the flue pipe is adequate for the size furnace being installed.

The position of the furnace is determined to a large extent by the location of the chimney. Locate a furnace as close to a chimney as a damper in flue pipe permits, Illus. 327. An exception is sometimes made when a slightly longer flue pipe permits using shorter runs to main branches.

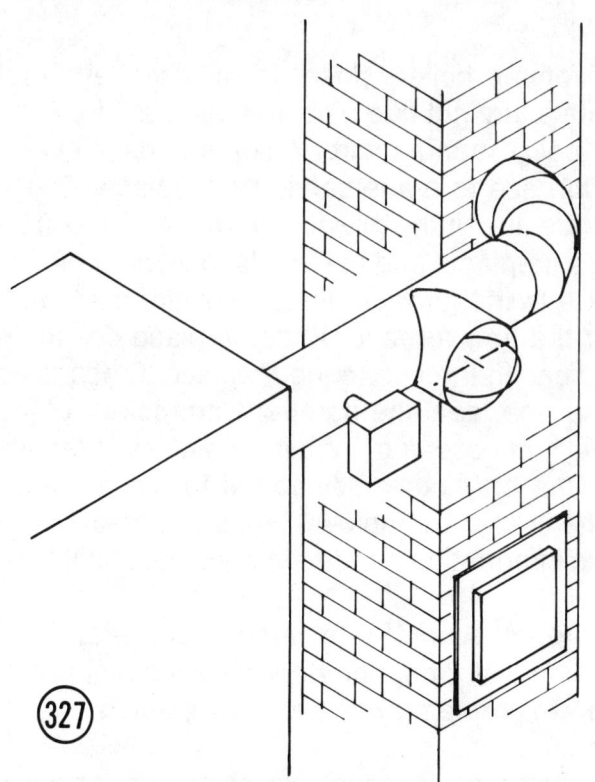

Use extreme care not to box a furnace into a tight corner. The air supply needed for combustion must not only meet local ordinances but must also be in abundance needed. Where a furnace room is vented with an outside vent, in a well below grade, Illus. 328. Consider whether the vent will still be open after a snow fall.

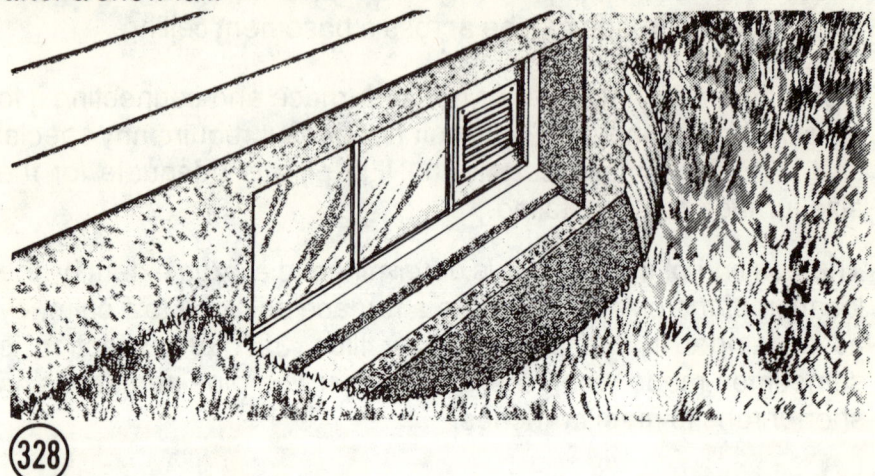

(328)

Besides positioning boiler close to a chimney, make the connection with a straight flue pipe if at all possible. Always use size flue pipe boiler manufacturer recommends. Never attempt to connect a furnace to a flue serving a fireplace. Each should be on a separate flue. If the previous furnace was connected to a flue serving a fireplace, and the fireplace works well, you could seal off the flue to the furnace. Install a prefabricated chimney, Illus. 329, for the new furnace. If the fireplace doesn't perform satisfactorily, seal off the flue to the fireplace. Close the damper if fireplace had one, seal the damper with rock wool insulation before sealing up opening. While losing a fireplace is a heartbreaker, the only other solution is to run a prefabricated chimney for the fireplace. Book #674 How To Install A Fireplace contains all the information needed to make an installation.

Underwriters Approved prefab chimneys are easy to install. If you plan a wall-to-wall closet on each wall containing a chimney you can solve two problems with two plus features.

If your house happens to have two chimneys, one within the house and the other on the outside, you normally get a better draft and more mileage out of your oil or gas if you connect to the inside chimney.

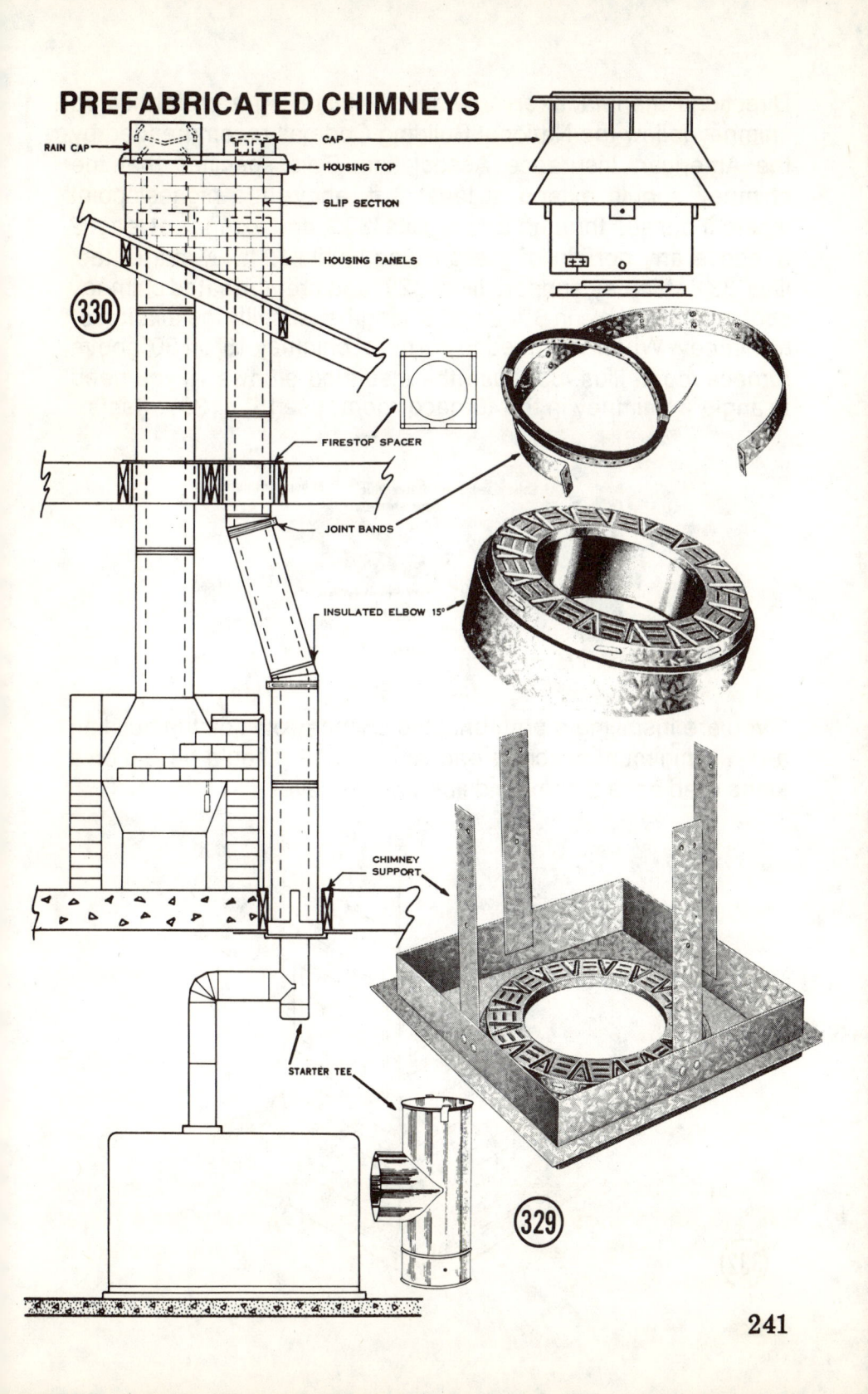

PREFABRICATED CHIMNEYS

(330)

- RAIN CAP
- CAP
- HOUSING TOP
- SLIP SECTION
- HOUSING PANELS
- FIRESTOP SPACER
- JOINT BANDS
- INSULATED ELBOW 15°
- CHIMNEY SUPPORT
- STARTER TEE

(329)

241

Directions manufacturer provides for installing a prefabricated chimney follow the National Building Code as recommended by the American Insurance Association. This specifies that the chimney should extend at least 3 ft. above the highest point where it passes through a roof, Illus. 330, and extends at least 2 ft. above any portion of the building within 10 ft. A starter tee, Illus. 331, chimney support, Illus. 329, and prefabricated chimney sections, available in 6", 2 and 3' lengths, simplify installation of a chimney. When you need to corbel a chimney 15° or 30° above furnace room, Illus. 330, use the insulated elbows. If you need to angle a chimney in the furnace room, use 15° or 30° offsets.

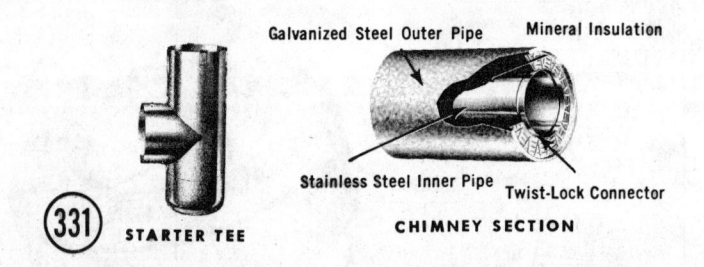

(331) STARTER TEE

Galvanized Steel Outer Pipe — Mineral Insulation — Stainless Steel Inner Pipe — Twist-Lock Connector
CHIMNEY SECTION

If you are installing a prefabricated chimney outside the building a 3½" minimum concrete pad A, Illus. 332, should be laid on a stone filled base that extends below frost level.

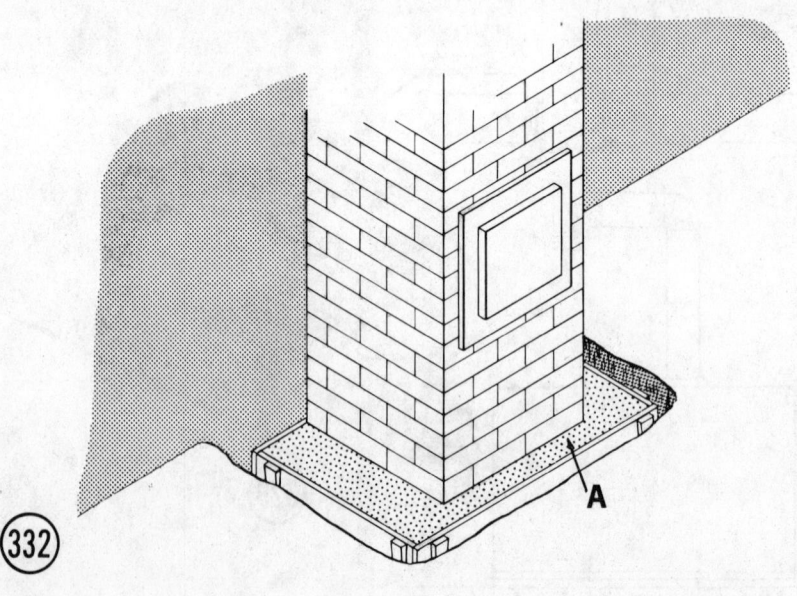

(332)

BASEBOARD RADIATION

The single supply line from a radiant hot water heating system can be roughed in at any stage of the job.

Illus. 333 indicates a forced hot water heating radiator. The easy to install radiators and 1" or ¾" main supply line takes a minimum of space. The supply line A, Illus. 334, makes a complete circuit and returns to heating unit as line B. This is called a single circuit.

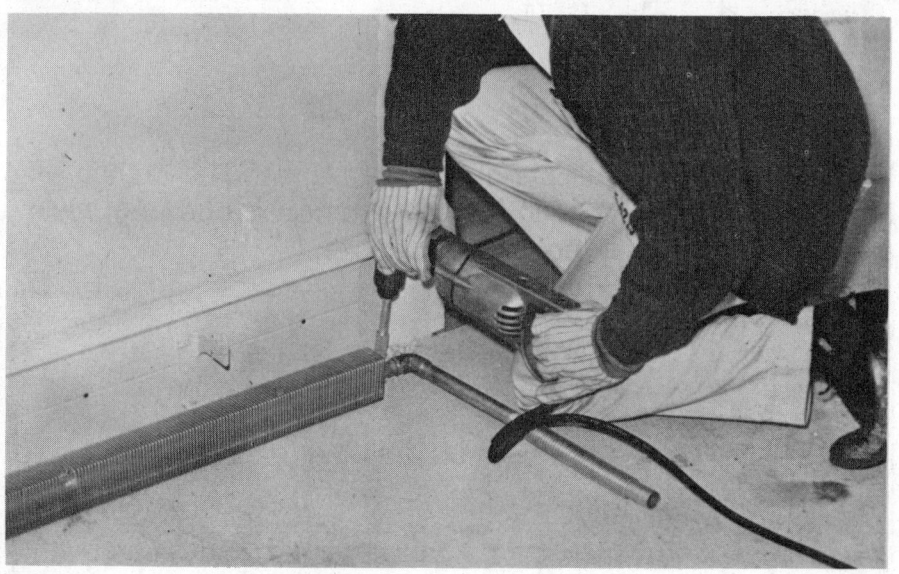

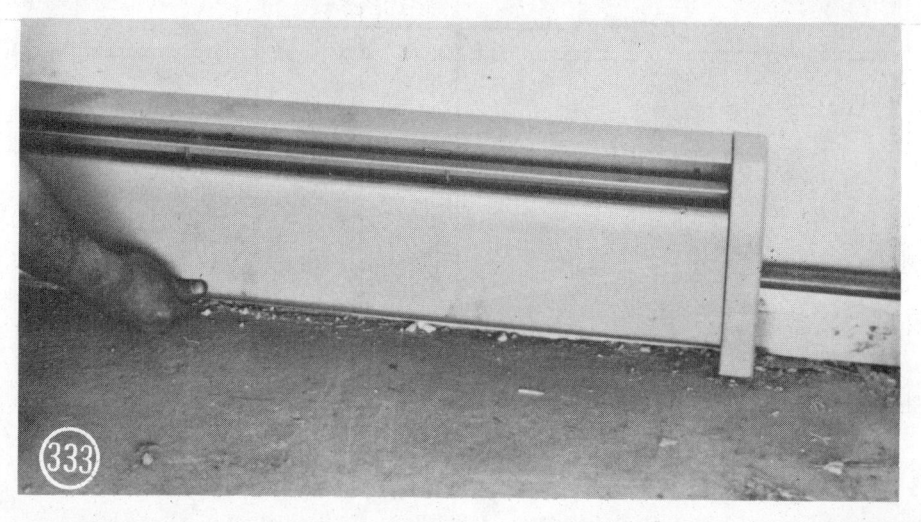

333

243

(334)

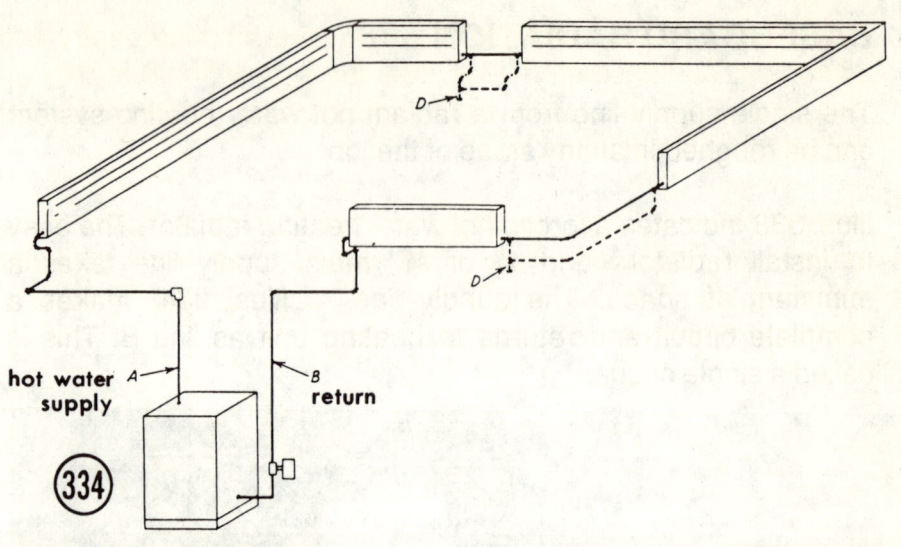

hot water supply — A
return — B

Illus. 335 shows a multiple circuit installation. One branch off boiler serves a bathroom and two bedrooms with one loop, while a second loop heats living room and kitchen.

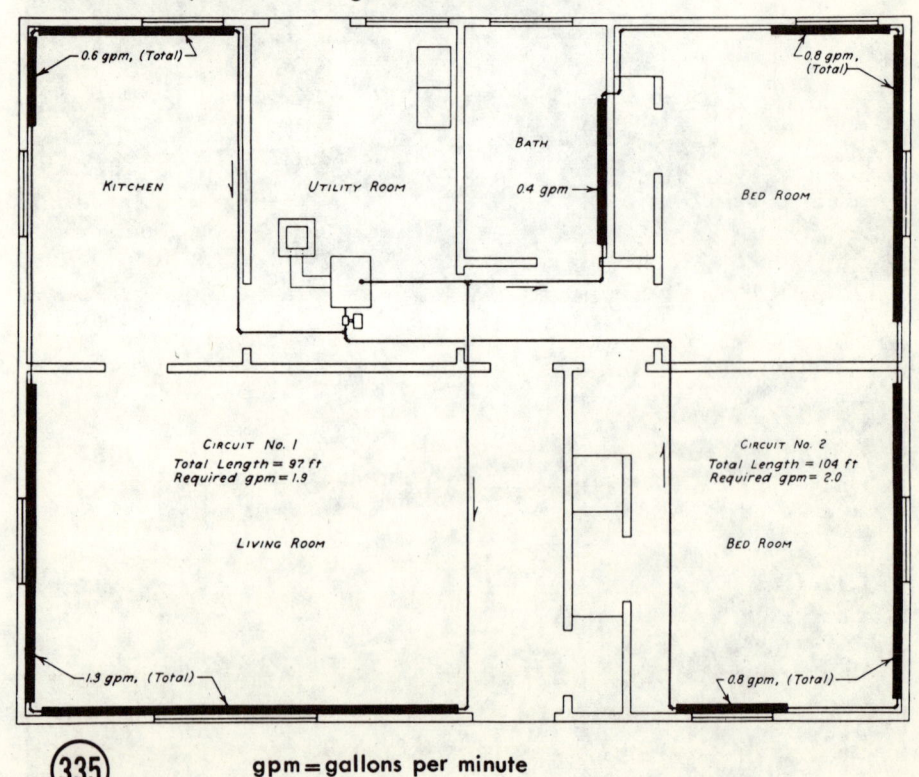

0.6 gpm, (Total)
KITCHEN
UTILITY ROOM
BATH 0.4 gpm
BED ROOM
0.8 gpm, (Total)

CIRCUIT No. 1
Total Length = 97 ft
Required gpm = 1.9

LIVING ROOM

CIRCUIT No. 2
Total Length = 104 ft
Required gpm = 2.0

BED ROOM

1.3 gpm, (Total)
0.8 gpm, (Total)

(335) gpm = gallons per minute

Baseboard radiation requires the least amount of carpentry and plumbing. As indicated in Illus. 334, the supply line A makes an end to end hook-up with each radiator. Only radiator drain D requires drilling an extra hole.

Always remove shoe molding and baseboard prior to installing baseboard radiation. Illus. 336 shows one way plywood paneling can be cut length required and applied to face of baseboard radiator with clips or brackets.

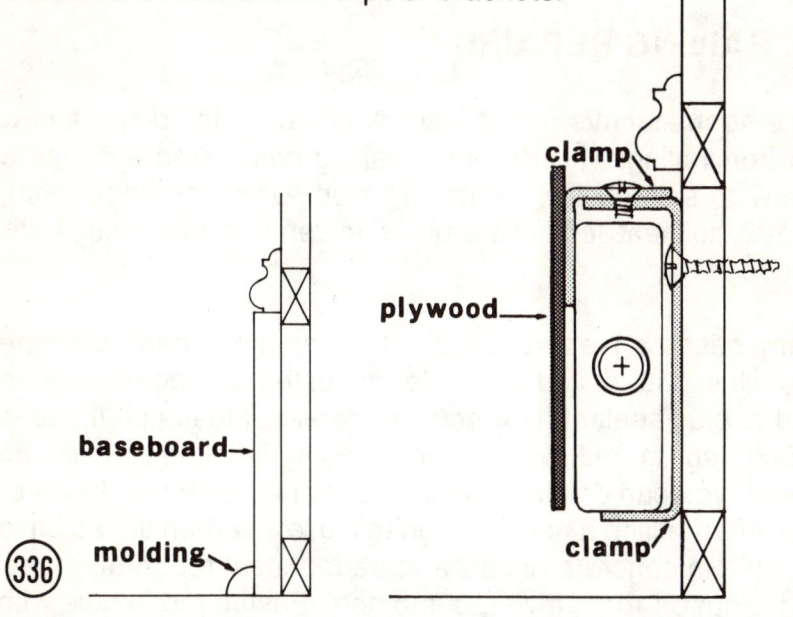

Since most boilers are equipped with a built in hot water circulator that connects to a storage tank, leave ample space for the tank. If the basement floor requires a sump pump, or shows any sign of previous flooding, set up 2 x 4 or 2 x 6 forms on edge, Illus. 337, and pour a raised platform for the furnace. Be sure to make the platform large enough for the hot water tank plus ample space to service the equipment. Use a waterproofing additive when mixing concrete as explained on page 53.

Depending on the kind of heating selected, hot air with floor or wall registers, or hot water with baseboard radiation, the size of the duct or pipe, and placement of radiation as recommended by the gas or oil company or heating supplier must be adhered to.

(337) 2x4 or 2x6

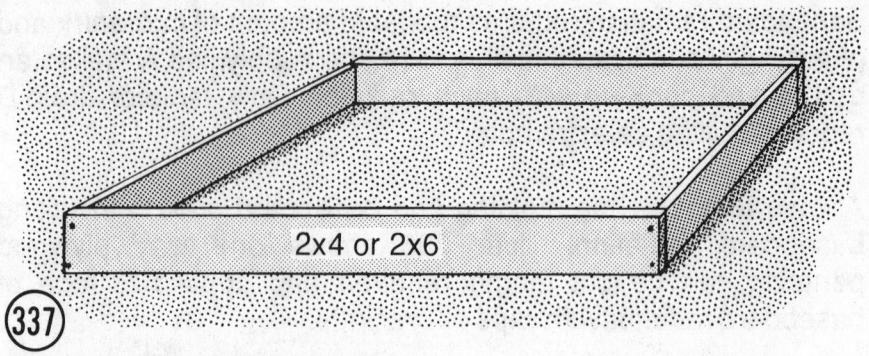

IRON RAILING REPAIRS

Plug cement sealants or hot lead can be used to anchor a new leg to iron railings. If a leg on a railing has rusted out, use a hacksaw to saw off any remaining stud. Use a propane torch, Illus. 162, to heat lead. Use pliers to remove any pieces still embedded.

In many cases a piece of 3/16 x 1" strap steel, bent to shape shown, Illus. 338, drilled with holes indicated, can be embedded in lead or plug sealant. Drill holes in lower rail to match those in leg. Bolt leg to rail. Where an existing leg can't easily be removed, you can drill through the bottom rail with a 5/16, ⅜ or ½" bit. After drilling a hole through rail, use a carbon tipped bit to drill a hole in concrete. Insert a threaded steel rod through rail, thread a nut on rod. Drive rod into hole. Fasten rod in hole with lead. When lead sets, snug up nut to bottom of rail. Place another nut, Illus. 339, in position shown and cut surplus rod with a hacksaw.

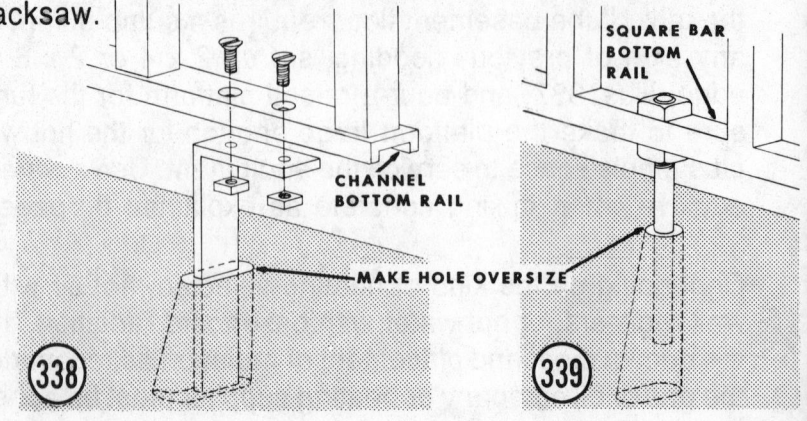

(338) CHANNEL BOTTOM RAIL — MAKE HOLE OVERSIZE

(339) SQUARE BAR BOTTOM RAIL

FRONT STEP REPAIRS

Many brownstone houses boasted handsome steps with wrought iron railings, Illus. 340. Many of these steps have been badly damaged. To shape a rounded edge, cut a metal or hardboard form to match shape of edge, Illus. 341. Fasten form to 1 x 2, Illus. 342. Cut A and B to width and length required. These position form.

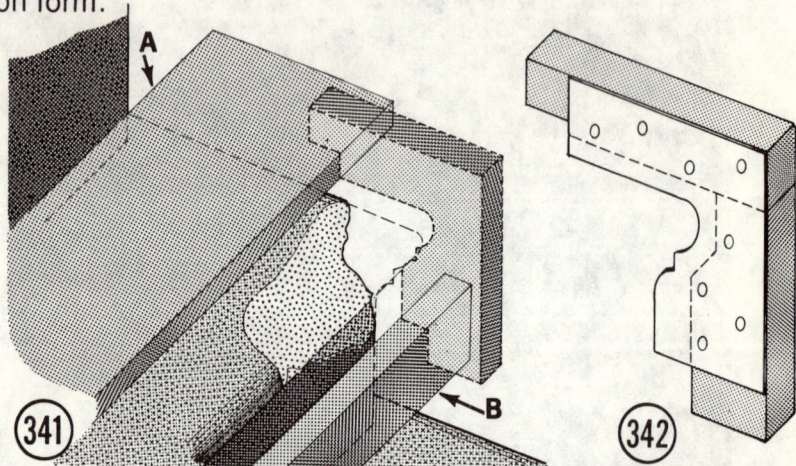

Adding the exact amount of color to concrete used for patching is very important. Ask an owner of a modernized brownstone where they obtained the concrete color they used. Mix concrete with only enough water so a handful holds its shape when squeezed. Apply where needed and shape edge with form. Protect steps for three days until concrete hardens.

IMPORTANT DO'S AND DON'TS

Time is life's most precious asset, yet it's one we squander without thought. Harness the stimulating power of a problem, learn to use it constructively and you begin to live some of life's happiest hours. But use time with caution. Never use a new hand or electric tool, or attempt to apply a new material or install equipment when you are tired or angry. It's at this point errors and accidents occur that could be avoided.

If you wake up in the middle of the night with your mind in a muddle, don't lie hour after hour twisting and turning, start patching that hole in the ceiling or preparing a wall where a new heating line needs to be installed. While you lose some sleep, you save yourself from ulcers or a nervous breakdown.

Today's fast changing world subjects each of us to stress and strain that's far beyond any we have previously experienced. Marriages break faster, a child gets hooked, salaries seldom equal rising living costs—each day brings problems with little or no relief in sight. To start a new way of life, one that can help rehabilitate a marriage as readily as a house, invest every spare hour doing what this book suggests. Make a pact to work without words.

Rehabilitation work requires far more physical effort each hour and day than most people presently get in a week or month. It also requires stretching your mind to encompass new areas of activity. When the mind is focused on a new task, one that also requires more than average physical effort, the activity provides instant escape from pressing problems.

Never use a paint thinner, carbon tet, latex, acrylic or any paint in a closed room. Unless you can open a window and get lots and lots of fresh air DON'T OPEN A CAN. Before any pollutant can create a stagnant air mass, place a fan in front of an opened window and pull room air out.

Never smoke or allow anyone else to smoke in a room when painting or using paint thinners, even with windows open.

Since few people think clearly when tired, angry or worried, when in this condition only do what you have successfully done before. Never attempt anything new.

THE MAGIC OF GOOD DIRECTION

The before and after pictures on the following pages illustrate how man can make like magic when he follows good directions. Under the guidance of the Brooklyn Union Gas Company the abandoned buildings and junk filled backyards were transformed into prime living space.

BEFORE

AFTER

(343)

(344)

251

FROM THIS
TO THIS

(345)

HOW TO THINK METRIC

Government officials concerned with the adoption of the metric system are quick to warn anyone from attempting to make precise conversions. One quickly accepts this advice when they begin to convert yards to meters or vice versa. Place a metric ruler alongside a foot ruler and you get the message fast.

Since a meter equals 1.09361 yards, or 39⅜"+, the decimals can drive you up a creek. The government men suggest accepting a rough, rather than an exact equivalent. They recommend considering a meter in the same way you presently use a yard. A kilometer as 0.6 of a mile. A kilogram or kilo as just over two pounds. A liter, a quart, with a small extra swig.

To more fully appreciate why a rough conversion is preferable, note the 6" rule alongside the metric rule. A meter contains 100 centimeters. A centimeter contains 10 millimeters.

As an introduction to the metric system, we used a metric rule to measure standard U.S. building materials. Since a 1x2 measures anywheres from ¾ to ²⁵⁄₃₂ x 1½", which is typical of U.S. lumber sizes, the metric equivalents shown are only approximate.

Consider 1" equal to 2.54 centimeters;
10" = 25.4 cm.
To multiply 4¼" into centimeters: 4.25 × 2.54 = 10.795 or 10.8 cm.

253

CEILING GRID

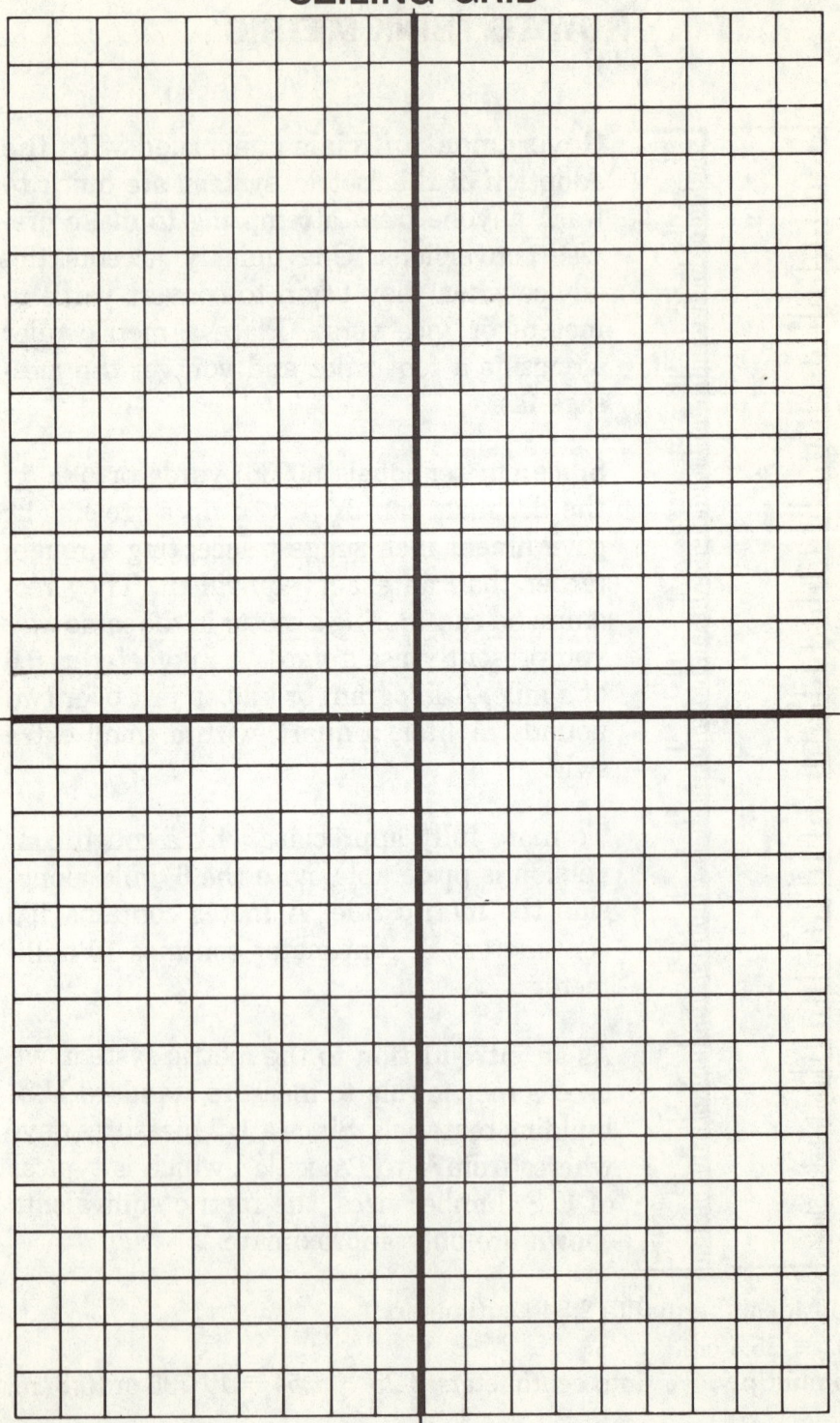

CENTER LINE

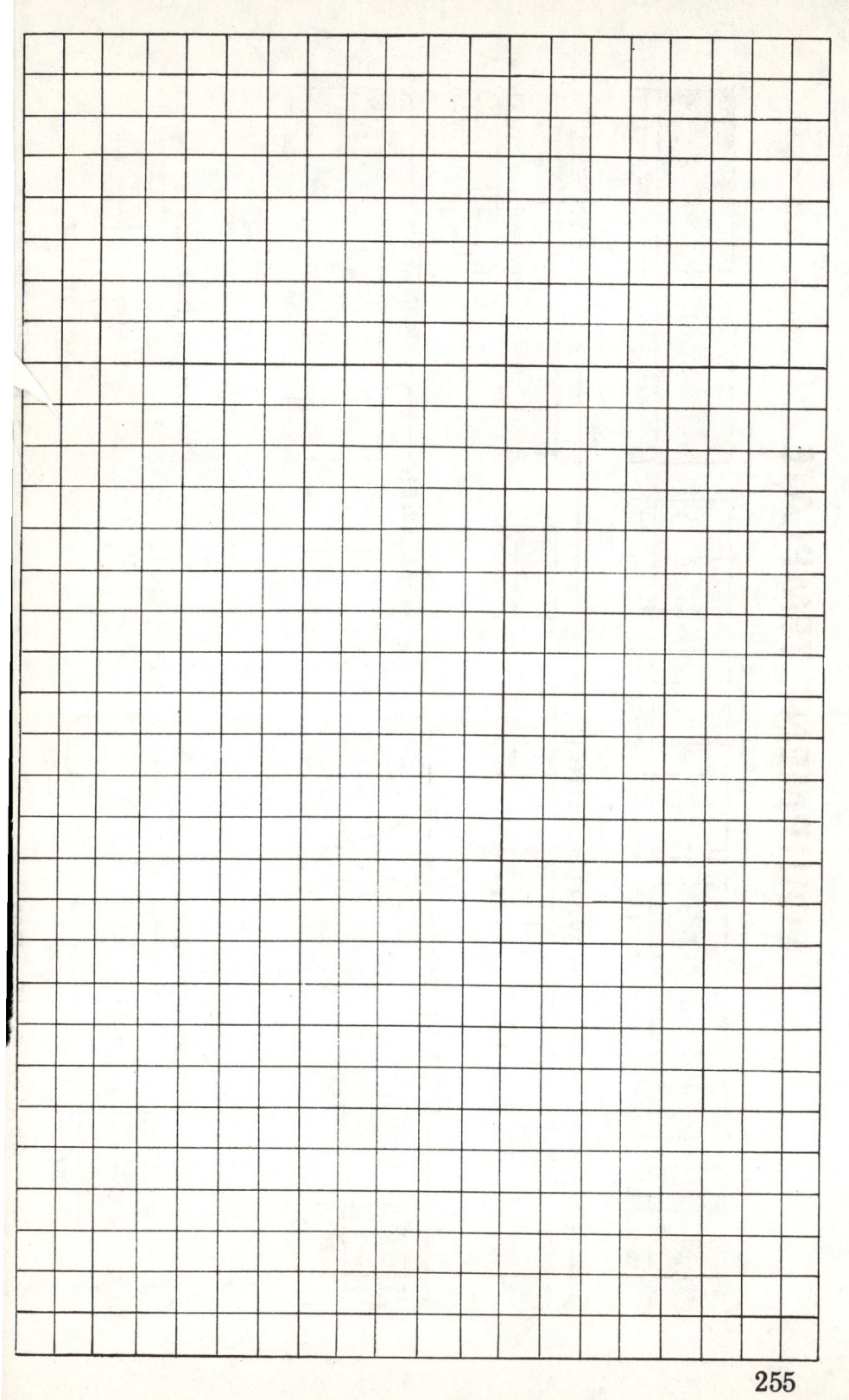

EQUIPMENT TEMPLATE Scale—1/4"=1 Ft.

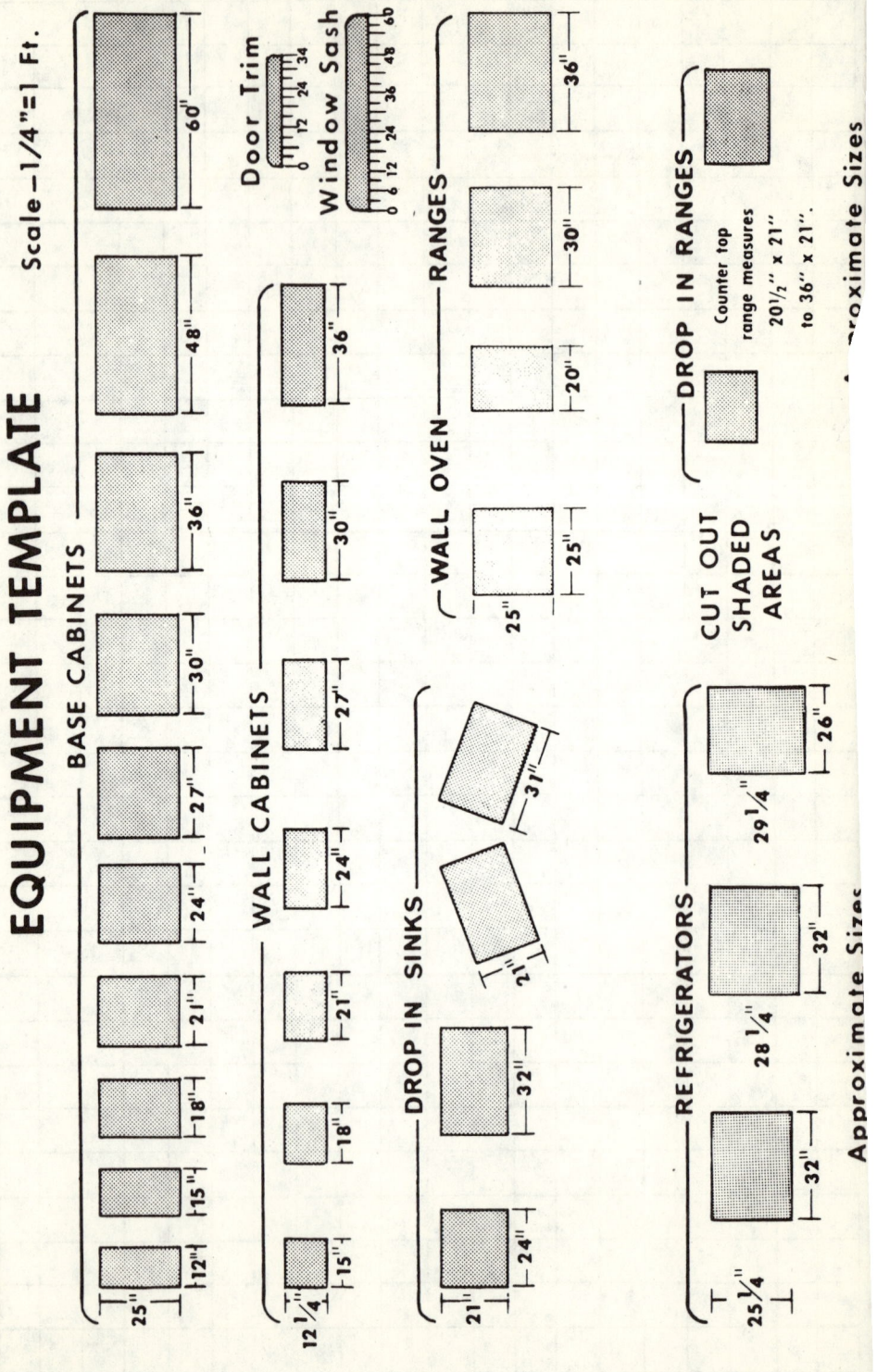

BASE CABINETS
60", 48", 36", 30", 27", 24", 21", 18", 15", 12" (25" depth)

WALL CABINETS
36", 30", 27", 24", 21", 18", 15" (12 1/4" depth)

Door Trim
Window Sash

RANGES
36", 30", 20"

WALL OVEN
25"

DROP IN SINKS
31", 21", 32", 24" (21" depth)

REFRIGERATORS
26" (29 1/4"), 32" (28 1/4"), 32" (25 1/4")

DROP IN RANGES
Counter top range measures 20½" x 21" to 36" x 21".

CUT OUT SHADED AREAS

Approximate Sizes

METRIC EQUIVALENTS

12"	30.5cm
12-1/4"	31.1
15"	38.1
18"	45.7
20"	50.8
20-1/2"	52.1
21"	53.3
24"	61.0
25"	63.5
25-1/4"	64.1
26"	66.0
27"	68.6
28-1/4"	71.8
29-1/4"	74.3
30"	76.2
31"	78.7
32"	81.3
36"	91.4
48"	121.9
60"	152.4

HANDY - REFERENCE - LUMBER

PLYWOOD - FLAKEBOARD - HARDBOARD - MOULDINGS

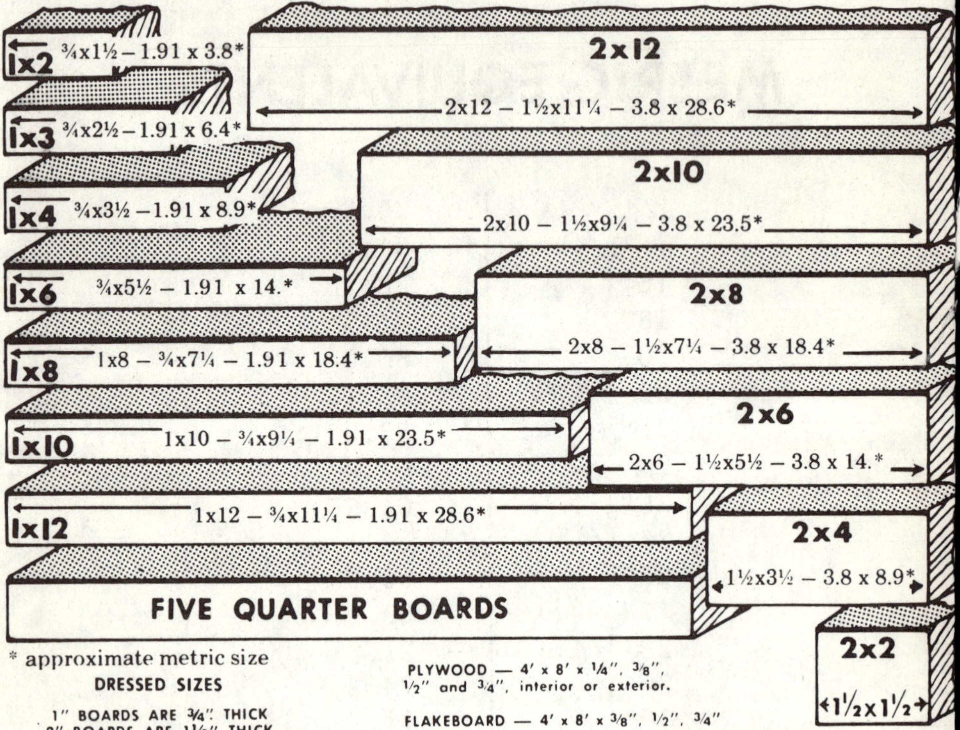

1x2 ¾x1½ – 1.91 x 3.8*
1x3 ¾x2½ – 1.91 x 6.4*
1x4 ¾x3½ – 1.91 x 8.9*
1x6 ¾x5½ – 1.91 x 14.*
1x8 1x8 – ¾x7¼ – 1.91 x 18.4*
1x10 1x10 – ¾x9¼ – 1.91 x 23.5*
1x12 1x12 – ¾x11¼ – 1.91 x 28.6*
FIVE QUARTER BOARDS
2x12
2x12 – 1½x11¼ – 3.8 x 28.6*
2x10
2x10 – 1½x9¼ – 3.8 x 23.5*
2x8
2x8 – 1½x7¼ – 3.8 x 18.4*
2x6
2x6 – 1½x5½ – 3.8 x 14.*
2x4
1½x3½ – 3.8 x 8.9*
2x2
1½x1½

* approximate metric size

DRESSED SIZES

1" BOARDS ARE ¾" THICK
2" BOARDS ARE 1½" THICK
5/4" BOARDS ARE 1-1/16" THICK

PLYWOOD — 4' x 8' x ¼", ⅜", ½" and ¾", interior or exterior.

FLAKEBOARD — 4' x 8' x ⅜", ½", ¾"

HARDBOARD — 4' x 6', 4' x 8' x ⅛", ¼", standard and tempered.

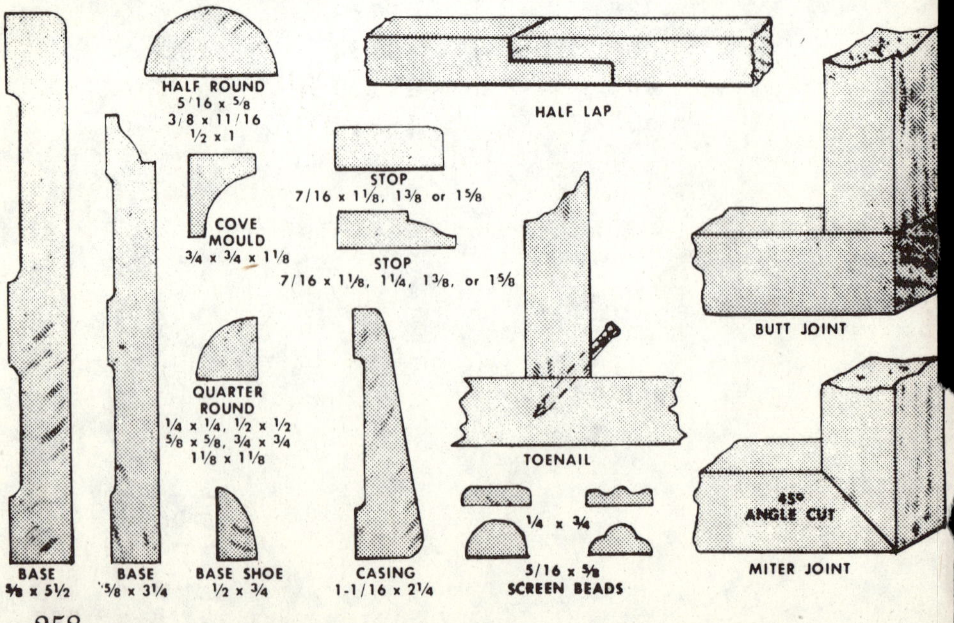

HALF ROUND
5/16 x ⅝
3/8 x 11/16
½ x 1
COVE MOULD
¾ x ¾ x 1⅛
STOP
7/16 x 1⅛, 1⅜ or 1⅝
STOP
7/16 x 1⅛, 1¼, 1⅜, or 1⅝
QUARTER ROUND
¼ x ¼, ½ x ½
⅝ x ⅝, ¾ x ¾
1⅛ x 1⅛
BASE
⅝ x 5½
BASE
⅝ x 3¼
BASE SHOE
½ x ¾
CASING
1-1/16 x 2¼
HALF LAP
TOENAIL
¼ x ¾
5/16 x ⅝
SCREEN BEADS
BUTT JOINT
45° ANGLE CUT
MITER JOINT